# WILD THEATRE

# WILD THEATRE

## THE HISTORY OF
## ONE YELLOW RABBIT

### Martin Morrow

THE BANFF CENTRE
PRESS

National Library of Canada Cataloguing in Publication

Morrow, Martin, 1958–
  Wild theatre : the history of One Yellow Rabbit / Martin Morrow.



  Includes bibliographical references and index.
  ISBN 0-920159-97-4

  1. One Yellow Rabbit (Theater company)—History.   2. Experimental theater—Alberta—Calgary—History.   I. Title.
PN2306.C32O53 2003          792'.097123'38          C2003-910161-4

The diary entries in Chapter 7 were originally published in a much-abbreviated form as "How I Spent My Scottish Vacation: Running with the Rabbits in Glasgow and Edinburgh," in the *Calgary Straight*, 7–13 September 2000.

Permission to use the Frank Zappa quotation on page 190 courtesy Gail Zappa. Permission to use excerpts from Blake Brooker's plays throughout this book courtesy Blake Brooker.

Book design by Janine Vangool
Edited by Lori Burwash
Proofread by Meaghan Craven
Index by Elizabeth Bell
Printed and bound in Canada by Houghton Boston, Saskatoon
Cover photograph (clockwise from top left) Denise Clarke, Michael Green, and Andy Curtis in *Thunderstruck* (1999). Photo by Jason Stang

The Canada Council | Le Conseil des Arts
FOR THE ARTS | DU CANADA
SINCE 1957 | DEPUIS 1957

The Banff Centre Press gratefully acknowledges the Canada Council for the Arts for its support of its publishing program.

THE BANFF CENTRE

Banff Centre Press
Box 1020
Banff, AB T1L 1H5
www.banffcentre.ca/press

For Adrian, Julian, and Andrea

# Contents

It was the end of the 1970s, the era of punk rock, a time when suburban kids who barely had a clue about chord changes were picking up instruments and forming bands. Ambitious young rebels Blake Brooker and Michael Green were bitten by that same DIY bug. But they and their theatre-crazy pals had something other than a rock group in mind.

One Yellow Rabbit makes a grand, blood-and-vomit-spattered debut at Edmonton's first fringe festival, gets censored at Vancouver's Expo, and goes looking for a home.

In which the Rabbits find a hidden hutch in Calgary's palatial performing arts centre and turn it into a laboratory of madness

In which the company loses a feminist postmodernist and gains a ballet-dancing diva

Or: How a hate-mongering social studies teacher in rural Alberta and a Nazi porn flick inspired a brilliant satire — and landed OYR in court

# Acknowledgements

**F**irst of all, I must thank the Canada Council for the Arts and the Alberta Foundation for the Arts for their pecuniary support, which allowed me the time to research and write this book.

Second, and no less importantly, a big, warm thank-you to the five principal Rabbits — Blake Brooker, Michael Green, Denise Clarke, Andy Curtis, and Richard McDowell. This project got its start one spring morning in 2000 at Caffè Beano, a tiny but popular Calgary coffee bar, where Brooker and Green enthusiastically welcomed my suggestion that it was high time someone wrote a book about their company and that someone should be me. From that day forward, all five have been more than generous with their time and memories. As well as granting my numerous requests for interviews and answering my endless e-mails, they gave me carte blanche to sit in on rehearsals, rifle through their files and photos, observe the Summer Lab Intensive and, in their usual convivial style, made sure I also partied with them at home and on tour.

The OYR office has been just as helpful. I am particularly grateful to managing producer Stephen Schroeder, a man with enough manic energy to run two theatre companies, who has channeled some of it into eagerly promoting this book. The ever-ebullient operations manager, Johnny Dunn, shared both his memories of the young Michael Green and his key to the OYR "vault" (actually a basement storage area in the Epcor Centre for the Performing Arts). The ever-efficient Daphne Bain, the Rabbits' publicist, cheerfully fielded my many interview requests and let me use the OYR archives as a lending library, minus the overdue fines. Also, a thank-you to Kathryn Osterberg, who introduced me to those archives and swapped impressions of the Rabbits with me as she completed her thesis on the troupe.

Much of the information in this book is based on interviews with the many people who have been involved over the years with One Yellow Rabbit. For offering up their memories and impressions, I'd like to thank, in alphabetical order: Paul Anderson, Penny Arcade, Mark Bellamy, Kevin Brooker, Ian Brown, Ronnie Burkett, Grant Burns, Neil Cadger, Ken Cameron, Ralph Christoffersen, Doug Curtis, Joyce Doolittle, Warren Fick, Karen Finley, Anne Flynn, Brad Fraser, Ken Gass, Don Gillmor, James Gottselig, Anne Green, Zaide Silvia Gutiérrez, Christopher Hunt, Daniel MacIvor, Bruce McCulloch, George McFaul, Mark McKinney, Ewan McLaren, Kirk Miles, Jim Millan, Peter Moller, Marianne Moroney, Michele Moss, Neil Murray, John Murrell, Brian Paisley, Laura Parken, Gyllian Raby, David Rhymer, Nigel Scott, Sandi Somers, Elizabeth Stepkowski, Jan Stirling, Gary Stromsmoe, Gerald Thurston, Keith Turnbull, Sheri-D Wilson, and Kate Zimmerman.

In the autumn of 2002, once again at Caffè Beano, I first met with The Banff Centre Press's managing editor, Lauri Seidlitz, who expressed the same enthusiasm for my manuscript that Green and Brooker had shown for the initial proposal. Like all the best editors, she has proved sensitive and encouraging while tactfully pointing out weaknesses and offering many valuable suggestions. I am indebted, too, to the astute copy editing of Lori Burwash and to the imagination of designer Janine Vangool, who perfectly captured the spirit of my writing in visual terms.

Finally, my thanks to Cheryl for the use of her superior computer, Julian for his technical support, Adrian for his provocative opinions, and especially Andrea, whose love has, in the words of Nick Drake, brightened my northern sky.

**Martin Morrow**
Calgary
12 December 2002

# Preface

"The Wild West" conjures images of gun-toting loners roaming the plains, stoic individualists battling the elements to claim their own piece of heaven on Earth. But other pioneers have also claimed this land as home and brought their own brand of wildness to the wilderness and, indeed, the world.

One Yellow Rabbit is Western and Canadian in the best possible sense, composed of colourful individuals with divergent beginnings and outlooks, joined together in the creation of a brave new world. Like the west itself, the Rabbits can never be totally tamed, and that is precisely why they are beautiful, frightening, and awesome.

Martin Morrow's delightful chronicle of the Rabbits details the history of the wildest bunch of freaks I've ever had the privilege of encountering. It's all here: the chance meetings and singular dreams that came together into a collective vision, first steps that mark the beginnings of a canon of work, discipline and focus married into a unique vocabulary. And of course the parties — from the best club Calgary ever knew, Ten Foot Henry's, to the Secret Theatre, and onward and outward into the world, Edinburgh, Mexico, Prague, Perth, and beyond.

Yet for all the steps into the world, it is the sense of home that perhaps best identifies the Rabbits' strength. From their example, and within the safe haven they created in the maddeningly confusing landscape called Alberta, many artists have unleashed their own wildness. In a city obsessed with being "world class," OYR's High Performance

Rodeo has brought world-class freaks, poets, shockmeisters, and experimentalists to Calgary's doorstep. And the Summer Intensive continues to be boot camp for dreamers.

The Rabbits are my extended family, my contemporaries, my inspiration, and my friends. Over the years, Denise Clarke and I have discussed our favourite element of the prairies: the sky, vast and clear, daring you to be equally limitless, hopeful, and upward-reaching. It's the thing that has defined so many Westerners, and the thing I miss most. No one would have expected the emergence of Canadian theatre's avant-garde from such an unlikely place, which, perhaps, is the very reason it happened.

I would suggest that this history have "Part One" added to its title, because I have a feeling that these wild things have only begun. While One Yellow Rabbit continues to create its history in the Wild West, the sky is indeed the limit. Fly, little bunnies, fly!

**Ronnie Burkett**

# The Emergence of Wild Theatre in Canada

**L**ate February 2000, Calgary. I take a break from Alberta Theatre Projects' playRites Festival "Blitz Weekend" to visit the Rabbits. They are in an early stage of rehearsals for a show Blake Brooker is directing called *The History of Wild Theatre*. It is a large collective project, and joining the core company are a few guest performers from Scotland. I am there to watch, but in the round-table discussion, Blake begins to interrogate me. What does "wild theatre" mean to me? What kind of "wild theatre" took place at the Factory Theatre and elsewhere in Toronto in the early 1970s?

I find the question curious. Perhaps it is simply the freshness of the appellation that intrigues me. "Experimental theatre" implies a focus on aesthetic exploration. "Avant-garde" defines itself in terms of the cutting edge. "Radical theatre" suggests a social or political impetus behind the work. "Underground theatre," in the true sense, is also political, operating beyond the mainstream, perhaps even in a clandestine or subversive manner. "Alternate (Alternative) Theatre"[1] has been widely used in the Canadian context to describe the small to mid-sized theatres, predicated largely on new work, that grew up in the 1970s and 1980s as an alternative to the staid regional theatres of the time. But "wild theatre"?

Reflecting on the term now, I would perhaps answer that wild theatre is one that remains untamed, bowing neither to classic traditions nor to the rigours of contemporary theatre fashion. Wild theatre is willing to break all rules, to shift terrain on impulse; it requires directors and co-creators who hunt by instinct. It is not so much a question of breaking conventions; rather, in the spirit of blazing the untamed wilderness, practitioners invent their own rules and discover their own means of survival. This requires not only enormous strength of purpose and resilience, but also, inevitably, a hunger. As such, the term aptly encompasses One Yellow Rabbit's large body of work over the past two decades and the modus operandi of OYR's core members.

It seems somewhat ironic that One Yellow Rabbit, perhaps the most successful wild bunch of theatre artists in English Canada (certainly no other collective has survived so long and earned such a pedigree), began in that most conservative period, the 1980s, in that most conservative of Canadian provinces, Alberta. At this juncture, the huge adrenalin rush of theatre energy that had burst forth in Toronto and elsewhere in the 1970s was beginning to wane as conservative policies within the arts councils, such as tying grant increases to increases in private sector fundraising, began to dampen the fires of experimentation and risk-taking. The point that emerges is that new ideas, and even *nouvelles vagues,* can start anywhere, and indeed at any time, if the right combustible mix of artistic ideas and obsessive individuals converge. The accidental meeting of a few like-minded theatre artists whom fate has settled in a single setting can, if they survive the inevitable initial bouts of friction, create a permanent collective or performance ensemble that launches a movement and defines an era.

In Toronto, in the late 1960s, the revolution began in that mythically wild and free institution Rochdale College, in the basement of which Jim Garrard founded Theatre Passe Muraille, or "theatre beyond walls." Like OYR, Garrard first tackled the wilder plays of off-off-Broadway, including Rochelle Owens's *Futz,* a play about a farmer having an affair with a pig (curiously parallel to Edward Albee's Broadway hit, *The Goat*). *Futz* fell immediately afoul of Toronto's morality squad and pitted the satirical values of this experimentally minded company against the established mores of Toronto the Good. In 1969, John Palmer and Martin Kinch were taking on the Stratford establishment by opening a storefront operation across from the Avon called Canadian

Place Theatre, producing wild, in-your-face theatre with a season of Canadian scripts, including two of Palmer's own.

Canadian Place Theatre was a short-lived venture, but the sheer audacity of the project had a reverberant effect that cemented the Kinch/Palmer creative partnership and drew in Tom Hendry, Stratford's literary manager and also a playwright, whose admiration for the effort led to him joining forces with the two to create Toronto Free Theatre in 1972. The wild efforts of Canadian Place had also caught the attention of Garrard, who invited Kinch and Palmer to launch the 1969–70 Passe Muraille season with Palmer's sprawling *Memories for My Brother,* performed on a tall scaffolding set, followed by another off-off-Broadway classic, Paul Foster's *Tom Paine,* a politically charged ensemble piece directed by Kinch. Certainly the critical reception to these works branded the company as wild and distinctly untempered but — though acknowledging the performers' energy and creativity — such critics also castigated them for an apparent lack of technical finesse.

Given the performers' youth, criticisms were certainly valid, but there is also the incongruity of judging performers bent on inventing new forms of theatre by the traditional criteria of the colonial masters. The true sources of inspiration for these new directors, aside from one another, was the explosive energy of Ellen Stewart's La Mama, and the Open Theatre founded by Joseph Chaikin, both pillars of the off-off-Broadway revolution of the 1960s and, to a significantly lesser extent, the European avant-garde. At the same time, the spate of US political assassinations, the Vietnam War, and the racial riots in the ghettos of Detroit and Los Angeles, coupled with the post-Expo pride of neo-nascent Canadian nationalism, led to the souring of the American Dream, causing directors to turn inward for inspiration. After the founding of the Factory Theatre in 1970, with my own admittedly headstrong policy of producing only Canadian plays, the centre of gravity for wild and original theatre in Toronto shifted from an off-off-Broadway sensibility (which I too had shared) toward markedly nationalistic aspirations.

As Jim Garrard became mired in the financial burdens of Passe Muraille, he briefly turned the artistic reins over to Martin Kinch. But as Kinch was finding opportunities to work at Stratford and elsewhere in the mainstream, it seemed logical that Paul Thompson (who had joined the company as stage manager but "had an opinion on everything" and had also apprenticed under Roger Planchon in France) should take over. Thompson quickly adopted the Factory's Canadian-only mandate, but also pioneered the collective creation, literally taking actors into the wilds (well, Clinton and Cobalt, Ontario) to create such extraordinary works as *The Farm Show* and *Under the Greywacke*. Without the company of Passe Muraille, the Factory would have had far less impact on the Canadian theatre scene — both theatres maintained an eclectic mix of original programming and nurtured independent projects as well as those favoured by their artistic directors. As Bill Glassco, who had directed two productions in the Factory's first season, including the groundbreaking *Creeps* by David Freeman, broke off to create Tarragon Theatre in the fall of 1971, and Kinch, Palmer, and Hendry founded Toronto Free Theatre a year later, a nucleus was formed with enough power to permanently transform Canadian theatre.

Garrard's enormous impact on the new theatre movement had as much to do with his conceptual thinking and generous, eclectic personality as his actual work as a stage director. It was Garrard who envisioned the New Directors Group, an association of several upstart directors, including Palmer; Kinch; Thompson; Martin Brenzell, a Hamilton, Ontario, director with strong ties to La Mama in New York; Henry Tarvainen, a young resident director at Toronto Arts Production, the regional theatre entity housed at the newly built St. Lawrence Centre; and myself. Reading here the minutiae of Michael Green, Blake Brooker, and Denise Clarke's first forays into theatre and performance art, I am struck with a sense of déjà vu over the parallels between the founding of One Yellow Rabbit and the New Directors Group more than a decade earlier. Unlike the Rabbits, the New Directors Group never coalesced into a theatre company, the need for such being obviated by the eclectic natures of both Passe Muraille and the Factory, which had several associate directors in tow at all times. Yet, from the fall of 1969 through the spring of 1970, just before the emergence of the

Factory, these very disparate directors met informally, occasionally smoked dope, but seriously began to ruminate on the state of Canadian theatre and to explore how to expand the current rumblings into a bona fide revolution. After an overexposed, grainy photograph of Garrard, Kinch, Tarvainen, and myself was published in the *Globe and Mail* magazine with an accompanying article by Betty Lee, the association gained enough credibility to be called as a witness regarding the artistic merits of Ivan Reitman's early experimental film *Columbus on Sex,* which was charged with obscenity after a screening in Hamilton, Ontario. The group contemplated guerrilla actions, such as chaining ourselves to the pillars of Stratford during a blackout to protest the stranglehold this institution had on our national psyche, but wisely refrained despite elaborate discussions of the idea's merits. Instead, the group seized an opportunity suggested by Tarvainen and staged a major festival event in the Town Hall area of the St. Lawrence Centre, which was in need of community-oriented projects to justify its costly existence.

The FUT! Festival (or Festival of Underground Theatre) was an extraordinary nineteen-day event in the summer of 1970, replete with many productions and events that can retrospectively be viewed as pure "wild theatre." What is astonishing is how swiftly it all happened. The project was conceived in mid-April, and on 1 May, the Ontario Arts Council (OAC) provided $1,000 toward a feasibility study. The study (essentially a detailed critical path and raison d'être) was completed in three weeks and submitted along with a request for $15,000, which the OAC granted shortly afterwards. FUT! imported the legendary New York–based Bread and Puppet Theatre and Jerome Savary's Panic Circus, or Théâtre de la Grande Panique, from Paris. John Juliani's Vancouver-based Savage God company and Jean-Claude Germaine's Théâtre du Même Nom from Montreal gave the festival a national perspective, and each of us in the New Directors Group had funds to direct a full professional production. In addition to the three weeks of performances at the 400-seat Town Hall, a Fringe Festival emerged at the 150-seat Global Village space, featuring imports from Buffalo and Boston (the outrageously black-humoured Swamp Fox and Burning

City, the latter a "women's liberation company") along with numerous other small-scale and spontaneous locally bred performances. There was a large, noisy street parade from Queen's Park to the St. Lawrence Centre involving several companies and theatre groupies lead by the Bread and Puppet ensemble with their signature twelve-foot puppet caricature of Uncle Sam. The baffled police threatened to arrest a Cuban dancer whose raunchy and muscular bare-torsoed performance on the back of a flat-bed truck suggested he was about to rip off his jeans. During the festival, performances constantly overflowed from the two theatres onto nearby streets. The entire spectacle, featuring a dozen major productions and thirty smaller shows, was complete by early September, barely four months from conception to completion.

While the artistic results of the New Directors Group were decidedly mixed (little surprise, considering the rush and limited budgets), the spirit of the event would have tickled the imagination of the Rabbits. Jerome Savary presented an erotic, carnivalesque anti-colonial extravaganza inspired in part by Tarzan stories; Paul Thompson created a fantastical Alfred Jarry adaptation called *Ubu Raw,* which featured a ten-foot penis on wheels; John Palmer's act of subversion was an ultrarealistic production of Ibsen's *A Doll's House* with a hundred and fifty lighting cues. A fringe performance featuring the highly theatrical Marcel Horne with a fire-breathing and sword-swallowing act, accompanied by John Mills-Cockell's Moog synthesizer music, was imported into the Town Hall program as part of a special program thrown together overnight to replace a suddenly cancelled production from Martin Brenzell. The Panic Circus also contributed to that night and got the audience participating in egg and spoon races up and down the aisles. As some of the eggs were raw, the results on the newly minted red carpets were not appreciated by the St. Lawrence Centre management. Wild? Untamed? Most definitely. The FUT! Festival quickly achieved legendary status in the annals of Toronto theatre and remained a touchstone for directors in the decade that followed.

Ignited in Toronto, the alternate theatre movement spread quickly across the country, spawning theatres that were in varying degrees wild, innovative, or simply focused on new playwriting. On the west coast, John Juliani had established himself since the late 1960s as the *enfant terrible* of Vancouver with hard-hitting experimental productions of leading contemporary iconoclasts such as Arrabal and de Ghelderode. Juliani, though aggressive, was less "wild" in that his productions, as I remember them, were sharply delineated and produced with a detail and care that reflected his rigorous theatre training. While Juliani also took theatre beyond traditional walls, notably with a production of Beckett's *Happy Days* in a Stanley Park tree trunk, the most memorable "wild" incident in his 1970s career was probably his letter challenging English-bred Robin Phillips to a duel to "avenge the honour of Canadian directors," after Phillips's appointment as artistic director of the Stratford Festival in 1974. Subsequently, Tamahnous Theatre, founded by John Gray in 1971, established itself as Vancouver's leading alternate theatre company, producing a steady and vibrant mix of new plays, collective creations, and edgy works from the contemporary repertoire. In Saskatoon, 25th Street Theatre gained a foothold as a prairie theatre collective in 1972, two years prior to the establishment of its regional theatre counterpart, Persephone Theatre. Theatre Network led the way for a number of important alternate theatre companies in Edmonton that would later also include Catalyst Theatre, Workshop West, and Northern Light.

On the east coast, Chris Brookes founded the Mummers' Troupe in Newfoundland in 1971. Employing a mix of docudrama, agitprop techniques, and medieval theatre traditions, the Mummers were less noted for wildness, but rather as a successful proponent of theatre as a political and social force. A few years later, the first of the Codco creations emerged, prompted by Paul Thompson, who offered to program the work at Theatre Passe Muraille. Thus the hilarious antics of Andy Jones, Cathy Jones, Tommy Sexton, Greg Malone, and their successors launched a whole movement, indeed a whole industry, based on unabashed and unbridled Newfie humour.

In fact, comedy, especially in its more outrageous veins, finds a natural affinity with the principles of wild theatre, where humour becomes a weapon in the rebellion against social convention, and where performers test boundaries of propriety to ridicule venerated idols of authority. Similarly, nudity seems to be a natural ingredient for wild theatre; the act of presenting the naked body in public defies society's strictures, but equally allows the performer to achieve an untamed state of being. That such is often deemed gratuitous or immoral perhaps may reveal more about the repressed state of the viewer than the wild performer. Certainly newspaper reviews for a number of early productions at Theatre Passe Muraille and One Yellow Rabbit constantly headlined the nudity, making it seem salacious, even in instances where it was only a minor aspect of the production.

Another attribute that wild theatre readily embraces is breaking the boundaries between actor and performer and constantly re-inventing the notion of theatrical space. In a similar way, traditional dramatic form, as the One Yellow Rabbit repertoire reveals, is transplanted by looser structures that easily encompass poetry, dance, and elements of performance art. Of course, playwrights emerge, even within the framework of conventional theatres, who develop their own notions of wild theatre — it is no surprise to note the affinity between the Rabbits and Brad Fraser, Ronnie Burkett, and Daniel MacIvor. Similarly, as the Factory Theatre settled into more structured seasons, it was the visceral energy and uncharted psychic landscape in the early plays of George F. Walker (such as *Beyond Mozambique* and *Ramona and the White Slaves*) that best reflected its still unbridled spirit.

The wild rebels of Toronto theatre in the 1970s, as well as the Rabbits in the 1980s, had become, by the end of their respective first decades, firmly entrenched within the Canadian theatrical establishment. Indeed, as the alternate theatre movement gained wider audiences and eventually a broader measure of public subsidy, these companies became the defining element of Canadian theatre, with the regionals struggling to keep up, particularly in terms of innovation and artistic excitement. The gentrification of the erstwhile rebels often came about in tandem with the acquisition of real estate. As OYR moved into the Secret Theatre in the Calgary Centre for Performing Arts, it was suddenly given *licence* to be wild — within limits, of course, which the company constantly tests — but a form of containment, or caging of the wild beast, might nonetheless be assumed.

Politically, one can argue that the radical elements in our theatres have simply been co-opted, but increased stability has, in my view, only enriched the work, allowing far more complex and multi-layered productions to emerge. A case in point is *Thunderstruck, or The Song of the Say-Sayer*, a poetic, rather difficult play by Quebec dramatist Daniel Danis. Though greatly undervalued by critics and audiences alike, OYR's production of this work, which also played at the Factory in 2000, was simply masterful. Full of visual astonishments, *Thunderstruck* proved a sublime example of ritualized storytelling with chorus work that oddly embellished character and added humour while intensifying the horrifying sense of impending tragedy. Under Blake Brooker's razor direction, not only did the production reveal the company as an exceptionally mature and versatile ensemble, but the complex layers of performance and theatrical invention sharply illuminated Danis's opaque text.

Of course, new generations of wild theatre artists continue to emerge from fringe festivals coast to coast and from structures such as Rhubarb! at Buddies in Bad Times Theatre, as well as OYR's own High Performance Rodeo, both of which actively foment experimentation and acts of rebellion. Companies like Boca del Lupo in Vancouver and artists such as Darren O'Donnell in Toronto suggest that wild theatre is a self-renewing phenomenon whose litmus test lies in the continuous shattering of boundaries in search of new forms and new theatrically engendered social experiences.

**Ken Gass**
Artistic Director, Factory Theatre
December 2002

---

1    Both "Alternate" and "Alternative" have been used to describe this movement. Denis Johnston, in his landmark book *Up the Mainstream: The Rise of Toronto's Alternative Theatres* (1991), clearly uses the latter, which he claims was the first label that stuck. However, he also acknowledges that "Alternate" has become the most popular now (p.5).

# 1. Bunnies

It was the end of the 1970s and the beginning of the 1980s, when that rude boy Punk and his kid sister New Wave were in full pubescent flower. Rock 'n' roll, which had grown all slick and polished and professional in the preceding years, was suddenly rough and ragged again, and accessible to all. Any kid who could get his hands on an electric guitar could be a musician, anybody with a garage or a basement could start a band. The prototype was the Sex Pistols, a crude, surly quartet of London boys for whom sneering and spitting came easier than melody and whose debut LP was an unremitting blast of nihilistic white noise, devoid of the flashy guitar solos and pseudo-poetic lyrics that had become rock's stock in trade. If the Pistols' Sid Vicious could play the bass (which he couldn't), then anybody could — and did.

Calgary, an oil-enriched Canadian city of 600,000, spread at the foothills of the Rocky Mountains, was a far cry from the futureless England the Pistols were railing against. While Sid, Johnny Rotten et al. were the product of generations grown up on the dole, living in tiny, squalid council flats, and oppressed by a country in love with its past, kids in Calgary knew none of those social ills. The city was enjoying a period of heady prosperity; the past was being torn down and replaced with gleaming skyscrapers whose reflecting glass mirrored the pristine blue skies. The suburbs had private lakes where families could swim and sunbathe in the summer and skate around bonfires in the winter. Jobs were there for the picking, white collar and blue collar, and free-spending bosses drove Jaguars and Mercedes while treating their employees to staff parties awash in Dom Perignon. But, as Marlon Brando and James Dean had asserted two decades before, you don't need a cause to be a rebel.

The white-bread kids from the suburbs bought the Pistols' album, learned their required two chords and headed downtown to create Calgary's own punk scene. Only the seediest, grungiest watering holes would do, and they chose such fleabag hotels as the Calgarian and the National, whose clientele consisted mainly of burly bikers and Aboriginals on the skids. As comedian Bruce McCulloch put it: "First we took the Indians' land, then we took their bar." Bands with sharp, ugly names sprang up, played a few gigs, and just as quickly disappeared. The Pistols didn't come to Calgary on their notorious, aborted North American tour, but other outside influences did. A strange geezer from England who looked like a wired Buddy Holly and called himself Elvis Costello rocked the genteel Jubilee Auditorium with hyper-clever lyrics and slashing guitars. Devo, an American band that sounded and acted like robots, paid a disconcerting visit to the Max Bell Arena — the typical Canadian hockey rink-cum-rock venue — as if they were landed aliens. Two of punk's old gunslingers, John Cale and Iggy Pop, blazed their way through memorable sets in the MacEwan Hall Ballroom at the University of Calgary.

Cale, the ex–Velvet Underground violist, had always been a schizoid personality, sometimes penning lovely, string-laden art rock, other times spitting out violent fantasies that ended in twisted screams and, on one infamous occasion, beheading a chicken with a meat cleaver on stage. Andy Curtis, an art student at the university at the time, remembers Cale's first appearance there and a second gig about a year later. "The first time he came through he was this bloated mess. It looked like he had some big-time substance abuse problem. The second time he came through he was trim and fit and lucid. It was like one of those before-and-after diet ads."

Calgary dispensed some wild music of its own, via such bands as the Verdix and the Rip Chords. The Chords' bass player, Richard McDowell, was the classic punk convert, in spirit if not spiked dog collar. A high school dropout at sixteen, he'd spent a decade of floundering, working on the oil rigs up north, and trying to figure out where he fit in. Then, at twenty-six, he picked up a musical instrument for the first time. In his own words: "That's when the world got happy again." He quickly went from making "horrible sounds" in a buddy's basement apartment to playing gigs with the Rip Chords that included opening for the popular British "haircut" bands of the day. McDowell also ran his own club, Ten Foot Henry's, a funky hole in the wall named after its on-site icon, a large wooden cut-out of Henry, the bald, mute little boy in Carl Anderson's venerable King Features comic strip. There, punk and new wave slam-danced against Warholesque film and light shows *à la* the Exploding Plastic Inevitable, topped off with modern dance and poetry jams — a multimedia concept McDowell had eagerly lifted from clubs in Amsterdam and Copenhagen. It was a crazy cocktail but it worked, rock and the arts mixing with remarkable equanimity. People who'd come to see a band would fall silent and listen intently when a poet took the stage, or watch eagerly as ex-ballerina Denise Clarke, McDowell's on-and-off girlfriend, and her partner, Anne Flynn, tried out their latest dance creations. The place even had its own resident visual artist, Rita McKeough, who lived and worked in the cellar. "We had a great sense of community there," says McDowell. "It was a small club, but when things were happening it was pretty unique and great fun." Bruce McCulloch, at the time a business student at Mount Royal College, knew about Henry's but never dared to penetrate its bohemian interior. If he had, he was later to muse, he might have come across his future best friend and the co-founder of One Yellow Rabbit, Blake Brooker.

Henry's housed some of Calgary's first stabs at performance art, as did the back room of the Off Centre Centre, an artist-run gallery presided over by Dadaist mail-out artist Don Mabie (alias Chuck Stake), a man famous for posting slices of bologna to politicians at election time. As for avant-garde theatre, there were a few glimmerings here and there, although mostly amid the foliage of academe. The city's three professional theatre companies, Theatre Calgary, Alberta Theatre Projects, and Lunchbox Theatre, were still relatively new entities, building subscription audiences by reproducing the latest hits from New York and London. Local playwrights wrote plays about local history, in styles that recalled Arthur Miller or Joan Littlewood's Theatre Workshop and could hardly be considered radical. Theatre Calgary did take a brief stroll into rougher territory for a couple of seasons, producing a midnight series of youth-oriented fare. Its first show remained its most successful: a staging of the young David Mamet's *Sexual Perversity in Chicago,* which packed the theatre with a rock 'n' roll audience thanks partly to vigorous cross-promotion with the city's new FM rock station. For the length of its run, it was the hottest thing outside late-night screenings of *The Rocky Horror Picture Show.* Martin Fishman, who directed the play, still remembers the opening night. "I'll never forget. The house lights go down, and all you hear are beer bottles being opened. It was that kind of crowd. And they turned it into a melodrama; they were booing some characters and cheering others. Word of mouth spread and it had an incredible following. People would come back dressed up as the characters in the play. It really tapped into the sexual revolution going on at the time."

But the real theatrical revolution was taking place on that northwest hill where the University of Calgary stood. It was there that a madman from England was trying out his improvisational experiments on an innocent student body.

Drama professor Keith Johnstone, bespectacled and long-haired, resembled the neurotic psychiatrist played by Peter Sellers in *What's New, Pussycat?* He had come to the U of C from London's seminal Royal Court Theatre, where he had run the company's Writers' Group (participants included Edward Bond and Ann Jellicoe) and used to lunch with Samuel Beckett. Johnstone, who professed no reverence for Beckett or anybody else, had come to see improvisation as the key to freer, deeper acting, and competitive improvisation as a means of getting audiences directly involved in performance. His book on the subject, *Impro,* would soon become a bible for young actors, and his influence would eventually rival that of Viola Spolin, the Chicago acting teacher whose improvised "theatre games" formed the bedrock for post-war American comedy, from Nichols and May to the Second City.

At the end of the '70s, Johnstone was an English legend in exile, a prophet in a cultural desert called Calgary. He made no bones about its arid arts scene. "I'm living in a city at the edge of the Rocky Mountains; the population is much greater than it was in Shakespearian London, and almost everyone here is literate," he wrote in *Impro*, published in 1979. "Where are the poets, and playwrights, and painters, and composers? … The great art of this part of the world was the art of the native peoples. The whites flounder about trying to be 'original' and failing miserably." He didn't just complain, he took action, forming a theatre company with his students called — in a fitting nod to his wild Canadian surroundings — Loose Moose. And the company did its share of wild theatre, from sacrilegious versions of *Waiting for Godot* to Johnstone's own odd plays, such as a revisionist *Robinson Crusoe* in which Friday eats the shipwrecked hero. If the work wasn't brilliant, it often left a lasting impression. Young Andy Curtis was blown away by a production of a Johnstone script called *Mindswop.* "I remember [actor] Grant Linneberg with an android mask and three legs, bursting out of an elevator and sending all these people in wheelchairs in the front row into spasms. That was cool."

However, Loose Moose's staple was Theatresports, Johnstone's improvisation games, held on weekends and drawing maximum participation from its young audiences. It made converts of the most unlikely kids. McCulloch, whose *American Graffiti* idea of a fun weekend was cruising the length of neon-lit Macleod Trail, rock music blasting from his car radio, or hanging at Tom's House of Pizza, thought theatre was for sissies. Then one night he ventured through the doors of the Loose Moose Simplex and the scales fell from his eyes. "I'd heard there was a place that had improv comedy and I'd been starting to write stuff," he says. "I walked in there and it was the only time in my life I thought: This is my calling. I started the way everybody did there at the time, which was going through classes. Then I started getting on stage and that's when I hooked up with Mark McKinney." The pair began doing a late-night comedy show Saturdays, for which McCulloch adopted Iggy Pop's "Lust For Life" as his personal theme and motto. Their lust for laughs was insatiable. Within a few years, the two had moved to Toronto and, along with Dave Foley, Kevin McDonald, and Scott Thompson, formed the Kids in the Hall.

Blake Brooker was more bookish than McCulloch but equally naive when it came to the stage. "I wasn't interested in theatre at all," he says. "When I was in high school at Crescent Heights, I remember there was a drama club that would come trooping into the lunchroom singing songs from some musical like *Oklahoma!* and I'd wonder what planet they were from. I could never see myself as part of that group. I had what I considered to be more serious and rigorous interests, and perhaps wilder interests, than knowing the songs to *Jesus Christ Superstar*." By the time he came to study liberal arts at the University of Calgary, Brooker was a voracious reader, mostly of modern fiction and poetry. His favourites, he remembers, included Franz Kafka, Thomas Mann, Henry Miller, Laurence Durrell, Carson McCullers, Don DeLillo, and, a particular hero, Leonard Cohen. For a little light refreshment, he turned to *Rolling Stone* — which, back then, was still a cutting-edge rock zine, not the glossy read for the frat-house crowd it has since become. That's where he stumbled upon the Ramones. "He was the guy who introduced us to the Ramones, in 1975," says his younger brother, Kevin. "Soon as they came out, he read a tiny blurb about them in *Rolling Stone,* said 'That band sounds interesting,' and went out and bought their album."

Along with a hunger to explore, Blake and Kevin were also determined nonconformists. They came by it naturally. They had grown up in what was, on the surface, the typical hard-working, hockey-loving, blue-collar Canadian family — but with a difference. Their father, who had never finished high school, had a keen and active mind and, in Blake's words, "always used to bring ideas into the house." There was talk of Shakespeare and Picasso at their dinner table and a Mercedes Benz in their driveway when the neighbours had Chevys and Fords. In the late 1960s, when the boys were barely in their teens, their dad suddenly quit his oil-refinery job, sold their suburban home, and enrolled in university. As if that wasn't enough of a mid-life challenge, he also set about designing a new house for his family and built the entire thing himself, with the help of his wife and kids. It was a do-it-yourself example that, as much as punk, left a lasting imprint on his oldest son.

After leaving school, the Brooker boys formed their own little band of outsiders. They all wore funny clothes, they read the Beat writers, and they travelled constantly, restlessly. There were road trips to California and backpacking adventures in North Africa and the South Pacific. And like Sal and Dean in Jack Kerouac's *On the Road,* they were always ready to jump in a car and just go. "We loved going on those long drives," says Warren Fick, who was one of the gang — although he won't claim it was entirely under the influence of Kerouac. "A lot of it was just fuelled by alcohol. We also read a lot of Hunter Thompson."

In the summer of 1979, they ended up sharing an old two-storey house in the inner city with the inauspicious address of 1313–13 Avenue SW. The Brookers, Fick, and Doug Grant were the main tenants but the place was always swarming with people. "We had a lot of dudes come through that house, just rockin' and rollin' and partyin'," says Kevin. "We had a real beatnik jungle going there." Richard McDowell made regular safaris, bringing along his high school sweetheart, Denise Clarke. "The first time I met those guys," she says, "they were all wearing pyjamas. Richard was an outrageous dresser, too. He would wear these wild-looking floral pants and he made his own leather boots and moccasins. And then we meet Blake and Kevin and Warren Fick and the rest, and these guys were the same! They'd actually go out in a group and go to the bars in their jammies." Or to a rock concert dressed as chefs. Fick says a bunch of them went to the Elvis Costello show in the little white jackets worn by kitchen staff.

Their quirky sense of humour also gave birth to Ten Foot Henry, the icon. Blake commissioned the giant figure from another buddy, musician-artist Gregg Casselman. By then, the gang had relocated to an old house beside the Elbow River, not far from the Calgary Stampede grounds. "Gregg got this traceable stencil and just blew the cartoon up and made a ten-foot Henry," recalls McDowell, "and they put it up against the clothesline in the backyard of the house. They used to give it ever-changing thought bubbles. During the Stampede one year, it read 'Depressing, isn't it?'" When Blake moved out, in the summer of 1982, McDowell asked if he could adopt the enormous boy for his newly opened club. "We hauled the character in and stood him up against the wall and he fit, like, within a quarter of an inch. We thought, That's perfect. Let's call the place Ten Foot Henry's."

The Brookers, McDowell, and their friends were always being razzed on the street for their unusual attire. At the time Calgary had more money than sophistication and there were plenty of ignorant hicks itching to stomp anyone who looked different. John Dunn, who'd just arrived from Montreal, where punk was an established trend, weathered a rain of abuse whenever he stepped out with his leather jacket and Day-Glo hair. "I used to get chased down the streets by pickup trucks full of guys yelling 'Hey, fag! C'mere!' They had never seen punk rockers before." The same thing was always happening to his best pal, Michael Green.

One day, Green, a skinny guy with unruly black hair and a hawk-like nose, chanced to wheel past 1313. "I was bicycling by on my antique bicycle, wearing my leathers," he recalls, "and I heard what I figured were these rednecks just haranguing me. So I thought I should go confront them. And when I went up to the house there were Blake and his brother, Kevin."

It was destiny. If the Brooker boys were offbeat, Green was a total zany. Raised on a diet of vintage *Goon Show* recordings by his British-immigrant parents, to which he added heavy teenage doses of Frank Zappa, he had sensibilities that tended toward the freaky, the sick, and the strange. With his high school drama teacher, Gary Stromsmoe, he had started a ragged little theatre group called Ikarus, which was defiantly outrageous. Many remember seeing Green act for the first time in a piece called *Meatsong,* performed in an old house across from the city's planetarium on Halloween. He opened the show with a quirky *coup de théâtre:* "I was in this bag, this sort of plastic, metallic womb that was hanging in the closet," he explains. "It started writhing and the thing inside cut itself out with a gigantic Bowie knife and I just came spilling out, all sweaty and Vaselined up, onto the floor." A television reporter was there to shoot a Halloween item and the scene was caught on camera. "I think I managed to get full frontal nudity on the local CBC-TV channel for the first time ever," says Green proudly. The house was owned by the city and slated for demolition. Ikarus dubbed it "the McPhail Secret Theatre" (after its original owners) and revealed its location over the phone to only the trusted few, so the company wouldn't get caught squatting.

When not staging clandestine acts of madness, Ikarus occupied the funky Pumphouse Theatres, where it liked to mangle the classics and infuriate the purists. Philip McCoy, a formidably erudite University of Calgary professor who also served as a freelance drama critic, was regularly appalled by the troupe. Stromsmoe still quotes his reviews with relish. "When we did *Deathwatch*, the Jean Genet play, he felt it was a disaster. He said 'It's good to see Genet being done in Calgary, but this production is worse than no production at all.'" But Ikarus, like its high-flying namesake, wasn't listening to authority. One of the group's craziest outings was an assault on Shakespeare. *Titus Androctopus, or: Scrotum's Revenge* was an outdoor show that took the already over-the-top tragedy to the point of ridiculousness. "It was done with total disrespect," says Stromsmoe. "It was a huge, deliberate mishmash of styles, some very slick and some totally laughable." Among the spurious characters added to Shakespeare's dramatis personae were a tree-dwelling clown called Scrotum and the perverted teenage Roman emperor Heliogabalus, played by Green as a Dickie Dee ice cream vendor on a bicycle.

Behind Green's lunacy lay unfettered energy and a passion for rough 'n' tumble theatre. He'd been turned on to it in high school, courtesy of Stromsmoe. The young teacher at Western Canada High had scarcely more experience with drama than his students, but he knew what he liked. Instead of producing a cheery *Music Man* or *West Side Story,* he opted to direct his Grade 12 students in a staging of Peter Weiss's anarchic classic, *The Persecution and Assassination of Jean-Paul Marat as Performed by the Inmates of the Asylum of Charenton under the Direction of the Marquis de Sade.* "We basically attempted to in some way emulate Peter Brook's production," says Green. "It was a real indication of how permissive society was then. All we had to do was take out a couple of 'fucks,' and we did it. And, as I recall, the students put the 'fucks' back in 'cause they felt like it." After graduation in 1975, Green helped Stromsmoe found the amateur Ikarus. "In all our naïveté, we were going to introduce Calgary to experimental theatre." As well as dismembering famous plays, Ikarus also created its own material. Stromsmoe had introduced Green to the Dadaists and the Surrealists, with their love of odd juxtapositions and their sense of mischief, and Ikarus scripts were often composed out of random texts that had been sliced and diced into "concrete poetry." For titles, they turned to such chance sources as a message on a lamppost or a poster in a bar. The latter, spotted by Stromsmoe in a Greenwich Village joint during a visit to New York, inspired a show called *First Aid for the Choking Victim.* The resulting confusion, Stromsmoe remembers, was delightful. "We had people showing up at the Pumphouse thinking that it was a presentation on the Heimlich manoeuvre."

While wreaking havoc at the Pumphouse, Green attempted a more formal study of drama at the University of Calgary. He eventually gave up, in mid-degree, when he came to the realization he'd rather make theatre than learn about it. By the time he and Blake Brooker had become good friends, Green was running Ikarus, improvising with Loose Moose, acting with various little Edmonton companies, working as a performing arts coordinator for the City of Calgary, and touring the province as stage manager for Theatre Calgary's Stage Coach Players.

He was also learning to be an impresario, arranging gigs for such visiting performers as San Francisco comedian David Schein. A member of the avant-garde, Berkeley-based Blake Street Hawkeyes Theatre, Schein paid two visits to Calgary. When he came the second time, in 1982, he brought along his girlfriend and fellow Hawkeye, Caryn Johnson, a young woman who had taken her stage name from that puerile practical-joke item, the whoopee cushion. David Schein and Whoopi Goldberg gave several workshops and performed at a vocational school and the Off Centre Centre. George McFaul, an aspiring young actor and clown, remembers catching Goldberg's act. "I will never forget Whoopi Goldberg coming out, doing this improv mime scene where she's an old woman in the park, bent over and coaxing the pigeons, like she's going to feed them. She's got this bag in her hand. And a pigeon comes up and — swoop! — she suddenly stuffs it in the bag. She's catching her supper! It was pretty clear at the time she was amazing; she was obviously a burning light." But most people didn't realize they had a future star in their midst. One of Schein and Goldberg's performances was called off when the cast and crew outnumbered the audience. "Whoopi refused to perform," says John Dunn, who was backstage. "So we all went back to Michael's house and got drunk." A year later, Goldberg would be performing her material at New York's Dance Theater Workshop, where Mike Nichols spotted her. A solo show on Broadway followed, then a leading role in Steven Spielberg's *The Color Purple* and, by 1985, Goldberg was a Hollywood star. Green, thinking of her performing to a handful of people in the back of a Calgary art gallery, still laughs about it. "She probably considers that one of the low points in her career."

Green soon had an on-stage/off-stage partner of his own. He'd met, and fallen head over heels for, Jan Stirling, one of the actors in the Stage Coach Players troupe. Stirling had grown up in Peterborough, Ontario, in a theatrical family. Her mother, Annie, taught drama and was involved with the city's amateur theatre guild, and Jan had been acting from the age of seven. After graduating from Sheridan College's theatre program, she had done a national audition and was hired for Stage Coach by Theatre Calgary artistic director Rick McNair. It was in 1981, during her second year with the company, that she encountered the manic Michael. "She was so pretty and I was out-of-my-head crazy," he says. "And I have to say I was a lousy stage manager. She used to haul me out on the carpet over things I'd done, in front of my bosses. And after a while I began to like it."

That little S&M frisson, unfolding behind the scenes as the troupe toured Alberta schools, would lead to a more serious relationship. Green knew Stirling was the right girl for him. He also knew she was the right girl to help start a theatre company.

Green had been nursing that dream for a while. He used to mull it over in his little basement apartment with another theatrical couple he'd become friends with. "It was like a Hobbit dwelling," remembers Gyllian Raby of Green's murky digs. She and boyfriend Nigel Scott would "visit and talk for hours. Periodically, Michael would talk about founding a theatre company with higher production values than Ikarus's community mandate permitted, but we were all too busy to catch the ball."

Green and Scott had met as drama students at the University of Calgary, where Scott was dabbling in acting and studying design. The two found themselves in a criticism course taught by Philip McCoy, and Scott admired Green's chutzpah in challenging the imperious pro-fessor. "Michael was a very outspoken, charismatic kind of guy. We hit it off big-time." Like Green, Scott was the child of Brits and had been born in Malta when it was still a British colony. Shortly afterwards, the family emigrated to the United States, then Canada, and Scott grew up in Calgary. There, he attended Central Memorial High and fell under the influence of an energetic English teacher named Louis B. Hobson, who staged the school's big theatrical productions. (Hobson later became well known as a drama and movie critic for the *Calgary Sun*.) After high school, Scott bounced between the U of C and the University of Alberta in Edmonton, finally settling on the former because it had a) Keith Johnstone and, b) a more creative approach to theatrical design. He became fascinated with the kind of environmental theatre preached and practised by Richard Schechner, founder of New York's hippie-era Performance Group (predecessor to the Wooster Group). Schechner believed in using the entire theatre as a set, in which actors and audi-ence members mingled in an act of communion.

Gyllian Raby, better known as Gyl, shared Scott and Green's taste for the avant-garde and, in fact, knew more about it than either of them. Fiercely intelligent, political, and opinionated, Raby had a much wider experience of theatrical styles. She'd come to the U of C on a research scholarship, fresh from her native Britain, where she had stud-ied drama at the University of Manchester, performed at the Edinburgh

Festival Fringe, and formed some decided opinions about what kind of experimenting she wanted to do. Although drawn ideologically to the kind of left-wing theatre practised in the UK by such '70s alternative companies as Joint Stock and 7:84, she felt their brand of social realism lacked imagination and theatricality. "I wanted the sort of total theatre [theorist Edward] Gordon Craig wrote about, that would wreak a voodoo effect."

Raby came from a country that, if it had no future as the Sex Pistols claimed, certainly had a monumental past. It was a millstone, she suggests. "Keith Johnstone once said to me that England was so weighed down with its self-image it couldn't move anymore." She had spent her childhood in Shropshire, whose "blue remembered hills" were immortalized by A. E. Housman, in the city of Shrewsbury, scene of Henry IV's victory against the rebel Harry Percy, immortalized in Shakespeare's *Henry IV, Part I*. She grew up reading the Bard — usually while blow-drying her hair. "The only plug the dryer would fit was next to the *Collected Works*." The stage was an obsession from an early age. "I think I was thirteen when I adapted Sophocles' *Oedipus*," she recalls, "and played the power-blinded king wrapped in a sheet toga." From the time she realized that her sex need not be her destiny (it was the dawn of the women's movement), she was set on a career in theatre.

Raby was also determined to one day emigrate to Canada. She saw her homeland as oppressive, all the more so because she was part Welsh and knew how that language and culture were belittled. As a teenager she fancied herself a Welsh Nationalist and tried to learn its consonant-packed Celtic. "Wales felt as if it was a huge and illicit part of my iden-tity," she says. Gazing across the Atlantic, she imagined Canada as a clean, sweet country free from class snobbery. Her student vacations eventually brought her to Calgary in the summer of 1978, when she got a job landscaping and was amazed to find artistic people who made a living as roughnecks on the oil rigs up north. "I found the culture raw, wild," she says. And full of potential. Upon graduating from Manchester, she headed out to the Wild West again to do a master's degree in dramatic literature. The move didn't disappoint her. "I had the strongest sensation of 'coming home' in Calgary," she says. "I felt surrounded by passionate, inquiring people in a way I hadn't in [Europe]." As she studied the work of experimental Canadian writer Beverley Simons for her master's thesis, Raby also tried her hand at improv with Loose Moose and formed a little group at the university, Double Vision Theatre, which staged work by Genet and a funny young chap named Ben Elton, who'd been a fellow student of Raby's at Manchester. She and Scott moved in together in 1981, as he entered his final year at the U of C. They rented an old house near the Bow River, not far from Green's basement burrow.

It was in an elevator, en route to a show at the University Theatre, that the strong-minded Raby found herself butting heads with an equally argumentative young man on the issue of shelters for battered women. "We didn't hit it off right away," Raby says of her first encounter with Blake Brooker. "Neither of us was actually listening to what the other was saying." She had no idea who Brooker was, or that Green had been confiding his theatre dream to him, too. Still, he quickly impressed her as no ordinary adversary. "I was intrigued with Blake," she says. "He was so weirdly passionate and didn't toe a party line on anything, always coming from a different perspective." Raby also noticed something else. "In Alberta, land of gingham shirts and blue jeans, Blake was wearing kind of striped pyjamas and flip-flops." Which, in a city where a man could get beaten up for wearing a pink shirt in public, she saw as a singular act of sartorial bravery.

There were other brave, odd souls out there who would soon become part of the growing circle of friends.

Kirk Miles was a young man with the broad, cheerful face of a farmer but the sensitivity of a poet — which is what he aspired to be. Visions of Cohen and Dylan brooded in his head. He also had an aptitude for theatre, getting top marks in his high school drama classes. His background, however, was solidly non-literary, and parental encouragement was scant. So Miles played the role of dutiful son, studying for a political science degree at the University of Calgary and planning to enter law school when he graduated. "I went the route that I thought I was supposed to go, to please my parents," he says. Then, in his final year, he snapped. "That was the year I really started to go 'I don't want to do this.' I got into law school, I achieved what they wanted me to achieve, and then I just decided, fuck it. I got drunk at the dean's reception and just said 'I'm gonna be a poet!' and walked out, kinda like [Charles] Bukowski. I didn't know how to be an artist, but I decided I was going to try it out, for a little while anyhow. I'd been into political science and now suddenly I was totally immersed in poetry and art."

Miles decided to take a second degree in English and began hanging with the local poetry crowd. That's when he got to know Blake Brooker. "I was acquainted with Blake," he recalls. "We'd formed a fairly strong acquaintance, almost turning into a friendship but not really."

While Miles was having his crisis at the U of C, George McFaul had returned there to flirt with the theatre — the latest kick for a footloose young man who couldn't stay put academically or geographically. As a nineteen-year-old from small-town Saskatchewan, he'd arrived in Calgary in 1974 and enrolled at Mount Royal College in its public relations program. It turned him off. He left after six months and shifted to the U of C, where he took political science. Before long that, too, palled, and McFaul dropped out to work and travel for a couple of years. He got a full-time job with the City of Calgary's social services, babysitting young offenders — "juvenile delinquents, as we would call them then. It was a really well-paying job for a twenty-one-year-old." With the money he earned, he travelled, and his wanderings made him realize his linguistic limits. "When I came back about a year later I wanted to learn a second language," he recalls, "and obviously the one to learn in this country is French, so I started doing immersion programs. I re-enrolled in the university and took every French-preferred class I could." The religious studies department was just starting up at the time and it was recruiting students. "It seemed as interesting as anything else, so I enrolled in religious studies and French programs."

After graduating, McFaul wanted to pursue his French further and received a bursary to spend a year at Laval University in Quebec City. It was there, while taking extracurricular classes, that he got plugged in to theatre. "I didn't have any previous history with it, but I started taking everything I could take that was about theatre and culture and clowning and improv, in French. I found that, as well as being a lot of fun, it was a fantastic way to develop the language." Arriving back in Calgary, he returned to the U of C and auditioned for its summer drama project, Theatre 21:00 (the name referred to its 9:00 P.M. curtain). The lean, lanky McFaul was cast in a production of Steve Gooch's feminist Botany Bay drama, *Female Transport,* where he played the role of a ship's surgeon and caught the eye of Gyl Raby. The year was 1982.

Calgary in 1982 was a small city that kept getting bigger, with one foot in the urban jungle and the other still planted on the frontier. Its skyscraper skyline was impressive enough to double as Metropolis in Hollywood's *Superman* films, while the back doors of its ever-sprawling suburbs opened onto untamed wilderness. Gophers, jack rabbits, deer, even the occasional cougar or black bear, would wander in from the foothills to appear suddenly, incongruously, amid the tidy lawns and freshly paved roads.

As an incorporated city, Calgary was less than a century old. It had begun as a North-West Mounted Police fort in 1875, established at the junction of the Bow River and its quaintly named tributary, the Elbow. The fort was christened with the Gaelic word "Calgary" by the NWMP commissioner, a sentimental Scot named James Macleod, whose maternal relatives owned a house of that name on the Isle of Mull. "The history of any city begins with an ending," wrote Blake Brooker when contemplating his hometown. "Each foundation laid is also an eviction notice." Up until 1875, the area had been prime buffalo-hunting ground for its indigenous peoples, the Blackfoot, Blood, Piegan, and Sarcee. The NWMP, sent to subdue renegade whisky traders who preyed on the Aboriginals, prepared the way for a more refined form of exploitation by the Canadian government. Aboriginal people were shuffled on to reserves, the land was leased, and cattle imported from the United States. Queen Victoria's son-in-law dropped by and saw that it was good. With the arrival of Canada's transcontinental railway, the settlement rapidly grew from a town (1884) to a city (1893). Farming and ranching were its principal industries — the latter celebrated with the world-famous Calgary Stampede — until the discovery of oil and gas fields in nearby Turner Valley in 1914. Then came the major find in Leduc in 1947, when the geologists discovered that Alberta, already famous for its dinosaur fossils, was also a vast depository of fossil fuels. The drilling rigs moved in and the province turned into Canada's primary oil producer, with Calgary as the centre of the industry.

In 1971, after thirty-six years of Social Credit rule, the Progressive Conservatives swept to power in Alberta, led by a shrewd Harvard-trained Calgary lawyer named Peter Lougheed. He saw to it that his government got a larger share of the oil wealth, and channelled it into upgrading the province. Like Texas, to which it is often compared, Alberta has a history as a haven of political and religious conservatism. Yet Lougheed's Conservatives, wherever they may have stood morally, practised a fiscal liberality that would inspire nostalgia by the time of the tight-fisted '90s. Among the many beneficiaries of their largesse were the arts. Money was pumped into projects large and small, and the smiling man with his hand on the pump was Minister of Culture Horst Schmid, a flamboyant visionary who stimulated activity by matching earned revenue dollar-for-dollar with grants. "It was an extraordinary time in this province," recalls Anne Green, who served with the ministry's performing arts foundation. "At one period, Alberta and Quebec were the leading provinces in their support of arts and culture in Canada." And Alberta's population was only one-third of Quebec's.

The spending was scarcely reined in when, at the outset of the 1980s, the oil bubble burst and Calgary's growth spurt ground to a halt. The city would recover from the recession by the end of the decade, but in the meantime it was hard times. Bankruptcies. Foreclosures. An exodus of skilled and unskilled labour. For starving artists, however, it was a time of unexpected opportunity. Suddenly, rents were dropping, vacancies climbing, and you could actually live well with very little money, even open a rock club or a theatre in one of the many empty buildings. And the arts funding was still there. Where some saw a crisis, others saw a chance to buy in.

There would be some new gamblers and prospectors in this Wild West town.

Calgary had always been Canaan for entrepreneurs. It was the metaphorical small pond, where a tetra could make like Moby Dick. Where even a scrawny little punk like the teenaged Michael Green could walk the streets as if he owned them and sniff the scent of promise in the unpolluted air.

"When I was sixteen, I remember there were places in downtown Calgary where you could stand and you could see the edge of the city in all directions," Green says. "It was a small place and that makes you feel powerful. And anything you wanted to do in this town, you could do it. No one had been doing it first; there was nobody saying things like 'You can't do that, it's been done before' or 'It would never work.'" So, if you wanted to start a professional avant-garde theatre, what was there to stop you? It was almost as easily done as said. And Green's Sal Paradise had Brooker's Dean Moriarty tugging at his sleeve, saying "Lessgo!"

"Blake said 'I'll provide the wine. You go out and enlist all the people that you think we'll need,'" recalls Green. He rounded them up and, at the appointed hour, they met at Brooker's house by the river, at the sign of Ten Foot Henry.

# 2. Leonardo, Batman, and the Juggler

"In dreams begins responsibility." — W. B. YEATS

The 1970s saw a revolution in Canadian theatre. Like young people all over the western world, Canadian kids entered the decade pumped with hippie idealism and primed for anarchy, and the youth tumbling out of Canada's theatre schools were prepared to give the finger to the theatre establishment. Never mind that the establishment — largely represented by Ontario's Stratford and Shaw Festivals — was scarcely two decades old. Or that the first of these festivals was run by Robin Phillips, a cocky young Brit in his early thirties. Shrines to Shakespeare and G. B. S., those institutions stood for Canada's colonial past. It was time to get out there and find Canada's stories and tell them to the average Canadian. A bushy-bearded director named Paul Thompson dropped a clutch of eager young actors in the middle of an Ontario farming community and had them collectively create a show about the folks they met. Socially conscious dramatists Sharon Pollock and Rick Salutin poked their noses into unexplored crannies of Canada's past and emerged with powerful plays. Michel Tremblay held up a mirror to the Caliban of the working-class Québécois family. John Juliani and his Savage God gang took their theatre to the streets, enlivening the public spaces of languid Vancouver. Alternative theatres sprouted up and took the communal-living trend a step further, with communal writing. The unexpected success of Thompson's *Farm Show* for Theatre Passe Muraille led to a flood of collective creations, about miners, loggers, oil-rig workers — the common man and woman. Individual playwrights also used the documentary method, and among the most successful efforts was John Murrell's *Waiting for the Parade.* A play shaped from the recollections of Calgary women on the homefront during the Second World War, it would go on to receive countless productions and launch Murrell's career.

Hand in hand with the idealism came the shock tactics of the counterculture. Tom Hendry, Martin Kinch, and John Palmer started Toronto Free, a theatre that charged no admission (at least for a little while) and relentlessly needled the puritan sensibilities of its buttoned-down host city. There, young poet Michael Ondaatje worked out his obsession with violence in the bloody, bullet-shattered lyricism of *The Collected Works of Billy the Kid.* There, ex-rocker Michael Hollingsworth tested the stomachs of theatregoers with *Clear Light,* a foul stew of brutal sex, cannibalism, and psychedelic drugs. Kinch, director of these and other controversial shows, came to be dubbed "Mr. Sex-and-Violence." Meanwhile, Ken Gass's Factory Theatre Lab, another new Toronto company, lodged in an old candle factory, wowed the critics with *Creeps,* an obscenely funny play about five men with cerebral palsy. Or, for Canadian history as horrific Greek tragedy, you could take in James Reaney's sprawling trilogy on the infamous Donnelly clan of southern Ontario. Staged with Brechtian brio by a tousle-headed twenty-nine-year-old named Keith Turnbull, it premiered to raves in Toronto, then toured from coast to coast.

In Calgary, Christopher Newton, another cocky young Brit *à la* Phillips, had arrived in 1968 to kick-start the city's first professional theatre. Born out of an earlier merger of Workshop 14 (director Betty Mitchell's award-winning amateur company) and the Musicians and Actors Club, Theatre Calgary joined the chain of regional theatres being set up across Canada. By 1972, Calgary's second professional theatre had been formed. Alberta Theatre Projects began playing to schoolkids but quickly metamorphosed into an adult company. Both theatres had modest beginnings: TC made its downtown home in a renovated tractor warehouse, while ATP occupied a log-built prairie "opera house" inside a suburban theme park. TC followed the regional formula from the start, reaching for the widest audience by programming classics and the

Broadway/West End hits of the day. Tellingly, its first show was Neil Simon's *The Odd Couple*. That didn't keep Newton from also serving some homegrown Calgary fare, in the form of musical revues he wrote with composer Allan Rae. Later, his successors, Harold Baldridge and Rick McNair, would make room for locally written plays by Pollock and the best-selling novelist W. O. Mitchell. ATP, which leaned more toward the alternative modes, was equally aggressive about putting Calgary on stage. Playwright Paddy Campbell, then married to artistic director Douglas Riske, penned local history lessons for all ages and turned the life of pioneer newspaperman Bob Edwards into musical comedy. John Murrell, a high school English teacher, also began writing for the company, which premiered *Waiting for the Parade* in 1977.

By the dawn of the 1980s, the alternative theatres that had stuck out the decade began to grow up, acquire solid reputations, and find a niche. If the regionals were the department stores of theatre, then the alternative theatres were the boutiques — a suitable metaphor for the '80s, when hippies grew into yuppies and the commune was replaced by commerce. The young rebels inevitably became the establishment. Newton took the helm of the Shaw Festival. Pollock became artistic director of Theatre Calgary, left after three strife-torn months, and was replaced by Mr. Sex-and-Violence himself, Martin Kinch. Shortly after his arrival, TC moved into a new state-of-the-art, 750-seat proscenium theatre in the city's $82–million Centre for Performing Arts. Kinch introduced himself with a season that included Shakes-peare's *Twelfth Night* and Chekhov's *Uncle Vanya* in a translation by Murrell. ATP, too, had its own custom-built venue in the arts centre, a 400-seat Georgian courtyard theatre, and a playbill favouring off-Broadway fare.

The time was ripe for a new avant-garde, a new wave of Canadian theatre, this time based less on playwriting than performance, with emphasis on a total experience in which text was only one component and expression came equally from movement, music, design. It would draw on European theories, which in turn were often inspired by the ancient theatre forms of non-European cultures. It's true that some of these ideas had already informed the alternative theatre of the '60s and

'70s, but in the end the emphasis had settled on building a body of Canadian dramatic literature. It was from that corpus that Ikarus had pulled David Freeman's *Creeps* for a 1981 revival to mark the International Year of the Disabled Person. It would be Blake Brooker's entry into the theatre.

The idea for the revival was Michael Green's. He was co-directing the play with Gerry Thurston, a professor in the University of Calgary's drama department, and during the casting process his thoughts turned to Brooker. "At that point, I'd been bumping into Blake on and off at parties for a couple of years," says Green, "and I asked him if he would come and consider auditioning. I think the audition consisted of Gerry getting Blake to read a couple of pages of *National Geographic* or something like that. And he got cast as the guy in the wheelchair." Brooker played Sam, a diaplegic, in the production, which was presented that March in the Pumphouse. He took the role very seriously, even riding the Handi-Bus, a bus service for the handicapped, to get a better idea of the challenges faced by his character. Kevin Brooker's pithy assessment of his brother's debut performance? "He was kind of a shitty actor but he got good at using a wheelchair."

Whatever his thespian abilities, Blake Brooker had finally crossed the footlights. The Ikarus experience excited him and he began to share in Green's daydreams about a professional avant-garde company. That encouragement was all Green needed. The talk turned serious and finally, almost exactly a year after the *Creeps* production, they decided it was time to act.

On a cold, dismal February evening in 1982, five people arrived at Blake Brooker's riverside house for that first exploratory meeting. Michael Green had invited Jan Stirling ("She was the first person I approached," he says, "because she had more administrative experience than Blake and I did"), Gyl Raby, Nigel Scott, and another friend named Keith Marion. Over Brooker's wine, they began to express their theatrical wants and desires. Raby remembers it distinctly. "Michael wanted an irreverent theatre of bold performance that had high production values.

Blake wanted a writer's theatre that featured a poet's view, offering anything but Broadway. I was in the same camp, interested in disrupting naturalism and investigating ideas that ran counter [to] consumer culture. Nige wanted to explore minimalist material-based imagist design, and Jan wanted to escape the ingenue roles she was being cast in repeatedly." Clearly, they were all on the same page. "Very early on, if not at that first meeting, we hit on the phrase 'vital and surprising theatre,'" recalls Stirling. "That was our vision, that's what we wanted to create. We also had a strong sense of what we *didn't* want to be. We didn't want to be mainstream or commercial or to play to the lowest common denominator." (Marion was the only one to opt out of the plans, although he would later become a cofounder of Ten Foot Henry's.)

Green was eager to fill out the application forms to start a not-for-profit theatre society, but the others were hesitant. After all, while they were all friends of Michael, they didn't really know one another. They decided instead to mount a production together and see how it went. Over subsequent gatherings, they settled on a venue and a play.

In retrospect, two incidents during those early meetings were harbingers of the future. At their second get-together, Brooker gave Scott an impromptu gift of Italo Calvino's novel *If on a Winter's Night a Traveler,* which had recently been published in English. "It was my birthday," recalls Scott, "and there was some mention of that, and Blake ran to his bookshelf and pulled out this book. He said 'You've gotta read this guy. He's brilliant.'" Soon after, the whole gang was reading and loving Calvino, and they would begin to share their other enthusiasms, too. Personal obsessions, shared and shaped into group projects, would drive the company creatively for the next twenty years. The other bit of foreshadowing occurred at the first meeting. When the six conspirators began their huddle at Brooker's house, there was a seventh person in the room — Blake's new girlfriend, Denise Clarke. Raby remembers that she was doing stretching exercises "as dancers do, but she wasn't intending to participate in the meeting and soon left."

## Old Master, New Fringe

Given her directing experience at the university, it was natural that Gyl Raby should direct the group's first show. She had also read more plays than the others and proposed a British one, *Leonardo's Last Supper* by Peter Barnes, for their debut. Today, Barnes is still best known for his 1968 play, *The Ruling Class,* a brilliant, brutal satire of the English peerage in which a young earl is thought mad when he fancies himself Christ — and sane when he switches to Jack the Ripper. Filmed from Barnes's own screenplay, it became the vehicle for a bravura performance by Peter O'Toole. *Leonardo's Last Supper,* a one-act, comes from the same period and was first produced in London in 1969, directed by Charles Marowitz. The play is set in 1519, in a French charnel house run by a family of Florentine exiles, the Lascas, who find their fortunes made when they are given the job of burying their fellow countryman, the late Leonardo da Vinci. The disgraced Lascas see the rare honour as their ticket back to Florence and fame, but their hopes are rudely dashed when it turns out Leonardo isn't dead yet — just the victim of a catatonic trance. The great man wakes and, realizing he's been given a second lease on life, prepares to finish all those unfinished masterpieces of his and assure his immortality. The Lascas, philistine capitalists, won't have it and end up drowning him in the same bucket that their drunken son Alphonso has been puking in.

Coarse, scatological comedy plays piggyback with tragedy as Barnes uses the sharp contrasts of the Renaissance — time of exquisite art and horrific plague, scientific revelation and ignorant superstition — to satirize the ageless struggle between humanity's loftiest and basest aspirations. Leonardo enjoys his own renaissance in the Lascas' charnel house until he is laid low by the greed of those for whom genius is no match against money. The script had obvious appeal for young actors, with its grotesque characterizations and broad physical antics, its dialogue full of gleeful, pseudo-archaic obscenities, and its use of juggling and masks. Not to mention an anachronistic finale in which the cast bursts into a rendition of the Nat King Cole ballad "Mona Lisa."

"In retrospect," says Raby, "Barnes's play provided the common thread that bound us. It had the rich language and dark humour, the attitude to materialism and authority, the wacky disregard for naturalism, and the potential for expressionist performance to which we were all keen to commit." To cast the play, the group held a reading/audition at Raby and Scott's. Brooker invited fellow poet Kirk Miles and an old university buddy, George McFaul, now a burgeoning actor whom Raby had just seen in *Female Transport*. Everyone was impressed with Miles's wild energy and McFaul's eagerness to tackle the tumbling and juggling the play required. They were immediately welcomed into the ranks. McFaul was cast as Leonardo. Miles was given the role of the besotted Alphonso Lasca, with Jan Stirling playing his mother, Maria, and Blake Brooker his father, Angelo. Michael Green served as stage manager. (He would later play Angelo in the company's 1985 revival.) Raby used her university connections to help scrape together costumes and props. According to Stirling, the company's future bean counter, the budget was a princely $375. It would cover production costs and marketing, the latter consisting of photcopied posters touched up with lurid blasts of orange and green spray paint.

By now, the new troupe had also found an ideal showcase for its first effort. Green had recently met Brian Paisley, the artistic director of Edmonton's Chinook Theatre, who had just been handed $50,000 to produce a theatrical component to the city's SummerFest activities, which already included popular folk and jazz festivals. Paisley had been to the impressive Edinburgh Festival Fringe the year before and saw the potential for a similar event, with one significant difference. Where Edinburgh's Fringe was a fend-for-yourself affair for the artists participating, Edmonton's Fringe would provide the makeshift venues as well as technical and other assistance. Green was there when Paisley floated the idea. Back in Calgary, he proposed the gang take *Leonardo* to the festival. Raby, who had played the Edinburgh Fringe as a student with Manchester Umbrella Theatre, was quick to second the motion. Now, what were they going to call themselves?

Deliberately or not, the company has always kept the meaning and origins of its name shrouded in mystery. In a 1985 interview, a po-faced Michael Green told CBC Radio critic Louise Bresky that the "One" stood for unity among the collective, "Yellow" was the colour symbolizing intelligence, and "Rabbit," well … That's where his improvisation broke down. In fact, it was Blake Brooker who dreamed up the name, well before that fateful first meeting in the winter of 1982. Inspired by his work with Green's Ikarus group, he'd attended an Alberta Culture workshop designed to instruct neophytes how to incorporate and run a not-for-profit theatre. Needing a company to register, he wrote down "One Yellow Rabbit." "I just made it up 'cause I needed a name," he says. "And when we got together a year later and had to come up with something to call our company, I said 'How about One Yellow Rabbit? It's got a bit of colour, it's somewhat poetic. Let's fly with it and see what happens.' No one came up with a better name, so we just stuck with it." Yes, but why "one yellow rabbit"? "It had a personal significance for me. It referred to one in my menagerie of childhood animals." We turn to kid brother Kevin to elucidate. "Every child has a favourite toy animal," he says. "Blake's was a very moth-eaten little bunny in a piss-yellow garment like a child's sleeper." To picture it, he adds, check out the episode of *The Simpsons* in which Bart Simpson's little friend is referred to. He's called Mr. Honey-Bunny "and he looked a lot like Blake's rabbit."

Gyl Raby says there were misgivings about choosing a name that could have them mistaken for a children's theatre or confused with Loose Moose. However, the other would-be clever suggestions — "Theatre X," "Theatre Station," "Know Theatre" — finally "rang vain and pretentious in our ears. I think we accepted the name One Yellow Rabbit to be perverse, because it was a-commercial, a challenging marketing tool, and it made us snicker." And so it was One Yellow Rabbit that would produce and perform *Leonardo's Last Supper* in the summer of 1982, first in the back space of the Off Centre Centre, then — and most spectacularly — at the Edmonton Fringe.

Belfast-born, Vancouver-raised, Brian Paisley had moved to Edmonton from little Fort St. John, on the British Columbia–Alberta border, in

1980, bringing Chinook, a young people's company, along with him. By then, Alberta's capital city was well on its way to becoming a theatre mecca, and well worth a pilgrimage. At the centre stood the spanking-new, three-venue Citadel Theatre, a major regional company run by such Brit heavyweights as John Neville and Peter Coe and known as a tryout house for Broadway-bound shows. Around it had grown an ever-widening circle of small professional theatres — Network, Northern Light, Workshop West, Phoenix, Catalyst — thanks largely to the superb drama conservatory at the local University of Alberta, which churned out graduates keen to create work for themselves. A fringe was, in retrospect, an obvious third ring, and one that would service Edmonton's eager playgoers in the dog days of summer. Paisley secured five venues in the amiably seedy Old Strathcona District and put out the call for shows. "I thought I was going to get twenty," he recalls. "I got forty-five." Groups came, not only from Alberta, but from other provinces too, while Mansamente, a visiting Brazilian puppet troupe, became the Edmonton Fringe's first international act. Calgary's wild contributions included One Yellow Rabbit's *Leonardo,* a staging of Snoo Wilson's *Blowjob* by Studio Theatre II (a group that included alumni of Theatre Calgary's midnight series), freewheeling improv by Loose Moose, cheeky puppetry by Ronnie Burkett, and Ikarus Theatre's mad mauling of Shakespeare, *Titus Androctopus.*

"They were like cousins coming out of the hills," says Paisley, evoking an image of avant-garde hillbillies descending on the capital. "It was an odd situation. [Edmonton] had the better set-up, but our people were not as theatrically adventurous as the ones coming out of Calgary." *Leonardo's Last Supper* won an enthusiastic endorsement from the *Edmonton Journal*'s drama critic, Keith Ashwell, who pronounced it "great saucy theatre" when he caught it on day four. "Once you forgive the fact that Jan Stirling can't possibly be Kirk Miles's mother, you'll just love her full-blooded, grubby performance," he wrote (18 August 1982). "Miles himself is a touch coy about his characterization but Blake Brooker just loves the malodorous nature of his trade and George McFaul is a lordly Leonardo. Gyl Raby's direction takes the show almost to the hilt of its outrageous and outrageously funny possibilities." Paisley remembers it as "a crackerjack show" that was pretty offbeat for the time and place. "People didn't know Peter Barnes," he says. "It was a whole different genre for Edmonton audiences; they'd never seen anything like that before." *Blowjob,* a violent British drama about two skinheads trying to blast open a safe, launched the Fringe tradition of drawing audiences with provocative titles (which would get much dirtier as time went on). *Titus Androctopus,* presented outdoors at midnight in an alley behind the Commercial Hotel, became the Fringe's first site-specific show and one of the first "you should have been there" productions. "That was a hoot. A wonderful show," says Paisley fondly. "It was supposed to be done two nights but only ended up being done once. There were sixty-five people in the audience, I think, but if you talk to people now, there were sixty-five hundred." The second night proved too cold and was called off, but Paisley and the Ikarus gang found a way to appease disappointed patrons. "At the same time, they were opening Hanratty's [restaurant] beside the Princess [Theatre] and they had a reception. We went in to the Hanratty's reception and they hadn't eaten all the hors d'oeuvres, so we scooped up the trays and when people came to the alley expecting to see the show at midnight, we greeted them and said 'Sorry, it's too damn cold, but here, have an hors d'oeuvre.'"

Paisley thinks the Fringe was a natural habitat for OYR and company and they took to it from the very start. "The Calgary contingent kept my energy up. It was refreshing to see that there were people who were immediately attuned to the idea. A lot of the groups were asking 'How does it work? What do we do?' while the guys from Calgary seemed to know already. It was a perfect match for them." George McFaul says the Rabbits' instincts for self-promotion came into play that August. When they weren't performing *Leonardo* in their ad hoc venue, a 150-seat space in the Tower Mortgage Building, they were working the pavement. "There wasn't a lot of presence for the festival in Edmonton that first year," he notes. "They were trying — they tried to have a parade and stuff — but we were the only company that really took this public face to heart. We got out there in our characters and paraded around, did little scenes on the street, to get attention — which nobody else was doing. They were sticking inside their theatres. But there we were, with a demented Leonardo wandering around the streets, reciting prophecies. We had a ball." The Rabbits' street show couldn't help but get attention, with Miles in a death-skull mask, Stirling dripping blood from her hands, Green thumping a military drum, and McFaul juggling as he made his predictions. Every now and then, they'd halt the parade and sing "Mona Lisa" with gusto. The antics paid off. "Our show rapidly gained a reputation as a must-see," recalls Raby, "and we swaggered about."

Not that it always ran smoothly. According to Raby, there was one lunchtime performance "where the troupe was possibly hungover" and everything started to fall apart. "The acrobatics went awry, with Blake accidentally being catapulted offstage and George's Leonardo wig getting pulled off." As juggling balls and lines were missed, the audience roared with laughter; but Raby, who was running the sound, became so humiliated that in a fit of pique, she bit the wrist of the lighting operator. "I've never run tech for another show," she says, "and I understand why Equity has a rule that keeps directors out of the booth."

In the end, the nine-day festival, Canada's very first fringe, had presented 220 performances, sold 7,500 tickets, and unknowingly kicked off what would soon be a national — and then international — trend. Michael Green, who had starred in the aborted *Titus* and stage-managed *Leonardo*, remembers an overall sense of elation. "It was wonderful. We didn't care that no one knew that it was going on. In our leather jackets, in the rain and the cold, we really got the feeling that we were involved in something very important."

Back home in Calgary, the Rabbits were mightily pleased. They'd invested $375 in their first production and earned some $1,200 at the gate. They were in the black and it was time to think of the next step. Buoyed by their Fringe experience, Miles and McFaul were keen to keep the company alive and be an integral part of it. Scott also wanted to carry it forward, as did Raby once she'd obtained her work visa. Blake Brooker, however, was not happy that summer. Perhaps torn up over his unsteady relationship with Denise Clarke (who was still involved with old boyfriend Richard McDowell), perhaps feeling he should leave theatre to the people with theatre degrees (Raby and Scott), he decided it was time to split. He left Calgary and the Rabbits and moved to Vancouver with his brother Kevin.

Michael Green and Jan Stirling, on the other hand, had become blissfully committed to each other and to the company. They got married in October in Stirling's hometown of Peterborough, entwined their last names into Stirling Green, and spent some of the money given them as a wedding gift to buy the troupe an electric typewriter and an answering machine. Their house, a rundown little bungalow in the downtown Mission neighbourhood, became One Yellow Rabbit's first office.

While the six were taking other jobs to pay the bills, they began to negotiate with the Off Centre Centre for rent-free use of the gallery's back space and sift through scripts in search of their next project. Impressed with the collective structure of the artist-run Off Centre Centre, they decided to adopt it themselves. Raby admits there was some uneasiness when she insisted on the title of artistic director — but after all, she had chosen to stay in Calgary to work with the company and she did have a master's degree. Otherwise, it would be a non-hierarchical outfit, where the actors also wrote grant applications and kept the accounts, the designer also acted, the playwright designed. Thanks to the determination of all concerned, it worked — for a time. "The philosophy of the company was that everybody could do everything," says Miles. "We were so idealistic and naive at the time. We had all these different talents, so we thought everyone could teach everybody else their skills and then we could all do it and we'd all take turns."

Miles and Raby approached the Off Centre Centre board with the request that One Yellow Rabbit become a subsidiary. The board was hesitant, believing it should be supporting performance art rather than theatre. The Rabbits argued that their work was a hybrid of both and, in the process of defining it, came up with the term "performance theatre." "It wasn't just expedience, a gambit for free rent," says Raby. Loathing the conventional work of the city's mainstream companies, "we thought there was a desperate need for a mixed-media approach to theatre." Their second show would be a vigorous — if not extreme — example of what they had in mind.

By now, Raby and Scott were living with Gerry Thurston, on the ground floor of his big, cozily cluttered old house in the southwest neighbourhood of Bankview. The university professor, an ardent supporter of all things experimental, was also an outspoken advocate of Canadian work. As Raby and Michael Green pored over the writings of the European absurdists, Thurston kept urging — in his grandly discursive style — that they forget Ionesco et al. and find a Canadian play. Raby finally agreed but, after plowing through a mountain of them, couldn't find anything that pleased both her and Green. Then she tentatively suggested *The Crusader,* a decidedly un-orthodox one-act by Beverley Simons, the Vancouver playwright on whose work she had written her recently completed master's thesis. The play was strange, cacophonous, disconcerting, and had, in the words of Green's idol Frank Zappa, no commercial potential. He couldn't wait to do it.

Beverley Rosen Simons had, by 1982, largely given up on the theatre and was writing prose fiction. A graduate of the University of British Columbia, she had been a favourite playwright of experimental director John Juliani, whose peripatetic Savage God project had produced several of her works, beginning in 1968 in Vancouver. Shortly thereafter, Simons scored her first — and only — mainstream success with *Crabdance.* An absurdist tragicomedy about an elderly woman's search for identity, it premiered in Seattle and went on to receive productions at four of Canada's regional theatres. Her other work, however, remained on the fringes and when One Yellow Rabbit picked up *The Crusader,* it had had only one previous production, by Juliani at York University in Toronto in 1977. It's easy to see why. A short, discordant piece, partly dance, partly pantomime, it's a broad allegory of the US involvement in Vietnam and, by extension, all western intervention in foreign wars. On one side of the stage a female victim is attacked by an invading soldier, who mimes raping, mutilating, and dismembering her. On the other side — separated by a ribbon border — the Crusader of the title debates whether to intervene. He is an imposing figure in a loincloth, whose face, torso, and limbs are studded with masks, representing multiple voices; his fingers sport long metal talons, and bells and mirrors dangle from his extremities. Simons, who in turn wears her Asian influences on her sleeve, has him posing in the stance of an Indian Kathakali dancer and speaking in the pitch-changes of a Japanese Kabuki actor. Also in Asian style, there is a fourth performer who serves as a visible stagehand, providing props and furnishing music and sound effects. Eventually, the Crusader decides to act, pushing his side of the border into the victim's territory and giving the soldier a taste of his own atrocities. Reading it, the play comes across as both visually striking and strikingly obvious.

Rosemary McCracken, who was then doubling as the *Calgary Herald*'s dance and second-string drama critic, gave One Yellow Rabbit its first review in that paper (10 November 1982). Clearly no convert to the virtues of Simons's work, she was nonetheless impressed with the multimedia staging: "Film clips, movement, monologue (minimal), costumes, masks and a collage [of] sound effects are combined to give a highly theatrical vision of the horrors of warfare past and present. ... The cohesive element in the production is provided by Michael Green. Masked, hooded and seated at the back of the set, Green keeps up an inspired cacophony of sound and chatter — everything from drum rolls, to playing taps on a harmonica, to offhand comments that bear ironic relevance to the 'action' of the play."

The Crusader was played by Nigel Scott, who also designed the production — his first work for the troupe. "There was no money for the design," he says, laughing, "so you could say that was the first show I scrounged." Jan Stirling was the female victim and recalls having "a huge allergic reaction" to her heavy makeup. "I thought the play was quite obtuse," she says, "but we certainly worked our buns off to give it some visual punch."

In the first month of 1983, the company took *The Crusader* on a small tour, in a double bill with *The Only Jealousy of Emer* by William

Butler Yeats. The latter choice was a throwback to the avant-garde of an earlier time. *Emer* (1919) was one in Yeats's series of plays about the Celtic hero Cuchulain (pronounced "Cuhoolin"), experimental works that used mask and dance and sought to emulate the ritual and stylization of fourteenth-century Japanese Noh theatre. Refined, elitist, the plays were chamber pieces and first performed in drawing-rooms for a few select patrons and fellow poets. Yeats later rewrote *Emer* in an "immediately intelligible" prose version for the masses. It was a far cry from the gross, shit-and-vomit-bespattered comedy of *Leonardo's Last Supper*. It may sound precious, but thanks to Yeats's vivid poetry, *The Only Jealousy of Emer* remains a profoundly sad little play, in which Emer, the loyal wife of the adulterous Cuchulain, faces the ultimate test of her unselfish love: in order to save her husband's life, she must renounce forever her one comfort — in her words, "the hope that some day, somewhere / We'll sit together at the hearth again."

Jan was cast as Emer and Michael and George played the two Cuchulains — the hero's ghost and his false double, Bricrui. For the dual roles of Eithne Inguba, Cuchulain's mistress, and Fand, the Woman of the Sidhe who attempts to woo his spirit away, director Raby enlisted Marianne Moroney. A young actor who had studied drama at the U of C, Moroney had previously acted in one of Raby's graduate directing projects there. For a newcomer, she was given a demanding assignment; not only did she have two roles, but Fand's dance of seduction was the climax of the play.

The company premiered *Emer* in the mountains, performing it alongside *The Crusader* at the Walter Phillips Gallery in Banff on 13 January 1983. The troupe then played two nights in nearby Canmore, at the Scout Hall, before returning to Calgary and the Off Centre Centre from 18 to 22 January. The *Herald*'s Rosemary McCracken gave the new work a tepid reception (20 January 1983). She praised Jan Stirling for bringing "human dimension to Emer's struggle" but felt Marianne Moroney had missed the mark. "Moroney's raunchy performance is a far cry from Yeats's idea of Fand as the embodiment of feminine beauty," she wrote. McCracken noted Raby's nod to the Noh conventions, while finding that they fell short: "Performers are dressed in kimonos and employ Oriental head and hand gestures; the traditional inturned Japanese knee and foot postures, however, have been neglected." She also complained that the actors' self-made masks hindered their speech and "with their pert, upturned noses, the masks worn by Emer and Eithne add confusing girlish qualities to these characters." (Without wishing to refute McCracken, it could be pointed out that the character of Eithne corresponded, in Yeats's mind, to Maud Gonne's beautiful young daughter Iseult, who, judging from photographs, did indeed have a pert nose.)

Despite the middling notices and some rough times backstage — "We all got sick and argued quite a lot," recalls Raby — the Rabbits felt they'd succeeded in raising their production standard with the two plays and were heartened when Simons flew out to see them and gave her seal of approval.

The company remounted *The Crusader* and *The Only Jealousy of Emer* for its second trip to the Edmonton Fringe in the summer of 1983. The bold little venture had caught the imagination of Edmontonians. Audiences had more than doubled in size in one year, and would continue to do so for the following three years.[1] Although their new shows didn't have the appeal of *Leonardo's Last Supper,* the Rabbits were becoming critical darlings. When they were overlooked at the festival's first awards night, the *Edmonton Journal's* new drama critic, Liz Nicholls, doled out her own prizes (the Wooden Nicholls) and gave the one for "most audacious experiment" to *The Crusader.* The experiments had only started, and the Rabbits felt they no longer needed to perform them on borrowed texts. The next time they visited the Fringe, it would be with a work that was entirely their own.

## The Juggling Doctor

*Juggler on a Drum* was the first Rabbit play to be written by the company. It grew out of a series of poems Kirk Miles had written, inspired by the life of Dr. Norman Bethune, the Canadian surgeon, communist, and medical innovator who became a hero in Red China. At first, Michael Green wasn't enthusiastic about the project, which smacked of the mainstream — Bethune's life had already been the subject of a successful television film starring Donald Sutherland a few years before. Michael sort of put up his nose," recalls Miles. "Gyl was really the driving force [behind it], saying, 'I think we could do this.' I sat down with Gyl and I'd never written a play in my life. Gyl wrote a lot of the dialogue and I wrote a lot of the juggler scenes and rewrote some of my poetry, and then I started getting into the dialogue, too. The next thing you know, we were both writing dialogue and in no time we had a script."

Green needn't have worried. What Miles and Raby came up with wasn't a docudrama but a graceful interpretation of the Bethune story through metaphor and symbol. The play juxtaposes key events in Bethune's life — his struggle with tuberculosis, his on-again, off-again marriage, his front-line work in the Spanish Civil War and the Sino-Japanese War — with poems, juggling, music, and dance. Bethune's life is bracketed throughout by two figures, the Angel of Death and a harlequin. The Angel, a beautiful woman *à la* Maria Casarès in Jean Cocteau's *Orphée,* flirts with Bethune while the harlequin teaches him to juggle and leads him to his fate like the Pied Piper. Although the life-as-circus motif is hardly new, the image of the driven Bethune as juggler, trying to keep aloft his many competing interests — medicine, politics, art — and responsibilities, seems very apt and pays homage to the artistic side of the great physician.

To stage the multidisciplinary show, the troupe received its first money from the Canada Council for the Arts, a $5,000 project grant, and brought in some outside artists. Dancer Denise Clarke created the choreography and performed as the Angel of Death, musician Brian Green laid down the score, and a young actor named Sheri Dayle Wilson — who would later remake herself as poet Sheri-D Wilson — played Bethune's long-suffering wife, Frances. The OYR performers were Michael Green as Bethune, George McFaul as the Juggler, and Kirk Miles in various roles. Nigel Scott did the design. For the first time on a

Rabbit show, he had a budget to work with — albeit a modest one. "We designed and built costumes, we all sewed them," he remembers, "and the set was essentially this big drum that was a projection backdrop." Also for the first time, the troupe was creating a work entirely from scratch. "That's what was so thrilling and addictive about it," remembers Gyl Raby. "I know it was the first time in my career that I'd been able to create, collaboratively, something completely new, out of nothing. And it worked." Her own devotion to the project was such that she spent all her time and money putting it together and ended up over a thousand dollars in debt. "We paid ourselves $350 each, but we worked on it for three months, full-time," she says. "It made it impossible to do any other work."

*Juggler on a Drum* received its test run in July 1983 — a five-night showing at the Loose Moose Simplex, the Moose company's new theatre near the Calgary International Airport. John Coulbourn, future theatre critic of the *Toronto Sun,* was doing duty with the paper's Calgary sister at the time and caught the short run. After cautioning the *Sun*'s downmarket readers that this was "experimental theatre," Coulbourn felt free to rave: "It is difficult to accept that *Juggler* is simply a play. Under the direction of Raby, it becomes a theatrical tapestry weaving poetry, music, dance, acrobatics and acting into a shimmering portrayal of human greatness — and frailty." He sprinkled praise liberally on the performers and politely reserved his constructive criticisms for the end of the review, pointing out sightline problems with the design and suggesting the "[s]ound and lighting effects could be put to much stronger use" (*Calgary Sun,* 22 July 1983).

The following winter, Miles and Raby's script placed third in Alberta Culture's seventeenth annual playwriting competition — a $100 cash prize — and that summer it was remounted for the Fringe. "They freaked when they saw it in Edmonton," says Miles, "they loved it." Among those who wigged out was the *Edmonton Journal*'s Liz Nicholls. "I couldn't take my eyes off the show," she wrote (22 August 1984). Nicholls also held up the company as the quintessence of fringe-style theatre. "If there is a troupe at the Fringe that knows, deep down, what to make of the event, it's surely One Yellow Rabbit," she noted. "The only assumptions you can safely make about a show by the Calgary collective is that it will be (a) thoughtful and (b) eager to toss some new theatrical ball into the air." After finishing its Fringe engagement at Chinook Theatre, the show returned for a second Calgary run at the Rabbits' new digs, the ION Performance Centre.

*Juggler on a Drum* also impressed somebody else. Blake Brooker, returning from his sojourn in Vancouver, saw the troupe's latest effort and wanted back in. This, clearly, was the poet's theatre he dreamed of. Thereafter, his commitment never wavered.

By now, One Yellow Rabbit was engaged in a dizzying number of activities that testified to the varied interests of its members. In the autumn of 1983, the company had launched *Winterplay,* a storytelling show consisting of folk tales, which would tour schools and retirement homes, and that winter it embarked on *Café Theatre,* a cabaret production for adults staged in a downtown club. The season also included sessions with two influential guests: Jan Henderson and Richard Fowler. Henderson was a pupil of beloved Toronto clown master Richard Pochinko and had her own mime-and-mask outfit, Small Change, in Edmonton. Jan and Michael Stirling Green had done a clown show with Henderson for Chinook Theatre, which prompted the first Jan to invite the second Jan to Calgary to lead a clowning workshop in January. The Rabbits immediately put her teaching into practice that same month, with a show called *Mr. Green Goes to Bottle Street.* Spring of 1984 saw more workshops with the arrival of Fowler. A Canadian actor-instructor associated with Eugenio Barba's Nordisk Teaterlaboratorium in Denmark, he was brought in to give lessons in pageant performance. In between, the troupe moved from its backroom venue in the Off Centre Centre to the ION Centre, a tiny performance space in a former stereo shop on 17 Avenue SW. That hectic summer included the mounting of a new play, *The Batman on a Dime,* and the Fringe remounting of *Juggler,* as well as efforts to put Fowler's training into practice with a roving show called *Festival Performance.*

*Winterplay*, the first production of the season, was a batch of British and Eastern European folk tales presented in a heightened story-telling style with mime, songs, sound effects, and other flourishes. After its debut at the Off Centre Centre in November 1983, it became a touring staple of the company for a couple of seasons. The repertoire was eventually expanded to include such popular Canadiana as Robert Service's poem "The Cremation of Sam McGee" and Roch Carrier's story "The Hockey Sweater," and a story exchange was set up for senior citizens who wanted to swap tales. (The OYR archives reveal that some took up the offer.) It was a curiously warm-and-fuzzy effort from the group that had begun by doing Peter Barnes and *The Crusader*. "*Winterplay* was a response to a certain criteria that was out there in the funding sector," explains Jan Stirling. "There was money to be had to do work in retirement homes and community venues. And we had an aesthetic interest in working with storytelling, so we combined the two." The province underwrote the tour to seniors facilities and also subsidized *Winterplay*'s school dates. "Alberta Culture had some funding where they would provide half the cost to the presenter," says McFaul. "So if we charged $350 for a performance, the school got back half of that."

Maybe the benign nature of *Winterplay* rubbed off on the Rabbits, because their next effort, *Mr. Green Goes to Bottle Street,* was a family show full of gentle whimsy. This was Jan Stirling's pet project, an attempt to create a work using the mask and movement techniques of clowning. "In retrospect, we developed that play too soon after the Jan Henderson workshop," she says. Partly inspired by a story she'd read as a schoolgirl, it was an environmental fantasy about an unhappy city planner who accidentally discovers an idyllic little neighbourhood not included on any maps. "It was kind of an idealistic story, but it suited the clown format." Jan wrote and directed it and Michael, Miles, McFaul, and Moroney made up the cast.

*Café Theatre*, in contrast, was brash and irreverent. McFaul claims credit for the idea. He had first encountered the concept as a student at Laval in Quebec City. "I thought it was just very cool. It was people doing theatre in cafés, just popping up here and there — sort of a hipster's version of dinner theatre, for people who didn't want to pay thirty bucks to see some has-been television star, but still liked the concept of seeing live theatre and being free to eat and drink at the same time." The show, which started out at Beggar's Banquet, a little downtown club just off Stephen Avenue Mall, offered a menu of poetry, skits, monologues, music, and juggling. Some of the material was original, some borrowed from the likes of David Mamet and E. E. Cummings. The tone could range from the sophisticated humour of a Fran Leibowitz piece to the pure Dadaist lunacy of the Juggle Boys. The latter act had echoes of Michael Green's Ikarus stunts. He cooked it up with Miles and McFaul, using the cut-and-paste writing technique he'd learned from Gary Stromsmoe. "We sat down and in two hours wrote out all the clichés for advertisements that we'd ever heard," says Miles, "then [Michael] went away and put those all together." Green recited the resultant farrago while Miles and McFaul juggled machetes. "We were in little shorts, underwear," says Miles. "It was so ridiculous, it was hilarious. It became famous. People would come to *Café Theatre* just to see Juggle Boys, and it was only a four-minute skit!"

Occasionally, the Rabbits got a little too outrageous for public tastes. "We'd consider doing anything," says Miles. "There was a poem George read one time about the pope fucking a chicken. The audience rebelled. It was out of a poetry journal produced in Saskatchewan and we'd said 'Sure, go for it George.' It wasn't till we had complaints from the restaurant ... that we had to pull the poem." McFaul remembers it differently, recalling it as a rare time when the company itself was offended. "Gyl's feminist take on it was 'What gets fucked, really? It's women who get fucked. So you're really talking about women, aren't you?' And Michael said 'I'm not a papist, George, but really — you're talking about the Pope of Rome fucking chickens!' I guess you can only go so far and even One Yellow Rabbit will censor you!" By and large, though, *Café Theatre* was a crowd pleaser. OYR performed it through the summer of 1984 and revived it the following summer at a different venue, Marty's Café. Over the years, the company would revisit the cabaret format and style again and again.

While *Café Theatre* was light entertainment, the Rabbits were taking their craft seriously, getting into the heavy-duty theories of Jerzy Grotowski via Richard Fowler. Grotowski was one of the big theatre gurus of the last half of the twentieth century. A Polish actor-turned-director, he promoted a rigorous, ascetic approach that began by stripping down theatre to its two essentials — the actor and the spectator. Like his English contemporary, Peter Brook, he founded a theatre laboratory and became more interested in process than production. His disciple, the Italian director Eugenio Barba, was similarly inclined and perpetuated Grotowski's "Poor Theatre" theories with his own company, the Odin Teatret, and his own research centre in Denmark. Fowler, in turn, had become Barba's Canadian emissary. An actor who had studied at the University of Alberta, Fowler had begun a career doing traditional theatre, from the regionals to summer stock, but found it unfulfilling. Then he learned about Barba's methods while working in Vancouver with American director Andre Gregory (loquacious star of Louis Malle's film *My Dinner with Andre*). Meeting Barba at the latter's International Symposium of Theatre Anthropology in Germany, Fowler became friendly with the director and wound up working as his assistant. By 1984, he had spent four years at Barba's Danish theatre lab and was assigned the task of spreading the Barba-Grotowski message to his homeland.

Gyl Raby and George McFaul were both familiar with Grotowski from university days. McFaul had studied him in Quebec, while Raby had seen his famous production of *The Constant Prince* in Manchester and briefly joined a student company that tried to adopt his principles. When they learned that one of his followers was near at hand, they determined to get his services. On the advice of Anne Green, Fowler's friend and manager, McFaul applied to Alberta Culture. "As I recall, we got a $15,000 grant to bring Fowler in, workshop a show, have some public workshops and public performances by him. Being the collective we were, every bit of money we got we used. So that $15,000 also covered our other projects that summer." Fowler would end up doing two retreats with the Rabbits, taking them and other participants into the countryside, where they lived communally, camping out and training in barns and small-town community halls. "It wasn't really a back-to-nature thing," explains Raby. "It was more a case of finding a cheap place where we could work eight hours a day."

In addition to teaching the Rabbits, Fowler performed his own one-man show, *Wait for the Dawn,* a tour de force based on Camus's *L'Étranger,* which also included lashings of Beckett, Genet, and T. S. Eliot. "I remember we particularly liked Fowler because he had this real macho approach," says Michael Green. "Like, any actor worth his salt should be able to recite all of Hamlet's soliloquies while standing on his head. That kind of thing." Moroney also recalls being impressed. "I remember being so overwhelmed watching his technique, and his daily workshop was very tough physically. I had come from a very athletic background and loved having the physical challenges thrown at me." Raby also appreciated the training, but she and Blake Brooker were less enthusiastic about the work that came out of it. "I found his images very powerful and disturbing, but they had no context," says Raby. (That would also be the criticism levelled at Primus Theatre, the Winnipeg company Fowler helped found a few years later.)

Fowler was preparing the Rabbits for outdoor pageant performances and they were keen to put their training to practice. McFaul remembers that at one point they took their routines to the city's busiest shopping mall to try them out. "It was just us trying to make some money and shop ourselves around. It was basically Michael on stilts and other weird characters doing Grotowski-esque stuff with props, doing some kind of confrontational interaction with drums and flags, et cetera. The mall people were okay with it until we started juggling with machetes. Then they shut it down." It may have been the first time a One Yellow Rabbit show was closed by the powers that be. It certainly wouldn't be the last. And the company's next production would wind up getting them kicked out of a far more prestigious venue.

## Batman with an X (or, Bob Kane, Meet R. Crumb)

The revitalized Blake Brooker took the acting workshops but, in the wake of *Juggler,* he was ready to begin writing plays. His first full-length effort for OYR was an immediate success, although it hardly presages the kind of dense, poetic texts he would soon compose. In fact, *The Batman on a Dime* was the company's most straightforward and accessible play to date.

Written for the *Café Theatre* program, *Batman* was a parody of Bob Kane's doughty DC Comics hero done as an extended comedy skit with songs. Thanks to a little nudity and some sexual content, the press referred to it on more than one occasion as an "X-rated" take on the comic book, but that's going a bit far. Try "naughty" and "irreverent" — not that there was much to revere in the Batman image by then. The campy 1960s TV series, which Brooker and his colleagues had grown up with, had effectively turned the Caped Crusader into a pompous ninny, even as it gave him a popularity that rivalled Superman's. Tim Burton's big-budget *Batman* film, which would rehabilitate the character and recapture his gloomy allure, was still five years away. However, as with Burton's movie, Brooker's play was hijacked by the flamboyant Joker, played to the gallery by Michael Green in one of his earliest scenery-chewing roles. *Calgary Herald* reporter Lisa Church was sent to review the show at Beggar's Banquet the summer of 1984 and wrote that "for sheer visual entertainment [he] steals the show. Decked out in a nauseating plaid suit and clunky orange boots which complement his green fright wig, Green waltzes around the small stage with the ease of a figure skater. His frantic eye-rolls and roller-coaster voice keep the audience mesmerized, and often draw attention away from the other characters" (25 July 1984).

Here, the Clown Prince of Crime teams up with the sexy Catwoman, alias Salina Kyle, manicurist, who is horny with unrequited love for Batman/Bruce Wayne. The Joker's cunning (or should that be baffling?) plot involves convincing the unmarried superhero that someone has run off with his spouse, a discovery that sends him into a mournful country-and-western ballad, "In a Letter She Wrote (Someone's Fucking My Wife)." As Catwoman stalks the heartbroken Batman, the Joker sets his sights on Robin, a bored alcoholic teenager of shaky sexual orientation, plying him with booze and attempting to seduce him. Their steamy scene is a neat spoof of the Batman comic's alleged "subtle homoeroticism," as detected by child psychologist Frederic Wertham in his infamous 1950s attack on the comic-book industry, *Seduction of the Innocent.* Brooker's most inspired touch, however, is to turn the climactic battle between the Dynamic Duo and their foes into a fashion show, with the over-costumed bunch trying to outdo one another on the runway. Will Batman's lithium-yellow utility belt and Robin's streamlined variant on the Zorro mask be able to compete with the Joker's "platform rock boots, circa '73"?

Brooker recalls that he wrote the play quickly and his only intent was to poke fun at the superhero image, but in retrospect he wonders if he wasn't on to something. "I still think that *Batman on a Dime,* with its portrayal of a brooding, suffering Batman, prefigured the *Dark Knight* series and the [Burton] movie," he says. (The controversial *Dark Knight* comics, in which author-artist Frank Miller envisioned Batman as an aging, angry vigilante, didn't make their debut until 1986.) In any event, with George McFaul as Batman, Kirk Miles as Robin, and Marianne Moroney as Catwoman, the show proved a hit and was reassembled for the by-now-annual trek to the Edmonton Fringe in 1985.

That year, entertainment scouts for the upcoming world exposition in Vancouver happened to be prowling the festival. They couldn't fail to notice *The Batman on a Dime.* It was so popular that people were queuing for up to five hours to get tickets. "It was in the Yardbird [Suite] and it was packed out," remembers Fringe producer Brian Paisley. "They could have run it all day and filled the house. They went on in the early evening and people were lining up at noon." In fact, the *Batman* lineups that year helped convince Paisley that he had to abandon his egalitarian, first-come, first-served policy at the Fringe and start selling advance tickets. The show must have looked like a surefire choice for Expo '86's comedy programming. The scouts quickly snapped it up —

as part of a One Yellow Rabbit package that would also include a piece of family-oriented street theatre called *The Pageant of the Comet* and the clown antics of Miles and McFaul.

For Expo '86, *The Batman on a Dime* was booked into the Flying Club, a 200-seat cabaret with an aeronautic motif and the second largest of the three venues in the fair's club complex. The original cast was reconvened for the gig with the exception of Moroney, who was unavailable. In her stead, Denise Clarke played the role of Catwoman. One Yellow Rabbit would be sharing the bill with such popular comedy acts as the Second City company and the Vancouver Theatresports League. The show was slotted for 26 May to 5 June, an eleven-day run. It ran a mere two performances and was promptly shut down.

Michael Green claims that Expo chair Jim Pattison pulled the plug. "Jim Pattison apparently showed up halfway through our disastrous opening night with a couple of diplomats from Sweden or some damn place, probably saw me kissing Robin or Denise flashing her tits or something, and made a phone call and that was that." The cancellation topped off a calamitous performance in what turned out to be an inadequate venue. "Frankly, it didn't work there at all," says Green. "We were furious. It was a club for stand-up comics and a disco. While they served drinks, mixed daiquiris and rang the cash register, and people spoke amongst themselves, there we were. They didn't give us any tech time. Boom, we were on. Nobody could hear us. I ran into the wall in a blackout, blood pouring down my face. It was disastrous."

"There *was* a sound problem," agrees George McFaul, whose memories of the opening night aren't as bitter. "We couldn't be heard. But it could've been solved. I guess the technical problems weren't worth solving for a show with what they saw as possibly controversial content. Expo '86 was a pretty sanitized place," he notes. "Not that this was a particularly raunchy show, but Denise's breasts are in most shows that she's in, and they were in that one." The Expo officials didn't break the contract, but the company was not allowed to perform *Batman* on-site or anywhere else in the city. "There we were, without our major show to do, but on full salary," says McFaul. "So we just stayed and played."

They still had their other gigs, notably the outdoor *Pageant of the Comet,* which Expo officials *did* like. So much so, that they moved it from the street to the Thunderbird Stage. "Funny," says Kirk Miles with a laugh, "[it] was a total success and we thought the show sucked." Miles helped Gyl Raby write the piece, another comic book–style spoof, which no one has fond memories of. Subtitled *The Wild West Travels to Outer Space,* it was a garbled, action-packed spectacle about solar-system shenanigans, ostensibly inspired by the 1986 appearance of Halley's comet. Michael Green, who played the Sun as a stilt-walking Rastafarian, remembers it as "a truly gruelling experience." Clarke, recruited for the role of the skateboarding Comet, calls it "the most important thing I've ever done, maybe, because I realized I will never do another thing that I hate." The show also featured non-Rabbits Bruce Hunter as SuperNaut, an egotistical space cowboy, and James Howley as his lofty musical mentor, the Sphinx. And Jan Stirling sharpened her clowning chops as Fetid, SuperNaut's comically odious sidekick. The show was Raby's attempt to wed the Fowler-style street pageant to a story with a message. SuperNaut represented overweening progress, attempting to lasso and subdue the Comet in his bid to colonize the "final frontier." A note in the rehearsal draft suggests the company was biting off more than it could chew: "The style of the show is a very curious hybrid [wrote Raby and Miles]. Essentially it is a satire, with farcical characterizations, occasionally degenerating into slapstick and facile one-liners (i.e. the climax). However, it is very important to tie it down in certain places to bring home a human reality and a political consciousness. At the other extreme, there are sections which are extremely lyrical and should be played as such for the sheer beauty of expression." The *Calgary Herald*'s Kate Zimmerman, reviewing it when it played a post-Expo run in Calgary, found it "almost overwhelming" and noted "there's almost too much to absorb in 45 minutes" (20 June 1986).

Expo also gave Miles and McFaul a chance to work on their newly acquired clown personas. The two, along with Jan, had benefitted the most from the sessions with Jan Henderson, in which they learned the basics of clowning. They came out of that intensive three-week workshop having created clowns that they still perform today. "That workshop was very powerful for me," says Miles. "The first thing I ever performed as a clown was my graduating skit, as they called it — the last thing you did on the last day of the workshop — and I did a three-minute version of *Hamlet*. So I called the clown Hamlet. I thought it was very apropos, 'cause I'm a literary guy but I'm also a bozo."

The workshop "was aimed at unearthing or discovering your clown," says McFaul, "but it was really valid for any kind of theatrical expression, just by freeing your persona and allowing it to come out and play. ... Mask building was very much a part of it, properties and costumes — not to cover anything up, but to uncover your own innocence. There were a lot of returning-to-childhood kinds of exercises. We took our characters from the workshop and just played, basically. I remember going out in the street and letting the clown roam around, to find out who he was."

Henderson and Fowler, Whoopi Goldberg and David Schein — the Rabbits were latching on to anyone who could teach them something, even as they continued to furiously mount show after show. "We all came from such different backgrounds," explains Michael Green, "and in order to act together on the same stage we needed to do these workshops." They were also a way to get public funding, says George McFaul. "There weren't grants specifically for training [artists], but if you could bring somebody in and demonstrate that you would have them do workshops for the community at large, and that you would also get a performance of your own out of it, then there was money available."

Part of the Rabbits' education involved learning how to access the grants available for their work. Some representatives of the government funding agencies took a shine to the plucky little troupe and began to nurture and encourage it. Canada Council officer Jeremy Long was one of them. "He'd come to town to view our work and then he'd take us out for dinner," says Gyl Raby. "Sometimes, that was the only really good meal that we had that month! To me, he was the only person who appreciated what we were going for. I really valued his feedback because he was seeing Théâtre du Soleil, Peter Brook's new work, the BAM festival in New York, and then coming to see us and comparing our work with theirs. He felt we were in the same league, which was deeply validating to a company that could only find thirteen hundred people for an audience at the time. It gave us confidence that, if we just kept creating, someday we'd be able to tour to places where people could immediately identify with our work." Richard Fowler's pal Anne Green, who served at various times with the Calgary Region Arts Foundation, Alberta Culture, and the Canada Council, was more circumspect. She never actually let on that she was a fan, but she continually offered valuable advice and got the Rabbits to think of theatre as a business as well as an art form. A former actor, Green knew whereof she spoke, having co-founded Edmonton's Theatre 3, an alternative company that had flourished in the 1970s. "I'd learned stuff along the line and wanted to pass it on," she says. She was attracted to the Rabbits because they were one of the few groups in western Canada attempting to create new, multidisciplinary work, something she was personally keen on. "I wanted to do what I could to help them move it forward," she recalls. "But I was always very careful not to cross the line into a conflict of interest."

While everyone in the troupe wrote grant applications, eventually the bulk of the administrative work fell to Kirk Miles, who had essentially become One Yellow Rabbit's general manager. Jan Stirling, meanwhile, had taken on the role of company accountant. While still functioning as a collective, OYR's loose structure was beginning to harden. "OYR is a weird mixture of communism and free enterprise," Blake Brooker told journalist Anne Georg in a profile published in *CityScope Magazine* in the spring of 1985. "Everyone does the dishes here." In fact, if "the dishes" included office duties, he was being disingenuous. "One problem with Blake is he never understood what was involved in the management of the company," says Miles. "He was always an artist, he never got his feet wet in the management side, and I think he underestimated it a lot. Arts administration takes some skill and I don't think he ever appreciated that." The fact was, once someone had shown an ability and willingness to do the dull stuff, they got stuck with it. And they quickly became adept. "I had absolutely no training in bookkeeping, I was just flying by the seat of my pants," says Stirling, who takes a perverse pleasure in recalling how much work it involved. "Every summer people knew they couldn't come to our house. Our fiscal year-end was July 31, I believe, and so much stuff had accumulated over the year. I did payroll, collected everybody's receipts, kept the chequebooks and deposit books, so by then there was a lot of arithmetic to do. So for about three weeks every July people steered clear of me, by George!"

The collective ideal included paying everyone equally. "As part of the troupe, you got a very meagre living wage," says Miles, "and then any money that you earned as a performer in a company booking would go into the company coffers." The Alberta Culture grant for the tour of *Winterplay* to retirement homes paid four of the company members $800 a month, but they'd cash their cheques, pool the money, and divide it equally so that the members not doing the tour also got paid. The final pay packet was well below the minimum wage. "I remember working sixteen-hour days," says Miles, "and having absolutely no money."

To survive, everyone had part-time jobs. Miles worked at the university's medical library. Brooker helped out with his dad's shelving business. The Stirling Greens performed with Edmonton's Chinook and Small Change Theatres, and Jan also waitressed and sold vintage clothing at Old Hat, a shop owned by Anne Green. Gyl Raby and Nigel Scott accepted work from the very theatres whose values they despised. Raby designed and built costumes for Stage West, Calgary's new commercial dinner theatre that specialized in sex farces, and Scott created its traditional box sets. (Soon, his sideline work became his full-time job. A temporary gig as draughtsman to Theatre Calgary's new in-house designer, Guido Tondino, stretched out into two years and saw him designing for the big house as well.) The troupe's youthful energy was often taxed to the limit. George McFaul, who had taken on some hours with his old employer, the Children's Service Centre, remembers being run ragged. There were times when he had to work the night shift, from 11:00 P.M. to 7:00 A.M., in-taking and watching young offenders, then race off to a school and do a morning performance of *Winterplay*. "I used to basically take speed to try and stay awake to do those shows."

The lack of money meant the company always had to live within its means. For Scott, it was a chance to put his minimalist aesthetic into practice, if for no other reason than a near-zero design budget. Even as he was helping Tondino plot grandiose sets for Theatre Calgary, such as an Olympic stadium and a Hungarian castle, he had to beg, borrow, and steal to create the Rabbit decor. "There were some amazing scams we pulled off," he says. "We called it the Midnight Props Service — running around, finding whatever bits and pieces we could." Old lumber left at a building site would often disappear in those late-night raids. "I think the most remarkable thing that I ever witnessed was when we needed some video for a show," says Scott, "and these guys in the video are supposed to be sharp dressers. Well, none of us were sharp dressers. So I remember going to a store and buying all these clothes, then doing the video shoot but keeping the price tags on the clothes and just carefully folding them inside so you couldn't see them, and then returning all the clothes the next day. And then we breezed into some wealthy neighbourhood, maybe Mount Royal, knocked on someone's door, and just begged them to let us use their front door to make it look like it was our house."

As with their sets and props, they had to make do with the cheapest venue they could find. For a while, the ION Centre did the job. It wasn't perfect, but then what fringe theatre is? What had been the sales floor of the electronics shop was painted black and turned into a black-box theatre. The basement became offices and rehearsal space. Their fellow tenant, mime artist David Cassel, was one man with two companies: Interlude Mime Theatre and the Nebulous Rebels. The theatre's name was an acronym: *I*nterlude Mime Theatre, *O*ne Yellow Rabbit, *N*ebulous Rebels.

When the Rabbits moved into the ION in the summer of 1984, they also tapped into a series of employment grants that would allow them to hire student help and pay a few of their own members full-time salaries. The federal and provincial money became the cornerstone of the company's funding in the early years. The financial statements for the 1985–86 season, for example, show revenues from employment programs of more than $85,000. These were not only far and away the company's biggest source of money at the time, they also covered almost a third of its $272,600 budget. In 1984, the Rabbits got an $8,448 Canada Works grant to pay a stage manager, secretary, and marketing representative; plus $18,000 from the province's Summer Temporary Employment Program to pay student apprentices. One of them was aspiring actor Laura Parken, who says her duties veered from office work to performing in the *Café Theatre* revues and tagging along for the Fowler-inspired *Festival Performance* outdoor show. "I played a goofy little character who pulled a wagon with all the props." She also pitched in for one of the company's first fundraisers, a spunky bid to cash in on the tourist trade at the Calgary Stampede.

A friend with a shoe store had unloaded a mess of cowboy boots on the Rabbits, and thrown in some cowboy hats, too. Since the ION was only a few blocks from the Stampede grounds, they decided to have a sale. "The building had these garage doors we could open up," says Parken, "and that became the shop. We made a big sign: 'A Whole Lot of Boots and Hats Galore.' I had a funny little mock country-and-western band at the time, called the Trouble with Lovin' Today, which was myself, Grant Burns, Gregg Casselman, and Peter Moller, Max and Adele Leger of the Rip Chords. We played out there on Friday and Saturday night, trying to hawk these wares. And Kevin Brooker did a whole line of boots for us that he hand-painted, that were totally wacky but very cool."

Despite such fun times, OYR's association with David Cassel eventually turned sour. "It was a roommate relationship with him," says George McFaul, "and we just couldn't get along with the guy." His memories of the mime are less than fond. "It was quite ugly when [our partnership] broke up." Cassel got the ION Centre and the troupe hunted for new accommodations.

In the early months of 1985, things were looking bright for One Yellow Rabbit. It had become a full-fledged professional company, having joined the Professional Association of Canadian Theatres. In three years it had done a tremendous amount of work, making a name for itself in Calgary and Edmonton. And it had proved the strength of a well-balanced collective. The Rabbits had never stopped running, even when some of their key players were sidelined. Along with Blake Brooker's year-long stay in Vancouver, there had been an eight-month period where Gyl Raby took a teaching position at the University of Manitoba in Winnipeg to pay off the debt she incurred from *Juggler on a Drum*. Both came back refreshed and ready to re-enter the game. "We were lucky," says Kirk Miles. "I've seen small companies start up and they'll have one or two people that drive the company. We had eight strong personalities driving our company, and if anyone burned out or got tired and fell along the roadside, there were seven other people to take the reins."

Now, they had happened upon a choice piece of vintage real estate, a spacious eyrie with a fanciful name. The SkyRoom was about to become One Yellow Rabbit's third home in three years. Once an old-time ballroom, more recently a new-wave nightclub, this was the Rabbits' dream — their own theatre.

---

1    Although it levelled off, Edmonton's Fringe remains the biggest fringe theatre festival in North America. By 2001, its twentieth anniversary, it had a budget of $1.5 million, featured 155 shows in thirty-five venues and attracted more than half a million visitors. In those two decades, the fringe concept spread like an Alberta grass fire, catching cities big and small across Canada and blazing into the United States. There are now some forty fringe festivals on the continent.

# 3. Secret and Not-So-Secret Theatres

*"We are a fragile unit surrounded by hostile facts."*
— TEARS OF A DINOSAUR

Sometime in the second week of March 1985, a scruffy young reporter on general assignment in the *Calgary Herald*'s entertainment department made his way to the SkyRoom at the corner of 11 Avenue and 6 Street SW. It was early in the day and only two or three people were moving about the space, finishing the set for the theatre's inaugural production, a revival of *Leonardo's Last Supper*. A fine-boned young woman of twenty-five, who spoke softly but ardently with a middle-class English accent, conducted a brief tour of the premises, waxing enthusiastic about its potential. I may have met Michael Green and possibly Nigel Scott for the first time that day, but I clearly remember Gyl Raby, who was visibly pregnant with her and Scott's first child, Xavier.

The SkyRoom was just south of the railway tracks and 9 Avenue, then the city's entertainment district: a thoroughfare studded with restaurants, clubs, and the QR Centre, home of Theatre Calgary. It seemed appropriate and symbolic that One Yellow Rabbit should settle on the other side of the tracks from Calgary's major mainstream theatre. The three-storey building, previously known as the Harris Skyroom, had once seen glamorous days as a ballroom in the 1950s, only to be later desecrated by chain-smoking bingo players. Before the Rabbits moved in, it had been suitably seasoned for anarchy as a punk nightclub called HC's — briefly a rival of Ten Foot Henry's. The troupe took over the dance floor on the top storey, a 5,000-square-foot room, of which 3,000 square feet would serve as stage and auditorium. The remainder, partitioned off, would become a green room, office, and workshop. Unlike some fringe theatre groups that are willing to live on the fly, the Rabbits had their minds set on a home base from the start. The company's proposal for a development grant, a year after the SkyRoom's opening, stated the theatre's significance: "The acquisition of a permanent venue has been essential for One Yellow Rabbit's ongoing activities, the constant rehearsals and office work necessary to run the company. It has also been highly beneficial for our audience development through means of identifying One Yellow Rabbit with a constant venue."

The old ballroom required major renovations to convert it to a theatre. Raby remembers that the city's fire inspectors became their particular bane during the first shows there. "We made improvements as much as we could, we worked our arses off, but the fire inspectors were never satisfied and they'd threaten to close us down. We'd arrive to do the show expecting to find the doors padlocked. It never happened, but the stress was something we could sure have done without." Kirk Miles called upon an old buddy to help with the improvements. Ralph Christoffersen was a big blond Viking of hearty appetites who knew how to wield a hammer. He had gone to Henry Wise Wood Senior High School with Miles and was now working in his family's drywalling business. He volunteered to spend a weekend helping build a wall to separate the main room from the office and workshop areas. "Just working with them that one weekend, I was blown away by the energy of everybody," he recalls. "I was coming from this dog-eat-dog, capitalist scene, and seeing people collaborating and co-operating that way, seeing how much they could do with next to nothing, was astounding to me. I thought: Who are these people?" So when Miles later approached him to do more upgrades, he accepted. Christoffersen didn't realize what he was getting into. "That project turned into a fifteen-year career in the theatre business."

The Rabbits had gotten some grant money for the renovations and there was plenty to be done to bring the theatre up to the fire inspectors' standards. "At the time, their lights were just coffee cans with light bulbs in them, plugged into lawnmower cords running through the ceiling," says Christoffersen. "They were run off the kind of dimmers you'd buy for the lights in your home. The whole thing was totally illegal." Christoffersen joined the Rabbits, hired with another grant from the Unemployment Insurance Commission to retrain workers. For a meagre wage ($2.50 an hour, he claims) he began to learn the craft of theatre building.

The SkyRoom opened for business that winter with a packed program. Along with the revival of *Leonardo,* in its first few weeks the theatre also hosted the dance team of Denise Clarke and Anne Flynn, a satirical group called the Art Ensemble of Calgary, and a concert by Louisiana's Queen Ida and the Bon Temps Zydeco Band. It looked as though the Rabbits would be able to make added revenue from rentals, with rates of $60 per night for a theatrical performance and $175 a night for other, non-theatrical bookings. To celebrate their big new space, they began to plan a big new show and they felt it was time to call in some outside help.

Keith Turnbull, of *Donnellys* fame, was the first outsider to direct a One Yellow Rabbit play. Turnbull was nearing the end of a four-year teaching stint at the University of Calgary when the troupe coaxed him downtown to direct *Ides,* a new script by Raby and Blake Brooker. Sitting in his flat in Montreal on a rainy summer morning, sipping cold coffee ("I like it that way"), the veteran director obligingly casts his mind back two decades and remembers that in 1980s Calgary, "if you were hunting for an interesting bunch of theatre people, all roads led to One Yellow Rabbit. They had the most stimulating ideas about the theatre," he says. "They were the ones with spunk, energy, and insightfulness. Everyone else was talking about subscriptions; they were talking about art." He had gotten to know the gang during his occasional visits to Ten Foot Henry's, and Marianne Moroney had been one of his students. So when they came looking for guidance on what would be their biggest project to date, Turnbull was happy to lend a hand.

In keeping with the collective spirit of the troupe, *Ides* had been instigated by designer Nigel Scott. He had read Russell Hoban's 1980 sci-fi novel *Riddley Walker,* an ambitious tale set in a post-atomic-apocalypse world, where the human race has been blasted back to the Dark Ages. "It was an amazing book about these people living in a medieval world in the future and uncovering their past," he says. "I just thought this was very cool, so I talked to Gyl and Blake about it and they co-wrote [the play]." As it happened, Hoban was already dramatizing his novel for a British production, which would premiere at the Manchester Royal Exchange in early 1986. Raby and Brooker weren't aware of that, but eventually scuttled the idea of adapting the novel and chose to go for an homage instead. "We made up our own world, but it was very much under the sway of Hoban's novel," says Brooker. Along with the post-nuclear premise, *Ides* borrowed a few other ideas from *Riddley Walker*. In both stories a form of religious ceremony is performed using puppets, and the young heroine Ides, like the young hero Riddley, is chosen to succeed the local prophet who interprets the puppet shows. Raby and Brooker also took a cue from Hoban by having their characters speak a hybrid language in which the Middle Ages collide with the twentieth century, although they hardly went as far as the novelist in this regard. The dialogue in *Ides* is closer to mock-Shakespeare than to Hoban's quite literally broken English.

In Raby and Brooker's imagined future, humans have been divided between the bourgeois, town-dwelling "traders" and the deformed "twists," wily outcasts who live in the bush or "scrubs" and are kept at bay with bribes. The traders are governed by a committee of Speakers, who in turn defer to the prophecies of the Doctor, a blind shaman whose messages are delivered in the form of puppetry. Ides, a wealthy trader's daughter betrothed to one of the Speakers, is chosen by the Doctor to be his successor — a job that requires blinding and celibacy. While Ides resists her calling and flees to the scrubs, her fiancé is secretly involved with a crafty female trader from another town who has arrived to undermine the Doctor's peaceful rule and foment war with the twists.

Brooker says that he and Raby wrote the play by deciding on the characters and plot structure and then divvying up the scenes. "I wrote a scene, she wrote a scene, then we'd give them to each other to rewrite.

It actually went very smoothly." Raby recalls that she gave birth to Xavier between the final rewrites and was back on the job shortly afterwards. "I brought Xav into rehearsals on the third day of his life."

*Ides* was more ambitious than anything the company had yet done. Scott recalls that it was months in development. He produced the show and handed off much of the design work to Laara Cassells (who would go on to design for the Stratford Festival) and an art student named Noreen Neu. "A woman had phoned me from the Alberta College of Art," says Scott. "She taught fabric art at the college and she had a student who was graduating that year, who was just amazing. She painted fabric, that was her forte. So we got Laara Cassells, who had just started the master's design program at U of C, to design the costumes and then Noreen would paint the fabric. Each and every costume was hand-painted. It really lent itself to the show, because it was the only way you could achieve a totally unique look."

Keith Turnbull's most enduring memory of the production is of a prop. In more than one sense of the word. He had some of the characters leaning on a pair of sticks attached to the sleeves of their garments. "We'd developed this idea that the terrain was so rough that it was actually better navigated with four feet rather than two. So we created these walking sticks that adapted the human body to a four-footed body, and then they also became magic wands and weapons and tools. And different lengths of stick gave different status to the characters. We developed a whole physical language around them." Although he worked on *Ides* as a dramaturge as well as director, he admits its Tolkien-ish fantasy wasn't really his cup of tea. Nor does he think the play would stand up today. "Those post-holocaust pieces are extremely dated now," he says, "but in the '80s it was a different matter. The possibility of world nuclear destruction was a really significant question for a lot of young people; they lived in terror of it. We forget that now."

The company responded well to the director's expertise. "I remember the cold and clear professionalism that Keith Turnbull brought to the project," says Brooker. "I always felt he was a great asset to it. And he must have thought we were fucking crazy." Brooker, a fledgling director, watched over Turnbull's shoulder and learned much. "He brought a series of techniques to constructing new theatre that I've used to this day and found very useful. He really understood the changes that a new script will undergo, and to keep track of them you have to be a clever record-keeper." While most directors replace each draft of a script as it gets rewritten, Turnbull would keep all the drafts before him so that if there were problems with a scene, he could refer to the earlier versions for possible solutions. "I also liked the way he handled everyone," adds Brooker. "He was very good for a young company. And he was always there earlier than everyone else and always stayed later than everyone else. He always did his homework." Turnbull also liked to pull all-nighters, which impressed the young playwright. "I remember going over to his house for rewriting sessions and we'd be out there, sitting on his balcony, drinking and eating his homemade gourmet delicacies, till three o'clock in the morning. And rehearsals were at ten o'clock."

After a gestation period that didn't quite rival Xavier's, but was lengthy nonetheless, *Ides* premiered in June 1985 at the SkyRoom Theatre. The immediate critical reaction was mixed. Kate Zimmerman, in the *Calgary Herald* (23 June 1985), found the show "a visually exciting piece of theatre with a confusing storyline. … Who the characters are and how they relate to the other characters is often cloudy." Louise Bresky, on CBC Radio (24 June 1985), chose to see that cloudiness as an intellectual challenge. "*Ides* succeeds for anyone willing to plunge, without a map, into a murky fantasy world. It means work. … *Ides* is complex, it demands your imagination." She did concede, however, that the play had problems with clarity. "It has moments of beauty, but too often it leaves you wondering what is going on."

Marianne Moroney, who played the play's rebellious heroine, remembers being dissatisfied with the result. "I still wonder about *Ides*," she says, "wonder if the acting company was able to bring the story to the height it needed to be." At the same time, she adds: "We really had a collective feel with *Ides* and coming from the Fowler workshop we were in dynamite shape, and I think we did some pretty amazing stuff." In fact, while the show was in rehearsal, Richard Fowler's boss, Eugenio Barba, stopped by to watch. The famed Italian director was in town for a series of workshops, organized by Anne Green and held at the University of Calgary. The sessions attracted a slew of theatre artists from Canada and the United States and culminated in a gruelling, Grotowski-style performance marathon from dusk to dawn. Unfortunately, *Ides* kept the Rabbits from participating and their only contact with Barba was that brief visit. Anne Green, who accompanied him to the SkyRoom, recalls that, while Barba's directorial approach was diametrically opposed to Turnbull's, he politely bit his tongue and said nothing.

Looking back, Turnbull thinks *Ides* was a watershed for the Rabbits, not in what it achieved so much as in what it taught the troupe. He believes it helped them realize that their forte wasn't in the area of traditional dramatic structures and naturalistic acting. At the time, Turnbull himself didn't recognize their strengths, especially when directing Michael Green, who played the puppet-wielding Doctor. "The difficulty I had directing Michael was that I was treating him as an actor, which was kind of a mistake. He isn't — he's a performer, and an extraordinary one. The style they've developed since is based more on performance, whereas at the time of *Ides* they were still stuck on this idea of doing a kind of alternative drama. I think this was probably the show where they said 'Enough of this! We don't like acting. We like to perform.'"

The Rabbits' next big production took them far away from the world of the Method and the well-made play. It would find them performing as talking (and singing) mice in a modern fable by a Beat poet.

### Of Mice and Fish (and Bears)

Michael McClure is one of the original Beats. He was one of the five poets featured at the legendary Six Gallery reading in San Francisco in 1955 — the one where Allen Ginsberg unleashed "Howl" upon the world. He appears, thinly fictionalized, as a character in *Big Sur,* Jack

Kerouac's late, despairing novel of unattained enlightenment. He moved into theatre in the 1960s and became a prolific, if decidedly experimental, playwright with such plays as *The Beard, Spider Rabbit,* and *Minnie Mouse and the Tap-Dancing Buddha.* Michael Green was first turned on to him when Gary Stromsmoe made one of his pilgrimages to San Francisco and came back with a copy of McClure's 1976 play *Gorf,* which Ikarus staged in Calgary. "I liked it so much that I ended up digging up a lot of his scripts," says Green. "I came across him when I was at a somewhat impressionable age and frame of mind and I really liked what he was doing; it made a lasting impression on me. He represented so much of what I thought was beautiful about theatre in the '60s and '70s — lots of nudity, Beat poetry, uninhibited."

The McClure script that One Yellow Rabbit decided to produce in the fall of 1985 was his most critically acclaimed. A play based on Kafka's last published short story, "Josephine the Singer, or the Mouse Folk," it had been produced at New York's WPA Theater in 1978 and won the Village Voice OBIE Award for best off-Broadway play of the year. (As it happened, the title role in the WPA production was played by a Canadian — Gale Garnett, an erstwhile pop singer/songwriter best known for the 1964 hit "We'll Sing in the Sunshine.") "Josephine" deals with one of Kafka's pet themes, the artist's role in society, here couched in the fable of a singing mouse whose artistry leaves her fellow mice ambivalent. Seduced as they are by her songs, they are unwilling to go so far as to recognize her contribution to the colony by making her exempt from regular mousework. McClure's play sticks closely to the original story, building a dramatic structure out of Josephine's increasing efforts to convince the colony's judges that she should be liberated from common labour. His only significant addition to Kafka is a subplot in which Josephine refuses to marry and be a mousewife and mother — her art is her only love. It leads one heartbroken admirer to kill himself over her, inspiring a wave of copycat suicides by her other spurned suitors.

The Rabbits had begun to think big and they wanted to make their production of *Josephine: The Mouse Singer* into a real event, by inviting McClure up from San Francisco to see it. As with Richard Fowler and Jan Henderson, the plan was to have the poet also do workshops during his visit. This time, getting funding wasn't so easy. Kirk Miles remembers the reaction of the Alberta Foundation for the Literary Arts: "They said 'You're not bringing up some has-been American Beat poet and paying him an outrageous amount of money.' We said 'Fine. You don't want to pay for him, we're bringing him up anyway.' Nothing stopped us." (By pitching McClure as a dramatist who would give a playwriting workshop, the company obtained a small grant from the province's performing arts branch instead. So there.)

With Gyl Raby busy learning to be a mother, the Rabbits hired their Fringe friend and mentor, Brian Paisley, to direct the show. Paisley had to cast the net beyond the collective to fill the play's many rodent roles. For the part of the diva Josephine, he chose Katherine Schlemmer, an actor with whom he'd worked at Chinook Theatre. Paisley also chose to ignore McClure's instructions that the mice be kitted out in Victorian and Edwardian garb. Instead, he saw them as a colony of farmers in homespun. The costumes were designed by Ronnie Burkett, a gifted young puppeteer who had begun moving in the Rabbits' circle. "The whole concept for the costumes was Amish quilting," Burkett says. "So we had these big, foam-rubber mouse bodies that were all quilted and tufted." The show was a chance for Nigel Scott to try some Schechner-influenced environmental design. He and Burkett collaborated on the striking decor, a magnified field with towering grass spears through which the mice scurried — and through which the audience had to make its way as it entered the theatre. Again, Scott applied minimal material to maximum imagination. The field was constructed out of yards of cheap muslin, painted green. There were also some gigantic props and, like Kafka's hard-working mice, everyone in the company pitched in to build them. "I remember helping to make the large vegetables," says Sheri-D Wilson. "I was hired as an actor, but I was also making a huge oversized carrot in my spare time."

If One Yellow Rabbit hadn't yet registered on the radar for most Calgarians, the production of *Josephine* and the presence of Michael

McClure sent a small but distinct thrill through the city's arts community. Critic Kate Zimmerman, who had arrived in Calgary from Ottawa a few years before, remembers how the event lit up the city's hitherto drab theatre scene. "There was a real buzz just going into the SkyRoom — you had to go up some stairs and check your coat and you could tell that a lot of the cool, young crowd were there — which was not a feeling I remember having at other theatre openings. It felt like a 'happening.'" In the *Herald* (2 November 1985), Zimmerman called the play "thought-provoking" and loved the production design, especially Burkett's mouse costumes, which "give the actors an endearing pear shape." However, she found Schlemmer's intellectual Josephine too dry and pedantic. The *Calgary Sun's* Andrew Penner (3 November 1985) was also laudatory, but seemed to think McClure and the company were confusing the story's theme by also making Josephine a feminist (that is, she doesn't want to have babies).

McClure arrived after the opening and spent a week signing books, giving poetry readings, conducting a playwriting workshop, and generally playing Beat sage to a gaggle of enthusiastic young theatre guerrillas. A dapper, greying fifty-three-year-old, he held court at the Metropol Café, where his plays *The Deuces* and *The Velvet Edge* were read by actors from the *Josephine* cast. Zimmerman, covering the event for the *Herald* (6 November 1985), couldn't help noting that "[i]t was far from the wild time the Six Gallery reading was." She interviewed McClure, who sipped decaffeinated coffee as he reminisced fondly about the sex-and-drug excesses of his youth. Shifting into his sage role, he explained: "Part of gaining temperance is to experiment with extremes."

Director Paisley got the impression McClure wasn't entirely pleased with the *Josephine* production. "He was a neat guy, I liked him, but I remember he was dubious about what we were doing." Others remember differently. "He really got into it," claims Laura Parken. She played one of the mice. "When we weren't on stage, we were under the risers, making mouse noises, scratching and peeping. His last night there, I remember Michael was underneath the seats, too, going 'peep-peep-peep.'" Gyl Raby preferred McClure's poetry to his plays, but says his playwriting workshop had a big influence on her — "mainly in his approach to automatic writing and the luminosity that emerges once chronology is disturbed." One young person, however, was totally in awe of him. Cast member Wilson, a dancer and actor with aspirations to become a poet, adored the Beats. She couldn't believe she was meeting one in the flesh. "The Beats had always been distant to me, unattainable, people from faraway lands," she says. "How do you meet the Beatniks when you're from Calgary? And because of their celebrity, I thought they were unapproachable." McClure put her at ease, reading her work and encouraging her to keep writing.[1]

The next Rabbit show was more modest in scale but again preoccupied with the lower species, and could also be seen as the company's own clever inversion of another Kafka tale. In Kafka's long-story masterpiece, *The Metamorphosis,* the travelling salesman Gregor Samsa awakes to find himself, to his despair, transformed into an enormous dung beetle. In Blake Brooker's *Changing Bodies,* the nerdy, disaffected Rev Kev *wants* to be transformed into another creature; he's trying like mad to morph into a fish.

Alone in his bedroom, Rev Kev carries out various experiments that he hopes will lead to a change from man to fish — or crustacean or poultry. He's not too particular. When he isn't submerging himself in a huge tank of water, he's donning a lobster suit and engaging in reveries about undersea explorer Jacques-Yves Cousteau or trying to do a brain swap with a chicken. In between, he reveals to us bits of his sad outsider life: his high school years, when he was ridiculed for being the lone member of the school's religious studies club and tagged with the nickname Reverend Kevin; his first job, in a fish factory, where he was fired for pocketing the air bladders of gutted fish. A sense of doom hangs heavy in his room. British philosopher J. G. Bennett warns of impending natural disasters on the radio and a toy passenger jet circles above, containing, Rev Kev tells us, a pair of grenade-bearing terrorists ready to blow the plane out of the sky.

Although the play wasn't directly inspired by Kafka, Brooker says the great writer's work was definitely in the back of his mind. "In my twenties, Kafka was a constant companion. A dog-eared copy of his short pieces, which I loved, was always close to hand on my bookshelf." Indeed, his choice for a folk tale in the *Winterplay* show was "Before the Law," that haunting little allegory found in *The Trial*. Kafka's themes of transformation and a world gone wrong became Brooker's own themes, rippling through this and his subsequent plays. Here, his first tentative exploration of those ideas was spurred by a hand-me-down title. *Changing Bodies: Patterns of Danger* was the name chosen by Gyl Raby and Michael Green for a play they'd planned to do in the spirit of Italo Calvino's sci-fi novel *Cosmicomics*. Raby had gotten as far as creating a character named Rev Kev who was obsessed with fish. "I don't know what happened, but Gyl dropped out of the project," recalls Brooker. "So I just stepped in and wrote a play of my own based on the title. It was about people hating the conditions of their lives. It grew out of this line: 'I would trade places with you, or any one of you.' That feeling of misery and imagining that something else is perfect just by its exterior appearance, in this case being attracted to that beauty and coolness and calmness suggested by a fish. It's a naive view, of course."

Michael Green played Rev Kev in the one-man show, which premiered with a three-night run at the SkyRoom in January 1986. Brooker directed and Richard McDowell, working with his new band Infradig, composed and performed the score. After that brief debut, the show toured to the Edmonton Fringe and its new Vancouver cousin, then played a gig in San Francisco. It resurfaced in Calgary for a run at the Pumphouse in October of that year and would eventually be re-mounted for The Banff Centre (1987) and Toronto's Factory Theatre (1988). People still speak of the striking decor, with Rev Kev's outsized aquarium tank set alongside his pet goldfish's bowl and a battery-powered toy airplane that circled above the stage. They also remember Green/Rev Kev's "entrance," suddenly emerging from the tank in his goggles and flippers to consult his bedroom mirror for signs of gills. It was a *coup de théâtre*, with echoes of Green's memorable entrance in Ikarus's *Meatsong*, bursting forth naked from a giant sac of fluid. *Changing Bodies* is a comic play with its fair share of funny lines (at his high school, says Rev Kev, "there wasn't an aquarium club — I went to a Catholic school, and they didn't want to encourage snacking on Fridays"). More significantly, Brooker found a style in which the comedy is inseparable from the poetry, where an eloquent image or metaphor often bumps up against an absurd one. At one moment, Rev Kev is contrasting himself with fellow dropout Robinson Crusoe: "Rather than clinging vainly to floating wreckage and hoping for an island to drift into view, I would relax my failing grip, forsake the future footprints in the virgin sand and sink softly into the tender wet." The next, he's describing that TV hawker of fish sticks, Captain Highliner, his "voice purring like Marlon Perkins on Spanish Fly."

*Changing Bodies* proved a mini acting showcase for Green, a chance to prove he could be freaky *and* sensitive. Kate Zimmerman's *Calgary Herald* review (24 January 1986) noted approvingly that he "curbed his usual orotund manner of speaking in order to bring this odd character an air of reality — a wise choice." Brooker says Green played Rev Kev "with a gentleness and a kind of sweetness that I really liked." The reviews were excellent. The show even brought out the *Herald*'s acerbic chief drama critic, Brian Brennan, whose columns until then had paid scant attention to the exciting young troupe in his midst. Catching the return engagement at the Pumphouse, he called the play "a charming, Ionesco-style absurdist joke" (evidently seeing a resemblance to Ionesco's *Rhinoceros*). Though, as was his wont, he thought the piece fell short. "*Changing Bodies* imaginatively defies convention and category, but never quite manages to defy gravity" (21 October 1986).

The play's premiere was the Rabbits' last in the SkyRoom. The strip of 11 Avenue on which the theatre was located had been undergoing a transformation of its own. Singles bars, sardine-packed with sweaty, sex-hungry yuppies, were taking over, filling the night air with the disco-rock come-ons of Madonna and Duran Duran and the rank scent of hormones in overdrive. Restless queues formed outside the hottest spots, and young males, like rival stags, battled and bloodied one another over the blond babes with the tightest tank tops. For the cops, it was a busy beat. The strip became known as Electric Avenue — the title of a hit song by reggae singer Eddy Grant. A nightclub of that name would eventually occupy the Rabbits' third-storey warren. When the building's owner, the Royal Bank of Canada, sold it to a restaurateur, the company was suddenly forced to abandon the venue on which it had lavished so much time and labour. "That was a huge blow," says Gyl Raby. Adding insult to injury, the new owner blithely appropriated the SkyRoom sign that Nigel Scott had designed for the theatre. "We wanted to sue them," recalls Raby, laughing in retrospect, "but we never got round to it."

Even before the eviction, the Rabbits had been living close to the bone. Artistic principles sometimes had to be compromised to keep the landlord-wolf from the door. Company members still remember, with a mixture of laughter and embarrassment, the time they agreed to don a Paddington Bear costume and cavort in a shopping centre for cash. "We had to meet the SkyRoom rent, which was a thousand dollars, and we were totally broke," says Kirk Miles. "Mount Royal Village called us up — we used to get a lot of calls [for entertainers] — and they wanted someone to do Paddington the Bear. They had the costume, so I agreed to it. I said we'd do it for $300 a day. They wanted us for five days, so there was our rent and a few hundred extra. They sent over the costume and we had a sign-up sheet. You had to try on the costume and sign up. Well, Michael and Jan just signed up right away. I signed up. George tried the costume on and it didn't fit. Gyl absolutely refused, she wouldn't stoop to do Paddington the Bear in a mall, no matter how broke the company was." It was December and the shopping centre wanted to give its customers a little festive entertainment as they did their Christmas shopping. Jan made the perfect Paddington, in part because she fit the costume perfectly, in part because it suited her clown sensibilities. Michael had a rough time of it. The bear head wouldn't fit over his own while he was wearing his glasses, so he was forced to play the role half blind. "He had to follow Santa Claus around the mall," says Miles, "and he kept running into things." The whole silly experience has become a part of Rabbit lore, complete with its own naughty little legend. Apparently one male member of the troupe (who shall remain nameless) was in his bear suit in a change room when a flock of pretty young ballerinas, also part of the Christmas activities, entered and began undressing. Finding himself aroused, and conveniently concealed by a bulky costume, he discreetly pulled his arm out of the sleeve and jerked off.

Laura Parken remembers the troupe doing at least one other mascot gig, a not-inappropriate stint as the Easter Bunny. Marianne Moroney recalls a slightly more dignified hiring, a week-long engagement at the Banff Springs Hotel. "We were given medieval costumes and we were to entertain the people at this conference," she says. "We were given a lot of time off and we all enjoyed the benefits of a big hotel. Late one night several of us climbed the fence that surrounded the pool and we skinny-dipped."

The loss of the SkyRoom meant the company was compelled to tour out of necessity as much as desire. While Brooker and Green went on the road with *Changing Bodies*, others in the troupe hit the school gymnasium circuit with a play commissioned by the Alberta Alcohol and Drug Abuse Commission. *Buy In/Sell Out*, written and directed by Gyl Raby with music by Gregg Casselman, was a didactic piece for teenagers about lifestyle choices. It was performed by Jan Stirling and two other young actors, Gordon Harris and Archer Mayling, and toured local schools in February 1986. (*Buy In/Sell Out* marked the Rabbits' next-to-last involvement in children's theatre and school touring. The following year, the troupe would stage *The Field*, a drama about prejudice by Calgary playwright Clem Martini, in co-operation with the Canadian Council of Christians and Jews and other anti-intolerance groups.)

The spring of '86 brought the Expo adventure in Vancouver. One might say "misadventure," given the shut-down of *The Batman on a Dime* and the tensions surrounding *The Pageant of the Comet*. The latter had been blighted by resentments and creative differences from the start. Actor and composer James Howley, a New Yorker, felt the show was too anti-American in its satire. Denise Clarke, who wanted desperately to act, felt she was being used merely for her physical skills. Gyl Raby felt her vision as playwright and director was being undermined. "It was an awful time," says Raby. "Emotions got ragged, nerves got frazzled. We were a pretty functional family a lot of the time," she adds, "but as with any group that's been together for four years, working without very much money, for very long hours in very intense creative conditions, it becomes like being in a bell jar."

However, as if in compensation, the Rabbits reaped some unexpected benefits from Expo. The previous year, the company had learned about an Alberta government grant to help build theatres. The Community Recreation/Cultural grant had been milked in previous years by the ongoing construction of the Calgary Centre for Performing Arts, but when that mammoth facility was completed in 1985, it freed up funding for smaller groups. As Nigel Scott recalls: "One of the kindly Alberta Culture reps tapped our shoulder and said 'Listen, the CCPA is finishing this year and next year there's going to be a half-million dollars available. Why don't you guys put together a proposal for a theatre?' Now the first thing we lacked was real estate, so we developed the idea of building a theatre we could put in a box and take with us anywhere — just put everything on movable platforms, design the lighting grid so we could install it, or rip it out, of any place we happened to be." The proposal was accepted and a chunk of grant money arrived in the autumn, just as the world's fair was winding down. "In October I drove to Vancouver with $20,000 in my pocket," says Scott, "and there was all this lighting and sound equipment that had only been used for this one six-month festival, going for very, very cheap. I was able to get a major deal. We were able to take that grant and stretch it way beyond what it would have got us just six months earlier."

Meanwhile, when *Batman* returned to Calgary from Vancouver, it ran into another stroke of bad luck that would end in a positive outcome. The musical was booked for a post-Expo run at the Ace of Clubs, a nightclub occupying the QR Centre, which Theatre Calgary had recently vacated in its move to the new performing arts centre. The show was cancelled when the club went under, and Kirk Miles turned it to OYR's advantage. "I got all the seats from the QR Centre for a bottle of Scotch," he boasts. "The club had to renege on our contract and I said 'I need something in return.' And they said 'Well, we have all these chairs.'" The seats were left over from Theatre Calgary days but still in good condition. Only they weren't mounted on anything. "In order to get the chairs installed on risers it was going to cost us $4,000," says Miles. "We were up for a government grant which would help cover the cost, but we had to prove that the chairs were worth something. So we phoned up an auction house and talked to the auctioneer and said 'We need someone to go in and say our chairs are worth $30 a piece.' He said 'Okay, I'll do that, but I want a bottle of Scotch.' So we got him the bottle, he assessed the chairs, and we got our grant."

## Finding the Secret Theatre

By the end of 1986, the Rabbits had amassed an impressive pile of equipment and furnishings. And as the days grew shorter and colder, they could hunker down in a new office — a pair of rooms in the eighth-floor penthouse of the downtown SOMA building, which Blake Brooker's dad had put them on to. Now what they needed was a theatre. Michael Green, never one to be put off by the lack of a traditional venue, had plans for a clandestine, Ikarus-style performance event to be staged in a secret location. A permanent home, however, remained elusive. What about looking in the most obvious place?

The trouble was, One Yellow Rabbit wasn't even in the picture when they drew up the blueprints for Calgary's new Centre for Performing Arts. It had been built for the city's big arts players: the Calgary Philharmonic Orchestra was given the Jack Singer, a 1,800-seat acoustic jewel of a concert hall, while Theatre Calgary and Alberta Theatre Projects occupied the plush Max Bell and Martha Cohen Theatres, respectively. When it opened in 1985 there were no small venues, no studio theatres. This wasn't entirely an oversight. First, there was no immediate demand for them. Calgary's smaller professional companies, Lunchbox and

Loose Moose, had their own theatres. The city's numerous community groups could choose between the little Dr. Betty Mitchell Theatre in the basement of the Jubilee Auditorium or the two-theatre Pumphouse on the banks of the Bow River. Second, there actually was a small venue in the Centre's future plans — the proposed Empress Theatre. A space on the building's southeast side, it sat hollow, a concrete shell, waiting for more funding to finish it. Even then, the Centre's general manager, Doug Lauchlan, fancied it would be used mostly for chamber music concerts and literary readings.

The day the Centre magnanimously announced that it would be making the Jack Singer Concert Hall available for small companies to rent, Michael Green scoffed. What was his little troupe supposed to do in such a grand room, and how could it fill all those seats? When a CBC-TV reporter looking for a comment thrust a microphone at his mouth, Green let it be known that what the Rabbits needed wasn't a concert hall but a hutch. As he remembers it, Larry Lorimer, the Centre's director of operations, saw him on the news and invited him down for a talk. "I told him we were never going to use the Jack Singer," says Green. "I said 'Don't you have anything else for us, like, even a big closet?'" Lorimer suggested he take a look about. At the time, the central courtyard and connecting corridors of the complex remained eerily empty, dotted with virgin glass-front spaces still waiting for commercial tenants. Hmmm … why not? If you've spent your career doing plays in abandoned houses, art galleries, and ex-stereo shops, you learn to use your imagination.

"Future Cocktail Lounge." The sign now graces the bar of One Yellow Rabbit's theatre but, in 1986, it was stuck to the window of one of those vacant spaces, which was tucked away in a corner on the arts centre's third level. The spot was obscure, but not entirely out of the way. People crossing from City Hall to the Centre for Performing Arts over the connecting +15 bridge that spanned Macleod Trail would see it as they entered. It was right by the stairs that led to the ground level and the main venues. Given that Calgary is in the grip of cold weather for at least six months of the year (and often longer), the +15 system, a series of enclosed bridges fifteen feet above street level that connect many of the city's larger downtown buildings, is frequently used. (Its hermetic effects were satirized by Calgary filmmaker Gary Burns in his quirky comedy *waydowntown*.) Still, it was not where you'd expect to find a theatre. When the Rabbits moved in, blackened the windows, and set up their second-hand seats, it felt as though they were gate-crashing the city's culture palace — as if a bunch of unruly art barbarians had invaded that brass-and-brick citadel of decorum and taste via a Trojan horse they called the Secret Theatre.

Soon it would be the locus for some of the most original and exciting theatre work in Canada. The stuff you can't buy. In that unlikely little space, One Yellow Rabbit would prove the virtues of Grotowski's "Poor Theatre" as it sat flanked by two big companies with seven-figure budgets. Alberta Theatre Projects, which received a $400,000 oil-company sponsorship to develop and produce five new Canadian plays as part of Calgary's 1988 Winter Olympic Arts Festival, was unable to come up with anything remotely as powerful or durable as *Ilsa, Queen of the Nazi Love Camp*, staged on a shoestring budget in the Rabbits' first Secret Theatre season. A patron who saw *Rembrandt Brown*, another show that season, felt moved to write in a letter to the *Herald* that "the arts centre at last [has] a tenant worthy of it" (15 June 1987). Among the Secret Theatre's patrons in those early years was ex-theatre rebel Martin Kinch. As he sat in that tiny, sixty-seat black box, he may have thought of his daily woes as the beleaguered artistic director of Theatre Calgary, which had been pummelled by the critics since moving into its posh new facility and was hemorrhaging subscribers by the hundreds. Maybe he wished he was back at Toronto Free in the early '70s and envied the Rabbits' creative licence. Maybe he remembered Bob Dylan: "When you got nothing, you got nothing to lose."

Kinch wasn't the only Centre resident lending support to the Rabbits. The moment they got inside, they discovered allies who were ready to help them out "under the counter." Ralph Christoffersen was duly impressed as he set about building his second theatre in two years. "There was a steady procession of folks who walked in, introduced themselves, and said 'I can get you this.' There was an underground economy there, people who'd bend over backwards to help you out." Of course, the Rabbits already had a man inside with Nigel Scott, who was helping design shows for Theatre Calgary. "I had an 'in' with the big theatre," he says, "and I had a key to the Joint Venture shop." Joint Venture was the in-house company formed in partnership by Theatre Calgary and Alberta Theatre Projects to construct their sets and properties. Scott would use his trusty key to sneak his Rabbit cohorts into the shop so they could do a little set painting on the sly. He also saw to it that the fire marshal wouldn't give them grief. "One of the problems was that we had these inspectors coming through, looking at our electronics, our lighting system, and I was able to wheel and deal with Theatre Calgary to get these boxes to make ours code-compliant. The people at Theatre Calgary helped us out and showed us how to do things all the time." Perhaps, like Christoffersen, they appreciated the irony. "In this $130 million building we walked in and built a working theatre for just $30,000," Christoffersen says proudly. After a year as technical director, he would leave the Rabbits to take a job with Joint Venture, where he'd continue to assist his pals.

Not everyone was pleased with the Rabbits' presence. Larry Lorimer recalls that D. Michael Dobbin, producing director of Alberta Theatre Projects, was concerned that the little troupe would be invading his turf. ATP had already staked its claim as the city's "daring" professional theatre and didn't need a bunch of avant-garde upstarts operating on its doorstep. "I think it was Michael pounding his chest, as he does from time to time," says Lorimer. "He said to us 'What right do you have to bring in another theatre company? We should have been consulted.'" Normally, the Centre's resident companies would have had a say on whether to allow another arts group into the building, notes Lorimer, but the Centre bypassed that by renting the Rabbits the lounge space temporarily, as if they were retail occupants. Officially, the Centre still intended to make the space available if an interested restaurateur was found. "But to be honest," says Lorimer, "we didn't go look for one." Dobbin says now that there was some resentment because the Centre's main tenants were having a hard time getting anything from management, "then they go and adopt this little theatre company. It became a standing joke in the building that what One Yellow Rabbit wants, One Yellow Rabbit gets. It seemed to be the golden child." Dobbin eventually became reconciled to the cocky kids next door, although the ATP-OYR relationship would not always be an easy one.

Now, having insinuated themselves into the Centre, the Rabbits began inviting in other fringe groups. In the summer of 1988, they turned the Secret Theatre into a tryout house for the Calgary acts heading north to the Edmonton Fringe. The following summer, Richard Fowler came back, this time as director of Winnipeg's Primus Theatre, to do another taxing Grotowski/Barba-style show. For a time, the Rabbits' space became a whistlestop on the fringe-festival circuit for troupes such as the English Suitcase Theatre — although, for reasons that will become clear later, OYR always resisted the impulse to give Calgary that long-overdue fringe festival of its own. In 1989, another little Calgary company, Live Arts Theatre Alberta, began mounting a season of shows in the Secret that alternated with the Rabbits' fare. LATA, which had started in 1985 with an Equity Co-op production of Sam Shepard's *Buried Child,* directed by Sharon Pollock, tended to swim closer to the mainstream than OYR. Its programming leaned toward the off-Broadway plays of the time, such as Terrence McNally's *Frankie and Johnny in the Claire de Lune,* Athol Fugard's *The Road to Mecca,* and Christopher Durang's *Laughing Wild.* Perhaps its wildest venture was a co-production with One Yellow Rabbit of an original script called *Lives of the Saints,* but that was largely a Rabbit creation. Scripted by Michael Green with actor Laura Parken and comedians Andy Curtis and Owen Demers, it was a rare OYR foray into religious comedy that fell midway between a Monty Python–style satire of the Roman Catholic Church and a sympathetic portrayal of its gutsy saints and martyrs. Today, it lingers in the memory mainly for its haunting score (composed by Richard McDowell and Tim Campbell) and for the performance of a tonsured Curtis, who was engagingly goofy as the bird-loving St. Francis of Assisi.

## *The Collective Explodes (And the Board Freaks Out)*

Just as One Yellow Rabbit was heading into the Secret Theatre, its tight little collective burst into pieces.

The company had already lost one member in 1984, when late-comer Marianne Moroney left to do an internship at Theatre Calgary. "I didn't think I was going to part forever, originally," she says. "Michael constantly chatted with me to keep me interested." But her acting career took off at TC and ATP, and she never went back. Then, shortly after Expo, the restless George McFaul packed his bags and departed Calgary for another sojourn in Quebec. He returned two years later, but his subsequent work with OYR was limited to the occasional acting role and guest appearances as part of his wife Laurie Montemurro's Springboard Dance Collective.

Jan Stirling would leave late in 1986 — just in time for the office to finally get its first computer. Although that might've made her bookkeeping easier, it wouldn't have been enough to keep her with the Rabbits. She felt she had become pigeonholed as an administrator when she really wanted to create. Besides, the company's work was getting darker and quirkier and less to her liking. "I felt I needed to make a clean break and begin a new phase in my life," she says. She went to Toronto to continue her clown training, studying with Richard Pochinko. "I really liked mask work and improvisation and wanted to develop more in that direction." A year later, she and Michael separated.

Kirk Miles had a taste for administrative work, but he was disgruntled at having to work as a general manager without a proper GM's salary. He quit to take on a more lucrative job as the box office manager of the newly hatched Calgary International Children's Festival. However, he remained on the company's board of directors. A young man named Craig Laven was hired to replace him. Looking back, Miles remembers One Yellow Rabbit's formative years as an exhausting and penurious time. "There's no question, those six years were the hardest I've ever worked in my life. They were sixteen-hour days: Write grants in the morning, rehearse in the afternoon, write plays in the evening, rehearse again until late at night, wake up and do the whole thing again — for very, very little money. It was really a subsistence wage the first six years. In fact, the first two years I don't think we were paid much at all, and yet [the company] demanded all this time."

But there was another reason why the collective broke up. Gyl Raby felt the company was being held back artistically by limiting itself to the use of its own in-house performers for shows. It was brought home to her when she sat down with Keith Turnbull to do a post-mortem of *Ides*. "Keith said to me, very forcefully, that the problems with the play weren't with the script or the production, they were innate within the company and the fact that there wasn't sufficient basic act-ing training. So I started to feel: Okay, if we're going to evolve, we need to be able to bring in other actors sometimes so that there can be a shar-ing of new skills. It would be a way of replacing the workshops, which were so expensive, and there were other people, exciting artists, I wanted to work with." Michael Green backed the idea, but there was resistance from the other actors in the troupe. Raby recalls some "fairly bitter exchanges" over what she saw as a closed-shop mentality. In ret-rospect, she thinks the ill feelings may have been triggered by the *Comet* clashes at Expo. Certainly, George McFaul and Jan Stirling both left later that same year.

Raby had her way. The inaugural show in the Secret Theatre, *Disrobing the Bride* by Harry Kondoleon, involved only two of the original Rabbits. Raby adapted the play and directed, while Michael Green was in the cast. The other performers were Lesley Ewen and Sheri Dayle Wilson and the production team was made up of Rabbit new-comers. One of them was Sandi Somers. Originally from Cape Breton, Nova Scotia, she'd studied scenography at Halifax's Dalhousie Univer-sity, then come to Calgary to begin her professional career designing the lighting for Stage West. Before her first year was out, she'd had her fill of placing aging celebrities in a kind light, and when fellow designer Nigel Scott told her that his quirky little troupe was hiring, her ears perked up. "I was looking for something like the Rabbits," she says, "something a little more creative and less traditional." OYR would offer her a spate of new challenges, not all of them creative. To begin with, she had to learn how to be an electrician. Arriving in time to help Ralph Christoffersen build the Secret Theatre, Somers discovered that, before she could design any lights, she had to wire the place first. "I remember walking in and it was literally just two walls and a floor, with no electricity. So I put all the circuit systems in, which was quite educational."

*Disrobing the Bride,* which ran in the Secret Theatre 6 to 21 March 1987, was an early experimental work by New York poet and playwright Kondoleon, who would go on to fitful success as an off-Broadway dramatist before dying of AIDS in 1993. (One of his more memorable — I won't say apt — stage creations was a vampire drama critic.) A long poem written in monologues, the piece took the form of a mock fairy tale, alternately satirizing and sympathizing with the innocent hopes and dreams of the young bride, doomed to be shattered by a selfish and devious groom. The play appealed to Raby's feminist sensibilities as well as her interests in poetry-as-theatre, freshly charged by the Michael McClure workshop. Although its original and published title was *The Brides,* she favoured *Disrobing the Bride,* the name used for its New York premiere in 1981, because it suggested the famous oil-on-glass master-work of artist/prankster Marcel Duchamp, *The Bride Stripped Bare by Her Bachelors, Even.* Witek Wisniewski, a local television and theatre designer, created decor for the show inspired by Duchamp. "I remember it had a lot of mannequins that glowed in the dark," says Somers. "After my fifth all-nighter in the theatre, they started to move." Freed from her Stage West boredom, Somers burned the candle at both ends to help realize Raby's vision. She says the show was so visually complex that she had to use three lighting boards, all running simultaneously.

Meanwhile, playwright Blake Brooker was burning up the word processor. On the heels of *Changing Bodies* came *Rembrandt Brown,* a satire of corporate skulduggery and a dark comedy about the trauma of unemployment. As he was shortly to do with *Ilsa, Queen of the Nazi Love Camp,* Brooker was now responding directly to the concerns of his local audience. Many were still struggling to recover from the oil bust at the start of the 1980s and "downsizing" was, or soon would be, a familiar word in the corporate lexicon.

Rembrandt, like many a yuppie in those Calgary office towers, goes swiftly from a cocksure employee to the hurt and dazed casualty of budget cutbacks and "restructuring." To make things worse, he also loses his long-distance girlfriend, a workaholic, to one of her co-workers. Rembrandt, unable to bounce back, slides into a semi-catatonic state, holed up in his bedroom, unshaven and pyjama-clad, watching his big-screen television and brushing off the concerns of his worried pal Deanie. "I've got an important meeting right now," he says, clicking on his TV — "with *Donahue.*" His unemployment spurs an identity crisis, which is not helped by Ms. Childs, the job counsellor he eventually consults. Instead of encouragement, she offers existential quandaries. "Who are we now?" she asks him — a question that reverberates through Brooker's plays.

As Rembrandt sinks deeper into despair, the play becomes more surreal and absurd. Its funniest scenes are a series of nightmare interviews with prospective employers, including one whose hilariously convoluted questions sound like the Q & A in the penultimate chapter of Joyce's *Ulysses,* and another who insists on believing that Rembrandt is really Neil Diamond: "What did you really mean to say in 'Forever in Blue Jeans'?" As an added touch of fantasy, throughout the play a team of Uzi-wielding Ninja warriors swarms over the set, at first assisting and then bedevilling Rembrandt as his fortunes turn. In the climactic scene, they become his torturers.

"It was a piece that reflected, almost exclusively, my personal fear of economic uncertainty and insecurity," says Brooker. He channelled his own anxieties as a struggling young writer into the corporate milieu without, he admits, much experience of it. Apart from pitching in at his dad's industrial shelving operation, he had little contact with the workaday business world. "I always had a fear and loathing of corporate life that was intuitive. There's something about it that always gave me the willies. The play grew out of this irritation and repulsion at what corporations do to people."

Gyl Raby directed the production, which opened in late April 1987 at the Secret Theatre. The set was by Nigel Scott, the music by Richard McDowell and Kevin Labchuk (performing as Infradig), and the cast included Michael Green, Alexandria Patience Thom, Paul Punyi, and Almeda Cowper. Against his older brother's wishes, Kevin Brooker played Rembrandt. "That was back when there was somebody who could steamroll Blake," he recalls with a laugh. The "somebody" being Raby. "Blake had written this play about a yuppie, a bit of a smart aleck, who had been fired, and there was something about the way I was as a person that said 'He's a guy like that.' Gyl was casting it, and she said to Blake, 'What about your brother? He's exactly the kind of guy you're writing about.'" He claims Blake objected but was overruled. (Blake refutes the story. "I wanted him to do it! I thought it was cool. I don't know why Kevin says that." Ah, siblings.) Kevin wasn't shy about performing. He had dabbled a bit in theatre, doing an improv show at the Edmonton Fringe, and also spun discs for the U of C's campus radio station. But this part was no walk in the park. "I had a five-minute nude scene, three torture sequences, two love scenes, I had to enter from the rafters Ninja-style, on ropes. And I had to finish the play with maniacal laughter evolving into maniacal crying. It was a super-demanding role," Kevin says. "I was just doing it to see if I could remember an hour-and-a-half worth of dialogue. They said I did okay, but I haven't acted since, so I couldn't have been that good." Kate Zimmerman's *Herald* review (25 April 1987) deemed him "equal to his brother's fine script," but she was particularly intrigued to see Michael Green in "an unusually low-key role" as Deanie. "It's interesting to see him do so well in this unprepossessing persona; he holds his shoulders hunched, as if he had been hit in the solar plexus with a medicine ball as a youth, and never fully recovered."

One Yellow Rabbit closed out its first season in the Secret Theatre with *Ilsa, Queen of the Nazi Love Camp,* a cunning musical satire written by Blake Brooker and composer David Rhymer in cahoots with Kirk Miles and Clem Martini. Its subject matter — not S&M porn flicks, as the title suggests, but a certain highly publicized court case —

would send the company's board members running scared over fears of a lawsuit. And the first show of the following season would prompt more defections — this time out of disgust. The Rabbits may have upped their professional profile by moving into the Centre for Performing Arts, but clearly they weren't about to compromise their ingrained desire to shock and provoke. The Centre had let in a bunch of troublemakers.

It was as if Michael Green had been waiting patiently for the troupe to break in the Secret Theatre and its audience to get comfortable before going completely gonzo. One can imagine him, acting quietly, sensitively in *Rembrandt Brown,* and all the while grinning wickedly inside, knowing that his old Ikarus mate, Gary Stromsmoe, was patiently birthing a sick, ugly little monster to let loose in season number two. *Fall of the House of Krebbs* premiered in October 1987 and, as its Poe-inspired title suggests, it was a tale of the grotesque — big time. Stromsmoe, abetted by Green, had served up a rancid slice of American pie, teeming with maggots; a sordid study in Midwestern Gothic, peopled by Bible-thumping perverts, ghoulish cripples, and idiot children. Kate Zimmerman's review in the *Calgary Herald* (2 October 1987) reads like one of those Victorian notices for Ibsen's *Ghosts:* "Stromsmoe peels back a bandage to expose an oozing societal sore"; an "atmosphere of fetid, violence-tinged perversion"; "the outlook ... is as bleak as that of a person with a terminal disease." But she was willing to see beyond her revulsion and her overall impression was favourable. Too bad she didn't sit on the One Yellow Rabbit board.

Kirk Miles remembers it as a fiasco. With the move to the arts centre, the company had been wooing members of the corporate community to join its volunteer board of directors. That meant a better chance of accessing donations from the private sector. *Krebbs* spoiled it all. "It was just a horrid show," says Miles. "It was so awful, we had board members quit. They took one look at that and said 'I don't want to be part of the company.'"

The play grew out of a news story Stromsmoe had read about a wacko in rural Wyoming who had traded a car to a young woman in return for sexual favours, then tried to sue her when she reneged on the deal. When Stromsmoe was finished with it, it had become the tale of a creepily dysfunctional family: deranged daddy Rusty Krebbs, a self-styled politician and evangelist; his twin sons Wingo and Yorky — the former a moron who digs up worms, the latter a zombie poet kept under a sheet — and his wife, Meg, whose feet Rusty has encased in cement. There was also Mother Gertrude, played in drag by Michael Green who looked, Zimmerman reported, like the transvestite rock singer Boy George.

It was an elaborate production, with a cast of nine, a lurid haunted-house set with eerie effects designed by Sandi Somers, and a country music score by the local band Sacred Heart of Elvis. It was Somers' set-design debut with the Rabbits and she pulled out all the stops. The scenery filled the entire theatre and included crumbling walls and a false wooden floor. Red light glowed through the cracks in the floor-boards at the climax when all hell broke loose. Somers remembers pushing the limits of the tiny space. At one point Andy Curtis, who played Yorky, was even hoisted up into the theatre's non-existent flies. "We found one little open area in the ceiling where all the ductwork went," says Somers, "so we actually had him ascending into the ceiling."

Dennis Cahill, artistic director of Loose Moose, played Rusty as a psychotic clown, complete with red nose and floppy shoes. Laura Parken had the role of Meg, his oddly abused spouse, who moved about in a washtub equipped with wheels, using a hook to pull herself forward. "I've rarely had so much fun doing theatre," says Parken, still relishing the memory. "Nobody knew what to make of it. It was way too weird for most people."

Stromsmoe wasn't just being weird for weird's sake. He took his writing seriously and *Krebbs,* like *Marat/Sade,* the show that launched Ikarus, was partly an attempt to practise Antonin Artaud's Theatre of Cruelty. Indeed, the zoned-out Yorky, who sporadically breaks out of his trance to make poetic utterances, was meant to represent Artaud himself. The tortured French theatre iconoclast spent the last years of his life in a madness broken by occasional spells of lucidity. Green, who took a co-author credit, still defends the show. "I think the people who were offended by it just missed the mark. For what it was, it was a tremendous piece of work. I know Gary wasn't happy with how much cutting I had to do to his script. But I've had people come up to me and say that seeing *Fall of the House of Krebbs* was what inspired them to get into theatre." ("No one has said that about my other shows," he adds with a mock sigh, "just that one.")

Bad or good, the board's reaction to *Krebbs* was not going to change the Rabbits. "We trusted ourselves," says Miles. "Despite our failures, we knew the big picture. We knew artists fail. Nobody goes out to write a bad show; we knew that. The board members didn't. We thought: If they can't get behind us, we don't give a shit." One Yellow Rabbit would eventually attract the right people to its board, but those early years in the Secret Theatre were rocky ones. Miles remembers how some members even tried to influence the company's work. "They were always trying to tell us 'You've got to do something about oil, it's an oil town.' They were going 'You've got to speak to the people. You can't be a company that does such wild things.'" Perhaps if those board members had listened more closely, they might have realized that One Yellow Rabbit was often speaking directly to them. The next new show that season was another family play — one more melancholy and poetic — which had "Alberta" stamped all over it.

In 1987, the province's ruling Conservatives were swinging further to the right, as talk of a need to return to "family values" surfaced in the speeches of Lougheed's pallid successor, Don Getty. It may have been a dodge to deflect Albertans' attentions from their ailing economy, but it smacked of the kind of moralizing that hadn't been heard from a premier since the high days of Social Credit under Bible Bill Aberhart. And it rang hollow in an era when changes both cultural and economic were making the traditional nuclear family a thing of the past. Meanwhile, in the arid badlands east of Calgary, the new Royal Tyrrell Museum of paleontology was drawing visitors from all over the province and beyond. The impressive, state-of-the-science museum, which had opened in the fall of 1985, celebrated Alberta's reputation as a major repository of prehistoric remains. So families and fossils were in the forefront of Albertans' minds when Blake Brooker set out to write *Tears of a Dinosaur,* a play that suggests the nuclear family is going the way of the Albertosaurus.

Brooker says the piece was triggered by one of the many enthusiasms of Michael Green. At the time, he recalls, Green was fascinated by Roy Chapman Andrews, the paleontologist and adventurer who, in 1923, made the first discovery of dinosaur eggs while exploring the Gobi Desert. Perhaps Green fancied himself swaggering about on stage with Chapman's trademark broad-brimmed hat and revolver, re-enacting his often hair-raising exploits. Brooker had other ideas. In *Tears of a Dinosaur,* he would have Green portray a paleontologist named Roy, but this one would be seeking something even rarer than dinosaur eggs — a happy family.

Roy is a firm believer in family values, a man determined to build his own nuclear unit despite the misgivings of his wife, Liz. The couple adopt a grown-up son, Ray — a glum orphan who first appears, unforgettably, as half-dinosaur, half–St. Sebastian. With a little James Dean thrown in. An unwanted foster child, the shafts bristling from his body represent the felicitous memories of his foster families, which he can never share. In one of the play's most inspired passages, Brooker moves the saint's martyrdom from the usual "scrawny linden tree" to the family supper table, where each family anecdote zings him until he has "arrows sprouting from every sad limb, and all this before the Jell-O has been served." Roy makes some comic efforts to impose the template of the traditional family on his ambivalent wife and damaged son, but in the end neither he nor they are very happy. Brooker arrives at no conclusion, only the final image of a dinosaur being sucked down into a bog, dragging its rider, Roy the family man, along with it. The play is, to use one of Brooker's favoured terms, a meditation; it mulls over the fate of the family but doesn't presume to suggest how it might be saved or even question if it is worth saving. "One Yellow Rabbit could almost be considered to be an issue-oriented theatre company at times," says Brooker, "almost doing popular or social action theatre in the style of

[Brazilian director] Augusto Boal. Only," he laughs ruefully, "ours was social *inaction* theatre."

*Tears of a Dinosaur* was developed at The Banff Centre, where it premiered in November 1987. Brooker wasn't happy with the results and did extensive revisions — changing one of the three main characters, cutting a fourth — before the show was re-assembled for its run at the Secret Theatre in May 1988. He may have felt more than the usual pressure to get it right. The company's reputation was riding on this one — *Tears of a Dinosaur* was also scheduled to visit international theatre festivals in Toronto and Quebec. Apart from Green's solo turn that winter in *Changing Bodies* at Toronto's Factory Theatre, One Yellow Rabbit had yet to tour eastern Canada. Brooker directed the production, Richard McDowell created an original score, and Sandi Somers and Ronnie Burkett collaborated on the design, which ranged from an eight-metre dinosaur skeleton as backdrop to a child's little dinosaur figurines. Burkett provided marionettes for the actors to manipulate while Somers created the big dino, dubbed Gracie. Denise Clarke and a young actor named Jarvis Hall, who had the perfect sad demeanour for Ray, joined Green in the cast.

Following its Calgary debut, the production headed east, playing Quebec City's Quinzaine Internationale du Théâtre as well as the du Maurier World Stage festival in Toronto and the Centaur Theatre in Montreal. Critic Marianne Ackerman, writing in the *Montreal Daily News* (17 June 1988), accurately pinpointed the play's virtues and flaws in a predominantly positive review. "The strength of the piece lies more with the richness and moment-to-moment power of the writing than with plot," she observed. As for the production, it was "one of the most aesthetically imaginative shows to come along in ages." (Quite a compliment coming from Montreal, Canada's font of theatrical imagination.) *Tears of a Dinosaur* then turned and padded back west to more familiar ground: the Edmonton and Vancouver Fringe Festivals. By now, the Rabbits were stars of the Edmonton Fringe and their latest work was greeted with a fanfare. The *Edmonton Journal*'s Liz Nicholls chose to lead off her annual Fringe preview by spotlighting the play and declaring: "I wouldn't willingly miss a One Yellow Rabbit show" (13 August 1988). Indeed, she caught *Tears* as soon as it opened and, while a bit daunted, was not disappointed. "Chances are you'll see nothing at the Fringe remotely like this fascinating, difficult, elusive, new show," she reported in the paper's 15 August edition, urging readers to catch it and then argue about it afterwards.

Not everyone was convinced of its merits, however. The play received one particularly brutal notice, in the hitherto supportive *Calgary Herald.* I wrote it.

By 1988, I had graduated from general arts reporter to angry young drama critic and, given that my predecessor Brian Brennan had been notoriously difficult to please, I felt it was expected of me that I should slay anything that didn't suit my tastes. This was one of my first experiences with Brooker's writing and I didn't yet know what to make of it, so I attacked it as "an amorphous muddle." Brooker was still finding his voice and deserved a more perceptive appraisal. *Tears of a Dinosaur* was clearly a further step away from the formal dramatic structures he was still relying on as recently as *Rembrandt Brown* and a move toward the kind of poet's theatre he and Raby had envisioned. I still think some of my criticisms were valid — the show had some splendidly surreal images but was too static (the playwright was also a novice director), it made little use of its puppets, and it ended in that anticlimactic whimper. Eventually, I'd begin to appreciate what Brooker was doing — and trying to do — but it would take a few years and a few more harsh reviews.

---

1    Shortly after meeting McClure, Wilson went to study at the Buddhist Naropa Institute in Colorado, home of the Jack Kerouac School of Disembodied Poetics, where she met most of the Beat icons, including Ginsberg and Burroughs, and was befriended by the likes of poet Anne Waldman and rock singer Marianne Faithfull. Today, Wilson is a published poet and playwright, writing in the neo-Beat tradition, whose books include *Swerve* and *Girls' Guide to Giving Head.*

# 4. Exit Gyl, Enter Denise

**T**he eyes of the world were on Calgary in February 1988 — or at least, the eyes of those who watch winter Olympic sports, which, thanks to network television, is a not inconsiderable number. The city was host to the XV Winter Olympic Games, and even those Calgarians who had never strapped on a ski or heard of a luge were caught up in the excitement. The event included a $10 million Olympic Arts Festival, a banquet of international music, dance, and theatre the likes of which the city had never seen. True, the menu — the Joffrey Ballet, Cirque du Soleil, Peter Brook's *La Tragédie de Carmen,* the Juilliard String Quartet, Robert Lepage's *Vinci,* to name a few items — was nothing you wouldn't find during a regular season in London or New York, perhaps even Toronto. And some of the dishes weren't especially fresh (Calgary got the seven-year-old *Carmen* at a time when Brook had just sent forth his acclaimed *Mahabharata*). No matter. For a city Calgary's size, this sudden cornucopia of culture was almost overwhelming.

The local artists and arts groups contributed, too — sometimes superbly (Calgary Opera's *Porgy and Bess,* directed by Christopher Newton), sometimes lamely (Theatre Calgary's revival of Sharon Pollock's *Walsh,* directed by Keith Turnbull). On the dance front, one local artist shone brightly. The Olympic Modern Dance Commissions showcased the work of six choreographers from across Canada, including Montreal's well-known Margie Gillis and Marie Chouinard, but Calgarian Denise Clarke blew everyone else off the stage with her creation, a high-octane ensemble piece called *The Blind Struggle* about the Darwinian battle for survival among a team of athletic women. "The whooping and cheering that greeted the premiere of Calgary choreographer Denise Clark's [*sic*] work might have been attributed to her being a home-town girl," wrote critic Stephen Godfrey in the *Globe and Mail* (1 February 1988), "except for the fact that it was a terrific dance." Godfrey enjoyed the irony that "the best piece among these commissions … turned out to be the local one." The dance's driving music was created by Richard McDowell, who had whipped it up while also scoring *Tears of a Dinosaur* in Banff in the fall of 1987.

One Yellow Rabbit, however, had no official part in the festival. Whether too new or too small — or both — it had been left off the guest list. Nor did it have much interest in contributing in the aftermath of Expo '86. "The world's fair was not a good experience for us," says Michael Green, "and I'm sure it tempered our enthusiasm toward getting involved in something like that again right away." Besides, in the midst of all the Olympic hoopla, the Rabbits were recovering from yet another loss.

By the time of the 1987–88 season, the company had three co-artistic directors: Gyl Raby, Blake Brooker, and Michael Green. And Raby was beginning to feel that she was the odd one out. It came to a head when the budgets for Brooker's *Tears of a Dinosaur* and Green's *Fall of the House of Krebs* left her with not enough money to stage her own pet project — a multimedia musical called *Treacheries of the Blue Angel* — in the manner she had hoped. Stuck in the office that winter, filling out grant forms while new manager Craig Laven was away getting training and her fellow Rabbits were off creating, she panicked. "I looked at the amount of administration and production work that I was doing," she recalls, "and at what I was not achieving artistically. I was in a big hurry back then. I had a kid and, since so much of my time was taken up parenting, the rest of the time had to be spent on art or I would not be an artist anymore. I was afraid I'd be subsumed by the company and my artistic identity was in danger of evaporating. So I resigned."

Raby went to Quebec City to work with Robert Lepage on the English translation of his psychological thriller *Polygraph*. While there, she was offered the job of artistic director at Edmonton's little Northern Light Theatre and accepted it. She eventually staged *Treacheries of the Blue Angel* at Northern Light in 1989.

Tough and prickly as she sometimes was, Raby still inspires respect and gratitude from her former colleagues. "She was such a driving force in the company, such a teacher," says Kirk Miles. "With Gyl, nothing was perfect. She was such a perfectionist, nothing was good enough, ever. There was always something that could've been improved, and that drove the quality up all the time. We were always reaching for Gyl's sensibility. I think at the beginning of the company, the one who had the real artistic vision, who was the real artistic director, was Gyl. In a way, she kind of taught Michael and Blake how to be artistic directors. She taught them how to have a vision and how to make it happen. She was an incredibly talented woman." Although in a new city, with a new company, Raby didn't sever her ties with the troupe. At Northern Light, she revived Brooker's *Rembrandt Brown* and hosted an OYR tour of *Ilsa, Queen of the Nazi Love Camp* that would cause a storm of controversy — more of which, later.

As Raby was leaving, another dynamic woman was moving in. Denise Clarke, long flirting on the edges of the company, was suddenly centre stage. In quick order, she performed in *Tears*, almost stole the show in *Serpent Kills*, took over the title role of *Ilsa*, and created the show that would realize Raby's dream of an international tour.

Clarke has also been flirting on the edges of this book so far and it's time she was properly introduced. Denise (Dee to her friends) is a big cat of a woman, tall (just a shade under six feet) and blond, with a long, supple body. She moves with the strength and grace of a lioness and holds her head high like a queen. Her eyes, protruding blue orbs half hid by heavy lids, smoulder with sensuality from countless One Yellow Rabbit posters. Her nose is *retroussé,* her mouth a tiny pout. Her natural roles are divas and femme fatales, and she has played her fair share of them — from Sarah Bernhardt to Mata Hari, not to mention one heartbreaker of a golden eagle. That is her aura. Meet her and you'll find she's the antithesis of regal and aloof. She greets you warmly and laughs easily. Her wide smile reveals crooked teeth she's never bothered to fix. She talks in slang like a teenager and burbles with enthusiasm like a little girl.

Another child of the Calgary suburbs, Clarke grew up in the southeast neighbourhood of Acadia, the youngest of four siblings. Entranced, like so many baby bunheads, by the tutus and tiaras of *Swan Lake,* she began ballet lessons at the tender age of three and her natural talent was recognized immediately (in her very first recital she danced the lead role — principal teddy in *The Teddy Bears' Picnic*). When she was only fourteen, she attained the prestigious Solo Seal from the Royal Academy of Dance, and by sixteen, she had left home to join Alberta Ballet, then based in Edmonton. Clarke was on the fast track to a professional career as a ballerina when, at eighteen, she had a career crisis. By now she was with the Royal Winnipeg Ballet and set to tour with its corps in *The Nutcracker.* She was smoking and popping pills to stay rod thin, nursing compound injuries and, suddenly, the idea of working like a horse and wrecking her health just to flit about in the wake of the Sugar Plum Fairy no longer held any appeal. "It became increasingly evident to me that, while I wanted to be a prima absoluta, a star ballerina, I didn't really want to dance too many fairy parts," Clarke says. "So I just completely quit."

A bohemian period followed in which she hung out in Montreal, disco dancing on a TV variety show, apprenticing with Les Ballets Jazz, and dabbling in poetry and drugs, before she landed back in Calgary. At home, she found her community and her calling. She was hired to teach ballet and jazz dance at the University of Calgary and proved so good at it that her classes were filled to the rafters. At the same time, she began creating and performing her own work, both solo and with her U of C colleague Anne Flynn, a modern dancer from New York. Like the Rabbits, Clarke found Calgary's artistic naïveté an asset. "There was no imprinting, it was a blank canvas, so there were absolutely no rules, and we would do these crazy, freaky performances." But to her experiments she brought a ballerina's discipline and determination. Kirk Miles recalls watching her and Flynn in performance and getting a sense of what One Yellow Rabbit could be. "I remember thinking: Boy, if the Rabbits could come up to this standard of professionalism, there'd be no stopping us!"

Clarke didn't exactly swoop in to take advantage of Gyl Raby's departure, but she admits Raby had been the impediment that kept her from greater involvement with the troupe. While the two women respected each other, they had never quite seen eye to eye. At the start, it was simply a difference of taste. Clarke was unimpressed with such excursions into the "old" avant-garde as *The Crusader* and *Emer*. She was, however, delighted to be part of *Juggler on a Drum*, for which she was allowed to stage her own movement, and got a kick out of playing Catwoman in *The Batman on a Dime*. Then came the falling-out over her role in *The Pageant of the Comet*, when Clarke tried to quit and Raby wouldn't let her. "It made me realize that, no matter how fond I was of Gyllian, I couldn't work with her anymore. I was ready to pull away from the company if need be, when it exploded. She left. She had already had a creative difference with George and Kirk. She had to tell them that she just didn't think they had the chops as actors, which was very painful and difficult. Then, the next thing I knew, she left, too. I really was blissfully ignorant of all this, but what it did was open my involvement full tilt. At that point I could come in as an associate artist."

Raby says she was pleased that Clarke moved in to replace her. She believed One Yellow Rabbit needed a strong female voice. "I felt I had been very important to the company because I brought a woman's perspective to Michael and Blake who, much as I love them, are not particularly concerned with any kind of feminism or a woman's take on the world. I remember early fights with Blake over his plays, where I'd say 'There are no women here. Where are the women characters?'" Apart from desiring that a female view be represented, Raby was keenly aware that there was a paucity of roles for women actors in Canadian theatre.

Once in place as an associate artist, Clarke was quick to assert herself. In the 1988–89 season, she conceived, choreographed, and starred in a guest production with actor pals Neil Cadger and Mark Christmann. Not only was it the hit of the season, it would go on to be One Yellow Rabbit's first international touring show and, in its adroit mixture of dancing and acting, presage the kind of physical theatre that would come to define the troupe's house style. Its unwieldy and mystifying title: *The Erotic Irony of Old Glory.*

Clarke also opened the following season, playing the title role of *Mata Hari,* a new musical written by her new husband, Blake Brooker. After years of vacillating between Blake and her old high school sweetheart, Richard McDowell, Clarke finally took the plunge. She and Brooker were married in April 1989, in a classy ceremony held at the Alberta Ballet studio in Calgary's Nat Christie Centre. It was a double wedding, with the couple's close friends, Shawna Helland and Grant Burns, also tying the knot.

## ... And Then There Was Ronnie

One Yellow Rabbit began another significant relationship during its second season in the Secret Theatre, also following a lengthy courtship. In January 1988, the company hosted a naughty musical trifle called *Fool's Edge* at the Secret Theatre. It marked the auspicious OYR debut of the Ronnie Burkett Theatre of Marionettes, a little puppet company destined to do great things.

Burkett, you'll remember, had designed the lovable mouse costumes for *Josephine* and contributed to *Tears of a Dinosaur* as well as co-designing the costumes for Denise Clarke's Olympic dance commission. He'd been friends with the Rabbits for several years and even shared digs with Brooker and Clarke for a short period. It was during their time as housemates that he and Brooker began to discuss ideas for a puppet show that would bring the dirty comic sensibility of *The Batman on a Dime* to *commedia dell'arte.* In 1986, the project took off under the aegis of Alberta Theatre Projects, which would give it a test run that August as part of a short-lived summer comedy season.

Burkett, at twenty-eight, already had solid credentials as a puppeteer: he had apprenticed under the legendary Bil Baird at the latter's theatre in New York and won an Emmy Award for his work on American television. Yet he'd set that success aside and come to Calgary, near his hometown of Medicine Hat, to fulfill his dream of starting a marionette theatre. An *adult* marionette theatre. *Fool's Edge* was not a kiddie show, it was smut with strings — very funny smut, delivered from the mouth of the puckish Burkett through the bodies of nine lovingly crafted, delightfully grotesque wooden dolls. (Eighteen if you count their hand-puppet doubles.) Brooker's ribald *commedia* scenario had the lecherous miser Pantalone trying to get his grubby paws on the buxom wench Colombina and at the same time give away his pretty daughter to his creditor, the impotent Dottore. Meanwhile, in a salacious subplot, the cavalier Capitano has been diddling Brighella the stable boy.

Burkett had originally imagined a carefully researched homage to the sixteenth-century Italian theatre tradition, then realized he was missing the spirit of the genre. "The whole point of *commedia* was that it was brash and lewd and funny. So we said 'Okay, let's just go for it.'" Burkett, Brooker, and composer Edward Connell chucked the textbooks and went to town, throwing in sado-masochistic references and even a bit of marionette sodomy. (The latter scene was cut after the first performance — only because it didn't get a laugh.) Burkett says the process was a lot of good dirty fun. "It really was like three twelve-year-old boys getting together and writing a show."

By the time he brought *Fool's Edge* to the Secret Theatre, Burkett had become heavily involved with OYR. Not only did he design and act in the Banff version of *Tears of a Dinosaur,* he also donned drag to originate the role of the Nazi prostitute Ilsa in that other Brooker play. And when *Tears* toured to Toronto's World Stage, Burkett was there, too, with *Fool's Edge.* After that, his Theatre of Marionettes would drift away to more mainstream theatres for a few seasons, only to return to One Yellow Rabbit in 1993 with the experimental *Daisy Theatre.*

## Dancing Spies, Drunken Quakers

For someone who claimed to loathe musical theatre and hated watching musical variety shows on TV as a kid, it's ironic that Blake Brooker's first play, *The Batman on a Dime,* and his most successful, *Ilsa, Queen of the Nazi Love Camp,* are musicals. Today, he puts down his distaste to youthful ignorance. "Now I can see the charm of, say, *Jesus Christ Superstar* or *The Music Man.* I guess it was contempt before investigation. I just never associated myself with musical theatre and I felt contempt before I'd even experienced it. But until my first visit to New York in 1980, where I saw a fantastic revival of *West Side Story* on Broadway, I didn't understand the power of a musical. After that, I could see how a musical could be cool." Still, Brooker's experiments with the genre have been a far cry from Broadway song-and-dance shows. His dark sensibilities lean more toward the decadent, satiric milieu of European cabaret. Indeed, if there is a West End/Broadway model for OYR's musicals, it would be *Cabaret.* And the influences behind that show also run through the Rabbits' musicals — from the art songs of Brecht and Weill to the 1930 German film classic *The Blue Angel.* Brooker's tastes are shared by Denise Clarke, who says she was "blown away" by the 1972 movie of *Cabaret* and whose dance style owes a debt to the brilliant Bob Fosse, its director and choreographer. Then there is Clarke's performance as the Nazi madam Ilsa, which is partly a send-up of Marlene Dietrich's *Blue Angel* persona, the whorish cabaret singer Lola Lola.

*Mata Hari,* Brooker's third musical for OYR, fit naturally into that mould. Its real-life heroine was a Dutch cabaret dancer shot by the French as a spy during the First World War. Part artiste, part whore, she was the toast of *fin de siècle* Paris for her steamy performances, which introduced the striptease to genteel European audiences under the guise of exotic Oriental dancing. Brooker and his collaborator, composer David Rhymer, found her to be a fascinating figure, a precursor to such shrewd pop stars as Madonna and Prince, who immersed herself in a sexy public alter ego concocted out of inscrutable Asian clichés and biblical erotica. Behind her Malayan stage name and Salome veils, she was really a middle-aged single mother named Margaretha Geertruida Zelle. In the end, however, the French may have had the last laugh. They accused her of being a German double agent (a claim still in doubt) and had her executed by firing squad. Today her name has become synonymous, not with the art of dance, but with the seductive female spy.

It was Rhymer who was first drawn to Mata Hari's story. Originally from Montreal, he'd arrived in Calgary in 1987 with a reputation as a playwright, but aspirations to be a composer. (He was also known then as David Rimmer, a name he later felt compelled to change to avoid confusion with a Vancouver filmmaker.) He had come west armed with tapes full of lyrics and tunes that he hoped to develop, including a song cycle about Mata Hari, which had been performed in recital at McGill University in 1981. Reading about the Rabbits in the newspaper, he went downtown to meet them and bonded instantly with Blake Brooker. Eventually, Rhymer would get his new friend hooked on his old project and the pair would proceed to rework the original cycle and spin it out into a full-length show. Their first version was a sung-through piece for one female singer/actor and a supporting ensemble of a dozen men. Rhymer says the operatic structure was a nod to the mega-successful mega-musicals of the time. "*Phantom of the Opera* and *Les Misérables* were our models." Rhymer had received a commission from Alberta Theatre Projects to develop the musical, and the songs were given a tryout in a free recital at playRites, the company's newly minted festival of new Canadian plays, during the Olympic Arts Festival in 1988. If ATP liked the results, there was the possibility that it would produce *Mata Hari* at a future edition of playRites. Instead, the experience became a sobering lesson in the ways of large regional theatres.

When Brooker and Rhymer arrived for a meeting with ATP's autocratic boss, D. Michael Dobbin, they were left to cool their heels in reception for a hour and in the meantime handed an extensive critique of the playRites presentation by Roger Perkins, the music director of the Shaw Festival in Ontario. "Roger didn't seem to appreciate that this presentation wasn't a finished product," says Brooker, "the songs weren't even in order, yet he was giving us all these detailed notes." When the young songwriting team was finally ushered into Dobbin's presence, Brooker was livid. "I told him 'This is bullshit. We didn't do this to be criticized and evaluated.' I felt ambushed. I couldn't work under those circumstances, so we just got up and walked out of the room. We withdrew the project. In retrospect, it was naive on my part, I should have at least gone through the process of listening to the notes before making any decisions." Dobbin still stands by Perkins' critique. "I think Roger's perspective on the music was pretty accurate," he says. "I would have loved to have seen the music become as sophisticated and commanding as the story, which I don't think it ever has." ATP was thinking Sondheim; Rhymer and Brooker were rock 'n' roll people. In retrospect, the blow-up was probably a good thing — OYR needed to discover its own musical style in its own way, not try to conform to the expectations of others. So much bad art gets created that way. Still, the criticism came at a sensitive time for the Rabbits, who had begun to feel that, despite their national success, they weren't being taken seriously in their own city and getting the respect they deserved. (That perception was rectified somewhat in 1991, when Brooker and Michael Green were given the annual Harry and Martha Cohen Award for their outstanding contribution to Calgary theatre.)

Instead of getting a lavish ATP production, *Mata Hari* made its debut in 1989 with a stark staging, aggressively choreographed by — and starring — Denise Clarke. The male supporting cast was reduced to four, says Brooker, "because we couldn't afford the twelve men I would've loved to have." As if to emphasize its pared-down nature, everybody in the cast had their hair cut short. The set consisted of nothing more than four intersecting boardwalks. Rhymer played the score solo on keyboard and synthesizer. It was essentially an animated song cycle. "I thought [the production] was interesting but unsuccessful," says Brooker. "However, there was a spark there that made us want to do it again." The play would undergo an extensive overhaul, to the point that when it finally resurfaced in 1996 as *Mata Hari: Tigress at the City Gates*, it bore little resemblance to the initial production. No longer sung-through like an opera, it now included dialogue and narrative. It also became an out-and-out cabaret entertainment, with Mata Hari's life (reviewed in flashbacks from her prison cell) told through a series of songs, monologues, comic skits, and, of course, Clarke's witty re-creation of her controversial performances. This cabaret also had a hot band, with Rhymer on keyboards, Peter Moller on percussion, and the dexterous Jonathan Lewis of the klezmer-rock group the Plaid Tongued Devils on viola, clarinet, and accordion.

Following its Calgary debut, the new *Mata Hari* stormed Edmonton's Citadel Theatre in the spring of 1997, where it won four of the city's Elizabeth Sterling Haynes Awards — the most received by any show that year. It was named outstanding musical production and also picked up prizes for Clarke's choreography and Rhymer's composition and musical direction. The *Edmonton Journal*'s Liz Nicholls loved it, bestowing on it a four-and-a-half-star rating out of five and pronouncing it dazzling. "The irony that Mata Hari, a fabulous self-creation, born of self-absorption and fuelled by self-interest, should be felled, in the end, by the accusation that she is working for some interest other than her own, is at the heart of this mesmerizing piece of musical theatre," she wrote (18 April 1997). She went on to praise Clarke's "riveting" performance, "Rimmer's [Rhymer's] allusive, elliptical songs," and every other aspect of the production. Still, Brooker isn't done with it, which is one reason why, as of 2002, it had yet to tour beyond Edmonton. "I'd love to revisit it. I think some of the songs are beautiful and some of the ideas are interesting," he says, "but it's still not finished, it's quite flawed. It's not a nice little gem or a sea-rubbed stone. It's still rough in places." Rhymer concurs. "It still has one more hoop to jump through."

From *Juggler on a Drum* onward, One Yellow Rabbit was and is primarily a creation company, making original works of theatre. There have been occasions, however, when it has produced other people's plays or, more rarely, dramatized literature for the stage. *Barbarians*, OYR's final offering of 1989, was adapted by Blake Brooker from J. M. Coetzee's novel *Waiting for the Barbarians*. The play had begun as a commission from Gerry Potter, artistic director of Edmonton's Workshop West Theatre. At the time, Potter was cultivating young Alberta playwrights with great success (bad boy Brad Fraser, the prolific Frank Moher, and the endearingly quirky Stewart Lemoine were among his contributors), and he gave Brooker carte blanche. Brooker had read and admired Coetzee's 1980 novel and proposed a dramatization. He then wrote the South African writer and received a reply that both did — and didn't — give him permission. "He sent me this letter, worthy of his compressed and enigmatic method of writing, which said he was afraid the rights to *Waiting for the Barbarians* were no longer his." The book had already been optioned by a British company; however, Coetzee suggested that a small production in an out-of-the-way place like Edmonton might not cause a fuss. "I interpreted the letter as saying 'Go for it' — even though he wasn't actually saying that," says Brooker with a smile. "So I went ahead and did it."

The book, an allegorical tale of political oppression, is the kind of Kafkaesque fable that would naturally appeal to Brooker, but he also saw in it a local relevance. Coetzee's novel sprang clearly, if not overtly, out of the apartheid policies of his homeland and the paranoia they engendered among the white ruling class. Brooker felt the story could also apply to Canada's treatment of its Aboriginal people. "I thought it was a way to provoke some thinking about that." The action is set in the remote desert outpost of an unnamed empire, where the local magistrate's easy way of life is suddenly disturbed by the arrival of a colonel with the secret service who has been sent to investigate an alleged uprising by the barbarian tribes living near the border. The magistrate insists that the barbarians are poor, harmless nomads, to no avail. When the colonel begins rounding up some of them and interrogating them under torture, the magistrate is torn between ignoring the outrage being perpetrated under his nose or trying to do something. He attempts to assuage his conscience by taking under his wing one of the victims, a blind beggar girl, and returning her to her people — an act that finds him accused of treason and tortured as well.

Coetzee's spare but vivid prose is by turns beautiful and harrowing, filled with sensual descriptions that make its allegory come palpably alive. Brooker's dramatization follows the text closely, lovingly. He remembers writing it in his friend Bruce McCulloch's apartment in Toronto. It was produced at Workshop West, with Potter directing, in 1988. Perhaps Brooker felt his faithful adaptation wasn't daring enough for One Yellow Rabbit, because when he staged it himself the next year, he decided to take some large liberties with the book. He changed the aging magistrate from a man to a woman, and the barbarian girl to a barbarian boy. The gender switch was problematic. Was Brooker undermining Coetzee's intentions by making the magistrate female, thereby implying that she was already something of an outsider in this patriarchal empire? Or, rather, did it give the magistrate further reason to feel empathy for the barbarians? Such questions were probably academic, given that so few people saw the show. "We did it at Christmastime," says Brooker, "which was spectacularly bad timing. Come and see a meditation on torture, 'tis the season."

For the role of the magistrate, Brooker approached long-time drama professor Joyce Doolittle, who had recently retired from the University of Calgary. A short, sturdy woman who wears her black hair in a Louise Brooks bob, Doolittle had been a mainstay of the city's theatre community since the 1960s, as a teacher, director, actor, and commentator. She especially loved intellectual and experimental theatre and had stirred up some controversy in her day, mounting a 1962 production of Aristophanes' *Lysistrata* that the *Calgary Herald*'s Jamie Portman called "the dirtiest play ever presented publicly in Calgary." She'd been watching the Rabbits avidly from the start and was flattered by the offer — if hesitant. "I had seen *Barbarians* in Edmonton and it was the kind of show where I had to cover my eyes during part of it, the things that happened in it were so awful. Besides, it was a very big part. I hadn't had that many lines since I'd played *The Madwoman of Chaillot* in graduate school." Nevertheless, Doolittle accepted and was happy that she did. Being in the play gave her an inside look at the Rabbits' creative process at that time. Denise Clarke's influence had obviously taken hold, for Doolittle felt their approach was closer to modern dance than to theatre. "We had sessions where we just made up movements," she recalls. "We each had a signature movement sequence and then they would be put together in different combinations." Adding the dialogue came later. Doolittle, familiar with the New York dance scene, says it reminded her of Merce Cunningham's method of choreographing his dances without playing the musical score. Clarke was only peripherally involved in the production, but Brooker used her techniques. "When he was directing us, Blake would say 'This is one of Denise's methods' or 'This is one of Denise's tricks.'"

As with *Mata Hari,* the production design was simple and symbolic. The central object was a four-metre refectory table, which bore a bowl of fruit and two microphones. It was flanked by a row of pine trees that had recently been cut down in the yard of Doolittle's house. The former represented the civilized comforts of the fortress, the latter the wilderness beyond its walls. Brooker assiduously avoided any suggestion of either South Africa or Canada, dressing his military officers in golfers casuals and his barbarians in sneakers. Michael Green, coiffed like a Cossack, gave a memorable performance as the barbarian boy, who is blinded with a hot fork by his torturers. Doolittle the critic foresaw plaudits. "I said to Michael 'You'll get wonderful reviews. Audiences always like blind people.'" Sure enough, he was singled out in a cast that also included such talented actors as Andy Curtis and Christopher Youngren. Otherwise, the notices were middling and the audiences small. Looking back, Brooker thinks the big mistake he made with *Barbarians* wasn't the gender reversal but the fact that nothing in the play was funny. "There was only one quasi-laugh in it. Even though it was a tragedy, I've understood since that you have to have some laughs. You can't do theatre without laughs; even the deepest tragedies need them. There have to be some moments to release the tension and let a body shift. I learned that lesson."

One Yellow Rabbit made up for the lack of comedy with its next show. Green's *Dreams of a Drunken Quaker* dealt with no issues, proffered no insights into the human condition. It was sheer nonsense, superbly done. Green had too much energy to concentrate only on being an actor — and a co-artistic director. To this day, he always has at least one side project on the go. The fact that the Rabbits now had a full-time dramatist in Blake Brooker didn't deter Green from writing his own plays — intimidated though he was. In the true punk-DIY spirit, he convinced himself he could do it and, for guidance, he turned to the Beats. Like Brooker (and like his hero, Frank Zappa), Green admired the way-out fantasies of William S. Burroughs and began putting Burroughs's cut-up method to practice. "It was a way for me to get over my fear of picking up a pen and facing an empty page," he says. "I'd long utilized those methods for coming up with performance artworks" — for example, his Ikarus pieces and *Café Theatre*'s Juggle Boys.

It should be noted here that the Burroughs technique traces its origins to a former Albertan. It was stumbled upon by Burroughs's friend, the artist Brion Gysin, when the two were living in Paris about the time of the publication of *Naked Lunch*. Gysin, a Swiss Canadian, spent his childhood in the Edmonton area, although by the time Burroughs first met him, he was running a restaurant in Tangier. The story is that Gysin had sliced up a pile of newspapers one day while mounting some drawings, and became fascinated upon noticing the unusual juxtapositions of words and phrases that resulted when strips from different pages were placed side by side. Burroughs seized on the random wordplay as a means of composition and went on to diligently explore it, first with Gysin and other collaborators, then on his own in his novels. His *Nova Express*, which was written using a similar technique, the "fold-in" (a process that involves placing two folded-in-half texts side by side), duly cites Gysin as the inventor of the cut-up.

Like Burroughs, Green experimented with various ways of "cutting up" texts. The ones he chose to mutilate were a Scandinavian folk tale, an Icelandic saga, and Robert Louis Stevenson's *The Strange Case of Dr. Jekyll and Mr. Hyde*. He described his method to me in an interview at the time: "I de-constructed this literature by reading through it frontwards or backwards and circling words that appealed to me and made a complete sentence. So, then I'd have a bucketful of sentences, apparently disconnected but unified in theme and coloured by vocabulary and by my own, apparently random, editorial process." He also admitted, ingenuously, that the process "allows me to come up with literature that I never would have thought in a million years that I could write" (*Calgary Herald,* 3 May 1989). He tried out the nonsensical results in three small doses, performed in workshop form at various venues (including the Buddies in Bad Times Rhubarb! Festival in Toronto) during the 1988–89 season. The shredded Stevenson text became a crime-and-punishment parody featuring a man and his mocking double and entitled *Blackmail House* (readers of Stevenson will recognize that as the name Enfield gives to Jekyll's mysterious laboratory). The Icelandic legend was reassembled as *Horse Killer,* the story of a plucky shepherd lad who becomes the hero in a war between horses and sheep. The Scandinavian tale turned into *King Scabbard & I,* a comedy routine featuring a squabbling two-headed giant with the grisly names of Flesh and Stump. When Green was ready to put the three together, he turned to Denise Clarke for help. Looking for a little unity, she pulled a copy of Carl Jung off the shelf and decided that in his absurd scenarios, Green was unwittingly dealing with dream symbols from the collective unconscious. Here, surely, was the archetype of the Shadow, as well as the mythic figures of the Simpleton and the Twins. More significantly, Clarke also saw the possibilities for physical comedy in two skinny rubber-faced men.

Green had found a perfect double-opposite-foil in Andy Curtis, who had essentially become a member of the company since his remarkable debut in *Ilsa, Queen of the Nazi Love Camp.* Curtis came from the comedy arm of Loose Moose and had the same surreal sensibilities as Bruce McCulloch and Mark McKinney, with whom he'd briefly worked. Rangy, fair-haired, with an open, amiable face, he was the sunny yang to Green's dark and sinister yin. Identically garbed as eighteenth-century Quakers, the pair was uproarious, executing Clarke's slapstick moves with balletic precision and somehow making sense out of the near-incomprehensible text of *Blackmail House.* More straightforward was the Monty Pythonesque *Horse Killer,* in which Curtis's shepherd fell for a pretty bit of regal mutton named Iseult. "Green's hilarious ewe with her speech impediment, saucer eyes and pigeon-toed gait is the most captivating element in the entire production," wrote the *Herald*'s Kate Zimmerman (9 March 1990). *King Scabbard & I* was a minimalist exercise in wordplay and repetition that Gertrude Stein would've appreciated. Clarke's conceit was that these three nutty skits were a series of dreams, and taped introductions linked them to Jungian theory. That may have satisfied her desire for some artistic rationale, but nonsense needs no excuse if it's entertaining and *Dreams of a Drunken Quaker* clearly was. It found fans in Calgary, Edmonton, and Vancouver — although not always among the critics. "Some people were laughing out loud," huffed Lloyd Dykk in the *Vancouver Sun* (17 October 1990). "Pardon my French, but they should have their heads examined." Green was as surprised as anyone that the crazy contraption of a show took flight. "I'd love to go back and do something else as ridiculous as *Dreams of a Drunken Quaker*," he says wistfully. "Few things ended up being as funny as that."

By the end of the 1980s, One Yellow Rabbit had left behind the collective ideal, but the company was still essentially a circle of friends. Grant Burns, who had known Brooker since 1982, left his job as manager of the University of Calgary's campus radio station and replaced Laven as GM. Richard McDowell, who against expectations had bonded with Brooker, his old rival in love, became the Rabbits' regular sound designer. And on stage, Green, Clarke, and Curtis were beginning to gel into an ensemble. This time, however, there weren't the weak links that had caused the "bitter exchanges" between Gyl Raby, Kirk Miles, and George McFaul and helped lead to the bust-up of the collective. The three worked like the proverbial well-oiled machine, whether they were playing a pair of ageless Nazis and a deluded social studies teacher in *Ilsa*, or a trio of lab-coated scientists investigating a curious suicide in one of the company's least-seen and most eloquent creations.

## The Land, The Animals

It was late on a sunny June morning. Blake and Denise were lying in bed, in their little house in Eau Claire that backed onto the Bow River, when they were roused by a knocking at the door. Dee sprang out of bed and ran downstairs. She opened the door to a tall, thin man carrying a bag. "Can I use your phone?" he asked in a worried tone. "There's someone in the water." Blake was making his way downstairs when he heard the stranger explain. He had been walking along the river and had spotted a man in the water. He went up and spoke to him and the man began muttering back. "He wasn't making any sense." Blake stepped into the warm wedge of sunlight from the open door. "Wait. You saw someone *in the water?*" The stranger shifted his bag nervously. Yes. He had just dropped off his wife at work and was taking his dog for a walk … "Your dog?" said Blake. "Yes," said the man, fumbling with the zipper of his bag. He opened it and a tiny Chihuahua poked out its pale round head. Blake was surprised and a little suspicious. He seems rather effeminate, he thought to himself, as he eyed the stranger in his doorway. He knew that their stretch of river, lined with bushes, was a popular gay stroll. The man reiterated. He had come across someone reclining in the water, with his head resting on the bank of rocks, muttering incoherently. "Wait here," said Blake, as he ran back upstairs to pull on his clothes. He was down in a moment. "Denise," he said, "call 911." Then he and the dog owner hurried down to the riverbank.

There was no one there. They walked up and down, scanning the sparkling Bow for any sign of the mysterious bather. It was a hot morning and Blake, sleuthlike, noted that there was no water on the gravel path. The white rocks of the bank had a thin film of dry mud on them. If someone had walked or dragged himself out of the river, surely the rocks would have been wet. Blake gazed at his tall companion, still wondering if he was telling the whole story. His doubts were soon erased. Sirens split the quiet, and police and fire department vehicles pulled up. The rescue squad came down to the riverbank, launched a rubber dinghy, and began to unhurriedly don their drysuits. They're taking their sweet time, thought Blake with mild annoyance. One of the squad waded slowly out into the river and, within minutes, found the body.

It was that of a middle-aged man — in his mid-forties, Blake guessed. He was lying face down, clad in a jogging suit and expensive sneakers. In the time that the Chihuahua's master had run to Blake and Denise's house, he had apparently slipped off his pillow of rock and slid into the icy flow. "The water at that time of the year is still extremely cold," Blake explained later, "and you can die if you stay in it for very long." His final babblings had likely been those of a man in the latter stages of hypothermia. Had he stumbled by the riverside and fallen in? The firemen discovered a note he had left for his brother, along with his car keys. He appeared to be a suicide. Blake and Dee watched the TV news that night and scoured the city's two daily papers for the next few days, in vain. No mention was made of the jogger who had slid, as smoothly as a fish, into the Bow. Blake never found out who he was. But he was going to write him a strange and moving memorial.

*The Land, The Animals,* which premiered in February 1991, is spoken of with such fondness by those who worked on it and those who saw it that it's surprising One Yellow Rabbit has never chosen to revive it. All Blake Brooker will say is: "I have a tender feeling for it. I kind of don't want to mess with it again." It began with the vaguest of premises. "I was thinking about the environment a lot back then," says Brooker, "and I thought: What's *our* environment? Not that of the rainforest, or the despoiled this and that, but what is the environment right here where we live?" He conceived a project in which he'd walk along the boundaries of Calgary and observe all the animals he saw living within the city limits. In the end, however, "it got too late and I didn't have the time or the discipline to pull it off." The Rabbits' habit of writing plays *after* they'd announced them in their season has often meant some artful fudging in the brochures and press releases. *The Land, The Animals* was one of those works that took a long time finding its focus, and Brooker turned his vacillations into a joke that opened the show. Under the title "What This Play Is Supposed to Be," three characters trace the evolving drafts of a play synopsis that reveal the playwright's slippery grasp on its content:

CAMPBELL: Apparently this play was meant to have been several
  things over the period of its development.
  When it began it was described as part fable,
  part agricultural chemical sales manual.
  A scream from the marsh's clogged throat,
  an elegant comedy from Canada's vanishing wetlands.
  As it turns out, it's not.

TED: Then it had a different description.
  A penetrating meditation on marsh ecology
  and not a high school textbook come to life.
  A farmer sports plastic genitalia.
  A Lesser Spotted Bittern imitates a swaying reed.
  This hunting/business trip into the wetlands
  assumes tragic dimensions when an agricultural sales agent takes
  a wrong turn.
  Part fable, part science lesson,
  it is a scream from a marsh's clogged throat …

And so on. Seven drafts later:

CAMPBELL: Finally it was:
  "If nature is so swell, why are animals always trying to relocate
  under the porch or up between the rafters in the garage?
  And what do scientists wear under those lab coats anyways?
  An eco-examination from the point of view of all animals who
  live in the city. Comedy that's certified dark green."

DORIS [*in a confiding tone*]: In the end, however, it was a difficult if not
  impossible task to describe what we would do.
  So many things were happening so fast.[1]

In other words, an opening night was fast approaching.

However, Brooker did find a hook on which to hang his ecological concerns: the death of the mysterious jogger in the Bow River. Campbell, Ted, and Doris — played by Michael Green, Andy Curtis, and Denise Clarke — are scientists in those aforementioned lab coats who have gathered to investigate the case and try to determine his motive for suicide. The jogger, they have ascertained, was one Cy Evans, "a normal coffee-drinking geologist" with a yen for the outdoors, a lonely guy who spent his days chained to a desk in an airless building, thinking about "techniques to extract poisonous liquids from deep inside the Earth's crust." The trio put Cy under the microscope, scrutinizing his habits, his diet, the contents of his closet and medicine cabinet, even his favourite comic strip *(Mark Trail)*. At the same time, his plight is compared and contrasted with that of other animals in the city, from a cougar that unwisely strays inside the boundary to an escaped pet ferret that discovers a "sweet blue drink" under a tool bench in a garage. Brooker shares the viewpoint of, among others, zoologist and author Desmond Morris, who has argued that the city is as unnatural a habitat for humans as a zoo is for beasts.

As usual, the Rabbits were attuned to the issues of the day and, as usual, they had taken an unexpected approach to them. The dawn of the 1990s was bringing a renewed concern for the environment. In 1989, the *Exxon Valdez* oil tanker had accidentally spilled its cargo into the Alaskan waters, with devastating effects on the area's marine life. Scientists warned that carbon dioxide emissions were hastening global warming and punching a hole in Earth's protective ozone layer. Rock stars and other celebrities rallied to save the Amazon rainforest. Recycling was all the rage. The troupe could have added its voice to the outcry with a piece of theatrical agitprop, but instead Brooker chose to ask a broader question: What are these insalubrious artificial environments we have built for ourselves, that willfully subdue and damage nature, and that may be killing us slowly as well? Calgary was a particularly good city in which to pose it. On the one hand, its economy was based on the extraction and sale of fossil fuels, making it a source of the world's pollution. On the other, it was still a new city, surrounded by great natural beauty and an abundance of wildlife, with lakes you could swim in and blue sky that had yet to turn death-pale from industrial fumes. Calgary had a high proportion of oil executives, but it also had a high proportion of conservationists and nature-lovers — and sometimes they were one and the same.

Brooker underscored that irony in the play, as well as satirizing the arrogance and myopia of career scientists, in the person of his team of investigators — the imperious Campbell, macho Ted, and mousy Doris. Yet, as with *Tears of a Dinosaur,* the overriding tone is one of melancholy mixed with absurdity. Cy is as sad and doomed as that scared ferret that seeks sweet respite in a container of antifreeze. His slide into the river is suicide as relief, a slip back into the primordial soup. Brooker imagines the shallow thoughts of the lonely jogger's co-workers after his untimely death: "It was a shame … And he was in such good shape, too."

Some of Brooker's best poetic writing is here and it inspired everyone to enhance it. Clarke transformed the geologist's watery "release" into a poignant ballet. Richard McDowell composed an eerie and menacing score. For the decor, Brooker called upon a friend from Vancouver, painter Martin Guderna. A Czech Canadian, Guderna was the son of well-known Surrealist painter Ladislav Guderna and had become friends with Brooker during the latter's retreat to the West Coast in 1982. Brooker and Sandi Somers had designed a box set with two telescoping side walls to represent the scientists' laboratory and Guderna proceeded to cover it with squiggly animal-like shapes that, up close, resembled ancient glyphs on a cave wall and, from a distance, evoked the magnified contents of a microscope slide. The sinuous white figures, painted on a bluish surface, were at once cartoonlike and mysterious. In an interview with the *Calgary Herald*'s visual arts critic, Nancy Tousley, Guderna said he extracted the images from his subconscious, in true Surrealist style. "When we started, I didn't know how the set would turn out," he told her (7 February 1991). "I listened to a reading of the play and slept on it. I wanted to dream about it." He painted the shapes directly onto the set over four days, making random marks on all three walls from which the figures gradually emerged and then interlocked. To indicate the play's Calgary setting, he also painted a range of snow-capped mountains at the foot of the upstage wall. The show's visual element was further enriched with sequences of slides, taken from photos Brooker had shot while rambling about the city.

That February, the Rabbits had come close to achieving all that they had aimed for exactly nine years before at their first meeting. *The Land, The Animals* was the total theatre Gyl Raby had imagined, with poetry as theatre, dance as theatre, visual art as theatre, electronic music as theatre. The only thing missing was that silly old thing, dramatic conflict (unless you count Cy's inner conflict, which is hypothesized more than dramatized). It was also the theatre of minimal means but high production values that Nigel Scott and Michael Green had aspired to. You could take exception to the "hazy, barely realized drama" at its core — as I did, still judging by traditional values, in my *Calgary Herald* review (2 February 1991) — but you couldn't deny the excellence of the execution, from Sandi Somers's aquatic lighting to the crack perform- ances of the ensemble. Green's pal John Dunn felt the Rabbits came into their own with that show. "Before, they'd always been raw and rough and ready. This was sophisticated, magical." Anne Flynn saw it a num- ber of times and fell in love with the text. "Blake's writing can be too dense on a one-time hearing, but it's work you can go back to again and again and think: Oh, these words are so beautiful! It's a reminder that Blake is a poet at heart." Novelist Paul Anderson feels the play wasn't fully appreciated at the time. "It was a beautiful myth about this city, which I don't think people recognized. In Calgary, unlike the big centres, if you're an artist you can't hive yourself off from the rest of the community, hang out in cafés, and do things just for your fellow artists. The Rabbits have always been responsive to their community, they're adamant about their responsibility to this city."

The play was also a personal coup for Denise Clarke. Beginning with *The Pageant of the Comet*, she had been bucking to act as well as dance. Since then, One Yellow Rabbit had given her numerous roles, but they were always extensions of her own persona — tall, sexy, flamboyant creatures. Finally, she was able to do a real chameleon turn and even fool the one person it is hardest to fool. "I loved *The Land, The Animals*. I just loved it," she says. "And I know why, too. Because I changed my appearance and when I came out the first night, in the little Secret Theatre, and began speaking, I had very low status as a character; I was really, really shy and I had a quiet little British accent. And it wasn't until halfway through my first speech that my mother recognized me and went 'Oh! It's Denise!' I just got such a kick out of it. I couldn't believe, first of all, that my mother was talking in the audience, and then that she didn't know it was me. That's a transformation, when you start to understand 'Ah, wow! I can fool people.'"

*The Land, The Animals* was cited by the *Globe and Mail*'s chief drama critic, Ray Conlogue, as one of the highlights of Canada's 1991 theatre season. However, it never went on tour, nor was it remounted in Calgary. It remains, like so much theatre, a cherished memory for a small audience. The next year, One Yellow Rabbit chose to revive another play and take it on the road. Its destiny would be very different. It would be banned by a judge, land its playwright in court, prompt an RCMP investigation, thrill international audiences from Scotland to Australia — and wind up on TV.

---

1    Blake Brooker, *Ilsa, Queen of the Nazi Love Camp and Other Plays* (Red Deer, AB: Red Deer College Press, 1993), 74–75.

# 5. Ilsa

"What you call truth I call lies."

— ILSA, QUEEN OF THE NAZI LOVE CAMP

**T**all and broad-shouldered, with a luxuriant sweep of silver hair and a penchant for big cowboy belt buckles, Jim Keegstra looked like the classic small-town man of the people, as upright as Jimmy Stewart, as wholesome as Andy of Mayberry. And in his mind's eye, the auto mechanic, high school teacher, and mayor of Eckville, Alberta, probably saw himself as the Jimmy Stewart hero in a Frank Capra–style scenario — the decent, God-fearing, modest-living citizen who stumbles upon a widespread conspiracy and has to battle the authorities in a fight to reveal the truth. On 9 April 1985, Mr. Keegstra was going to Red Deer, to the Court of Queen's Bench, to bravely face the wrath of a government that wanted to gag him and discredit his views. The national media had turned out in force — had even reserved their seats in the courthouse — to watch the fateful show-down between the mighty Province of Alberta and the lone teacher from Eckville.

Only, what if the hero is really a crackpot? What if his "conspiracy" is a load of horse manure, a heap of foul, anti-Semitic rubbish, culled from the most dubious sources, which he had foisted upon his innocent social studies students for a decade? Jim Keegstra was being tried under Section 281.2 of the Criminal Code of Canada for wilfully promoting hatred against an identifiable group. In his classes at Eckville's junior and senior high school, Keegstra — a teacher looked up to by his pupils and admired by his peers — taught that the Holocaust was a sham, part of a gigantic Zionist Jewish plot that had also engineered the French and Russian revolutions, brought about the American Civil War, and was probably behind fluoridation, too. Among his more amusing claims: that John Wilkes Booth, President Lincoln's assassin, was a Jew, and that Canadian Prime Minister Pierre Trudeau wore the trademark red rose in his lapel to show he was a communist. Among his more egregious ones: that the Nazis and the Jews were actually in cahoots and the horrifying photographs and film footage from the death camps were fake. Far from being a shiny-eyed Capra hero, this Mr. Smith was a paranoid menace.

Keegstra, fifty-one at the time of his trial, had been teaching in Eckville, a town with a population of less than a thousand, since 1968. A fundamentalist Christian who regarded the standard social studies text-books as the skewed work of socialists and humanists, he had built up his own conception of world history and taught it with utter conviction. As studious as he was wrongheaded, he had absorbed a vast amount of hate literature, published under the guise of historical theory, and it came to form the syllabus of his grade nine and grade twelve social studies classes, to the exclusion of any other point of view. Students were actively discouraged from reading sources other than those he provided in class. The kids who faithfully regurgitated his rot in their essays got high marks; more inquiring minds were rewarded with low grades.

It took far too long before Keegstra's tainted teaching was exposed — thanks to some outraged parents who'd finally had enough — and by then simply firing him from his post wasn't deemed adequate pun-ishment. The Alberta government felt increasing pressure to prove it didn't tolerate racism in its schools and, finally, in the wake of an RCMP investigation, Attorney General Neil Crawford laid charges. The jury trial lasted a numbing seventy days and in the end Keegstra was found guilty and fined $5,000.

Down in Calgary, 150 kilometres away, members of the little One Yellow Rabbit theatre troupe had been watching the Keegstra case unfold with disbelief and disgust. While Keegstra harboured a host of delusions, the media coverage had mostly emphasized his refusal to believe that Jews had been systematically rounded up and exterminated in the Nazi death camps. "We couldn't believe it," recalls Blake Brooker. "I've been to a number of Holocaust memorials. If these things didn't happen, then how come so many families disappeared, how come so many living people saw it happen? The whole concept of being a Holocaust denier is repellent, and the idea of a Holocaust denier teaching it in high school is even worse." Not only that, as Alice B. Toklas's father said of the San Francisco earthquake, this would give westerners a black eye in the East. "Here we are, living in Alberta, and again being tarred and feathered with the image that the rest of the country has of us, that we're a bunch of religious racists and anti-Semite rednecks. It's not true."

Up until then, the three-year-old troupe had dabbled a bit in topical satire, mostly through its *Café Theatre* cabarets, but the circumstances of the Keegstra case cried out for commentary. It began, casually enough, with one of poet Kirk Miles's famous kitchen-party riffs. "It was a regular house party at Blake's," remembers Miles. "We were laughing in the kitchen having heard about this Keegstra guy, we just thought it was so ridiculous that someone could say [the Holocaust] didn't happen. Then we thought: What if some of these icons from commercial porn showed up and told him that he'd got his facts wrong? I get into these kitchen riffs sometimes, when I've had a couple of beers; I just start making people laugh, I get on a roll, almost like I'm doing stand-up. I call it raving. So I was raving, just making everybody laugh."

Brooker claims the party was at Miles's apartment, but the riff is still stuck in his memory. "Kirk was singing this little snippet:

*I'm Ilsa,*
*Queen of the Nazi love camp,*
*Jim Keegstra says that I don't exist.*
*If this ain't flesh, baby,*
*What is?"*

Miles was doubtless thinking of a 1974 soft-porn flick entitled *Ilsa, She Wolf of the SS*, which starred an actress named Dyanne Thorne as the torture-loving commandant of a Nazi medical camp. The low-budget movie was the first in a series of Ilsa adventures, including 1979's *Ilsa, The Tigress of Siberia*, which had the nasty anti-heroine escaping to Canada. (Perhaps coincidentally, One Yellow Rabbit would end up subtitling its Mata Hari musical *Tigress at the City Gates*.) Whatever the source, Miles sang the lyric over and over, says Brooker, until it dawned on them that they might have the seeds of a musical satire. At first, they decided to approach it as a cabaret, with a string of songs and skits based loosely on the Keegstra theme. Miles went off and wrote a couple of scenes. Jim Millan, Brooker's friend and the founder of Crow's Theatre in Toronto, was also tapped for a contribution, as was up-and-coming Calgary playwright Clem Martini. "When the scenes came in, the scene Jim wrote was too pornographic, too hardcore," says Brooker. "It was all about kinky S&M. Clem's scene was a seance scene and it was really good. We used it almost word for word. I had gone off with David Rhymer and written a bunch of songs. We wrote the songs first, so that the order of the story was determined by them, and then filled in between the songs with the scenes."

Miles says that he did the bulk of the background research for the play. By then, he'd left his job as the Rabbits' de facto general manager and gone over to help run the new children's festival. "I really didn't have a lot of time when Blake was writing *Ilsa*," he says, "so I did all the research and handed it to him, along with my two scenes, and he took it over." (Miles and Clem Martini would be duly cited for their contributions when the work was produced and published.)

The cabaret idea soon gave way to a full-blown play, involving Keegstra, a pair of nostalgic ex-Nazis, and what Brooker calls a "cheesy, *Boys from Brazil* plotline" about genetic manipulation. It opens with the Colonel, former head of one of Adolf Hitler's concentration camps, in hiding in Uruguay and pining for his fallen Reich and his lost "queen" — Ilsa, the officers' favourite prostitute. Ilsa, meanwhile, is stuck in Hamburg, still turning tricks and wondering where the Colonel escaped to with the camp's ill-gotten riches. And in Eckville, a disgraced and depressed James Keegstra repairs cars while reflecting on how his own dreams of power went awry. "There was a real elementary playwriting technique at work," says Brooker with mild disparagement. "Each character had something they needed: James needed a job, the Colonel needed to find Ilsa, and Ilsa needed to find the Colonel."

Now comes the *Boys from Brazil* twist. At the camp, Ilsa and the Colonel had been involved in a top-secret project to save phials of Der Führer's sperm, so that he could pass on his genetic makeup should anything happen to him. However, six of the eight test tubes were broken by accident. The Colonel and Ilsa each believe that the other one would have stuck by the remaining test tubes out of loyalty to the Reich. Therefore, if they can track down those two specimens, they may also find each other. Both trace the first test tube to Mobile, Alabama, where Ilsa has a run-in with a pair of half-witted Ku Klux Klansmen while the Colonel learns that its seminal contents ended up with one Mrs. Lefkowitz, who unwittingly used it for axle grease. As for the second specimen, it apparently disappeared into the wilds of backwoods Alberta.

While this broad satire unreels, complete with flashbacks to the glory days at the camp, mock torch ballads *à la* Marlene Dietrich, and a beerhall-style singalong called "Blame It on Berlin," more subtle stuff is unfolding in the Eckville garage. Brooker's real achievement was to dig into the psyche of Keegstra and explain — convincingly and, one suspects, not inaccurately — how he came by his paranoia. Keegstra's hatred of Jews was, after all, largely abstract; there were few Jewish people in rural Alberta, let alone tiny Eckville, and Keegstra had spent most of his life in such small towns. His anti-Semitism had its roots in the religious and political milieux he grew up in. As a teenager, he heard his mother complain that the newly founded state of Israel was "anti-Scripture." As a hardline member of the Social Credit party — which governed Alberta from 1935 until 1971 — he imbibed the theories of Social Credit founder Clifford H. Douglas, a British civil engineer-turned-economist whose fans included the pro-Fascist poet Ezra Pound and whose views were so virulently racist that he wrote letters to Hitler telling him to keep up the good work. Brooker's monologues for Keegstra include succinct summaries of Douglas's worldview, which held that banks and lending institutions keep the consumer mired in debt. (Douglas's solution, social credit, involved government subsidy for either business or the consumer to close the gap between prices and wages.)

Brooker's regular-guy Keegstra, dirtying his hands under a car hood, begins by winning us over with a folksy analogy, comparing society to an internal combustion engine in which every part has a purpose. Only, these days he's not sure what his own part is. "I thought I was part of the motor," he says, "but now some people call me a crankshaft." But as the play progresses, his personality grows darker. The garage becomes a classroom and Keegstra is back in his teaching days, now lecturing us on the evils of credit, now getting angry with students who refuse to accept his version of history. At last, out comes the conspiracy theory, revealed in a coy song by Keegstra who, in his fervour, has unwittingly placed a dunce cap on his own head.

> *The means of production manufacturing quotas*
> *are controlled by the very few*
> *You can bet that rhymes with something and it sure as hell ain't you*
> *Banks and lending institutions, the media's in it too …*
>
> *Bet your life it rhymes with something and it rhymes with J-J-J*
>
> *Jot down these notes*
> *Just copy what you see …*
>
> *If you don't read or tell your mom*
> *You might just get a "B"* [1]

Back to Ilsa and the Colonel, who romantically reunite in the Calgary airport and begin the last leg of their journey, the drive to Eckville. In the play's climax, inspired by Kirk Miles's kitchen-party ditty, they finally encounter Keegstra in his garage, where they are shocked and appalled to hear his crackpot denial of the Holocaust. "Wait a minute," says the Colonel indignantly. "I was there." Ilsa, meanwhile, is beside herself with rage. "Who do you think you are? Those were the best damn days of our lives!" As added proof, the pair holds a seance to summon up the ghost of Adolf Hitler, now roasting in hell, who inhabits the body of the Colonel to join Ilsa in a chorus of "Those Were the Days." Then, with a song and dance, the two old Nazis shuffle off to Florida — but not before Ilsa thoughtfully writes her phone number on the inside of Jim's wrist. Alone and lonely again, Keegstra is left to make one last half-hearted stab at self-justification. "I don't think I'm crazy," he sings. "I just don't believe everything I hear."

Now comes the final, gut-wrenching twist. As Keegstra ends his lament, two grim, grey-clad prisoners slowly enter what was the garage. Gazing toward the audience imploringly, they begin to sing a dirge:

> *Can't the sun go down on Auschwitz*
> *End of day we beg for it*
> *The sun goes down inside of us*
> *Alone why don't you leave us alone* [2]

David Rhymer's music was crucial to the play. It was during his first visit to the One Yellow Rabbit offices, and his first meeting with Blake Brooker, that the aspiring tunesmith learned about the project. "Blake drove me home and we ended up talking for six hours," he remembers. "He mentioned he was doing this show." *Ilsa* needed songs and Rhymer had all sorts of melodies and lyrics to work with. Even better, a lot of them had a European cabaret flavour, having grown out of his Mata Hari song cycle several years before. Brooker listened to the bits and pieces and, along with Rhymer, began to expand and shape them to fit the play's scenario. One of those fragments became "What's a Good Man in Changing Times?," the dejected Keegstra's *cri de coeur* — his "Behind Blue Eyes," if you will. "Take a good look into my eyes," he sings. "What you call truth I call lies / Do you recognize what you despise?" "We were hellbent on not shooting trout in a barrel," says Rhymer of that song. "We wanted to look seriously at this guy and what makes a good man or a bad man."

*Ilsa* helped launch Rhymer on a new career as a theatrical song-writer and composer and marked the first of numerous collaborations with Brooker and the Rabbits. However, he says the big learning curve came, not in writing the musical, but in playing it live. A self-taught musician, he could plunk out a tune but didn't really know his way around the keyboard. "I learned to play piano on *Ilsa*," he recalls, shaking his shaggy grey head at the memory. "The first run of *Ilsa*, my goal was just to complete the show every night without making any mistakes! It was like running a gauntlet."

The original Ilsa was a man. Puppeteer Ronnie Burkett stepped into the prostitute's pumps for the play's initial production. He was over at Brooker and Denise Clarke's house one afternoon when Brooker was discussing the project and he jokingly proposed himself for the title role. "I said to him 'If you had any balls, you'd let me play her, 'cause you'll never find a woman who can pull it off.' Shortly after that," he adds with a laugh, "I was in rehearsal." Although Burkett had never acted professionally without some marionettes dangling from his fingers, he had been a musical-theatre major at university. He also had some definite ideas about drag roles and this one in particular. Gyl Raby had taken on the direction of the show (which would prove to be her last before leaving OYR) and at the outset she and Burkett clashed over what Ilsa should look like. Raby saw her as a curly-haired blond, Burkett recalls, while he imagined her as a tough little China doll — more Louise Brooks in *Pandora's Box* than Dietrich in *The Blue Angel*. To win her over, Burkett invited Raby to drop by his studio one Sunday morning at nine o'clock. "I got up at six o'clock, shaved, and did the whole drag-makeup thing, got a black China-doll wig, put on this little corset and fishnets. Gyl knocked on my door at nine and I greeted her as Ilsa. She just laughed and said 'Okay, you win.'"

However, the most propitious casting choice was the young actor picked to play Keegstra. Andy Curtis, then twenty-four, had been crossing paths with the Rabbits since their *Café Theatre* days. An alumnus of Loose Moose's *Late Nite Comedy* revue, he'd formed his own troupe, That Comedy Thing, which also played gigs at Beggar's Banquet. Schooled only in improv, he was impressed with the Rabbits' well-rehearsed timing and multiple skills. "I had bugged them for a year or two about letting me work with them," he recalls. The opportunity finally came one evening at a One Yellow Rabbit function in the upstairs bar of

Sorrenti's, a restaurant in the Centre for Performing Arts. "Blake came up to me, pulled my hair back, scrutinized my face. 'D'you know who Jim Keegstra is?' he said. 'Yeah.' 'You want to play him?' 'Okay.' And that was pretty much that."

The tall, wiry Curtis, with his boyish thatch of red hair and welcoming smile, was physically perfect for the role, and he also radiated a modest, aw-shucks affability that people immediately warmed to. His acting at that time had been limited to improvised comedy skits and some children's theatre, but experience wasn't a prerequisite at One Yellow Rabbit. The role called on him to sing and deliver monologues, but most importantly, to build a rapport with the audience. His Jim Keegstra came across as goofy but winning, a likeable square, not unlike many a popular teacher — until you caught on to what he was teaching. Curtis gives credit for his interpretation to Brooker. "Blake taught me to cultivate the opposite. I always look for the humanity in characters," he says. "I certainly got a lot of comments about it. 'Boy, he seemed like such a nice guy.' Yeah. You know, Hitler had a dog, man, he kissed babies, he wasn't such a bad guy — in some ways. It seems like kind of a basic premise, that evil is not always the guy in the black hat, but I guess some people haven't figured that out. That, in fact, is how people get sucked in. It's the reasonableness of someone like Keegstra."

With Rabbit newcomer Paul Punyi cast as the Colonel — Michael Green was touring the antipodes with Small Change Theatre — the play went into rehearsals. Meanwhile, there were rumblings of concern from the company's board of directors. The idea that, in lampooning a private citizen, the theatre was risking a lawsuit, led many of them to resign. When they did, says Gyl Raby, the chill was passed on to the actors. "There was a fear generated by the board members walking that, if we were sued, the actors' assets would be liable." One of the actors had drafted a letter saying the opinions in the play weren't necessarily his, and he was just doing a job. "I thought that was a good idea," recalls Raby. "I wouldn't want anyone to get their hands on my truck (which was all I had), so I drafted a similar letter." The following day, on her way to rehearsal, she was confronted by Blake Brooker. "He was in a white fury, saying 'What kind of a company are we, if everyone is saying they don't believe in the show? Why are we doing it then?'" Raby felt so ashamed, she yanked out the letter and tore it up on the spot. To cover its ass, however, the company had the play screened for any possible legal troubles. A specialist in the newly minted Canadian Charter of Rights and Freedoms was among the experts who agreed to watch a run-through. Burkett remembers it as "very surreal. I have a vivid memory of an early rehearsal, running around in a T-shirt, sweatpants, and high-heeled shoes, singing and dancing in front of a bunch of lawyers."

The satire was deemed safe and *Ilsa, Queen of the Nazi Love Camp* made its debut on 28 May 1987 in the Rabbits' new sixty-seat Secret Theatre at the Calgary Centre for Performing Arts. "It went very well and nobody sued us," says Raby. Its porn-parody title caused more problems than anything else. It attracted a few kooks to the theatre, including a pair who came dressed in SS uniforms. And the posters advertising the show kept getting torn down. "We had to keep putting them back up," says Raby. "We found out it was the administration of the Centre for Performing Arts that was ripping them down! We had to go challenge them, remind them that we were one of their tenant companies. There was a lot of tension in the air," she remembers, "but nothing happened." Although Keegstra had been convicted two years previously, his case was still fresh in Albertans' minds and many remained outraged. In fact, *Calgary Herald* critic Kate Zimmerman complained that *Ilsa* wasn't tough enough on its target. In her review (30 May 1987), she said the show "pussyfoots around its subject" and brought up a valid point: "[I]f the play is to err on the side of timidity, why call the Eckville mechanic character James Keegstra? If he were called John Geegstra, perhaps the script could be braver." Nonetheless, it was well-received by audiences, first in Calgary and then later that August at the Edmonton Fringe, where it was, in the words of onlooker Denise Clarke, "an underground smash-ola hit." After Edmonton, the Rabbits put *Ilsa* to bed and moved on to other projects.

But James Keegstra's legal saga was far from over. In 1988, the Alberta Court of Appeal overturned his conviction, declaring that the anti-hate law on which it was based was unconstitutional. In 1990, the Supreme Court of Canada ruled to the contrary and sent the case back to the appellate court. A year later, the provincial court would again overturn the conviction, this time on grounds that Keegstra's lawyer, Doug Christie, had not been allowed to challenge jurors at the trial. A retrial was ordered, and when it finally commenced in Red Deer on 2 March 1992, it would prove to be the worst thing that ever happened to One Yellow Rabbit. And the best.

### Ilsa, Bane of the Red Deer Courthouse (or: The Play-Maker Meets the Hate-Monger)

With the Keegstra case continually in the news, the play remained topical and the Rabbits finally decided to revive it, with some cast changes, in the summer of 1990. Michael Green, a master at sinister sliminess, took the role of the Colonel, which fit like an officer's kid glove. Denise Clarke slipped into Ilsa's black-lace lingerie and transformed the character from a drag spoof to a more potent parody of an Aryan sex fantasy — part Valkyrie maiden, part Sacher-Masoch Venus. Musically, Rhymer and Brooker altered the song arrangements, making them less campy, and Rhymer's live keyboard was now accompanied, with heart-tugging beauty, by the violin of Calgary jazz musician Karl Roth. By then, Gyl Raby had left to run Edmonton's Northern Light Theatre, so Brooker assumed the task of director while Clarke doubled as choreographer.

Ironically, Clarke, who would become the definitive Ilsa, had never imagined playing the Teutonic tart the first time out. On the contrary, she pushed for Burkett to do it. "I talked [Blake] into giving it to Ronnie. Ronnie said to me 'Oh, Dee, I'd kill for that part,' and I thought that was inspired. I did not in any way think I was an actress yet — at least to take that part on, at my age. After Ronnie did it, when Blake really wanted to do his own production after Gyl left the company, I finally had the chops to be able to sing and act the part."

The new *Ilsa* had a three-week run in Calgary at the Secret Theatre, which was both a critical and popular success. The Rabbits' general manager, Grant Burns, felt they had a hot property on their hands. "Every time we did it, it did really well," he says. "There seemed to be some name recognition. It had that crazy title, which was a fringe-theatre title for sure, the kind with a sex and comedy angle to it." Besides, the issues it raised had only increased in relevance since the first production. It turned out Keegstra was by no means a lone nutter. In 1988, Ernst Zundel, a Toronto-based neo-Nazi and publisher of racist literature, had been convicted for spreading false news (the charge didn't stick and the Supreme Court acquitted him in 1992). In 1990, Canadian members of the Idaho-based Church of Jesus Christ Christian: Aryan Nations had organized a Ku Klux Klan–style cross-burning in Provost, Alberta. The Aryan Nations' Canadian leader was another small-town Albertan, Terry Long of Caroline, a tiny burg just south of Eckville. And then there was Keegstra clone Malcolm Ross, a math teacher in rural New Brunswick and author of Jewish-conspiracy propaganda, who was banned from the classroom in 1991. Clearly, *Ilsa* deserved more widespread exposure.

Plans were made for another remount, this time for a national tour in early 1992. The play was originally to visit four cities, but Grant Burns couldn't get firm commitments from three of the presenters in time to meet his deadlines and in the end proposed dates in Sudbury, Vancouver, and Victoria had to be scrapped. Only Gyl Raby's Northern Light Theatre was left. So the Rabbits settled on a more modest tour: a two-week gig in Edmonton as part of the Northern Light season, after which the troupe would return to Calgary for a short engagement at the Pumphouse Theatres. The Northern Light run would open 25 February and continue to 8 March. Meanwhile, James Keegstra's new trial was scheduled to begin 2 March. Burns knows it's hard to believe that the company wasn't aware its tour would coincide with the trial, "but we were so busy it never occurred to us to check."

On 2 March, a Monday, Court of Queen's Bench Justice Arthur Lutz opened the trial in Red Deer by ordering a province-wide publication ban. The evidence heard at the previous Keegstra trial — and, as well, at the trials of fellow hate-mongers Ernst Zundel and Malcolm

Ross — and "any other matters that are of similar form," were not to be commented upon while the case was before the court. Mr. Justice Lutz extended the order, not just to the press, but to "any movies, newscasts, plays or documentaries and the like." The ban was Draconian, but Lutz had his reasons. Keegstra's first trial had been rendered invalid on a technicality and he didn't want to run that risk a second time by allowing anything that might prejudice the jury.

When the word came down, One Yellow Rabbit convened an emergency board meeting to discuss whether the Edmonton run should go ahead. A cancellation meant that the Rabbits and Northern Light each stood to lose as much as $10,000 — a big sum for small theatre companies. However, the lawyers on the board said it was the Rabbits' responsibility to seek clarification. So the 4 March performance was cancelled as a precaution and the following day lawyers-cum-board members Bill Christensen and Marian Bryant appeared before Mr. Justice Lutz in Red Deer to ask if *Ilsa* had, indeed, been banned. The judge was a bit bewildered. He had never heard of the play, or One Yellow Rabbit. Keegstra, on the other hand, knew all about them — or thought he did. His minions had gone to see the show and he now confidently told the judge that it was "perverse, mischievous," and even "pornographic." The ex-teacher, who for this trial had chosen to act as his own defence, did a slick turnaround, accusing One Yellow Rabbit of his own crime. The play, he said, promoted hatred against an individual (presumably himself) and against an identifiable group, "which I would call the German people." He characterized the show as a "villainous attack" and asked that it be included in the gag order. Mr. Justice Lutz decided that a hearing should be held to deal with the issue and, in the meantime, ordered that *Ilsa* be shut down.

Gyl Raby remembers well the night the Keegstra goon squad turned up to view the play. Northern Light's artistic director had arrived at the little Kaasa Theatre in Edmonton's Jubilee Auditorium to give her pre-show speech "and there were some weird-looking audience members grilling the woman in the box office, our publicist. I stepped in and fielded the questions, which were quite aggressive. 'What made us feel we had the right to present this show on James Keegstra?' After the show, those same people — there were about twelve of them — went around collecting the programs. As they were leaving I said 'I'm glad to see you need so many mementoes.' Their main spokesman turned on me and said 'These are going to be mailed to every arts funding organization in the country, so they can know what poisonous garbage you are putting on the stage. You're never going to get another penny by the time we've finished with you. You'll be out of town.'" Raby asked why he was so vengeful. "He launched into me, telling me how Keegstra was a spokesman for the free-thinking world and he was being persecuted by a conspiracy of liberal, left-wing communists." The conversation became a heated exchange. Raby recalls that four or five of them had her cornered in the lobby. A security guard came by, saw what was happening, and ran to fetch Ken Graham, manager of the Jubilee Auditorium. "The argument had gotten pretty loud," says Raby. "I was saying to them 'You do your show, and I'll come and see it.' And they were replying that theatre was sick and they wouldn't want to do a show to state their beliefs. I said 'Maybe your beliefs won't stand up under scrutiny.' It had an ugly feel, the scene. I was quite frightened." Graham finally arrived and broke things up.

Raby was still rattled when, a few days later, news came of the gag order. She mistakenly fancied that Keegstra's henchmen were making good their threats. The show's cancellation was greeted with outrage by the Rabbits, especially Denise Clarke. "Denise wanted to perform it anyway," recalls Raby, "but I said 'You can't. I'm not prepared to do that to my board or to Ken Graham.' She and I had a bit of a fracas about that, but I knew where she was coming from." Instead, Northern Light replaced the show with a forum on censorship, which was well-attended.

Friday, 13 March had been appointed as the day for the hearing, when Mr. Justice Lutz would decide if the show could go ahead. The Northern Light run had been scuttled, but the Rabbits were still hoping to play the Calgary dates. This time, Blake Brooker and Grant Burns would join Christensen and Bryant in the courtroom.

It was a beautiful morning in early spring and, as they made the ninety-minute drive to Red Deer, Brooker felt confident they had a strong argument to make to the judge. How could a little play staged in a small theatre in Edmonton or Calgary influence this jury? "Our contention was that, at the best of times, it's hard to get anyone in to see theatre," he says, "let alone to get someone into your theatre who is going to travel back to Red Deer and infect the jurors. I can understand a television ban, perhaps, or radio or any mass media. But our contention was that theatre is a specific place where only certain people will come and pay money to be entertained. And the jurors are given instructions to not watch television or read newspapers and magazines or look at anything that has to do with the case while they're involved in it. I think the judge was lazy and just decided on a general publication ban without taking into consideration our lawful and legitimate cultural/business activity."

However, the session began with a surprise for the Rabbit party. Keegstra had a witness — one of his cronies who had seen the play. Christensen expressed his dismay that someone without any expertise in theatre should be called upon to give a synopsis. He countered with the suggestion that a video of the play be screened in court. Mr. Justice Lutz — ever mindful that he had put a jury trial on hold to deal with this issue — said he had no problem with Keegstra's witness and instead of a video, gave Christensen the option of producing a witness of his own. That's when the lawyer spoke the fateful words: "I have the playwright here. Perhaps the most prudent course would be to just have him tell us what it's about." Burns says Christensen hadn't considered that, if he called Brooker to the stand to explain the Rabbits' point of view, it would then put the playwright in a position where he could be cross-examined by Keegstra. "It was a mistake, and we never saw it coming."

Keegstra's witness — no doubt one of the stooges who had crossed swords with Raby in the Kaasa lobby — described the plot of the play with a childlike simplicity that suggested some of it had gone over his head. He was, however, convinced that the show put Keegstra down — quite literally, in fact. He seemed particularly upset that, in the play's climax, the character of Jim is thrown to the ground before a map of Europe pinpointing the Nazi death camps. (By the way, he had also learned how tough it is to be a drama critic. He complained to the Crown prosecutor that his memory was vague because, in a darkened theatre, it's very hard to take notes.) Christensen didn't bother to cross-examine him.

Then Brooker took the stand. Christensen had him give a more detailed description of the play as well as discuss its history and reception. Brooker made the point that his Keegstra was a fictional character in a satirical fantasy, that he hadn't intended to write a biography or an in-depth analysis of the man. Keegstra couldn't get his head around that. When he stepped up to cross-examine Brooker, he challenged his claim that the Keegstra of the play was an imaginary figure.

KEEGSTRA: I would suggest that I'm standing right in front of you. I don't know whether I'm imaginary or not, am I?
BROOKER: You, yourself, are not imaginary, no. ... The character is imaginary.
KEEGSTRA: But has my name. Well, that's striking.[3]

"He couldn't make the distinction that there was a character in the play based on him," recalls Brooker, "based on information that had been in newspapers and on radio and television in the years before, when the play was being put together. The character was a representative. I tried to explain that *Ilsa, Queen of the Nazi Love Camp* is a satire, a work of fiction, the circumstances are outrageous, it's an entertainment, characters burst into song. It's based on a tradition in societies as old as ancient Rome and Greece." Brooker's undoing, however, was his almost insane caution in answering Keegstra's questions. As if fearing a trap, he insisted on a literal interpretation of every question, and both Keegstra and the judge started to get annoyed. Keegstra tried to get Brooker to say that he knew Keegstra had worked as a garage mechanic and that's why the character was fixing a car in the play:

KEEGSTRA: You're not going to say surely that that's coincidental that I happened to be [a mechanic]?

BROOKER: I don't know what you are. I know how my character came to be a garage mechanic. I don't know how you became [*sic*] to be one.

KEEGSTRA: I think — I'm not so sure that I understand what you're saying. I thought my questions were quite straightforward. [4]

Keegstra had a hard time getting what he wanted. He finally let it go when Brooker agreed his memory of the Keegstra affair "no doubt" had an effect on his imagination. Then it was Crown prosecutor George Combe's turn to grill the witness. Combe questioned Brooker on the descriptions of the play contained in my 1990 review of *Ilsa* in the *Calgary Herald* and Anika Van Wyk's in the *Calgary Sun,* as well as in a feature in that day's *Globe and Mail.* Again, Brooker became extremely literal and split hairs with the attorney over whether the play "focused" on intolerance (as the *Herald* headline claimed) or "meditated" on intolerance. Now Combe was irritated. He did get Brooker to explain how the production could inadvertently coincide with the trial, but he couldn't get an admission that the real Keegstra was the subject of the play. Finally, Christensen briefly re-examined Brooker in an attempt at damage control:

CHRISTENSEN: Did you caricature the real Jim Keegstra in your play?

BROOKER: Yes.

CHRISTENSEN: When you refer to the character James Keegstra as an imaginary character, are you referring to the words that come from his mouth?

BROOKER: In the play, yes. [5]

It may be that, when confronted by Keegstra and Combe, Brooker's natural recusancy, his lifelong habit of doubting and defying authority figures, came to the fore. If the teenage Blake Brooker had been a student in one of Keegstra's twisted social studies classes, you can be certain he would have blown the whistle.

Tense though it was, like every Rabbit performance, the Brooker cross-examination had its moments of comedy. Such as Keegstra's attempt to play his "good Christian" card:

KEEGSTRA: I'm asking, when you use somebody at the expense of humour, is that comedy? Because that's what I suggest you're using me as.

BROOKER: I think it can be.

KEEGSTRA: So you're not — you wouldn't have the — you wouldn't have a belief such as: you should love your neighbour as yourself. Do you have that kind of belief?

BROOKER: I think I do.

KEEGSTRA: Would you make fun of your neighbour? I mean, would you like — just suggest I came up and put myself up as a playwright and then I wrote a play on you which was not at all complimentary. And would you really like that?

BROOKER: I don't know. I'd have to see the play. [6]

Then there were those funny slips of the tongue, which may have betrayed a little wishful thinking on the part of Keegstra and Combe:

KEEGSTRA: And you say [the play] only lasted nine minutes?

BROOKER: Ninety.

KEEGSTRA: I'm sorry. I misread you that there [*sic*].[7]

COMBE: [The *Calgary Herald*'s review] says, "If, in real life, Keegstra took a German concentration camp tour and came home convinced, in Brooker's fantasy —"

THE COURT: "Unconvinced."

COMBE: "… unconvinced, in Brooker's fantasy …" [8]

However, the judge wasn't laughing, as he made clear later.

Brooker had felt he was playing to a hostile crowd. He remembers the courtroom was packed with Keegstra supporters and neither the Crown nor the Court were pleased with his responses. "The questions being asked of me I answered to the best of my ability," he says. "God knows why I would upset the judge, other than the fact that our being there at all was upsetting to him. Our presence there was unwelcome, we were upsetting the flow of how he wanted things to go."

After an adjournment, the hearing resumed at 11:30 A.M. with final arguments from Keegstra, Christensen, and Combe. Keegstra not only said that the *Ilsa* production interfered with his right to a fair trial, he asked the judge to ban it permanently on moral grounds. Christensen argued that, as a play, *Ilsa* fell outside the legal definitions of a media ban. Combe gave the Crown's position that *Ilsa* could potentially sway public opinion and was too much of a risk to the trial.

Keegstra was relatively tame in court. His written motion to have *Ilsa* banned was much more colourful, starting with his mistitling of the play, which he referred to as *Ilsa, Queen of the Nazi Love Camp Haunts Jim Keegstra*. He argued that it isn't protected by the Charter of Rights and Freedoms because it goes against the Christian principles upon which he believes the charter was framed. More specifically, One Yellow Rabbit's play was a work of socialism and, as we all know, "this political-religious ideology is atheistical at best and a worshipper of Satan at worst." After dragging in quotes from exiled Russian novelist Alexander Solzhenitsyn to back up his claims about the socialist menace, Keegstra went on to contend that this show he hadn't actually seen had "incorporated lies, deception, hate, sex perversion, pornography, filthy language, ridicule, vice and every other kind of evil. This can do nothing but destroy the mind [*sic*] of those who watch." Because *Ilsa* "has no redeeming value for the general good and welfare of society but rather the typical socialist distructive [*sic*] motive, and because it was deliberately designed to defame and ridiclue [*sic*] to promote hatred against the accused and the German people, this production should be shut down permanently." [9]

*This* is the real Keegstra's voice, not that of the character in Brooker's play. Andy Curtis's mild-mannered Jim never resorts to this kind of overheated raving. Given how deserving he was of savage satire, Keegstra should really have been grateful to the playwright for making him look better than he was. "That's the funny thing," says Grant Burns. "Blake always felt like he gave Keegstra a pretty fair treatment. He didn't want to be accused of shooting fish in a barrel."

Following a lunch break, the hearing concluded at 2:00 P.M. with a ruling from Mr. Justice Lutz. He declared that, in his opinion, continued production of the play posed "a significant and substantial risk to the ongoing fairness of the trial of Mr. Keegstra." He extended the ban until the trial was over. But there was more. Lutz had also taken exception to Brooker's replies on the stand. "I frankly found it very distressing to listen to him," he said. "I thought he had one of the more evasive and selective memories of any witness that I've ever heard in my many years on the bench." He announced that a transcript of Brooker's testimony would be sent to the Attorney General for investigation and possible prosecution.

Brooker and Burns were sweating bullets by the time the hearing was over. As Burns remembers it: "We walked out of the courtroom, said 'No comment' to the reporters trying to interview us — as we were advised by our lawyers — get in the car and drive back to Calgary. And the lead story on the CBC five o'clock news, across Canada, is about *Ilsa, Queen of the Nazi Love Camp.* And again at six o'clock, and on *As It Happens* [CBC Radio's popular news magazine]. We're getting calls from people all over the country. It was the best thing that could ever have happened to publicize the company and the play. I mean, when was the last time a play was the lead story on a national news broadcast?"

As Burns the general manager saw it, the whole episode was "a beautiful blunder. People thought it was a publicity stunt, that we'd gone to court, got Blake on the stand, and let Keegstra cross-examine him. I was being credited with being a publicity genius, but we didn't realize what we were doing."

For Brooker, who'd unwittingly roused the wrath of a Court of Queen's Bench judge, it was scary.

"There was one part of me that felt like I was floating in space," he says, recalling his time on the stand. "There was one part of me answering these questions and another part of me was almost laughing at how unreal it was. Not only is Keegstra questioning me, but the judge is making space for him and helping him to question me. Even the Crown prosecutor seemed to be helping Keegstra at that point. It had a peculiar effect on me, as if something was settling on my shoulders, a great wariness, a frustration, and an understanding, finally, of what the naked weight of the state could do to you without putting you in jail." For a long time afterwards, Brooker didn't want to talk about his experience. "It seemed like you're complaining compared to, say, a Chinese dissident who's thrown into jail. This was mild in comparison. But I was so naive, I never thought this could happen in our society, where a public figure could not be discussed just because he's on trial."

Meanwhile, back in Edmonton, Gyl Raby and Northern Light were finding the publicity unwanted and upsetting. She and the theatre's administrative director, Susan Moffatt, were interviewed by the media and soon the creeps began coming out of the woodwork. "We started getting calls from every twisted, right-wing weirdo in the Rocky Mountains," she says. "Susan was followed for a week. A man came into our offices one day and threatened us and we had to call the police. It was freaky. I'd get calls at home from anti-abortionists, tearing up one side of me and down the other. I'd get in and find hate messages on my answering machine. It was very stressful." By then the mother of two young children, Raby didn't need the stress or the fear and resigned from Northern Light at the end of the season.

On 1 April, the Rabbits' lawyers went back to court, this time in Calgary, to try to overturn Mr. Justice Lutz's ban. Madam Justice Mary Hetherington adjourned the appeal to later in the month. On 3 April, the Rabbits and their friends held a fundraiser to recoup some of the $10,000 lost due to the shutdown. The *Banned in Alberta Benefit Cabaret* was held at the Pumphouse, where *Ilsa* was to have made her Calgary encore. It featured entertainment by the Rabbits themselves as well as guests that included Ronnie Burkett, local CBC host David Brindle, Denise's musician brother Peter Clarke, *Ilsa*'s violinist Karl Roth, and the Huevos Rancheros band. The event was a smash success, pulling in over $9,500 and netting $6,728 after a few expenses (such as beer, wine, and tequila) had been deducted. "I don't even think I saw the first half of the show," says Grant Burns. "I was too busy trying to shoehorn people into the Pumphouse. Also, I had my eye out for the RCMP or anybody who looked like a lawyer or a Keegstra type. We were super-paranoid. We were told not to do anything from the show and, in fact, we did numbers from the show. Now, if you asked Blake he'd say 'Oh no. We only did numbers that were very *similar* to ones in the show.'"

In addition, the Colonel, a.k.a. Michael Green, performed *Yowl*, a Ginsberg-style "rant" he'd written in response to the ban. It had been prompted by a fact-finding visit from the RCMP — Mr. Justice Lutz had made good on his threat to have Blake Brooker investigated. "This guy interviewed me out on the Olympic Plaza," Green recalls. "I can't remember a single sensible question. I think the cop knew he was on a wild goose chase and just had to go through some motions. That's where the impulse for *Yowl* came from. I was so mad at circumstances. I had a small grant to write a play for Wagonstage [the University of Calgary's children's troupe]. I went up to The Banff Centre and I was supposed to write this nice play for kids and I just couldn't do it. *Yowl* came out instead."

Along with the benefit revenue, the Rabbits also received a donation of services from the law firm of Shea Nerland so the *Ilsa* appeal could proceed. The battle against the Lutz ruling would have the Shea Nerland lawyers in and out of court throughout the month of April. Finally, on 23 April, the Alberta Court of Appeal stated that it was upholding the ban. Keegstra was there to hear the verdict, and so was his doppelgänger, Andy Curtis. When the court adjourned, the two came face to face at last. "There he was in the foyer of the court building," recalls Curtis. "He was passing by and I had no particular desire to meet him, but as he passed he spotted me and stuck out his hand. I shook it. He seemed quite pleased, he had just won the appeal. He said 'Y'know, I can see the resemblance.' I said 'There ain't no resemblance. It's purely physical, sir.' I can't believe I called him sir!"

Interestingly enough, Curtis didn't really have a problem with the ban. "I suppose, in hindsight — and perhaps at the time, even — I agree with that decision. It made legal sense. Give the guy a fair trial. And if anything we do, by the remotest chance, jeopardizes the outcome of the trial, well okay, I guess there is a hierarchy of rights, and his right to a fair trial certainly surpasses our right to say what we want to say [about him]."

The appeal was over, but the criminal investigation of Blake Brooker continued until the end of the year. RCMP officers from Red Deer dutifully interviewed many of his friends and colleagues. "I had the RCMP in my office two or three times, asking me about Blake," says Grant Burns. "They were asking me 'Do you think he's a liar?' I don't think Blake lied in court but, was he contemptuous to the judge? Well, you know what Blake's like ..." Andy Curtis was also quizzed by a cop. "I can't remember what he wanted to know, but it seemed very odd. Keegstra's the bad guy and we're just pointing at him and laughing. Can't we do that here?"

Gyl Raby, who was interviewed, too, says she understood Lutz's desire to prevent a mistrial. "But part of me still subscribes to the romantic notion that we, as artists, were being censored and investigated instead of the true criminal." Denise Clarke still gets steamed at what she perceives as Lutz's ignorance. "Had a truly hip judge been able to communicate to us, 'You guys, I understand your dilemma, but this guy's the bad guy. Let's all join together and get him,' then it might have been different. But he didn't have a clue what we were doing. He didn't look into it, he didn't investigate our work. I'm sorry, but that play is a brilliant piece of social-political theatre, and its voice is powerful against Keegstra. [Lutz's] attitude was deeply disturbing."

Brooker himself refused to be interviewed, on advice from his lawyer. The detective work failed to turn up anything incriminating and, in December, the RCMP officer in charge phoned him one last time. "He said 'I've got a Christmas present for you. We've decided to stop investigating you.' I said 'Oh, thanks so much.' That was a spectacularly colossal waste of law enforcement resources, just in order to shut us up."

In Red Deer, Keegstra's second trial had dragged on for four months. It came to a close on 10 July when, after four days and thirty hours of deliberation, the jury re-convicted him. This time he was handed a $3,000 fine. One Yellow Rabbit was free to restage *Ilsa*.

### "Ilsa's Back and She's a Hit"

It took until the following spring for the Rabbits to revive their most controversial creation. The triumphant return of *Ilsa* seemed to require a bigger venue than the Secret Theatre and one of the company's stalwart board members had the answer. Blake O'Brien had become a co-owner of the Barron building, an eleven-storey office tower of 1950s vintage, which had once been the focal point of Calgary's budding oil industry but was better known to most Calgarians as the home of the twin-screen Uptown Cinemas. Cineplex Odeon had ditched the old movie house at the end of the 1980s, and O'Brien and his partners bought it at auction for a song. The plan was to turn the original theatre on the main floor into a repertory cinema and convert the upstairs one, a 1970s addition, into a 350-seat live performance space. O'Brien wanted *Ilsa* to christen the new space. Despite the previous year's publicity, One Yellow Rabbit was cautious. Given that the Uptown was five times the size of the Secret, the troupe decided to limit the run to a week.

The first night, Monday, 3 May 1993, was an eye-opener. People queued up halfway down the block to get in. Not an uncommon sight at the release of a new Hollywood blockbuster — but for an original play by a small local theatre company? And the audiences just kept coming. A gala performance on Thursday was sold out a week before the opening, despite the then-lofty $20 ticket price. The reviews were raves and the headline for the *Globe and Mail*'s four-star notice, by veteran critic Chris Dafoe (6 May 1993), summed them all up: "Ilsa's back and she's a hit." Grant Burns remembers that single production earned as much as the company usually made in an entire season. "At the time, the average yearly box office for the Rabbits was about $30,000. With that one-week run at the Uptown, seven or eight shows only, almost every one sold out, we made $25,000. I can't believe we only did it for a week!" Instead of holding it over, the troupe took the play on tour to the West Coast for a two-week gig at Vancouver's 130-seat Firehall Theatre and a further week at Victoria's Belfry Theatre.

The company is still rather painfully aware that it missed a golden opportunity. "You sure can't accuse us of milking something," says Denise Clarke ruefully. At the time, Theatre Calgary was being governed by Brian Rintoul, Martin Kinch's showman successor, who was continually extending popular shows and had even transferred one to Toronto for a commercial run. He went to see *Ilsa* at the Uptown and approached Clarke afterwards. "I remember Rintoul saying to me, 'Now, I just know you guys are not going to run this thing for the next month, or three or four months. You just don't get it, do you? If you kept holding it over, you could run that play five, six weeks, maybe five months.' That show was either the absolute making of us," she says, "or the reason we are still struggling financially in some respects. We have extraordinary acumen as far as art and politics are concerned, but we're the lamest fucking bunch of producers."

They would, however, do a one-week encore at the Uptown in April 1994, before launching a second *Ilsa* tour that would take them to Toronto and then abroad. By the time of the second Uptown engagement, others in the entertainment industry had awakened to *Ilsa*'s popularity. Namely, Larry Day, a Calgary television personality who had found a lucrative sideline developing and selling shows from the studios of his home station, CFAC or Channels 2 and 7. At the time, he was co-hosting (with his wife) a syndicated bit of Hollywood puffery called *The Movie Show*. Day sold the Rabbits, and the Superchannel pay TV service, on a film of *Ilsa*, to be shot live during the Uptown performances. Calgary filmmaker Jeth Weinrich would direct and Day said he envisioned it as a piece of filmed theatre in the style of *Swimming to Cambodia*, the 1987 Jonathan Demme movie of Spalding Gray's monologue. Day even spoke of taking the film to Cannes that May and shopping it around.

All went well from the Rabbits' point of view. By every account, they gave an electrifying performance before a wildly enthusiastic crowd. Then came the bad news. The film, shot with three cameras, had problems with colour matching and the footage was unusable. By this time, the troupe was in Toronto and had just finished an exciting engagement at the du Maurier World Stage festival. Day, who had pre-sold the show, needed to deliver something, so he hastily organized a morning studio shoot at his TV station. Back in Calgary, the bleary-eyed Rabbits slouched into CFAC at what, for any self-respecting actor, was the ungodly hour of seven (or eight, or nine — depending on who you speak to), where they were forced to go through their paces before a bussed-in gaggle of high school students. Denise Clarke remembers that the teenagers didn't get any of the jokes. "The only thing they howled with laughter at was the sperm scene. Just think, to have played two weeks ago to that audience at the Uptown, which was just so electric, and then to come back and shoot it again to these kids going 'Huh?'" To juice it up, some of the audience response from the Uptown show was inserted afterwards — and the laugh track wasn't the only cheesy thing about the production. "We had the same makeup as Larry Day," says Clarke. "We're all tanned! It's just so ugly — newsman pancake! He's the squarest fucking cube." "I still can't bear to watch it," adds Michael Green with a shudder. "I was so mad at Larry Day at the time. We had done such a brilliant job at the Uptown. In Toronto, I shaved off my moustache in celebration of the end of the tour and then the phone rang. And a few days later, there I was, at seven in the morning, trying to stick on a phoney moustache. I was not happy." The film ran its course on Superchannel — a service available only in western Canada — after which the Rabbits may have wished it would quietly sink into oblivion. Instead, it was sold to the cable empire of Toronto's Moses Znaimer and on 6 December 1995, it premiered nationally on the Bravo! arts channel. "That thing is years old now and it's still running all the time, in rotation," says Clarke. "It's brought us publicity, but at the cost of our extraordinary show becoming a sort of hack Bravo! TV program. Now, I may say that, but I get e-mails from people telling me 'That was one of the most amazing things I've ever seen on TV. It's so funny.' They should see it on a good night."

Like the audiences at World Stage did. The Toronto premiere of *Ilsa* was short but thrilling. The production visited the Brigantine Room of Harbourfront Centre, 13 to 16 April. Despite the brief run, it got plenty of press thanks to the gag-order controversy, and H. J. Kirchhoff, then the *Globe and Mail*'s chief drama critic, gave it another positive review, although he was stingier with his star rating than Dafoe. Kirchhoff awarded it three — perhaps because he felt the play was "sketchy." That hardly mattered. The public response was better than any rave notice. Ralph Christoffersen, the show's technical director, remembers that one of the last performances provoked the most powerful reaction *Ilsa* had yet received: "At the end of the show they had what they called 'the lampshade dancers' — a couple of concentration camp victims who came out and sprinkled sand on the stage. It was quite a sad and sombre moment. We used to drop the lights, go to a blackout, and wait for a response from the audience. It usually took from ten to thirty seconds. But this night the audience — and it was a full house — sat in silence for well over a minute. It was quite a poignant silence, just super heavy. It was getting to where we didn't know what to think. And then all of a sudden, the audience just burst into this thunderous applause. People just went wild. The actors were literally shaking backstage afterwards."

That summer, *Ilsa* sashayed across the pond to make her international debut in Scotland. One Yellow Rabbit was already becoming a known quantity there. Since 1991, the company had toured three shows to the Traverse, one of the hub theatres of the Edinburgh Festival Fringe, and the previous year it had begun a relationship with Glasgow's Tron Theatre as well. Still, the production was a risk. Where Canadian audiences saw controversy in the Rabbits' portrayal of James Keegstra, the British and European audiences that flocked to the Edinburgh Fringe would be more sensitive to a musical comedy about Nazis and the Second World War.

Sure enough, *Ilsa, Queen of the Nazi Love Camp* was labelled as tasteless as *Springtime for Hitler*, the joke Nazi musical in Mel Brooks's classic film comedy *The Producers* — and that was in one of the good notices. "We had a lot of mixed press," recalls Grant Burns. "Some people hated it. Anything to do with the war is a lot more of a loaded issue in Europe. I remember Blake and I talking to a cab driver on the way to the airport who was railing about the [euro], about how the British had whipped the Nazis and now they were going to have the same currency as them." Jeremy Kingston in the *Times of London* gave *Ilsa* its worst review ever, next only to Keegstra's — but one assumes Kingston actually saw the play. In the 30 August 1994 edition, he lambasted its "wretched taste" and "incompetent staging" and acidly concluded: "Inert dialogue, pathetic attempts at irony and self-indulgent acting by the man playing the teacher make this monstrous and rotten." Ouch! A more considered response came from Claire Armitstead in the *Guardian* (31 August 1994), who acknowledged the play's serious intent but felt One Yellow Rabbit had gone too far and "transform[ed] fascist archetypes into camp icons. Particularly Denise Clarke's Ilsa, in her plaits and fishnets, takes parody to that treacherous point when mockery verges on a celebration of style." All the same, the show sold well during its two-week run in the Traverse's 120-seat studio theatre and mightily impressed one important audience member — David Blenkinsop, the director of the venerable Festival of Perth in Australia. He'd been invited to the opening night performance and ran backstage afterwards, collaring Blake Brooker. "He walked up to me," recalls Brooker, "and said 'I understand you're the director of this show. Would you guys like to come to Australia?' He asked us if we were free in February of next year. I said we were and he shook my hand and said, 'Okay. See you in February.'"

The year 1995 marked the arts festival's forty-third season and was particularly significant as it had been designated the Year of Culture by the Australian Tourism Commission. Blenkinsop had a globe-girdling program lined up for Perth, from Britain's National Theatre with Stephen Daldry's hit revival of J. B. Priestley's *An Inspector Calls* to Ukraine's Odessa Philharmonic Orchestra to the Chinese Acrobats of Guangdong. One Yellow Rabbit was its sole Canadian act and, along with New York's Garth Fagan Dance Company, one of only two companies from North America. *Ilsa* played the 200-seat Dolphin

Theatre, one of several venues at the University of Western Australia, for two weeks and twelve performances. It was high summer down under and when the Rabbits touched down in Perth they were treated as distinguished guests. "David B. himself came and picked us up at the airport," recalls that happy road warrior, Ralph Christoffersen. They were booked into a posh downtown hotel, given their own van to use, and provided with complimentary surfboards. "They took us from party to party and introduced us to government officials and visiting theatre professionals from all over the world. It was quite the deluxe affair."

By now, the company realized their little local satire had international resonance. Denise Clarke remembers that Andy Curtis's delivery of Keegstra's "society is an engine" analogy was invariably riveting. "I used to lie on my bed on stage and listen to that monologue and every night you could hear a pin drop. Every audience was mesmerized. And also by [the song] 'What's a Good Man in Changing Times?'" Her own performance elicited as much sympathy as Curtis's Keegstra the aspect of the play that had troubled the *Guardian*'s Armitstead. "Men would say to me 'Oh God, Ilsa's sexy,'" Clarke recalls. "I'd say 'Really? You don't find her monstrous?' That's how it works. You buy into her. 'Oh, I love Ilsa, she's so cute and funny and sassy, this love-camp goddess.'

"When I took it on," she explains, "I understood that I had to really tread the line between an all-out, ridiculous, over-the-top performance as this whore and not lose the respect of the audience. So I began to play subtext, and from what I understood it was working — the audience could still be moved by this monster. And that came from me, in my deepest heart, believing that Ilsa was a Jew. Somehow that reads, people are sympathetic. And they buy the ending." Ah, that ending. "The reason *Ilsa* was always such an extraordinary experience to perform," says Clarke, "is that people would be screaming with laughter, pissing themselves all night, and then we'd come out and do the last song, which is like a prayer: 'Why don't you leave us alone?' It was very emotional. And there'd be dead silence. We felt so justified when we did that play all over the world and it was always the same reaction."

The Rabbits themselves were unabashed fans of their own work. Even hard-nosed Grant Burns went all soft during that final scene.

"Maybe it was just the violin," he says, in a futile effort at dismissal, "but I could never get through the closing number without crying. Ever. And I saw it a hundred times."

The courts hadn't yet dropped the curtain on the Keegstra follies. There was a third act in store when the Alberta Court of Appeal overturned his second trial on another technicality, ruling that Mr. Justice Lutz had not given appropriate directions to the jury. So Lutz's painstaking attempts to conduct a fair trial had been in vain. The case was lobbed back to Ottawa, where the Supreme Court reinstated the 1992 conviction.

Finally, on 26 September 1996, the appeal court had the last word, overturning Keegstra's $3,000 fine and replacing it with a one-year suspended jail sentence. The ex-teacher, now plying his original trade as an auto mechanic in Eckville, was also placed on a year's probation and ordered to do two hundred hours of community service, preferably working with refugees from political oppression. An unrepentant Keegstra, now sixty-two, schlepped back to his grease pit, mumbling that the courts had "criminalize[d] the truth." "I never was a racist or anything of that nature," he told Canadian Press.

One Yellow Rabbit, meanwhile, had packed away the riding crop and fishnet stockings and moved on. But the themes and issues raised by its most famous play — the conspiracy mentality, eugenics, rural eccentrics, not to mention the experience of seeking and being denied permission — would inform its work for years to come.

1    Blake Brooker, *Ilsa, Queen of the Nazi Love Camp and Other Plays* (Red Deer, AB: Red Deer College Press, 1993), 49–50.

2    Ibid., 68.

3    Transcript of proceedings with regard to *Ilsa, Queen of the Nazi Love Camp,* taken in the Court of Queen's Bench of Alberta, Red Deer, AB, 13 March 1992, 21–22.

4    Ibid., 24.

5    Ibid., 41.

6    Ibid., 27.

7    Ibid., 21.

8    Ibid., 33.

9    Motion of J. Keegstra filed in the Court of Queen's Bench of Alberta, Red Deer, AB, 13 March 1992.

# 6. From an Elevator to a Rodeo

"Nothing is true. Everything is permitted."
— HASSAN I SABBAH, AS QUOTED BY WILLIAM S. BURROUGHS

Press "Rewind" and go back to the middle of Chapter 3. There's a hidden track I've deliberately skipped over. In the first week of February 1987, after One Yellow Rabbit had been kicked out of the SkyRoom and before it moved into the Secret Theatre, a little "happening" occurred — surreptitiously, after hours in a downtown office building — that sowed the seeds for one of the troupe's grandest, craziest, and most successful achievements. Kate Zimmerman was there, and gave a first-hand account in the pages of the *Calgary Herald*: "Scurrying along a downtown alley in the darkness, it was difficult to guess which of the anonymous back doors would lead to One Yellow Rabbit's Secret Elevator Experimental Performance Festival. But there was a clue — a One Yellow Rabbit sign leaning casually on its side against a wall. The door opened, a head emerged and the intrepid patrons were welcomed into the mystery location, and ushered into a dark elevator. The black box opened onto the dingy third [*sic*] floor of an office building" (9 February 1987).

It was, in fact, the SOMA building, a nondescript edifice of paprika-red brick located on the north side of 8 Avenue SW, between 5 and 6 Streets, just a few doors down from the Uptown Cinemas. There, on the eighth floor, OYR general manager Craig Laven's office had been converted into a thirty-five-seat theatre, home to a week-long festival of new performance.

Michael Green, itching to perform and undaunted by the lack of a proper space, was up to his old Ikarus tricks again. Get people to call a number, give them instructions where to go, smuggle them into an illicit venue, and hope that one of them isn't a cop. The mainstay of the mini-festival was a new Green and Stromsmoe project with the vaguely smutty title of *Rusty Buster's Dimple and Wiener Review* — an early draft of the notorious *Fall of the House of Krebbs* — starring Green in a crimson fright wig as an evangelist-cum-clown. To bracket its four-night run, Green invited a motley bunch of friends and fellow artists to contribute performances. Local minimalist composer Windsor Viney tested the audience's concentration with works for child's metallo-phone and toy piano; Toronto playwright/actor Sky Gilbert, in town to participate in Alberta Theatre Projects' first playRites festival, enter-tained with a reading from one of his campy movie parodies; and poet Sheri-D Wilson partied on the rooftop.

Ralph Christoffersen was the guardian at the gate, meeting audience members in the alley. "We took them onto a black elevator with a flashlight, turned the flashlight out, went up in the elevator, and led them out into a darkened hallway. They were marshalled there and then they'd be led into the room." That room was spacious for Craig Laven; with thirty-five people, it was a sardine tin. It had been transformed into a theatre — of sorts. "We had a little stage," says Sandi Somers. "We put risers in there so the performers would be elevated. The actors' heads were inches from the ceiling." Lighting was improvised. "We used every alternative we could. Slide projectors, candles, [light bulbs in] tin cans." Dix Richards served as stage man-ager, while Somers operated the lights and sound. Her booth was a closet under some stairs. "The ceiling was slanted, so I spent every night with my head bent sideways," she says. "The whole thing was totally wacky."

Sheri-D Wilson, doing a poetry performance called *Dying to be Famous*, made the most of the unorthodox venue. She and Laura Parken, playing in Parken's words "a couple of lost party girls," refused to be confined to a stuffy office. "We climbed out the window," says Wilson, "and the audience had to follow us out onto the rooftop, in the freezing weather, to watch the rest of the show."

Word of the secret festival quickly spread and by its third night, the run was sold out. All the same, the other Rabbits watched Green's experiment warily. "We were all very nervous about it," says Gyl Raby, "because of our previous experience with the fire marshals [at the SkyRoom]. And the people on our board were *really* worriers by that point," she laughs. "We were always operating on the edge of the law."

Once the company was ensconced in its perfectly legal Secret Theatre at the Centre for Performing Arts, the festival seemed like a natural choice to keep the venue busy between Rabbit shows. First of all, a name change was required, and the felicitous choice was High Performance Rodeo. Michael Green remembers lifting the term "high performance" from the magazine of that name, a publication dedicated to performance art. "I fancied that 'high performance' was a whole genre, and that's what I wanted to see at the festival — whatever that meant." Also calling it a "rodeo" would seem a no-brainer in Calgary, home of the Rabbit-reviled Stampede, opening the way for all sorts of cowboy clichés in the marketing.

"Rodeo" also implied wild and dangerous — attributes the festival aimed for and, occasionally, achieved. More often, though, the early festival was like an avant-garde gong show, minus the gong. Artists — mostly local, largely inexperienced — presented experimental work, often conceived for the event itself, before an indulgent audience. Sometimes the experiments fizzled or blew up in everyone's face. Now and again, they'd be cool in indescribable ways. (I still remember Neil Cadger, as a modern-day Orpheus, playing a wire-strung "musical chair" with a bottleneck and violin bow.) The ever-supportive Kate Zimmerman, part of that indulgent audience, felt she had to remind *Calgary Herald* readers that this wasn't the Stratford Festival: "A rodeo, by its nature, is a dynamic and risky event" (29 March 1988).

In true Rabbit spirit, Green had started a festival without quite knowing what he was doing. For the first Rodeo, staged in March 1988 in the Secret Theatre, he took all comers. "I just went out into the community and asked anyone to please do it. We'd give them the gate, although we'd have to keep some of it to cover some overhead. That was really all I had to offer." Out of the $5.50 ticket price, the performers and technicians got $4. "There were a lot of artists just starting out in those early days," he says, "and it must have seemed like a good enough idea to them. And I didn't limit it to theatre; I really wanted it to be an open-ended expression of different forms of performance. It was a reflection of what One Yellow Rabbit's mandate was. In our own work we would try to create a new mix of different performance styles and genres."

The 1988 Rodeo, which ran two weeks, included a young woman doing a striptease while reading Descartes; a satire of homophobic AIDS propaganda involving dancers, musicians, and tape loops; and Green himself, encased in an acrylic box full of crumpled paper, where he blew a trumpet and played with feathers in yet another Stromsmoe/Green creation called *Baby's Breath*. Nobody quite knew what to make of it all, but coming on the heels of the big-name, big-ticket Olympic Arts Festival, this was clearly an alternative event in every way. It didn't even fit the formal definition of performance art — visual artists using a performance medium. Although visual artists would participate in the festival from time to time, they were heavily outweighed by dancers, musicians, poets, actors, and comedians.

It was, however, a good time to ride on the coattails of the performance art movement, which had finally penetrated the consciousness of John Q. Public. Laurie Anderson had scored an unexpected radio hit in 1981 with her single "O Superman" and her concert performances took the art form out of SoHo galleries and onto network television — from the US Public Broadcasting System to *Saturday Night Live* and Letterman. As well, category-defying performers from the margins of the mainstream, such as Eric Bogosian and Sandra Bernhard, were being tagged as performance artists. Michael Green had seen his first performance art at Calgary's more adventurous galleries, including Artons, Clouds 'n' Water, and the Off Centre Centre, and had strongly identified with it. "I used to think I was more of a performance artist than a theatre artist," he says.

Green likens himself to Tom Sawyer, suckering a bunch of locals into doing performance pieces so he could build a festival. Maybe he was also Andy Hardy, whipping up enthusiasm in the Calgary arts community: "Hey, gang! Let's do some performance art! I've got this retail space that we've turned into a theatre, and Sandi's made some lights out of juice cans, and ..." Although this was hardly Andy Hardy–style entertainment. Indeed, some thought it was most unwholesome.

"Quite early on in the Rodeo's development," says Green, "I was very conscious of attempting to give something back to the community that I felt had really supported us, and my growth in particular. So I was in discussion with the Calgary Board of Education to put a special night aside at the High Performance Rodeo to encourage any groups of high school students who weren't happy with doing *The Music Man* or *The Crucible* and maybe wanted to come forward and show some work that they had created themselves. And the man at the board was very polite, but he said 'You know, we can't possibly allow our students [to participate]. We can't condone this kind of event, because One Yellow Rabbit is experimental theatre and, well, frankly, everyone knows that experimental theatre is naked men swearing.' Now, it occurred to me that I had never had a naked man swearing in a show — and certainly *I* had never sworn naked — so Gary [Stromsmoe] and I put together a piece where we had a naked man chained up and I swore while I whipped him. I figure if they're going to accuse you of it, you may as well do it. Especially if it sounds like fun."

Although he couldn't sway the stuffy school board, Green did coax some high schoolers to contribute to the 1989 festival. Working under the banner of the Purple Cave Project, the teenagers staged something akin to a hybrid of satirical revue and school cafeteria free-for-all, trashing American consumerist culture while whacking wieners at the audience with a gigantic plastic baseball bat. They must have had a blast, because the next year they regrouped to thumb their noses at commercialized religion with a mock TV game show called *Wheel of Martyr*, featuring a crucified Christ at the centre of the spinning wheel. (Jesus eventually got down off his cross, led the audience faithful out the theatre doors, then climbed into a waiting van like a rock star and sped away.)

The Rodeo was an open invitation, not just for high school kids, but for any hipsters in the city with an interest in the avant-garde. There were plenty of one-off collaborations: poets with jazz musicians, rock bands with modern dancers. Even non-performers got involved. At one Rodeo, Heather Elton, then the editor of *Dance Connection* magazine, delivered a lecture on Antonin Artaud. For a time it looked as though the festival was becoming the highbrow or, dare we say, pretentious version of the Edmonton Fringe. Where participants at that big northern bacchanal liked to aim for the lowest common denominator with funny, dirty company names and show titles — who could resist, say, Three Dead Trolls in a Baggie performing *Kevin Costner's Naked Butt*? — down south their artsy-fartsy cousins were opting for the intellectual and the deliberately abstruse. These troupes called themselves Ceremony Chagall, 1500 Shadows, Colour Correction Theatre Peace, and performed such enticing works as *Typhoon Trilogy* and *Part No. 63A18: The Hook*. (The titles weren't always that solemn, mind you. Let's not forget *My Roommate the Antichrist* and *Tupperware on Fire*.) Whatever the label, the performances strove assiduously for the bizarre. The strange sights seen by early Rodeo-goers ranged from mime Monica Meneghetti carefully picking up 108 glass beads off the stage one at a time, to comedian Owen Demers ritualistically dismantling a sandwich and arranging the contents on his head. Was it art? A put-on? Just a lot of wanking in public? Michael Green, shrewdly anticipating criticism, staged a surprise incident in which the *Calgary Herald*'s head drama critic, Brian Brennan, stood up in the middle of one show, pronounced it a load of rubbish, and tossed a bucket of playing cards at the performers.

While there was a good deal of dabbling, and perhaps a little wanking, at those early festivals, some genuine talent was also finding its feet. One two-time Rodeo participant was Calgary singer/songwriter Anne Loree, who would go on to write "Insensitive," the first big hit for pop singer Jann Arden. Another musician, Edmonton's Lester Quitzau, delighted Rodeo patrons with his shit-hot slide-guitar playing en route to a Juno Award–winning recording career. And then there was Doug Curtis, who would introduce Quitzau to the Rodeo.

Curtis made his debut in the festival's fifth year, in the spring of 1991. Boyish, with a mop of sandy hair, he looked like the kid next door, Dennis the Menace just barely grown up, as he appeared in a lone spotlight on the Secret Theatre stage. Seated behind a desk, clutching a sheaf of papers, he read what sounded at first to be a suburban teenager's unusually well-written account of trying to get through a harsh prairie winter. There was talk of hockey and bumper-skiing (a favourite extreme sport of danger-loving Canadian boys: hanging on to the back bumpers of cars and "skiing" the icy roads), and getting drunk on stolen crème de menthe. It was all very innocent and engaging. Yet there was a certain wry, knowing tone to the young man's voice and unexpected touches of magic realism in his writing. Curtis was, in fact, an actor in his late twenties, the "read" story was a memorized monologue and the material was only loosely autobiographical. With the artful storytelling of *Black Ice and Red Adidas,* Curtis had found his métier and Calgary had found its Spalding Gray.

"I was influenced a bit by Spalding Gray," says Curtis, "and also Garrison Keillor. I knew I'd more than likely be compared to them, but I wanted to tell that kind of story people want to hear, that was unique to their circumstances and my experience."

A Calgarian, Curtis had left town to studying acting at Circle in the Square in New York, then started his career as a jobbing actor in Toronto. Between auditions and waiting tables, he hung out with a bunch of other hungry young actors and playwrights who read their work Monday nights at the Cabana Lounge in the Spadina Hotel. It was there that Curtis began writing and performing his own material, out of which *Black Ice* emerged. Returning to Calgary for an acting gig, he submitted the script to Alberta Theatre Projects, where it got a reading at the playRites festival, and then offered it to Michael Green as a potential Rodeo show. Although it was a far cry from the wild and woolly stuff Green was looking for, he accepted it, thereby launching Curtis's solo career and giving the festival one of its best-loved regulars.

The following festival, December 1991, Curtis would be back with an even better sequel, *Lester's Hat* — the Salingeresque tale of misadventures with a troubled teenager off his Ritalin — and a musical sidekick to underscore the narrative. Curtis had heard Lester Quitzau playing in a bar on Edmonton's Whyte Avenue and was amazed by his skill. "When I heard his name was Lester, I just about jumped out of my shirt," he recalls. "The character in the show I'd just written was this grade eight sociopath named Lester." Curtis got friendly with the guitarist and suggested he might want to embellish some storytelling with his bottleneck slide. The collaboration clicked and Quitzau would go on to accompany Curtis in his future shows *Mesa, Paranormal*, and *The Cruise*.

### "Anger Is an Energy" — John Lydon

At the same festival that Doug Curtis charmed listeners with the suburban nostalgia of *Black Ice and Red Adidas,* the Rodeo was rocked by a jolt of raw urban rage, administered by an angry young man from New York.

James Howley's *Almost in Exile,* a razor-sharp dissection of the rotten Big Apple in the midst of recession, performed with electrifying intensity, nearly blew the audience out of its seats. For eighty often-vitriolic minutes, the monologuist and musician spat out urgent dispatches from the urban combat zone. He reported on bystanders being shot in the street, sang about homeless people sleeping on sidewalk gratings and sheets of cardboard, zeroed in on the barely restrained hatred of Jews and Arabs in a Manhattan delicatessen. In one terrifying episode, half-hidden in darkness he re-enacted an overheard exchange at a motel, where a crazed, violent black man screamed obscenities at a white woman. He punctuated it by smashing a chair against the theatre wall. Between his tirades there were strange, gentle interludes, in which he cooled down the audience by serving it spring water in paper cups or, guitar in hand, shared a pretty tune he'd recently learned from Bob Dylan's old buddy, folk singer Dave Van Ronk.

On that stunning April night, Howley single-handedly raised the Rodeo's performance bar. *Almost in Exile* quickly made you realize how tame and silly a lot of the festival had been until then. A bit-part actor in American film and TV, Howley was an old friend of OYR. He had spent time in Calgary and Banff in the 1980s and worked with the Rabbits on *The Pageant of the Comet* and *Ides*. The timing of his Rodeo debut couldn't have been better, coming the night after Elton's lecture on Antonin Artaud. Howley was Artaud in practice, using theatre as provocation, shocking the spectator out of his apathy and critical distance. A more contemporary comparison, however, was with Eric Bogosian, the frenetic New York actor/playwright whose one-man shows also surveyed the city's ugly side (his *Sex, Drugs, Rock & Roll* had just premiered off-Broadway the previous year). Howley, dark and wiry, even looked a bit like Bogosian.

*Almost in Exile* was the first in a string of watershed performances that would grab the Rodeo audience by its lapels (or, more accurately, T-shirts) and demand attention. Amateur Hour was over — this was serious stuff.

There was a slight thrill of déjà vu at the next festival, in December 1991, when the house lights went down and a slender, dark, wild-eyed young man walked to centre stage, picked up a chair, and hurled it into the wings. He got another chair, tried it out, then threw *it* into the wings, too. Then he stepped before the shut doors of the Secret Theatre, a mad grin on his pasty face, barring our exit. Daniel MacIvor had arrived.

Or had he? Surely this wasn't the same actor we had seen playing the sensitive Tom in a Theatre Calgary production of *The Glass Menagerie* only a few seasons ago? This sour nut looked more like a leaner, meaner Rodney Dangerfield — or maybe the young Bob Hope tripping on speed and supremely pissed off. Just what was his problem anyway?

Everything and everybody. As MacIvor began to rant and spew, all the while rolling an invisible marble between finger and thumb, you looked about furtively to see where he'd shed his straitjacket. Turned out his name wasn't Daniel, it was Victor. He was in group therapy and, boy, did he have issues. There was his crummy job in the septic tank business. There was his cheating wife, who was leading a double life as an S&M dominatrix. And there was his dysfunctional family — dad the circus freak, mom, a TV junkie possessed by the devil, and sis, who did it with dogs. Victor's life was one big, crazy nightmare in which every mundane detail morphed into the hilariously surreal. It was like listening to a schizophrenic, his brain zooming from topic to topic, or a stand-up comic from hell. And there was no Howley-like respite, no cups of spring water. Whenever Victor took a time out, it was to menace the audience or maybe play the bagpipes on his throat.

Those who first saw *House* at the High Performance Rodeo probably didn't realize, as the critics would later helpfully point out, that Victor was a kindred spirit with the anti-heroes of Dostoevsky and Céline. (If only Dostoevsky was this funny — intentionally.) But it was clear that MacIvor, actor and playwright, had created a unique and unforgettable character. Behind the cranked-up figure of Victor and his colourful ravings lay a shadow of melancholy, a quiet sadness that lingered after the laughter. In his moments of peace, he kept returning to the idea of the house as home, refuge, idyll, the key to happiness. It was a dream that had failed him so far and yet he seemed to believe it might still be waiting over the horizon. *House* was a show you couldn't shake off. A fascinating new voice in Canadian theatre had been born.

MacIvor had written other plays, but this was his breakthrough. He'd tried out *House* at the Factory Theatre's Studio Café in Toronto earlier that year, before bringing it to the Rodeo. It went on to win the prestigious Floyd S. Chalmers Canadian Play Award and receive a Toronto remount on the mainstage of Theatre Passe Muraille. As with Doug Curtis, MacIvor's first Rodeo gig was the start of a continuing relationship with the Rabbits. In the next decade, Calgary audiences would watch him build a remarkable solo repertoire even as he began to establish a second career in television and film.

MacIvor, based in Toronto, had performed in Calgary only a couple of times, in roles at Theatre Calgary. When he arrived at the Rodeo that winter in 1991, he immediately got a sense that something exciting was happening. Something that, by rights, should be happening in the bigger urban centre but wasn't. "I felt Calgary had a closer connection to what was going on in New York than Toronto did," he recalls. "There was something about the energy at the Rodeo. It was more direct. As small as it was, it felt really important and cutting edge."

The New York connection was about to get closer.

## Bitch! Dyke! Faghag! Penny!

On a January evening in 1993, the second night of the sixth official High Performance Rodeo, a faithful audience gathered in the Secret Theatre to see a pair of solos by a modern dancer from Banff — interpretive works with a Wild West theme. Evoking a horse, the young woman tap danced a gallop and tossed her long chestnut mane. Then she rippled her body gracefully to suggest wind in a wheatfield. Then she galloped some more. As the piece went on, the polite silence of the spectators was broken somewhere in the back rows by snorts of derision and stabs of commentary: "What is this shit?" hissed the voice. "You call this a dance? Enough with the galloping already!" Those who overheard may have wondered: Had some philistine invaded this tiny temple of art? And wait — listen to her accent. Omigod, even worse, it was an *American* philistine!

No. It was Penny Arcade, a ballsy, no-guff performance artist from New York who didn't suffer foolishness gladly. And she was about to take the Rodeo on its wildest ride yet.

Two nights later, *Bitch! Dyke! Faghag! Whore! The Penny Arcade Sex and Censorship Show* made its international debut in a converted rehearsal hall in Calgary's Centre for Performing Arts. It contained satiric monologues, caustic social commentary, video vérité, nudity, and an orgy of go-go dancing. At the centre of it all was a buxom brunette in black lingerie, as bold as Lenny Bruce, as confiding as Oprah Winfrey, who proved that performance art and good ol' American showbiz savvy were not incompatible. No one had heard of her before, but word quickly got out, and by the third and final night of her too-brief run, it was standing room only in the hall, with people being turned away at the door.

Who was this magnetic woman? Penny Arcade was the alias of Susana Ventura, a battle-scarred veteran of the New York avant-garde who had grown up on the edges of Andy Warhol's fabled Factory scene. Born in a small town in Connecticut, she ran away at sixteen, in 1967, and wound up being adopted by the sexually diverse members of John Vaccaro's proto-queer theatre, the Playhouse of the Ridiculous. It was there that she was spotted by Warhol and ended up being cast alongside his transvestite superstars, Candy Darling, Jackie Curtis, and Holly Woodlawn, in the 1972 Paul Morrissey flick *Women in Revolt* — a campy send-up of the women's lib movement. By the '80s, she had begun writing and performing her own solo shows, often drawing on her colourful past. Her defiantly populist work was filled with passion and compassion and deliberately avoided the intellectual and obscure. *Bitch! Dyke! Faghag! Whore!* had been crafted as a response to the controversy stirred up by arch-conservative Republican senator Jesse Helms when he attacked the National Endowment for the Arts for funding allegedly obscene art. But it was not just a left-wing artist's knee-jerk reaction.

"The show was a criticism, not only of Senator Helms and the NEA, but also of the downtown art world's preoccupation with sensationalistic sex without content," Arcade says. "I wanted to show how it was all a hustle. We know there isn't any real controversy. How can there be? Every time you turn on the television in America, they're using sex to sell a can of soda or a car. And yet there is this big mythology that we're a moral country."

The show included shrewd Bruce-style riffs on America's sexual hypocrisy, at once angry and funny, as well as more personal material in which Arcade recalled the pain of watching gay friends die of AIDS and confronted her abusive mother on video. In between, she embraced all sexual orientations as equal and broke down the dehumanizing objectification of those who work in the sex trade. The overall effect was so candid and cathartic that she invariably had audiences up on their feet, happily dancing with her squad of strippers by the end of the performance. *Bitch! Dyke! Faghag! Whore!* premiered at Performance Space 122 in the East Village and did so well that it moved west to the Village Gate for a long run. Michael Green had caught it at PS 122 during a trip to New York and liked it so much that he approached Arcade and offered her a spot at the Rodeo. At that point, her work had never left the confines of New York and such alternative venues as the Knitting Factory and La Mama, and her knowledge of Canada was sketchy. "I'd never really heard anything about Calgary before," she says. "I had been approached in the past about going to Toronto, but they had a lot of censorship issues there and it had fallen through. I thought: Gee, Calgary, that sounds pretty backward, a cowtown. Someone I asked had compared it to Tulsa, Oklahoma. But I was very open to it."

When Arcade arrived in Calgary, her first concern was to round up some local exotic dancers, a necessary component of the show. There were ten in the New York production, but she settled for seven — a mix of men and women with names such as Malibu, Sensation, and Cherish. One of them, Gitanjali Varma, was even an old schoolfriend of Michael Green's. Penny was impressed with the assembled talent. "Canada has some of the best burlesque and erotic dancers in the world, because it still has a standard for that," she says. "It's not just about taking off your clothes. You have to have a gimmick, like Gypsy Rose Lee said." When the dancers were assembled, instead of making them audition, she auditioned for them. "I don't want to work with anybody who doesn't love the material." They did — and so did the Calgary audiences. Penny Arcade wasn't surprised — after all, the show had already been an underground success in New York. What did knock her out was that her work was suddenly being treated with respect.

"Up to that point, it had been running in New York for the better part of a year, yet it wasn't getting any publicity," she recalls. "It was running on word of mouth." The *New York Times,* the city's last word on theatre, had not only paid scant attention, it prudishly refused to print the show's full, exclamatory title in its listings. "And here I was in Calgary, performing at its civic centre to a diverse audience, and being very well-received. I thought that was pretty forward-thinking." Far from Tulsa, "I felt like I was in secessionist Vienna," she says, "where artists were at the top of the heap rather than the bottom."

Arcade apparently didn't know that Alberta had its own Jesse Helms types. Ken Kowalski, for one. Kowalski, then the province's deputy premier, had recently made the news fuming over a show by the lesbian artists collective Kiss and Tell at the publicly funded Banff Centre. But at the High Performance Rodeo there was no sense of art under siege. Quite the contrary. Penny Arcade was struck by how normal it all seemed. "I liked the whole approach of One Yellow Rabbit: We're going to put avant-garde work at the forefront and pretend it's not unusual, that it's what everybody wants to see. And consequently, that was the response they got."

Calgary proved a launch pad for the sex and censorship show. It went on to tour the UK, Ireland, Germany, Austria, Switzerland, Australia — with Arcade gathering exotic dancers everywhere she went. She'd be back at the Rodeo three years later with another production — by then, a well-travelled artist whose fame had spread beyond New York's downtown scene. Today, she still remembers the pleasant surprise of coming from Manhattan's Lower East Side and stepping into a bracing, salubrious prairie winter for the very first time. "Being in Calgary gives a sensation of enormous clarity, because the air is so crystalline and bright," she says. "Also, I'd never known what it was like for your nose hairs to freeze."

From the get-go, Michael Green had lassoed the odd out-of-towner for the Rodeo — Sky Gilbert at the pilot Secret Elevator event, Toronto dancer/performance artist Jill Rosenberg, Vancouver's Compagnie de Danse Monique Giard. Then, if you don't count British expatriate Alan Williams in 1990, the festival went international in the spring of 1991 with Howley, a troupe of ex-Muscovites called the Russian Theatre of Improvisation, and a Belgian/Canadian production of Mikhail Bulgakov's *Heart of a Dog*.

Penny Arcade had been picked up on Green's first shopping trip to New York. It had been paid for by the National Performance Network (NPN), a US-based organization looking to get American acts into Canada and vice versa. As a consequence, the 1993 Rodeo featured three New York acts: Arcade, Howley (who returned with a new show, *Their Land*), and Linda Mancini, a dancer, performance artist, and clown originally from Montreal. Mancini, like Penny/Susana, a dark, voluptuous woman of Italian heritage, presented her solo showcase, *Not Entirely Appropriate,* in which she revelled in displays of public misbehaviour. Green would subsequently make another trip to New York — where, in forehead-slapping retrospect, he passed up a solo show by then-unknown Camryn Manheim — but he found it difficult to maintain a relationship with the NPN. The organization wanted One Yellow Rabbit to participate in its meetings, but the busy troupe was seldom available. When the Rabbits did show up at a couple of NPN events, says Green, they felt out of place. "They were in the throes of political correctness — it was the heyday of all that — and we were the wrong colour, the wrong sex — they were really disappointed. We weren't even gay."

### Scraping Mashed Potato off Your Doc Martens

The Rodeo was growing by leaps and bounds, artistically and literally. For the January 1993 festival, the Rabbits added a second venue, using Theatre Calgary's rehearsal hall (with seating for about three hundred) to present Penny Arcade and a poetry cabaret featuring Rodeo regular Sheri-D Wilson and friends. Arcade's smash success and the extra seats pushed the total attendance to 1,343 — the festival's highest up to that point — and ticket sales exceeded their budget by $2,000. There had been twelve acts giving twenty performances over two weeks.

For the next Rodeo, held in November of the same year, the action spread beyond the Centre for Performing Arts, with four productions occupying the new Uptown Stage and one "performance spectacle" (which turned out to be a spectacular food fight) quartered in an art gallery. Michael Green wanted to be ready for another Arcade-style sell-out, but the choice of the Uptown — which the Rabbits had inaugurated as a live theatre with the return of *Ilsa, Queen of the Nazi Love*

*Camp* that May — was also partly dictated by the size of the incoming shows. The vigorous Montreal dance duo of Pierre-Paul Savoie and Jeff Hall, who had first energized the Rodeo with their high-speed antics in 1991, were bringing *Bagne,* a brutal piece about imprisonment employing a huge, cagelike set of metal scaffolding and chain-link fence. Vancouver's Dancecorps, meanwhile, was touring with *Rec Room,* a new work by choreographer Harvey Meller for eight dancers. That year, most of the visiting acts were prime Canadian performers, including Toronto's Mump and Smoot (alias Michael Kennard and John Turner), the "clowns of horror," who had already acquired cult status with their blood-spattered buffoonery. The only international artists were Oscar McLennan and Anne Seagrave from Dublin, who did their solo pieces as a double bill.

The presence of so many Canadian touring acts on the program was an indication that the High Performance Rodeo had begun to register on the country's cultural radar. The Canada Council didn't fund the Rodeo (or any other festival, for that matter), but Green says the agency would suggest it to artists who had received touring grants. "They'd say, 'One Yellow Rabbit has this funny little festival, you should talk to them.' That's how we got Pierre-Paul Savoie and Jeff Hall the first time. In some ways, [Savoie and Hall] changed the way I looked at the festival. They came into the little Secret Theatre with this touring show and put us on the map in terms of being one of those venues to which professional artists could go in the west. The audiences loved them, the artists were so grateful, and the Canada Council was very happy to encourage this sort of growth."

At the same time, local performers continued to find a berth in the Rodeo, and Green, if more selective, remained adamant about not abandoning the festival's rough-and-tumble beginnings. The one company that carried the banner for sloppy outrageousness year after year was a little mask-and-puppet troupe called the Green Fools. They did, indeed, seem green and foolish much of the time, but they could always be counted on to evoke the anarchic spirit of the original Secret Elevator event. The Fools, led by Dean Bareham and Christine Cook (like Michael Green, former students of Gary Stromsmoe), entered the Rodeo innocently enough, with a garden-variety birth-and-death allegory involving insects and dragons entitled *The Agony and the Egg*. That production, in 1991, was quickly forgettable. "Foggy symbolism, graceless movement, tedious plotline," summed up a certain critic in the *Calgary Herald* (16 December 1991). From then on, the Fools would make sure they left an impression. *The Idiot and the Odyssey*, in January 1993, had the troupe herding its sheeplike audience out of the theatre and into an elevator for a meandering journey through the labyrinthine innards of the Centre for Performing Arts. The idiotic odyssey came to a climax in a rehearsal hall, where spectators were prodded by devils and menaced by a gigantic vagina on stilts. Who could forget that vagina? Who could remember the story?

In compensation, for the next Rodeo the Green Fools staged a sit-down affair, a banquet held at the New Gallery. Guests were outfitted with plastic ponchos and hoods at the door, then seated and served heaping plates of mashed potatoes, carrots, and corn. Given the opportunity, the well-fed audience quickly regressed to infancy, hurling handfuls of vegetables at one another without even waiting for their hosts to encourage them. *Everybody Loves Dessert* was, perhaps, the most offensive thing that the Rodeo has ever presented — a gross demonstration of disrespect for food in a land of plenty. This time it wasn't Cook, Bareham, and company who were the fools — we, the audience, were. Try to explain this kind of entertainment to the Third World.

In subsequent years, the Green Fools would indulge their twisted sense of humour in plays about cannibalism and Hieronymus Bosch, and now and again drag audiences back into the bowels of the arts centre for more infernal fun and games. Perhaps their most satisfying Rodeo effort, however, came in 1995 with a hundredth-anniversary staging of Alfred Jarry's *Ubu Roi*. In their suitably raucous revival, re-dubbed *Ubu Wrecks*, the grotesque, gluttonous ruler of the title, flourishing a toilet-bowl brush as a sceptre, bore no little resemblance to Alberta's portly premier, Ralph Klein. It was a delicious bit of mischief, with Jarry's scatological schoolboy satire tailored to fit the current government, then on a budget-slashing spree. Surprisingly few alterations were needed. Michael Green orchestrated the lunacy, directing a cast of eleven masked actors, some of them cross-dressing *à la* British pantomime, while a seven-piece band, Street of Crocodiles, honked and clattered through a crazy, cacophonous score in which Bizet's "Toreadors' Song" bumped up against Bobby Vinton's "My Melody of Love." Blake Brooker just shook his head. This was the play that had caused a riot at its Paris premiere in 1896? But in Jarry's madcap classic, the Fools had finally found the perfect vehicle for their rude, unruly style.

Since we're on the topic of giving offence, has there ever been a Rodeo act that truly had audiences in an outrage? Yes, and it was not the Green Fools.

"Goat Island is still the most reviled, yet the most talked-about [company] ever at the High Performance Rodeo," claims Michael Green. "I love them so much, I don't care if no one else likes them," he adds with a note of petulant defiance. "People haven't stopped talking about them. At the time, I thought some people were going to take a swing at me, they were so angry. It's not too often these days that you can almost provoke a riot, but these guys practically did."

The Goat Island in question is the Goat Island Performance Group out of Chicago, which played the Rodeo in 1997, and its offensiveness had nothing to do with sex, violence, or flying mashed potatoes. The troupe was just wilfully — and for many, infuriatingly — obscure. Four vigorous, highly disciplined performers, clad alike in industrial-looking uniforms, the Goat Islanders engaged in strange ritualistic movements, from small hand motions to wild, jerky jumps, which went on interminably and drove some watchers to distraction. Perhaps the greatest sin you can commit in a North American theatre today is to stretch rather than compress time. Whatever it is they're watching, people don't want to sit still too long, and certainly not for something they don't understand. Goat Island's *How Dear to Me the Hour When Daylight Dies* came with copious program notes helpfully explaining its sources and inspirations, and the troupe performed with the audience sitting on stage, to tear down the old "fourth wall." But its style was so enigmatic that the performers remained remote even when they were an arm's length away. Which is not to say there weren't times when the foursome were amusing or moving in their cryptic way, notably in a late passage where they solemnly evoked an annual Irish Catholic pilgrimage up a mountainside in County Mayo by repeatedly climbing over a chair. In retrospect, Goat Island is what the Rabbits might have become had they fully embraced Grotowski in the 1980s. And if they hadn't had a saving sense of humour.

Still, the heated reaction of Rodeo patrons to this curious company was unusual. Did they forget they were at an experimental theatre festival? "Some people love to get up at cocktail parties and say how much they support experimental theatre," says Green, "but they sure as hell don't actually want to go and watch it. If we put on something that's a little out there on the contemporary scale of things, a little on the unusual side, they'll stay away or, if they don't, they'll complain. They'll hold me personally responsible for having the gall to subject them to that stuff. But as soon as we give them something that looks like it's going to be wild, but once they get there, it's actually a fairly traditional play, then they thank us with their money and their support." Perhaps, but once upon a time Rodeo-goers had been willing to watch work that was much less competent than Goat Island and just as obscure. As the festival's standards had gone up, so, too, had audience expectations.

### Karen Finley, sans Chocolat

By the mid-1990s, performance art had lost its mystique and been reduced to a popular joke:

Q: How many performance artists does it take
to screw in a light bulb?
A: I don't know. I left after four hours.

Even Michael Green was ready to admit the attraction had grown stale. In 1995, sounding like his Nazi colonel from *Ilsa*, he told me: "Today,

everyone who hears the words 'performance art' reaches for their Luger"
(*Calgary Herald,* 11 January). That year's Rodeo was heavy on comedy
— albeit the surreal comedy of people like Andy Curtis and the great
Newfoundland funnyman Andy Jones — and light on the kind of bizarre
demonstrations that had once been a staple of the festival. The Rodeo
audience, said Green, preferred to see interdisciplinary performances of
the kind created by One Yellow Rabbit itself — hybrids of theatre, comedy, and dance. In short, they wanted to be entertained.

Annoyed audience members weren't the only ones reaching for
their Lugers. In the United States, where the forces of the far right were
in the ascendant, where crusading right-wingers from Newt Gingrich
to Rush Limbaugh were the celebrities of the moment, performance art
had become a sitting-duck target. It was easy to get the supposed "moral
majority" to hate it. Performance art was often difficult to understand, it
generally involved nudity and other taboos, it was practised by society's
misfits and radicals — homosexuals, lesbians, feminists (the last two
often equated in the right-wing mind) — and, here was the clincher, *it
was publicly funded.* In 1990, four performance artists — Karen Finley,
John Fleck, Holly Hughes, and Tim Miller — were denied grants from
the National Endowment for the Arts despite unanimous recommen-
dations by a peer panel. The veto — by the NEA's chairman, John
Frohnmeyer, and its advisory board — came in the face of mounting
political pressure from the right, led by Jesse Helms, the redneck senator from North Carolina who had accused the agency of funding "filth
and sleaze." The "NEA Four" fought back with a lawsuit, and the resultant publicity put them smack in the public eye. For a time, it was a
frightening place to be. Conservative critics who have since accused
them of capitalizing on the controversy, conveniently forget that the four
were tormented with hate mail and death threats. "It was very scary,"
Holly Hughes told me in 1994 (*Calgary Herald,* 6 June). "I was getting
letters from people that said 'We know where you live, we have a gun
and we're coming to New York this summer. And, by the way, Jesus loves
you.'" Hughes's offending work was a monologue on lesbian sexuality.
But the artist who became, in the words of *USA Today,* "the whipping

girl in the ideological battle over federal funding of art" was Karen Finley. The lone heterosexual of the four, her colourful feminist shows were the kind that best fit all the negative clichés about performance art. Her most-often cited act of outrage was smearing her semi-nude body with chocolate frosting (in her 1989 show about patriarchal oppression called *We Keep Our Victims Ready*). If you were going to invite a truly provocative performance artist to your festival, this was her.

Michael Green thought the NEA notoriety might have made her unaffordable, but he was a Finley fan, so he decided to give it a shot. As it turned out, her fee was reasonable, but just a little beyond the reach of the Rodeo's budget. So he approached the Glenbow Museum, Calgary's major art institution, and suggested a collaboration. "They wouldn't go for it," he recalls, "so then I went to Josh Marantz [then the programming manager at the Centre for Performing Arts], a gentleman with a lot of vision. It was his job to program a lot of what went on in the Jack Singer Concert Hall. He had a penchant for some pretty wild things. I told him how much it cost and I said 'Why don't we bring this woman in, knock this city right on its ass?'" Marantz was game. The Centre teamed with One Yellow Rabbit as co-presenters and covered the expense.

Chicago native Karen Finley was not just a performance artist, but also a prolific painter, playwright, author, sculptor, songwriter, and creator of art installations. Like the Rabbits, she was a product of the punk-rock era, whose early gigs included opening for the Dead Kennedys. Later she would go on to collaborate with another outspoken (and vilified) young woman, Sinéad O'Connor. She would be bringing the Rabbits her solo show, *A Certain Level of Denial*, which had premiered in 1992 at Lincoln Center in New York and had just been released as a CD on the hip Rykodisc label. Like much of her work, it dealt with the dark side of American life: homophobia and AIDS, sexism and rape, police brutality, cruelty to animals, abortion, and suicide. The idea that Calgarians would flock to a 1,800-seat concert hall in the dead of winter to hear one woman rail against society's ills for ninety minutes seemed a crazy gamble. Would her infamy be enough to lure them? Would they expect some chocolate frosting?

Karen Finley was chocolate-free that night, but she did appear nude. She walked out on stage in nothing but a pair of pumps and a decorated hat, thereby satisfying the voyeurs at the top of the show, so they could go home and she could get down to business. As the evening progressed, she gradually donned items of clothing — a necklace, tights, a dress — in a reverse striptease. (The Rabbits cheerfully appropriated the idea a few years later for their tribute to Leonard Cohen, in which Michael Green entered naked and straight-faced to warn the audience, "There will be nudity in tonight's show." While he continued with a list of caveats, the other members of the company came on and dressed him.) But it wasn't Karen Finley's nude torso that commanded attention, it was her remarkable voice. She might have been a Northern woman possessed by Southern devils, reciting her text in tones that varied between a breathy, delicate, Blanche DuBois cry and the deep, undulating rant of a Bible Belt preacher. She had a way of radically changing pitch in mid-word, like a tape slowing down and speeding up. It was the voice of a seer, a contemporary Cassandra — weird, disturbing, abrasive. She treated many of the same subjects as Penny Arcade, but while the latter's anger had a warmth and humanity to it, Finley's was raw and scalding. Even when she spoke in her own gentle voice and chatted with the audience, she was not easy to like. Opinions were divided — Blake Brooker being among the ones who didn't care much for the show.

However, Michael Green and Rodeo producer Grant Burns weren't complaining. The entire main floor of the concert hall was packed. "It was a huge success," says Green. "Nine hundred people came to see her. Although, by the end of the show half the people had left." Burns says it did great things for the Rodeo's reputation. "The Canada Council were blown away that we could get nine hundred people out to see Karen Finley. Nobody believed we could make Karen Finley work in Calgary. I think it gave Michael credibility afterwards [when he was looking to attract artists to the festival]."

Finley herself remembers the trip to Calgary as a happy experience. The supposed enemy of American family values brought along an entourage that included her mother, her husband, and Violet, her eighteen-month-old daughter. "I remember it was the first time my daughter watched *Sesame Street* on television," she says.

"I liked the people of Calgary," she adds, "and I loved the severity of the landscape in winter, the beauty of it. It's a painter's landscape, white on white." In the wake of the NEA controversy, there were places where Karen Finley was no longer welcome and to have her to your festival was to take a stance in the dispute. "I felt honoured to be invited to Calgary," she says. "I felt I was being supported in my fight for the Fifth Amendment and freedom of speech. And I thought the audience was distinguished and understood my work, that I was respected and they got what I was talking about." Her battle was not irrelevant in Alberta, where politicians such as Kowalski had begun to spend their spare time raging against the funding of gay and lesbian art. In May 1994, eight months before Finley came to town, Gary Mar, the mild-mannered Alberta cabinet minister in charge of culture, was suggesting that the government might withhold grants to works that "offend the sensibilities of the community standards."

Whether or not the Calgarians who went to see Finley were making a statement, the surprising turnout encouraged the Centre for Performing Arts to continue its partnership with One Yellow Rabbit. For the next three Rodeos, OYR programmed one big act in one big venue to serve as the centrepiece of each festival. In 1996, it was Michel Lemieux and Victor Pilon's ambitious *Grand hôtel des étrangers*, a high-tech production using 3-D projections to create a hotel full of ghosts, which played in the Jack Singer. In 1997, the brilliant theatre-dance troupe Carbone 14 brought leader Gilles Maheu's latest work, *Les Âmes mortes* — a more successful treatment of the same idea without all the technical wizardry — to the Max Bell Theatre. In 1998, the Max Bell was used again for the Crow's Theatre tour of Lee MacDougall's gritty crime comedy *High Life*, starring Tony Award winner Brent Carver as a sickly morphine addict. None of the shows recouped their costs.

To some extent, the Rodeo was elbowing its way into the big leagues as a presenter, backed by the Centre, even though it didn't yet have the audience to justify it. Penny Arcade had marvelled that the Rabbits sold the avant-garde to Calgarians as if it were popular commercial fare, but the move into the larger venues stretched that illusion. "The Centre lost a fortune bringing in, combined, Karen Finley, Lemieux, Carbone 14, and *High Life*," says Green. One Yellow Rabbit dropped the Rodeo's big act/big venue format in 1999, but resumed it the next year with a new partner — local dance presenters Dancers' Studio West. Together, the pair imported top Quebec troupes La La La Human Steps and Compagnie Marie Chouinard, in 2000 and 2001 respectively. The big turnout and rapturous response for Chouinard's solo retrospective, which played two nights in the Max Bell, suggested that uniting the city's theatre and dance audiences was the way to go. (Finley, meanwhile, has since made two return visits to the Rodeo, in 1998 and 2003, performing her works *The American Chestnut* and *The Distribution of Empathy*, respectively, in the Rabbits' own theatre.)

If the Rodeo was expanding a step ahead of its audience, it was still amazing how far it had gone in nine years — from thirty-five people in a converted office in 1987 to nine hundred people in an elegant concert hall in 1995. The latter year would also be the last one in which the Rodeo and the Rabbits inhabited their tiny black box on the +15. They were a force that refused to be contained any longer. It was time to bust out.

## The Secret Theatre Gets Big

There was nowhere to go but down. Literally. Tear out the floor and take over the conference room directly under the theatre. In 1994, OYR approached Doug Lauchlan, the crinkly faced boss of the Centre for Performing Arts, and explained its need for more elbow room. The Rodeo was growing, the Rabbits had packed the Uptown with *Ilsa* the year before, and they were cramming more than the legal limit into the Secret Theatre for some shows (okay, maybe they didn't tell him *that*). Lauchlan thought it was a good idea. The proposal was approved by the

Centre's board of directors and architect Mark Chambers was hired
to design an elongated theatre, incorporating both the original Secret
Theatre and the downstairs meeting room. The result would more than
double both the height and capacity of the space. Before, the ceiling
had been a mere eight feet above the stage; now the Rabbits would
have to acquire some extension ladders, because the lighting grid was
twenty feet above them. The 30 x 31 foot playing space (non-elevated,
as before) was surrounded on three sides by risers at the main level
and on two sides by a balcony at the upper storey, allowing for a total of
162 seats. Thanks to the expanded area, the main floor could now
accommodate a small bar — the Future Cocktail Lounge (the sign had
indeed been an omen). The balcony — the remains of the original
theatre — also housed the technicians' booth and the dressing rooms,
accessed by a spiral staircase. The overall look was a black box with
attitude — basic without being stark, raw without looking rough. The
project was planned as a joint venture, with the Centre providing the
room, the Rabbits contributing the equipment, and the two splitting
the renovation costs.

Sure, the Rabbits had been doing well, but Grant Burns remembers the expansion as a risk taken partly out of frustration. "When we
developed the Big Secret Theatre, we kind of went out on a limb," he
says. "I was getting to a point with the company where my thinking was:
I'm totally fried, I'm working my ass off, and we're not getting anywhere. I feel like I'm pissing in a windstorm. I can't compete with [the
big theatre companies in town]. So around that time I said 'Okay, we
need a bigger theatre, a bigger potential audience, we need to spend
more money. It's either go big or go home.'" It was a gamble that meant
the company would have to go into debt to pay its share of the renovations while its lease with the Centre would be doubled from $1,500 to
$3,000 a month. To compensate, the Rabbits would be able to rent the
larger venue to more users and, besides, it now had an additional source
of revenue.

During its tours to the UK, the troupe had seen how small British
theatres were able to subsidize their work with food and beverage sales.

In particular, the Traverse in Edinburgh and the Tron in Glasgow had both become upscale variants on the pub theatre, with trendy bars from which they derived a healthy income. The Future Cocktail Lounge could do the same for the Rabbits — as Burns realized. During the Big Secret Theatre's first year, the Centre insisted on running the bar, but Burns kept agitating to take it over. "At the end of the year," he recalls, "they looked at it and said that they didn't make any money from it. I was in their face about it, a lot. I wanted it. So they said 'Fine. Take it.'" Michael Green's boyhood buddy, John Dunn, who'd had seventeen years of experience in the restaurant business, was hired to oversee it. "In the first year, we netted $10,000 from the bar operation," says Burns. "It offset the increase in our rent. And that was just year one." The Rabbits, inveterate party animals, could now throw big fundraising bashes in their own theatre. They could also revive a passion for cabaret that stretched back to the *Café Theatre* days.

To open the first season in the new digs, Blake Brooker and David Rhymer teamed up again to write the satirical *Conniption Cabaret,* a cranky jab at, in Brooker's words, "the irritating, arrogant, and embarrassing provincial government that existed at that point." As Ralph Klein's Tories began hacking away at health, education, and social services budgets, Brooker and Rhymer's lyrics summed up the mood of the time: "All we've built is under the knife." Yet the revue was very much a hit-and-miss affair, well-aimed barbs alternating with smugness and self-pity. It could be that, as Burns's remarks suggest, the Rabbits were operating in overdrive at the time. Penny Arcade says she noticed a change when she arrived two months later for the first Rodeo in the Big Secret Theatre. "I could see that, with the demands of running a company, touring, and putting on a yearly festival, the strain was starting to show."

The Big Secret, however, was an audience winner, with a friendly, informal ambience that encouraged patrons to take their drinks to their seats — an unheard-of thing in the Centre's other venues at the time. The only drawback was a back-row sightline problem on the main floor due to the overhanging balcony above. That wouldn't stop the Rabbits from eventually using the full two-storey height of the playing area for such shows as *Radioheaded* (in which Denise Clarke scaled the back wall like a superhero) and *Featherland* (in which dancer Christine Bandelow perched on its upper ledge as a golden eagle). Neil Cadger, who had been away from Calgary and OYR for years, living and working in Antwerp and Paris, visited the space for the first time in 2001 and was very impressed. "It's one of the best theatres I know, including European theatres," he says, "because it's so welcoming and very versatile. It's kind of in-your-face because it really has no upstage area. It has a great popular cabaret feel to it as well as being a place for serious theatre art." Mark Chambers won an award of excellence from the Alberta Association of Architects for his design.

*Conniption Cabaret* introduced more than just a new theatre to One Yellow Rabbit's audiences. It also introduced Elizabeth Stepkowski, the newest member of the ensemble. Stepkowski was already a familiar face to theatregoers in Calgary and Edmonton, often seen on the big stages in big musicals such as *Anne of Green Gables* and *Evita* (Theatre Calgary) and *Oliver!* and *Man of La Mancha* (Edmonton's Citadel). A trained singer with a drama degree from the U of C, she had just come off a four-year stint with Robin Phillips's acting stable at the Citadel when the Rabbits asked her to replace actor Lindsay Burns for a 1995 tour to Scotland. Her vocal skills made her a real asset as the troupe began exploring cabaret and musical theatre anew. Stepkowski says it was "a really big difference" going from Phillips's auteur style of directing to OYR's organic creative process. "I loved Robin Phillips and I learned tons from him," she says, "but he's extremely specific, he tells you how to move and when to move, how to say it, how to do it, every step of the way. The Rabbits have an incredible trust and faith that you as the artist will get there however you need to. Blake doesn't step on your toes as a director or make your role for you. He's only there to help you and guide you." Stepkowski would remain with OYR for the next five years.

When the Rabbits had finished their conniption fit, it was time to celebrate the tenth anniversary of the High Performance Rodeo. The occasion was marked by return visits from Rodeo sweethearts Penny Arcade, Daniel MacIvor, and Doug Curtis. All were in top form. This time out, Ms. Penny told *True Stories,* her own "Walk on the Wild Side" of New York's artistic and social fringe, in which she impersonated such real-life characters as forgotten Warhol superstar Andrea Whips and the hilariously hoity-toity drag queen Dame Margot Howard-Howard. MacIvor, meanwhile, embodied an incorrigible liar, stringing us along with one entertaining bullshit story after another, in *Here Lies Henry.* Curtis, on the other hand, simply convinced us he'd been tormented by a ghost in the spooky but thought-provoking *Paranormal.*

Michael Green once again found a way to be part of the festival while organizing it at the same time. His gleefully perverse Grand Guignol homage, *Zertrummerung,* was produced by the Art Ranch, a company started by aspiring director and playwright Ken Cameron, who would soon be joining the OYR backstage team.

At this point, one may wonder what the other Rabbits were doing every year come Rodeo time. Early on, Andy Curtis was quick to take advantage of the showcase, creating larky pieces with various collaborators, including musician/actor Peter Moller, dancer Nicole Mion, and his comic soulmate in Edmonton, the lovably geeky Neil Grahn of Three Dead Trolls in a Baggie. He also did some of his first directing at the Rodeo, guiding the ever-evolving monologues of Doug Curtis (no relation) starting with *The Cruise* in 1993. Blake Brooker and Denise Clarke, however, remained somewhat aloof from the festival in its first decade. Behind the scenes, there had been an ongoing dispute between Brooker and Green, as co-artistic directors, over the importance of the Rodeo. "I used to have to convince Blake that it was a legitimate activity, a part of the company," says Grant Burns. The fact that it had to be paid for out of OYR's operating budget was a sore point. Brooker didn't like that, says Green. "I had to make sure, to the best of my ability, that the festival didn't cost One Yellow Rabbit any money. But of course it almost always did, a little bit. That's one of the reasons why [as curator] I never took any money myself for years and years." There was also tension over the quality of some of the Rodeo acts in the start-up years.

Burns recalls that one year Brooker and Clarke decided to get involved in the programming after seeing a festival show that, in Burns's words, "they thought to be a piece of shit. There used to be meetings about who's coming to the Rodeo, that Blake would sit in on, and he'd say 'Did you see it? Can I see the tape? Let me see the material.'" With the opening of the Big Secret Theatre, however, Brooker was finally ready to acknowledge the Rodeo's significance. As of 1997, One Yellow Rabbit would become not just a presenter, but also one of the companies performing at the Rodeo. And Clarke and Brooker would also bring personal projects to the festival, such as Clarke's *Radioheaded* and *Blake with an Exclamation Mark,* Brooker's first solo show.

With the new theatre came a greater investment in the festival and, consequently, a greater payoff. Burns says the turning point was the '97 Rodeo, where the headliner was the Kids in the Hall's Bruce McCulloch. "We were attaching ourselves to a star, and we had a bigger theatre, so we decided to spend more money on marketing — distributing our program throughout the city." The marketing budget, which had been about $2,000 in the past, was more than tripled. The result was visible. A serpent of queuing Calgarians undulated through the Big Secret lobby, eager to see the hometown boy-turned-cult TV and film star, back to premiere a new one-man show called *Slightly Bigger Cities.* Thanks to McCulloch, and a generally strong festival that year, the Rodeo's box office also tripled. In terms of revenue, says Burns, the Rodeo suddenly "went from being like a pretty good Rabbit show to bigger than any Rabbit show."

After bouncing about on the calendar in its first nine years, the Rodeo finally settled into the January time slot, coming straight out of the chute after New Year's and dovetailing with the city's other, larger theatre festival, playRites at Alberta Theatre Projects. Burns says he and Green chose January because, at the time, there was no competition. "PlayRites didn't start till February. Nothing happened in the city in January. So even though it was potentially fucking freezing, the fact of the matter was, we were the only game in town." The two festivals turned Calgary at its coldest into a national hotspot for theatrical activity. Suddenly, it felt as if most of the country's theatre community was either rehearsing or performing in the Calgary Centre for Performing Arts. You never knew when you might bump into director Paul Thompson in an elevator, say, or find Brent Carver quaffing a brew in the Future Cocktail Lounge.

In 1993, the year that Penny Arcade first set the Rodeo on its ear, the then-record attendance at the festival was 1,350. By 2002, it was over 7,500. In 1993, there had been twelve acts; in 2002, double that. The budget, $40,000 in the Year of Our Penny, had grown to $200,000. Michael Green, who once parcelled out $300 "commissions" to get local artists to create stuff for the Rodeo, had a budget of $23,000 in 2001 to commission actor/playwright Lyle Victor Albert's *Jumpin' Jack*. The man who begged local people to be in his festival now travels to Ireland, Israel, Hungary, and other countries to suss out potential guests. For a long time, it wasn't easy being an international avant-garde festival in the middle of the Canadian prairies, with a shoestring budget and no major corporate sponsor. (playRites, a mainstream festival of new Canadian plays, has a history of being underwritten by oil and gas giants.) To bring in acts, Green had to find other presenters to make the trip worthwhile. In recent years it has gotten easier, as other small alternative festivals continue to sprout up. Green says he sees a circuit forming across the country: da da kamera, the company formed by Daniel MacIvor and director Daniel Brooks, with its Six Stages in Toronto; Workshop West with its KaBoom Performance Theatre Series in Edmonton; Théâtre la Chapelle's Vasistas in Montreal. "These are festivals that have decided to hitch their wagon to the same star as I have."

Green admits that for a long time he bluffed his way into presenters' and producers' circles, pretending the Rodeo was bigger and better known than it was. "There are incidents that still make my face burn when I think of what I did and said. But it was in order to make it seem that we had already arrived. Certainly we felt like we had in our own hometown." Today, he doesn't need to bullshit. "The Rodeo is formidable at this point," he says. "I don't think it was a major festival in Canada until 1998. It'll never be as big as those festivals in central

Canada, but it's important." Those festivals he refers to aren't Stratford and Shaw, of course, but the biennial World Stage in Toronto and Festival de théâtre des Amériques in Montreal — major international showcases he can't dream of competing with, certainly not without a corporate angel. "I suspect the Rodeo will always remain a fiercely independent voice of individualism," he says. "And that's great. I love that."

The Rodeo roundup in recent years has mixed veteran artists, from Canadian actor/playwright Linda Griffiths to legendary British loony Ken Campbell, with exciting new talent both from Canada (actor/playwright Michael Healey, protean comic actor Diane Flacks) and abroad (Israel's Theatre Clipa, Europe's Spymonkey). It also manages to lasso the occasional star — such as Philip Glass in 2003. Overall the artistic standard is high, but the days of encountering the inept and embarrassing have yet to pass. It may have drove Burns crazy and made Brooker want to exercise quality control, but Green still clings to the Rodeo's ragged roots by allowing a few amateur and amateurish acts into the festival every year. Some of them have been herded into special areas — such as the 10-Minute Play Festival, a challenge to little theatre groups to create and perform a short work within twenty-four hours — but the odd one escapes into the general program. "I like to think we haven't ever forgotten the origins or, indeed, in many ways the purpose of the festival," Green says.

It may be that he remembers when One Yellow Rabbit was also young and struggling. Or it may be that he just loves the thrill of discovery. Says ex-Rabbit and ex-wife Jan Stirling: "There's something about his creation of [the festival] that goes back to what he brought to the company in the first instance, which was a real capacity to create opportunity for people to come together and try new things. The High Performance Rodeo has been just another way of doing that, on a large scale."

For audiences, the festival has knocked down the barriers between art forms. It's still the place where you see rock musicians doing theatre, actors singing song cycles, dancers acting. Often, it's difficult to define exactly what you're watching. Neil Murray, director of Scotland's Tron Theatre, finds it all "very exciting. The shows aren't necessarily dance or aren't necessarily theatre. In Glasgow, we've had a festival of contemporary dance which really struggles because the audience and the work get pigeonholed, nobody takes the risk to come out and see it. Whereas the Rodeo seems to cross through those boundaries."

What makes the Rodeo special, in Penny Arcade's view, is that it is run by artists to support other artists. "That's pretty rare," she says. "Artists tend to be competitive and jealous, they're not fundamentally well-balanced people. Rarely do you see artists going out of their way to promote people who are unknown to their audiences. I was very impressed and moved by that." She quotes the avant-garde poet and publisher Charles Henri Ford, who introduced America to European artists during the 1940s in his influential *View* magazine. "When I asked him why he did that, promoting other artists, he said to me 'I wasn't promoting other artists! I was *exercising my taste.*' I think that's what Michael Green and One Yellow Rabbit are doing with the Rodeo."

# 7. On Tour I – 1991-2000

"Touring can make you crazy, ladies and gentlemen."
— FRANK ZAPPA, 200 MOTELS

*August 2000 — One Yellow Rabbit arrived in muggy Glasgow today with all four actors, director, assistant director, luggage, and some 320 kilograms worth of sets, costumes, and properties for two different productions. But a few items are missing — most crucially, composer Richard McDowell's synthesizers. It's one of those classic airline fuck-ups.*

*Now tour manager Ewan McLaren is trying to chase down the equipment via a rented mobile phone as he moves rapidly in and out of the Tron Theatre's bar, pausing only to roll the occasional cigarette with licorice-flavoured rolling papers. "Very '60s psychedelic," laughs Richard McDowell when he sees them. Very appropriate, too, given the Rabbits have come to the Tron with* Doing Leonard Cohen, *their homage to the poetry and prose of one of Canada's great '60s songwriters. The show's undoubted highlight is a second-act dramatization of Cohen's 1966 novel* Beautiful Losers, *a sex-and-drug-drenched slice of hippie-era excess.*

*Neil Murray, the Tron's administrative director, enters the bar. A small, dark, bearded man, he neither looks nor sounds Scottish. Indeed, as we sit down for a drink, he explains that he's originally from Newport in South Wales and studied business in Manchester before getting turned on to theatre after seeing the London premiere of Dario Fo's* Accidental Death of an Anarchist. *He has been in Scotland now for thirteen years — the last four at the Tron. His theatre, which includes a 246-seat auditorium, a restaurant, and the bar, dwells within the walls of an eighteenth-century kirk, whose steeple still serves as a landmark. "It was built in 1795 by [Glasgow architect] James Adam," explains Murray, "and it's been used as a theatre by the Tron since 1981." The name refers to a tron, or public weigh beam. For centuries, the building sat at the heart of Glasgow's trade district, where goods were weighed and taxed. Today, as a Glasgow theatre, it's engaged in another kind of balancing act. Artistically, it teeters between the kind of popular fare found at the more famous Citizens' Theatre, located in the legendary Gorbals, and the experimental programming of Tramway, a theatre established in 1989 in a converted railway tram-shed. Murray says the Tron "sits uneasily at times" on the Glasgow scene. "We're often thought of as an avant-garde venue but a lot of the work we do appeals to quite a mainstream audience." It was the Tron that introduced Scottish audiences to Quebec playwright Michel Tremblay back in 1989, via a translation of* Les Belles Soeurs *in Glaswegian dialect that proved a smash hit. The success of that and subsequent Tremblay productions in Scotland helped stimulate a British interest in Canadian playwriting that the Rabbits, among others, have benefited from.*

*Murray says* Doing Leonard Cohen, *which will run 8 to 12 August, is something of an experiment for the Tron — a summer show running head-to-head with the first week of the Edinburgh Festival Fringe. However, like Calgary and Edmonton, Glasgow and Edinburgh are rival cities and Glaswegians tend to turn up their noses at the mammoth festival just an hour's train ride away. The name "Leonard Cohen" should help sell tickets, too. "Leonard Cohen is very well known in the UK," Murray says. "*I'm Your Man *is still a hugely popular record over here, and the [tribute] collection* I'm Your Fan, *which featured a lot of British artists. But his poetry and novels are not as familiar, which is what intrigued me about the Rabbits' piece when I first saw it in Philadelphia. And they do it with a level of wit that's very refreshing."*

*Murray has been a One Yellow Rabbit fan since 1994, when the company brought Brad Fraser's* The Ugly Man *to the Tron. "I thought it was wonderful. It didn't sell out at the time, but it's one of those shows that people remember and still talk about here."*

The Rabbits have been touring since day one. That trip to the inaugural Edmonton Fringe with their inaugural production, *Leonardo's Last Supper,* began a pattern that has found them on the road every season since. The early years were filled with tours to schools and community halls in Calgary and round the province, as well as the annual August trek to Edmonton. Vancouver's Expo '86 took the troupe outside Alberta for the first time, and the *Changing Bodies* and *Tears of a Dinosaur* projects in 1988 were the first forays into the east, with engagements in Toronto, Montreal, and Quebec City. However, it was with its first international tour, a tough, fun, eye-opening slog through England, Scotland, and Ireland, with a side jaunt to Belgium, that One Yellow Rabbit began to get a real sense of where it stood in the wider world of experimental theatre.

The year was 1991 and the show was *The Erotic Irony of Old Glory.* This was Denise Clarke's first major work for the troupe and, in its initial form, had been more of a guest shot than a bona fide Rabbit production. Ever since quitting the university and amicably dissolving her partnership with Anne Flynn, she'd been looking for a new way to use dance in a theatrical context. "I hated dance theatre," Clarke remembers. "I would go and see it — and I was a part of dance theatre — and I would always be uncomfortable. I don't like watching dancers who can't act doing a monologue or a poem badly. And I really don't like watching actors who can't move do choreography badly. And I was getting a bit mouthy about it, so I thought if I was going to be this adamant I'd better put my money where my mouth is and try it myself. Really take charge and do something."

To create the piece, Clarke called upon two actor friends — Neil Cadger, a Calgarian living in Amsterdam, and Toronto-based Mark Christmann, a graduate of the famed Jacques Lecoq mime school. The project began with airy intellectual concepts. Clarke wanted to do a show illustrating what German author Thomas Mann referred to as "erotic irony" — the impulse to take apart and over-analyze what we love to the point where we no longer love it. Cadger, meanwhile, had a vague idea about a piece exploring the theme of decay to be called *Old*

*Glory, New Ruin.* Then Cadger showed Clarke *A Green Coupe,* a lurid 1930s radio script by Don Becker that he'd discovered in an old anthology, and the two realized it was the dramatic backbone they were looking for. Taking a page from Pirandello, they conceived a comedy about three characters trapped in the confines of a radio melodrama, where they try desperately to derail their prewritten fates. At the time, Clarke told the *Calgary Herald*'s Kate Zimmerman that the erotic irony theme applied to the characters' self-examination as they replay their deaths every time the script is performed. Looking back on it now, Cadger admits the conceit was rather tenuous. "I think the 'erotic irony' part is a bit of a weak link," he says, laughing. "It's not really about erotic irony at all. But it was a good title, very heavy. It promised all sorts of deep meaning and the play was really just a romp."

Whatever the case, when *The Erotic Irony of Old Glory* premiered at the Secret Theatre in January 1989, it was evident that Clarke had succeeded in achieving a compelling merger of theatre and dance. Her crisp, witty choreography didn't merely enhance the radio play — a pedestrian thriller about an adulterous love triangle that ends violently — it became the characters' alternate form of expression, their real thoughts and feelings made physical, often amusingly so. As critic Mary Brennan succinctly described it in the *Glasgow Herald* two years later: "Denise Clarke ... has choreographed sly asides of gesture, giveaway phrases of body language, exuberant subtexts of frenetic footwork and convulsing limbs as a running commentary on the somewhat banal exchanges between characters" (14 June 1991). The play was a hit with audiences as well as critics. and it toured to the Edmonton Fringe, Toronto's Tarragon Theatre, and Ottawa's Canada Dance Festival. Its Toronto run won Clarke, Cadger, and Christmann a 1990 Dora Mavor Moore Award for outstanding direction. It seemed the obvious candidate for One Yellow Rabbit's first trip abroad.

Michael Green did the initial legwork. "Michael got a grant to go to Ireland and England and research venues," says Grant Burns, "and he did a great job. He met a lot of people, made a lot of connections. He gave me a bunch of scrawled notes on scraps of paper and said 'Let's try and get an international tour together.'" The tour, a six-week, eight-city affair, was planned for the spring of 1991. Neil Cadger proved unavailable, having taken a teaching job at the University of Calgary, so Green stepped in to fill his shoes. Blake Brooker had already come on board to help restage the piece after its Calgary premiere and now, with the addition of Green, *Erotic Irony* was clearly a full-fledged OYR show.

After playing an engagement in Vancouver, the Rabbits flew to Britain to open the tour in London — "which sounds great," says Burns, "but it was at the Finborough Arms, a pub theatre, upstairs. It was very much like the original Secret Theatre, maybe smaller, held about fifty, sixty people. We went in, the place was a fucking mess — dust bunnies the size of dinner plates, layers of black paint on everything, that had chipped off, a really ancient lighting board and lights. I was the tour manager and sound operator, Blake was the director and lighting operator, Michael, Denise, and Mark were the performers, and Michael also helped us with the hang [hanging lights]. We basically built this show in the Finborough Arms for a four-night run and I was doing publicity on the side, trying to talk to thirty-five London press people. I tried to get dance reviewers out and was told Baryshnikov was in town and they wouldn't be able to cover us. But we somehow still managed to get a picture in *Time Out*." From there they travelled down to Brighton and a bar called the Zap Club, where they were slotted into a performance art festival. "And then we went to Ireland and started playing pubs and churches," says Burns. They performed dates in Limerick, Listowel, and Cork and, while their prudish Catholic presenters chose to promote it as *The "Exotic" Irony of Old Glory*, the middle-aged Irish audiences seemed to love the fast and sexy show. Then they crossed back to England for a gig in Manchester.

"It was a crazy little tour," says Burns. "I tried to get us to the Chapter Arts Centre in Cardiff, Wales, which is supposed to be an amazing place, something like The Banff Centre. But they thought we were far too polished. They'd seen a tape I'd sent them. And the Rabbits have gotten a lot of that over the years when we've been to Britain. We're not polished enough for the big London theatres and not coming from the right place in terms of creation and process for a place like the Chapter Arts Centre." There were no such qualms when they briefly crossed the Channel to play the Vooruit Centrum in Gent, Belgium, where they found themselves in front of a large and appreciative audience.

In retrospect, however, the most valuable connection made during that first European visit was with Edinburgh's Traverse Theatre, their final stop. The theatre, a British bastion of new writing, was about to go Canada-mad under artistic director Ian Brown. And both the *Glasgow Herald* and the *Scotsman*, Scotland's major dailies, gave *Erotic Irony* glowing reviews.

*8 August 2000* — Doing Leonard Cohen *opens in an hour and, as they say, it's all right on the night. Richard McDowell's stray synthesizers, located in London, arrived today, and now a grinning Neil Murray reports that the performance is sold out. Casually sipping white wine in the Tron bar, he admits that he wasn't sure what to expect. "When we announced we were going to do it we thought we'd get all the young hipsters coming in for tickets, all the Belle and Sebastian fans. Instead, it's been people in their mid- to late-fifties, the ones who come to see jazz gigs, saying 'When is this show about Leonard Cohen?'"*

*One of the Tron's black-clad bartenders runs up to consult Murray. "How do we make this wee drink?" he asks, referring to the Red Needle, Cohen's signature cocktail, which is being advertised at the bar. Murray shrugs his shoulders. "You'd better ask Blake." Brooker, expert on all things Cohen, is nearby and provides the recipe: tequila, cranberry juice, lots of crushed ice, and a squeeze of fresh lemon. Cohen describes the Red Needle in his prose poem "End of My Life in Art," where he also mentions serving one to a Buddhist monk. The Rabbits have been serving it to theatregoers ever since* Doing Leonard Cohen *premiered in Calgary in 1997, when the drink made a simultaneous debut at the Future Cocktail Lounge.*

*Murray knocks back his wine, I finish my Guinness, and we exit into the theatre. Seeking my seat in the steeply raked auditorium, I see that he is right: most of the audience is middle-aged, well-dressed, and probably, once*

*upon a time, listened moodily to "Suzanne" and "Sisters of Mercy" over
a bottle of cheap red wine in a squalid student bedsit with a coin-fed
gas meter.*

*The Rabbits are all Cohen fans, but this production was instigated
by Michael Green, who suggested an adaptation of* Beautiful Losers. *The
1966 novel, Cohen's second, is about a troubled Montreal Jewish scholar
who plunges into an obsession with Catherine Tekakwitha, a seventeenth-
century Iroquois virgin and saint, as a means of escaping the messy suicide
of his Aboriginal wife and the tormenting revelation that she bedded down
with his deceased best friend. Maddeningly uneven, the book at its worst is
full of purple-tinged erotic prose in the D. H. Lawrence vein and long,
barely readable ramblings. Its saving grace is a wild, black sense of humour
and a fascination with profane sex that's at least as strong as its hymns to
the sacred Lawrentian brand. The escapades with the narrator's cuckold-
ing pal F., a polymorphously perverse radical who shoots up Lourdes
water, blows up statues, and crashes his sports car while masturbating to
intensify an orgasm, are among Cohen's most hilarious and inspired feats
of prose. According to his biographer, Ira B. Nadel, Cohen wrote most of
the novel at his Greek retreat on the island of Hydra, on a regimen of fast-
ing and amphetamines — which may help explain its feverish, chimerical
qualities. Brooker tackled the adaptation and soon realized that chunks of
the book simply couldn't be dramatized. "Some of it resisted stage treatment so intensely I couldn't use it," he recalls. "We didn't even get into the
third section of the book, it would have been so hard to do." Then Denise
Clarke suggested they complement it with a reading of Cohen's poetry.
The result was a two-act show, the first consisting of forty-six poems
culled from six of Cohen's poetry collections, the second offering a con-
densed version of the novel, which skilfully retrieved its best scenes from
the morass of overwriting.*

*The production premiered in Calgary in February 1997. Kate Taylor,
theatre critic of the Toronto-based* Globe and Mail, *happened to be in
town, caught the show, and filed a rave. She was entranced by Clarke's
choreographing of the poems and Brooker's visualization of the novel.
"The images created on stage are as hallucinatory as those of the novel's*

*stream of consciousness," she wrote (24 February 1997). "It is a glorious evocation of the text." In November 1998, OYR toured* Doing Leonard Cohen *to Toronto's Factory Theatre, where it was a smash success. Taylor reiterated her initial enthusiasm, opening her second* Globe and Mail *review (23 November 1998) with an attention-grabbing statement: "If theatre is to survive, it must produce moments only possible on stage. Enter One Yellow Rabbit, the Calgary troupe with a genius for truly live performance." But more useful from a marketing standpoint was Susan Walker's notice in the* Toronto Star *(22 November 1998), which called* Doing Leonard Cohen *"probably the dirtiest literary stage show to have been mounted since* O Calcutta *[sic]." The reviews, combined with Leonard Cohen's name, worked their magic. Toronto celebs, from TV mogul Moses Znaimer to TV journalist (and future Governor General) Adrienne Clarkson, flocked to see it, and Cohen's sister Esther travelled from New York to check it out.*

*The show already had Leonard Cohen's blessing. How that came about is a favourite Rabbit anecdote. Michael Green had sent a formal request to Cohen's LA management, asking permission to use his work, and was waiting for a reply. One day the phone rang in the Rabbits' offices and an assistant picked it up. "Hey, Grant," he called to general manager Grant Burns, "some joker's on the line saying he's Leonard Cohen and he wants to talk to you." "Yeah, sure," said Burns, assuming it was a prank, and took the call. "How's it goin', Lenny?" he asked sarcastically. "Hello, Mr. Burns," said an unmistakable bass-baritone voice from the receiver. As Burns scrambled to regain his composure, Cohen asked what the company intended to do with his work. Burns filled him in on their plan. "Well," said Cohen amiably, "that sounds fine." Not long after, a formal letter from his management confirmed that the production could go ahead. The poet was invited to attend the Calgary premiere, but graciously declined. On opening night, however, a bouquet of a dozen yellow roses arrived at the theatre with a card. It was signed "Love, Leonard Cohen."*

*At the post-show reception in the Tron's restaurant, the Rabbit actors emerge, tired and sweaty (they don't call it "physical theatre" for nothing), and immediately begin dissecting the audience reaction. The punters certainly seemed riveted, especially during the darkly humorous* Beautiful Losers. *Still, a turtlenecked Michael Green, the show's surrogate Cohen figure, isn't sure. "They didn't laugh at the funny stuff," he grouses. "No, no," says co-star Denise Clarke, always the troupe's optimist. "I could see them out there, listening. They were hanging on every word."*

In the 1970s, the future members of One Yellow Rabbit were among the hordes of North American kids who headed to Europe, Asia, North Africa, and the Levant in search of adventure. They were the global-village hippies, wide-eyed successors to Kerouac and Cassady, equipped with little more than backpacks and sleeping bags, ready to rough it in hostels, crash with friendly strangers, wash dishes or work on kibbutzim, rent Vespas, thumb rides, or bang about in a second-hand van with a bunch of fellow thrill-seekers. It was never lonely on the road, since young people all over the Western world were doing the same thing. You got to know them better than the citizens of the countries you visited, because you shared a common purpose and a global youth culture. The lingua francas were drugs and rock 'n' roll. Kids who didn't speak the same language could bond over a hash pipe and a battered cassette of Led Zeppelin's *Houses of the Holy.* An impromptu international Jim Morrison fan club could be found gathered in Paris's Père Lechaise cemetery. In London, youth of all nations performed the solemn rite of strolling barefoot across the Beatles' Abbey Road.

Haight-Ashbury had moved sometime after the Summer of Love and taken up residence in Amsterdam, the new hippie-head mecca. But, if you weren't freaked out by the dirt and poverty of the Third World, the drugs got better and cheaper the closer you got to their source. Marrakesh. Bombay. Bangkok. It was like stepping inside the glossy photos of *National Geographic,* only more vivid and intense, the madding throngs loud and alive, and what better way to experience your first taste of opium than floating down the Chao Phraya or walking the beaches of Goa. For those with ragged copies of Hesse's *Siddhartha* or *The Autobiography of a Yogi* stuffed in their packs, there might also be spiritual enlightenment along the way.

With all these naive young tourists on the loose, Nikon cameras hanging from their necks, travellers cheques stuffed in their wallets, it was inevitable that they would attract predators. The most infamous was Charles Sobhraj, a part-Indian criminal who gave a new meaning to the term "snake charmer." Sobhraj, dubbed "the Serpent," was a con artist, thief, and killer who preyed on travellers, especially the backpacking set, by disarming them with his suave, worldly ways, then poisoning them with drugs and stealing their valuables and passports. Blake Brooker first heard about him while travelling in the South Pacific in 1979. By then, Sobhraj had left a trail of bodies in India and Thailand and had finally been caught and incarcerated after the mass poisoning of a French tour group. What made his tale especially intriguing to a young Canadian tourist was the revelation that one of Sobhraj's accomplices was from Quebec.

Marie-Andrée Leclerc was a young medical secretary from the small town of Levis who had met and been seduced by Sobhraj while on holidays. She became his unlikely partner in a year-long crime spree that ended, for her, with her arrest in 1976 on charges of conspiring to murder an Israeli tourist in the sacred Indian city of Varanasi. Her case would be Brooker's point of entry when he sat down, a decade later, to write a play about Sobhraj.

*Serpent Kills*, co-written with Jim Millan, was about the seduction of Marie-Andrée, but both playwrights also wanted to explore her experience in the greater context of the cultural fantasies that the West has about the East — and vice versa. If his victims were (to lift a line from Todd Rundgren) strung out on Eastern intrigue, Sobhraj was equally hooked on Western materialism. Born into an Indian-Vietnamese family in Saigon, he remade himself into a globe-trotting European entrepreneur, an urbane swinger, the Sort of Man Who Reads *Playboy*. His idol was that symbol of cool consumerism, James Bond. His dream was to open an international string of jewellery shops called Goldfinger's.

The resultant semi-fictional script was a dark, drug-riddled thriller, written film-style in short scenes that shuttled between Canada, India, Thailand, and Nepal. As an added cinematic touch, a soundtrack of classic '70s rock tunes was woven through the piece. The plot was based on Leclerc's story but, perhaps showing a lack of confidence in writing from a female, French viewpoint, the two male writers invented an introspective English-Canadian gang member named Gerry to serve as narrator.

Millan says they simply felt Leclerc was too passive a character. "Marie-Andrée ultimately floated along [with Sobhraj] and then she was captured. We needed somebody the audience would follow who actually made a choice in the end." Gerry befriends, then ultimately betrays, Marie, ripping off the gang and hightailing it back to Canada just before the heat closes in. As well, says Millan, Gerry "allowed us to have a fictional figure who could do the kind of philosophical rap that Blake loves to write."

Brooker and Millan had got together at the instigation of Michael Springate, an officer at the Canada Council who was a fan of both the Rabbits and Millan's little Toronto company, Crow's Theatre. "Michael said to us that we were the two most exciting companies in English Canada," recalls Millan, "and that we had to meet." Millan came out to Calgary in 1987 and got along famously with the troupe, and they began talking about a possible collaboration. "Blake told me the story of Charles Sobhraj while we were driving around in, I believe, his father's pickup truck." Millan, who had done his share of wandering in Europe, liked the idea, which would also allow them to dramatize the experiences of their generation "on the road." He did his research on Sobhraj, then he and Brooker began writing the play gradually over the next two years.

*Serpent Kills* made its debut as a co-production between One Yellow Rabbit and Crow's Theatre in the summer of 1989. Directed by Peter Hinton, it starred Damon D'Olivera as Sobhraj and Siobhan McCormick as Marie, with Denise Clarke, Guillermo Verdecchia, and Earl Pastko playing a variety of roles. Its premiere at the Tarragon Theatre Extra Space garnered great reviews, with Robert Crew of the *Toronto Star* calling it "everything theatre should be — daring, dangerous and disturbing." (Both the Rabbits and Crow's Theatre liked that line so much, they cheerfully yanked it out of context and made it a general encomium for their companies.) Brooker, however, wasn't satisfied with the result. Hinton's staging, he recalls, "was very high-concept" with a bizarre costume design by Denise Karn. "The guys in the play wore waiter jackets, Speedos, and combat boots. I never got it. I never thought it was that high, or that much of a concept." He also realized it should focus more clearly on the character of Marie, the good Catholic girl blinded by love. With Millan's blessing, he went back to the script, stripped it down, and rebuilt it as a vehicle for the One Yellow Rabbit ensemble.

The new version was presented in Calgary in the winter of 1992, with Michael Green as Sobhraj, Andy Curtis as Gerry, Denise Clarke (repeating her memorable role as a road-wise Aussie), and, as Marie, Gillian Ferrabee, a member of Montreal's avant-garde Carbone 14 dance troupe. That August, it became the second OYR show to travel to Edinburgh's Traverse and the first to play the Festival Fringe. The play was ideal fare for an international festival and, unlike many first-Fringers, OYR was making its debut in a choice venue. It was booked into the 100-seat secondary space of the Traverse's handsome new £3.4 million theatre complex next to venerable Usher Hall. The Traverse has long been at the hub of the massive Fringe, a position that virtually guarantees those all-important reviews that guide bewildered festivalgoers like flags above a crowd. Upon opening, *Serpent Kills* was nominated for one of the *Independent*'s Fringe Awards and got a thumbs-up in *The List*, the Edinburgh-Glasgow entertainment guide, which instructed readers to "cough up the seven quid and blister your hands during the curtain call."

Not everybody agreed with the critics. A prominent member of Scotland's landed gentry, the Laird of Gleneagles, who had evidently spent the previous decade or two under a rock, attended a performance and was disgusted. "In the newspapers, he condemned it as 'Fringe filth,'" recalls Jim Millan, who'd come along for the tour. "He said he would have walked out, but he was restrained by his companions, so he averted his eyes and did not look at the rest of the play." Millan was staying with Brooker and Clarke and remembers the morning phone call from the press that woke them up. A reporter told them about the laird's displeasure and asked for a comment. Brooker obliged, calmly explaining that the play's young characters and their drug-and-sex-driven lifestyle were true to life. "He was very articulate," says an admiring Millan, "considering it was first thing in the morning. Then at the end, just before the reporter hung up, Blake said 'Oh, just one thing. What exactly is a laird?'"

No one to worry about, apparently. Being dissed by an aristo was simply more publicity for the show. *Serpent Kills* played to solid houses (an average of eighty people a night), the Traverse was happy, and the buoyant Rabbits set about earning their famous Scottish reputation as hard-drinking Canucks. "They were a fun group to have at your party," says Ian Brown, who was running the Traverse at the time. "The Fringe was a good place for them." Calgary dancer Michele Moss had joined the cast for Edinburgh, replacing Ferrabee as Marie. She remembers the whole experience was rather overwhelming. As a novice actor, she was learning on her feet every night; as a festival tourist, she was trying to take in the plethora of shows in her spare time. On top of that, "there was a lot of partying. I'm a little pixie and it was hard to keep up, but I did try. I discovered raves that year." Richard McDowell, who had assembled the play's evocative period-pop score, discovered how lucky he was to be based in Canada. His impressions of Edinburgh, which he shared with the *Calgary Herald* shortly after his return, were of Scottish theatre artists with holes in their shoes, who could barely afford a pint in the pub after the show. And he couldn't wrap his head around the exorbitant price of a glass of whisky. "Scotch there is way more expensive than it is [in Canada], and you're only fifteen miles from the door of the distillery!"

Andy Curtis, also paying his first visit to Scotland, recalls a sobering moment in the midst of one of their big drunks. "We all had bottles of duty-free whisky we'd brought with us and we were passing them around one night at our flat, and smoking these big, fat hash joints. And there was this art student there, watching us try to guzzle as much whisky and suck as much hash into our lungs as possible, and at one point he called us a bunch of fucking selfish capitalists. I'd thought as a group we were sensitive to others — we took pride in that; we weren't greedy Americans, we were Canadians — but that night we'd crossed that invisible line and ruffled a feather or two. It made me think twice about our desire for speed, for instant gratification." Thereafter, he learned the mellow Scottish method of making one spliff last for hours.

*Postscript* — Like Brooker, Jim Millan would take another kick at the serpent. He, too, felt the character of Marie needed more work — especially after meeting a woman who had become friends with Leclerc during the latter's stay in India's Tihar prison. "I developed the role based on my reading of letters that Marie-Andrée wrote to her," he says. Millan staged *his* revised version of *Serpent Kills* at Ottawa's National Arts Centre in 1994, this time with Earl Pastko as Sobhraj. The text was published the same year and has since been produced by other companies. For a time there was also talk of doing a film version. "Atom Egoyan was a huge fan of the show and there were other people interested in it," says Millan, but nothing came to fruition. "I still think there's a good movie in there yet."

*9 August 2000 — Blake Brooker wants to introduce me to Glasgow's notoriously greasy gastronomy.*

*The city is cosmopolitan enough that we could easily find a savoury panini or a fragrant rogan josh for our lunch, but Brooker's having none of it. He leads us to a tiny, grubby, old-fashioned chip shop on the edge of Glasgow's working-class East End, an establishment purportedly famous for its "fish teas."*

*"When I first came here, I thought maybe they had some weird way of serving fish, dipping it in the tea," he admits with a laugh. Tea time is one British custom that never caught on in Canada. Anxious that I should have the full experience of Glaswegian fare, he even urges me to douse my chips with a bottle of something dubiously dubbed "brown sauce."*

*If Brooker knows his brown sauce and fish teas now, it's because this summer marks the fourth time One Yellow Rabbit has performed in Glasgow, and the seventh time it has played the Edinburgh Fringe. The Rabbits have become regulars at the Traverse Theatre, taking a new play to its Fringe season every couple of years. This time they'll be doing their English-language production of Daniel Danis's* Le Chant du Dire-Dire, *retitled* Thunderstruck, *which premiered in Calgary in 1999. The Traverse had a big hit a few years ago with Danis's* Stone and Ashes *and the last time the Rabbits visited there, in 1998, they won a* Scotsman *Fringe First Award for their production of John Murrell's* Death in New Orleans — *so the combination of Danis and OYR was clearly irresistible.*

*Brooker explains why the Rabbits keep coming back to the Traverse and the Tron. "In our early attempts at touring, we discovered it's not enough to just go some place, it has to be the* right *place for a successful tour. Our definition of success is that whatever we're doing is appropriate for where we are."*

*Aside from showcasing its own creations, the company has become an unofficial ambassador of new Canadian playwriting at the Traverse, bringing Scottish audiences the latest works of Edmonton's Brad Fraser, Calgary's Murrell, and now Danis, one of the most original playwrights to emerge from Quebec in recent years. Brooker and Denise Clarke first encountered* Thunderstruck *when Linda Gaboriau's translation was read at The Banff Centre's playwriting colony in 1997. Both were attracted to Danis's poetic, dreamlike writing, which reminded Clarke of the novelist Cormac McCarthy. And, like McCarthy, Danis has a taste for rural settings and shocking violence.* Thunderstruck *is a freakish family chronicle about the Lastings, three bumpkin brothers and their kid sister, who are orphaned after a thunderbolt of biblical proportions slays their parents. Naomi, the sister, is also skewered by the lightning, which endows her with an ethereal voice, leading her to seek her fortune as a country singer. Later, when she is deposited, comatose, on the Lastings' doorstep, her siblings try to nurse her while keeping the curious community at bay. However, word gets out that Naomi now glows in the dark, the gawkers and media hordes descend, and the play ends in a climax at once bloody and transcendent.*

*Danis was excited when One Yellow Rabbit decided to do his play. "I think it's a great company," he told me during an interview for the* Calgary Herald *(23 February 1999). "They have a very physical, comic style which fits very well with my writing." However, he had some reservations after seeing the production in Calgary, taking exception to the more grotesque and exaggerated aspects of the staging. "It wasn't exactly as he'd imagined it," says Brooker. Consequently, the troupe has toned it down for Edinburgh, making the Lasting boys a little less bizarre. Most noticeably Michael Green, who plays oldest brother Rock, will be abandoning his hunchback and horn-rimmed glasses.*

*At the same time, OYR was determined to put its own stamp on the play. "We weren't going to do it faux-Quebec backwoods," says Brooker. "The characters are wearing Albertan work greens. Go out into the Alberta countryside and you'll see farmers wearing the same clothes. And the actors are using rural Alberta accents. We can feel these brothers in our western souls, as it were."*

*What will the Edinburgh audiences make of it? Tough to say.*

*As we finish our mugs of tea, Brooker adds that one of the side benefits of touring is that it keeps the Rabbits "sharp." This tour especially, where the ensemble is performing two very different shows, both with dense, poetic texts. "Very few members of the public understand what a difficult undertaking that is for the actors, what kind of energy level and concentration they have to have. Of course," he laughs, "you wouldn't know from last night's party. We were letting off a little steam, drinking a few drinks. But rehearsals for* Thunderstruck *start tomorrow afternoon and we'll still be doing* Cohen *at night."*

If the Rabbits believe in a project, a certain bloody-mindedness sets in, which at times has clashed with the harsh realization that what they've created won't sell. There remains a cloud of frustration over two of their favourite works, *Alien Bait* and *Permission*, which for various possible reasons — timing, title, subject matter — have never done well at home or on tour.

*Alien Bait* was born out of one of Michael Green's stranger obsessions.

For years, nobody discussed it publicly, but Green was — psst! — a UFO freak. It all started innocently enough, as these things do. During one of his frequent stays in Edmonton, a bored Green began reading someone's copy of *Communion* by Whitley Strieber — the controversial 1987 best-seller in which Strieber, author of such horror novels as *The Wolfen* and *The Hunger,* claimed to have been abducted by strange beings with grey skins and almond eyes, who stuck needles in his brain and probes in his rectum. The writer's compelling argument that something is "out there," backed by the corroborating experiences of other alleged abductees, got Green hooked. Not one to do anything by halves, he began to seek out and devour other literature on the paranormal, attend UFO conferences — and pester his partners with the idea of staging a play about it all. At first they ignored him. "He kept saying 'Everybody's got to read *Communion!* You've got to read this book!'" recalls Denise Clarke. "And I was thinking: Get lost. I'm not the least bit interested in that phenomenon. Finally, I read the book just to sort of shut him up." Eventually, Green wore them down. They agreed to look at his stack of research, from reputable scientific papers to sensational pulp magazines, and suss out its dramatic potential. They listened to tapes of people recounting their too-close encounters under hypnosis. They began to get a sense of real loneliness and agony, whatever its cause may be. Then, with trusty pencil in hand, Blake Brooker proceeded to shape their impressions into a gripping piece of theatre.

Taking off from Green's experiences, *Alien Bait* was set at a UFO symposium, where a panel of egghead experts try to explain away the supposed visitations by extraterrestrials while the victims of those visitations, who've come looking for answers, are instead forced to turn to one another for support. As with his Jim Keegstra in *Ilsa, Queen of the Nazi Love Camp,* Brooker brought a disarming empathy to these loners, losers, and misfits who've become convinced that aliens have planted mechanisms in their nasal cavities or violated their genitalia. But unlike the infamous Mr. Keegstra, the "alien bait" are never held up to ridicule. With a respect stemming partly from Green's own convictions, they are treated as victims of an unidentified trauma that the scientists and psychiatrists are too quick to dismiss. As one frustrated panellist puts it pointedly: "In my day, we learned science is the investigation of the unexplained, not the explanation for the uninvestigated."

Brooker's writing had never been so poignant, and the ensemble complemented it with finely honed performances. Green, in particular, gave a deeply felt portrayal of a man in a state of excruciating distress. The actors (Green, Clarke, Andy Curtis, and Lindsay Burns) doubled as both the troubled victims and the panel of bickering pros, the latter providing the comic ballast to keep the play from tipping too far into the dark. Still, it was a creepy and at times harrowing work, staged with spine-tingling sci-fi effects including an otherworldly score by Richard McDowell and a phantasmagoria of visuals by Brad Struble, a designer of planetarium shows.

There are disadvantages to being a few steps ahead of popular culture. Chris Carter's *The X-Files* had made its TV debut just a year prior to *Alien Bait*'s premiere in the fall of 1994, but had yet to move into the forefront of public consciousness. If it had, perhaps the Rabbits' show would have drawn the same audience that followed FBI agents Mulder and Scully in their earnest efforts to expose an extraterrestrial conspiracy. But the company may have also shot itself in the foot by marketing the play as if it were some wacky comedy, with the catchphrase *"Alien Bait:* They'll do anything for a date." Not *quite* as powerful as "The truth is out there." In any event, despite excellent reviews, it proved a hard sell at home and abroad.

This time round, the troupe bypassed the Edinburgh Fringe and instead played the Tron and the Traverse post-festival, in the autumn of '95. Opening night in Edinburgh proved a technical nightmare. The show's intricate audiovisual element required a phalanx of slide projectors, operated along with the lighting by Ralph Christoffersen, as well as McDowell's computer-programmed synthesizers. The first thing to go was the sound. "Richard's gear went totally south that night," says Christoffersen. Due to a computer glitch, the musical intro didn't play, "so none of the actors knew what they were doing. They were sort of bumbling about on stage for those first few minutes." Finally they had to go off and start again from the top. Then it was Christoffersen's turn to screw up. "About halfway through the show, I pushed the wrong button and we wound up hammering back through a hundred slide cues, with all the projectors going at once. At the time, Michael was speaking this poetic passage about a field with a brown horse. It was probably the worst technical disaster I'd ever had on a show. And the reviews came out the next day and they were superb. The critics loved the show, nobody noticed that anything was amiss. They even mentioned the sound of the horse galloping down the cobblestone street in that scene — which was actually the clacking of all those slide projectors running backwards."

Funnily enough, Colin Donald in the *Scotsman* (21 October 1995) remarked that "*Alien Bait* is surprisingly restrained in its use of sound and slide effects." UFOs were a hot topic in Scotland at the time, where there had been an uncommon number of flying saucer sightings over the little town of Bonnybridge, but even that wasn't enough to fill the house. (*Fortean Times*, the popular British journal of strange phenomena, unhelpfully published its endorsement two months after the show had closed.)

The following year *Alien Bait* did a stint at Toronto's Factory Theatre, where again the critical reception was good — the *Toronto Star*'s Geoff Chapman called it "an eerie, thought-provoking ninety minutes of entertaining stagecraft combined with sophisticated barbs of wit" (14 March 1996) — and the audiences were small. But when it finally played Vancouver, where *The X-Files* was filmed, it didn't even get the critics' support. Renée Doruyter in the *Vancouver Province* (18 October 1996) was especially dismissive, finding the whole exercise "tedious." "After an hour," she wrote, "we were wishing we could have joined the four theatre patrons who left."

The Vancouver gig was so disheartening that OYR didn't tour *Alien Bait* again. But Michael Green felt it had succeeded, box office be damned. "It just scared the shit out of people, fucking terrified the impressionable ones," he insists. "When we did it in Vancouver I managed to organize a forum after one performance with a science fiction writer, the head of the Mutual UFO Network of Canada, and a woman

**1.** (L–R) Rodney Tuttle (not a company member), Michael Green, Kirk Miles, Nigel Scott, Jan Stirling, Gyl Raby, Marianne Moroney, George McFaul, January 1983, Ten Foot Henry's, Calgary. Photo courtesy of Michael Green

**2.** Michael Green and Jan Stirling, circa 1983. Photo courtesy of Michael Green

**3.** George McFaul, 1983, Edmonton. Photo courtesy of Michael Green

**4.** (L-R) Jan Stirling, Blake Brooker, and Kirk Miles in *Winterplay* (1983).

**5.** Kirk Miles performs at Ten Foot Henry's, 1983 or 1984. Photo courtesy of Michael Green

**6.** Company members for *Josephine the Mouse Singer* (1985). Back (L-R) Jim Leyden, Kirk Miles, Gregg Casselman, Denise Clarke, Ronnie Burkett. Centre (L-R) Brad Leavitt, Katherine Schlemmer. Front (L-R) Nicolaas Kocken, Graeme Davies, Nigel Scott, Laura Parken, Michael Green, Sheri-D Wilson, Brian Paisley (in cap).

**7.** Michael Green and James Howley in *Ides* (1985). Photo courtesy of Michael Green

**8.** Gyllian Raby, 1986. Photo by B. Checorr, Edmonton

**9.** (L-R) Denise Clarke, James Howley, Bruce Hunter, Michael Green, and Jan Stirling in *The Pageant of the Comet,* Expo '86, Vancouver.

**10.** Michael Green as Rev Kev in Blake Brooker's *Changing Bodies* (1986). Photo courtesy of Michael Green

**11.** Rev Kev (Michael Green) emerges from his tank in *Changing Bodies* (1986). Photo courtesy of Michael Green

**12.** Kevin Brooker is menaced by Michael Green in *Rembrandt Brown* (1987). Photo by Heather Elton

**13.** Michael Green as Rusty Buster in *Rusty Buster's Dimple and Wiener Review* (1987) at the First Annual High Performance Rodeo (the Secret Elevator Experimental Performance Festival). Photo by King Wilson, courtesy of Michael Green

**14.** Sheri-D Wilson with Michael Green in Wilson's *Hung, Drawn & Quartered* (1991), High Performance Rodeo. Photo courtesy of Michael Green

**15.** Penny Arcade with Calgary cast, including Gitanjali Varma to Penny's right (1993), High Performance Rodeo. Photo courtesy of Michael Green

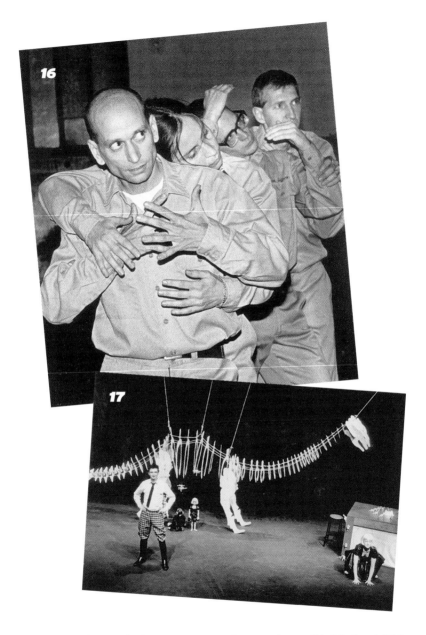

**16.** Chicago's Goat Island in *How Dear to Me the Hour When Daylight Dies* (1997), High Performance Rodeo. Photo by Nathan Mandell

**17.** Michael Green as Roy and Denise Clarke as Liz in *Tears of a Dinosaur* (1988). Photo by Trudy Taduska, courtesy of Michael Green

18. Denise Clarke and cast in *The Blind Struggle* (1988). Olympic Modern Dance Commissions, Olympic Arts Festival, Calgary. Photo courtesy of Denise Clarke

19. Me and My Shadow: Andy Curtis (left) and Michael Green in *Dreams of a Drunken Quaker* (1990).

20. Denise Clarke in *CD Dance* (1991), choreographed and performed by Denise Clarke. Photo by Trudie Lee

**21.** (L-R) Michael Green, Mark Christmann and Denise Clarke in *The Erotic Irony of Old Glory* (1991 tour). Photo by Trudie Lee

**22.** (L-R) Power struggle: OYR Co-artistic Directors Michael Green and Blake Brooker with General Manager Grant Burns, 1991.

**23.** Designer and original Rabbit Nigel Scott, 1992. Photo courtesy of Michael Green

**24.** Andy Curtis during the *Serpent Kills* tour (1992), Edinburgh. Photo courtesy of Michael Green

**25.** (L-R) Michael Green as the Colonel, Denise Clarke as Ilsa, and Andy Curtis as James Keegstra in *Ilsa, Queen of the Nazi Love Camp* (1993) by Blake Brooker. Photo by Trudie Lee

**26.** Denise Clarke (standing, left) and Blake Brooker (standing, far right) with the cast of *Under the Bed* (1993), Singapore. Photo courtesy of Denise Clarke

**27.** (L-R) Mark McKinney, actor Lenore Zann, and Michael Green during the *Ugly Man* tour (1993), Edinburgh. Photo courtesy of Michael Green

**28.** (clockwise from top) Andy Curtis, Michael Green, Lindsay Burns and Denise Clarke in *Alien Bait* (1994). Photo by Clint Adam Smyth

**29.** Front (L-R) Lindsay Burns, Mark Bellamy, Tanja Jacobs. Back: Denise Clarke in *Breeder* (1994) by Denise Clarke. Photo by Trudie Lee

**30.** The OYR Ensemble, 1995. (L-R) Andy Curtis, Denise Clarke, and Michael Green. Photo by Trudie Lee

**31.** (L-R) Andy Curtis, Michael Green, Denise Clarke and Lindsay Burns in *Permission* (original production 1995). Photo by John Hazlett

**32.** In Mexico for the *Hunger's Brides* tour (1996). (L-R) Denise Clarke, Richard McDowell, Zenaida Cruz (Zaide's mother), Paul Anderson, and Zaide Silvia Gutiérrez. Photo by Michael Green

**33.** Richard McDowell, OYR's resident composer/sound designer in action, 1996. Photo by Michael Green

**34.** Michael Green atop the bar of the Future Cocktail Lounge in the Big Secret Theatre, 1996. Photo by Rob Bitschofsky, courtesy of Michael Green

**35.** Michael Green and Denise Clarke pay homage to a poetic hero in *Doing Leonard Cohen* (1997). Photo by Jason Stang

**36.** Denise Clarke and Doug Curtis in a steamy publicity shot for *Death in New Orleans* (1998) by John Murrell. Photo by Jason Stang

**37.** Ronnie Burkett and Marionettes in a scene from *Happy* (2001). Photo by Trudie Lee

**38.** Daniel MacIvor (2000). Photo by Guntar Kravis Photography

**39.** Front (L-R) Andy Curtis, Michael Green, Denise Clarke. Back: Elizabeth Stepkowski in *Thunderstruck* (1999) by Daniel Danis. Translated by Linda Gaboriau, directed by Blake Brooker, staged by Denise Clarke. Photo by Jason Stang

**40.** Blake Brooker (1993). Photo by Mark Mennie

**41.** Denise Clarke in her solo dance/salon show, *Sign Language* (2001). Photo by Sean Dennie of Photoganda

**42.** (L-R) Michael Green, Andy Curtis, Denise Clarke, and Rita Bozi in Denise Clarke's *Featherland* (2001). Photo by Sean Dennie of Photoganda

**43.** Richard McDowell, founder of Ten Foot Henry's, nightclubbing in Prague, 2002. Photo by David van Belle

**44.** The OYR ensemble, 2002: (L-R) Michael Green, Denise Clarke, and Andy Curtis on the set of *Somalia Yellow*. Photo by Sean Dennie of Photoganda

who does a science program on CBC. It was full that night and there was a lively conversation afterwards. The president of MUFON Canada [Michael Strainic] took me aside and said he considered the show to be the most meaningful contribution to the field of UFOlogy from Canada that year."

If *Alien Bait* is Green's pet, then *Permission* is Clarke's favourite child. One of her craziest feats of choreography is hidden behind its enigmatic title — a word that means more to the Rabbits than to its audiences. The company has an uneven history of seeking — and not seeking — permission to perform other people's work. Sometimes, the outcome is good — as with Leonard Cohen's personal benediction over the phone. Sometimes it's open to interpretation — as with J. M. Coetzee's ambiguous letter to Blake Brooker. And sometimes, there's a flat refusal.

The company had no need to feel spurned when it was denied the professional rights to do a production of Edward Albee's *Who's Afraid of Virginia Woolf?* in 1995. First of all, it was a case of spectacular bad timing. Albee's star had long been on the descendant — many felt that, like the latter-day Tennessee Williams, he had entered an irreversible decline — when, in 1994, he suddenly soared to the top again, buoyed by his memory play, *Three Tall Women,* which became an off-Broadway hit and won that year's Pulitzer Prize. Suddenly, there was a rush to revive old Albee, notably the best of his past works, *Virginia Woolf* and *A Delicate Balance,* in New York and London. It was no surprise the rights were all sewn up when the Rabbits came calling. Second, Albee was notoriously protective of his plays anyway, even during his down cycle. In 1990, he refused to let the Stratford Festival mount a major revival of *A Delicate Balance* because it wouldn't also hire him to direct it. (David William, then Stratford's artistic director, likened him to "a ship in distress firing on its rescuers.") So if Stratford couldn't get Albee's permission, why should One Yellow Rabbit expect to? Grant Burns admits the company was naive. "We didn't know about all these other productions. We thought it was because we were minor players and he thought we were too bizarre and twisted."

Blake Brooker in particular took it personally. He was a fan of the 1966 film of *Virginia Woolf*, which starred Richard Burton and Elizabeth Taylor (his father had taken him to see it as a kid), and he'd envisioned the Rabbits' version as an homage to '60s cocktail culture, set in a living room filled with eleven hi-fis. When OYR's request to Albee's agent, the William Morris Agency, was turned down without an explanation, he was so miffed that he wanted to retaliate. "I'd decided to do a whole show on the idea of granting permission," he says, "which leads you right into the idea of power relationships and the concept of ownership and power over ideas." That winter, after the Rabbits wrapped their tour to Australia with *Ilsa, Queen of the Nazi Love Camp*, Brooker stayed on in Perth, rented a studio "in the back of someone's garden," and began to write. "I worked on it and worked on it and wrote a bunch of scenes, but toward the time when I had to come home with a draft, I just didn't like what I'd written. It didn't appeal to me at all. So just for the fun of it, one afternoon I went to a used bookstore in Perth and got a copy of *Who's Afraid of Virginia Woolf?* I went right through it and wrote down every stage direction. And there were so many, I began to think: Maybe there's something in this."

Inspired, he suggested to his wife that they skirt the rights problem by producing, not the spoken text, but the directions. "I said to Denise 'Let's make a movement or portion of physical vocabulary for each one of these instructions and we'll see what happens.'" What Clarke ended up creating was essentially a cross between a modern dance interpretation of Albee's play and a dumb-show re-enactment. The vitriolic exchanges between its battling, boozing couple, George and Martha, were physicalized into a comparably violent body language that ran the troupe ragged. Not entirely silent, the show also used a smattering of words and phrases — such as, "What a cluck!" "Georgie-Porgie, put-upon pie" "Booze angel" "Impotent lunkhead" — plucked from Albee's caustic text. The effect was like seeing the play performed behind a thick pane of glass, occasionally catching the odd shouted insult or a line that sounds vaguely familiar. For those who know Albee's play, it was amusing to watch the Rabbits take things just a hair's breadth from copyright infringement. Richard McDowell also got into the spirit with a teasing sound design that included a barely recognizable sound bite from the film and, where Albee's stage directions request Beethoven's Seventh Symphony, a fragment of the Fifth instead.

The ensemble fit the *Virginia Woolf* characters perfectly. Clarke, in black Liz Taylor wig, portrayed the incomparably bitchy and blowsy Martha, while Michael Green was her wilted, bitter husband, George. Andy Curtis and Lindsay Burns played their unwitting young guests, the affable Nick and his fragile wife, Honey, who drop by for a nightcap and wind up trapped in a domestic nightmare. As Brooker the naturalist neatly put it: "George and Martha are these two scorpions in a bottle and Nick and Honey are the two crickets that get drawn into it with them." Just as they had hired painter Martin Guderna for *The Land, The Animals,* the Rabbits called upon well-known Calgary artist Chris Cran to design *Permission*'s decor. Cran, whose own work is filled with wit, says he chose to underscore the humour in the piece. "I wanted the set to look as much like a cartoon as I could." He furnished George and Martha's pad with such bits of '60s kitsch as a green Naugahyde bar, a screen door embossed with pheasants, and a colourful abstract painting — all floating like isolated period relics against a black-and-red grid.

*Permission* was partly a parody, partly a genuine homage to Albee's work, and Clarke choreographed it with a zeal that went far beyond mere spoof. Green had requested a show that would really make the ensemble sweat, and Clarke obliged. Curtis says it "almost hurt. It was painful to do sometimes." In one scene, Clarke decided she wanted Curtis to sound out of breath. "She said to me 'I want to be able to hear it. And I don't want you to act it. So we're going to run around so that you are really out of breath.'" Not that Curtis is complaining. "I love that investment [in a performance], that feeling that you either totally go for it, or else you've let yourself and your colleagues down and you've ripped off the audience."

Those who saw *Permission* certainly didn't feel ripped off. But the trick was getting people in to see it. For some reason it proved box-office poison — and right at the time when the Rabbits were out to prove that they required a larger venue. The wheels were already in motion to create the Big Secret Theatre, the Centre for Performing Arts was on side, and suddenly the troupe had laid an egg. "We averaged something like twenty-five paid [customers] a night," says Grant Burns. "It was May, a bad time for a run; a stupid title; a modern dance play — product, marketing, title, time, everything went wrong. We just beat ourselves up over it, trying to figure out what happened: How could we make a play and nobody comes? We'd been at this for fifteen years."

Shortly afterwards, Lindsay Burns quit the ensemble. She'd decided to accept a role in a Theatre Calgary/Vancouver Playhouse co-production of *The Importance of Being Earnest* and, after her experiences with *Permission* and *Alien Bait,* no one could blame her. "A young, budding actor decides she'd rather play to seven hundred people than twenty people a night," says Burns with irony. "I don't know *why* she made that decision."

Still, the Rabbits refused to accept *Permission*'s failure. They performed it during a tour of Mexico in 1996, reasoning that its maximum physicality and minimal text would make it an accessible show for Spanish-speaking audiences. Then they revived it — almost defiantly — in the Big Secret Theatre in 1997 and took it to Toronto's Factory Theatre the following year with *Doing Leonard Cohen.* That only hammered home the show's lack of commercial appeal. While *Cohen* was a sold-out hit, *Permission* played to empty seats. Perhaps they should have retitled it *Doing Edward Albee* (or even better, *Screwing Edward Albee*).

Today, the Rabbits seem torn between shelving the show and trying to sell it again. "We love it," says Denise Clarke, "and we're convinced we'll keep doing it over and over." Blake Brooker isn't so sure. "We know what we like to do, but what we like to do and what people like to watch are possibly two different things at times. We have to be aware of public tastes and respect them. The public is right, not us. If they want to come, they'll come."

*12 August 2000 — Clad in sequined miniskirt and go-go boots, long blond hair caressing her shoulders, Denise Clarke's persona in* Doing Leonard Cohen *is an homage to a '60s icon: Nico, icy chanteuse of the Velvet Underground, Lou Reed's Germanic queen, and Cohen's unattainable dream. It's one of those femme fatale roles Clarke excels at, but she gets a much bigger kick running against the grain in* Thunderstruck. *In Danis's play she gives a delightfully atypical performance as Fred-James, the youngest of the three hick brothers, as eager as a puppy dog and so sensitive he swoons at the sight of blood. Like her mousy turn in* The Land, The Animals, *the part has fooled audience members expecting another Ilsa or Mata Hari. During the Calgary run, John Dunn overheard a woman expressing her disappointment in the lobby after a performance. "I enjoyed the show," she told her husband, "but I understood Denise Clarke was going to be in it and I like to see her work." In vain did her husband try to convince her that the young man they'd seen on stage was Clarke. "It was not!" she insisted, until Dunn stepped in to tactfully settle the matter. Clarke tells me the role isn't all that difficult, growing out of the natural dynamics between her and the guys when they're goofing around in rehearsal. "I've always felt like Michael and Andy's little brother," she says. "They've always allowed me to tag along with them when they're riffing and being playful."*

*Clarke sounds like she's already slipped into Fred-James mode as she arrives at the closing-night party for* Doing Leonard Cohen *— a reception hosted by the Canadian High Commission. "Hey, you guys, I'm gonna do it!" she announces excitedly to her colleagues. "I'm going to say those lines with a Scottish accent." And she launches into a passage from* Thunderstruck, *sounding like Jessica Lange in* Rob Roy: *"Yew shud all be placed in fooster homes. Yer all so yoong, who's going to coook?" Nothing like pandering to the locals, but if anyone can get away with it, it would be Denise.*

*While Clarke is at the centre of the party, Elizabeth Stepkowski is off to one side, leaning on the bar and sipping a beer by herself. Unlike the* Cohen *show, where she recites poetry and plays the unfaithful wife, Edith, in* Beautiful Losers, Thunderstruck *has handed her a pretty thankless role. As Naomi, the C & W–singing sister, she spends much of her time in a vegetable state, slumped pathetically like a big rag doll in the curious har-ness her brothers have constructed for her. And while her unearthly soprano is used to strong effect in Richard McDowell's sound design, her lines of dialogue are almost non-existent. Approaching her, I ask if the monolin-gual Rabbits are still considering the idea of performing Danis's play in the original French. "I think so," she nods. "What's the French word for 'and'?"*

*"Et."*

*"Well," she says with a sweet smile, "that's the only word I'll need to know."*

*The houses for* Cohen *were good throughout the week and tonight's finale was another near sell-out. "Neil seems to be happy," everyone keeps telling me. Neil does, indeed, seem happy. He's invited everyone back to his roomy flat in Glasgow's West End, which he shares with his charming partner, Ursula, a transplanted Irishwoman working in the British film industry. Now that the show is over, Neil admits that, truth be told, his favourite Canadian songwriter is actually his namesake, Neil Young.*

*Despite a supply of wine, beer, and other substances, there's little Cohen-style hedonism. The Rabbits have some hash, a few of the Scots are snorting coke (Clarke shakes her head indulgently — been there, done that), but nobody's really getting ripped. Friends drop by, bringing their sleeping baby, and a domestic theme runs through most of the conversa-tions. The Tron's techies, rough lads who look like they've stumbled out of* Trainspotting, *talk fondly of their wives and kids as they swig from their bottles of Stella Artois. Ewan McLaren's Czech wife just gave birth to their first child and he's anxious to rejoin them in Prague. But the guy who really has the warm fuzzies is Andy Curtis. The man who plays F., the bisexual, junkie anarchist of* Beautiful Losers, *confides to me that his real dream is to give up acting and spend all his time fishing, camping, and playing with his two-year-old daughter, Arielle.*

It began with a chance meeting in an Edinburgh bar and ended with a torrid little affair in Singapore.

Back in 1992, while playing the Fringe with *Serpent Kills*, Brooker and Clarke were having a drink in the bar of the Traverse Theatre when they were approached by a tall, attractive Chinese man who spoke in a soft British accent. He introduced himself as Ong Keng Sen, artistic director of Singapore's TheatreWorks, an English-language company that was making its UK debut at the Traverse with a solo play called *Madame Mao's Memories.* The couple found him brilliant and articulate and, after exchanging pleasantries, they agreed to check out each other's work. When the three reconvened, they were suitably enthusiastic. Keng Sen was excited by OYR's bold physicality and visual panache; Clarke and Brooker were impressed with *Madame Mao* — in particular the performance of its star, a gifted young actor named Claire Wong. As they traded compliments, Keng Sen warmed to the pair, slipping out of his formal British and into lively, lilting Singlish (the Singapore brand of pidgin English). Then he popped the question: Would they consider coming to Singapore to make a show for his company? Clarke, used to such come-ons, didn't take the proposition too seriously. "I recall being blasé about the whole thing," she says, "as it seemed like loads of people would ask you to collaborate in the fever heat of the Fringe event." But Brooker, who had travelled in Asia, was thrilled with the idea and so they accepted the offer.

Less than a year later, the couple was in a rehearsal hall in Singapore, putting sixteen local actors through their paces to the funky sounds of Prince and introducing them to the cut-up techniques of William S. Burroughs. From that eleven-day workshop in June of '93, they culled nine performers who would go on to help them create a steamy dance drama called *Under the Bed.*

The theme of the piece was "desperate romance" — arrived at by Brooker and Clarke as they looked about them and saw how difficult it must be for lovers in Singapore to be alone. The island republic was crammed with more than three million people, and most young, single Singaporeans still lived with their parents in matchbox housing developments; socializing took place mainly in the city's crowded food courts, while cars were prohibitively expensive and not allowed in certain zones at certain hours — so where did you go to make out? Not only that, when did you find the time? The company they had assembled was made up of hard-working young professionals, from lawyers and accountants to soldiers, who had enough stress just balancing their acting careers with their demanding day jobs. Clarke and Brooker figured they'd have plenty to say about the desire for intimacy. "We were right," says Clarke, "and, although occasionally I managed to shock them in rehearsal, they soon opened right up and told us all their secrets!" Putting those secrets on stage was another matter.

By 1993, Singapore's long-time leader, Lee Kuan Yu, had stepped down as prime minister, but his velvet-clad iron fist was still felt in Singaporean society, where public behaviour was repressed and a quietly efficient censorship existed. To do an openly sexual play was a risk, even if Singapore arts groups such as TheatreWorks had been encouraged to import and emulate Western culture. "We submitted our script to the censors and it passed," says Clarke, "however, we were warned repeatedly that no nudity would be tolerated." They were allowed to let the actors strip to their underwear, which is what the cast ended up doing in the play's final scene. (In Calgary, the Rabbits likely would have *started* such a play in the nude.) Instead, Clarke's sensual choreography would have to suggest intimacy through movement, gesture, and touch, the hands of the actors "just lingering over erogenous zones," as reporter Hannah Pandian observed in a feature for the *Straits Times* (16 November 1993). In a throwback to the pre-Stonewall era, there was only one homosexual character, and he was closeted and in torment.

Brooker and Clarke had returned to Singapore in the fall to build and rehearse the play for its November opening. *Madame Mao* star Claire Wong, a lawyer by day, was part of their hand-picked ensemble, along with six other Chinese Singaporeans, one Indian (Noorlinah Mohamed), and a Frenchman (Jean-Marc Favre). All of them were newcomers to the Rabbit style of theatrical creation. TheatreWorks was a green company, less than a decade old, and part of a contemporary arts scene that was just beginning to emerge alongside the Chinese opera and other traditional forms of entertainment. Ong Keng Sen, the theatre's visionary, turned out to be one of those tyrannical directors who liked to mould actors to his own specifications and motivate them through fear of his violent temper. Clarke was not impressed. "To me, he seemed like a cartoon of the genius director who had convinced them that his cruelty made them better artists. They were definitely baffled by our concern for their fatigue levels and well-being, until we made it clear that it was part of our aesthetic that they be relaxed and confident." One of the cast members, Verena Tay, described the unusual experience of working with Brooker and Clarke in an article in Singapore's *Hot Nouveau* magazine, published in advance of *Under the Bed*'s premiere (November/December 1993): "Ultimately, what was novel for the participants was the freedom and respect given to the actor as a writer and a performer," she wrote. "In the techniques Blake and Denise were sharing, the actor becomes responsible for writing his own text and performing the text the way he envisages it should be done." This was not democracy as Singapore knew it — and not the way most theatre is created anywhere. Clarke is certain that word of their kinder, gentler approach got back to Keng Sen, although he never mentioned it. "I think he may have been a bit embarrassed by how 'friendly' we got with the gang and were therefore breaking with his brand of protocol."

As well as picking their brains in rehearsal, the couple hung out with the actors, who introduced them to Singapore's serious food culture and one night took them for drinks at a soy-milk bar — much to Clarke's amusement and Brooker's disgust. Given the subject of their show, the two co-directors were hyperaware of the tacit sexuality surrounding them, from the gay cruisers in the parks who pretended to be jocks, to the gaggles of glamorous "she-boys" — transvestite prostitutes — in the food courts that everyone seemed to studiously ignore. Brooker told *Business Times* critic Claire Leow (16 November 1993) that, if sexual frustration emitted electricity, "Singapore as a city is glowing blue!" He and Clarke also took an opportunity to comment in the media on the city's rampant consumer culture — a Western import they were not proud of. "Consumerism," Brooker gently told Leow, "can interfere with [the] search for like souls." It's an opiate, added Clarke, who had found even the hip young actors of TheatreWorks were addicted. As she remembers, rather sadly, "shopping was hailed as the activity of choice, well above dating, for young Singaporean women."

The press, meanwhile, played up Clarke and Brooker's own romance. "They are such a sexy couple," cooed reporter Theresa Tan in the entertainment magazine 8 Days (20 – 27 November 1993), "even though he looks like a kid with worry lines, and she towers over him like a blonde guardian angel. They never answer a question without looking, asking, *flirting* with each other. They will kiss passionately in front of *anybody*." Nobody knew that, in fact, these two exhibitionist Canadians were going through a rough patch in their marriage. Clarke had come to Singapore in the midst of mid-life turmoil. She thought she had fallen in love with someone else and was considering leaving Brooker, the Rabbits, and Calgary. Along with her pleasant memories of Singapore are unhappy ones of feeling cooped up and angry on the thirty-eighth floor of one of the twin Westin Hotel towers, drinking a lot of gin and tonic, and trying to sort out her conflicted feelings. She was also trying to write her first full-blown play — a futuristic fantasy about procreating prostitutes called *Breeder*.

*Under the Bed* ran for eleven nights at the Drama Centre on Fort Canning Hill and was well received — although natural Asian politeness made it difficult for Clarke and Brooker to tell how people actually felt about it. "The real kick was seeing the actors committed to the playing and finding naturalism with poetics and physicality," says Clarke. Before they left, the cast urged them to visit nearby Bali — a travel tip that Clarke would be grateful for. The Indonesian island provided the same creative retreat for her that the Greek island of Sifnos would for Brooker when he penned *Alien Bait* a year later. "I grew very happy there," she recalls, "and wrote ten pages a day in a jungle garden surrounded by flowers that give off their scent at different hours of the day. I could tell how long I'd been working by which flower was releasing its wild perfume." She came back to Calgary refreshed and ready to re-commit to the troupe and her husband.

The Rabbits would thrive and *Breeder* would prove to be a huge hit. Clarke's marriage to Brooker would last another four years.

*16 August 2000 — Edinburgh in high summer is a startling contrast to Glasgow. The latter is bustling but serious, a workaday city with a working-class feel, where even the theatre types are embroiled in the local obsession with football (that is, soccer) and the enduring rivalry between the Catholic-supported Celtic team and the Protestant-backed Rangers. It's Billy Bragg country, "just a northern industrial town."*

*Get off the train at Edinburgh's Waverley Station, however, and you arrive in a joyous, festive city. Its landmark castle, which appears so bleak and forbidding in a rain-lashed Scottish winter, sits atop its sunlit crag like a picture in a storybook. Crowds of tourists pour through Princes Street, spilling down into the gardens below the castle where tents and outdoor stages have been pitched, or flowing north to Rose Street with its pubs and sidewalk cafés. For one jam-packed month, the city is as lively and pan-cultural as London. Not only does it host the small, prestigious Edinburgh International Festival and its huge, unruly Fringe, it also crams book and film festivals into the calendar — not to mention its famous military tattoo, an orgy of kilts and bagpipes let loose in the castle grounds. There is far too much to take in. Should you try to catch Björk's film debut in this year's controversial Cannes Palme d'Or winner,* Dancer in the Dark, *or see the Abbey Theatre's epic staging of Valle-Inclán's* Barbaric Comedies? *View the Dalí retrospective at the Dean Gallery, check out Susannah York's solo tour de force as Jacqueline Picasso, or try to snag a ticket to comedy sensation The Boosh? Michael Green always does a little scouting for the Rodeo while in town, but this year he also had high hopes of meeting Frank Zappa's oldest daughter, Moon Unit, who was at the book fair to flog her first novel. However, rehearsals wouldn't permit it.*

*It would be easy to spend most of the Fringe just hanging at the Traverse, where a dozen shows are rotating in its two theatres and the building's various bars and restaurants make it tempting to stay put. But it's hardly an oasis of calm. For the Rabbits, the stakes are higher here, the play they're doing is more difficult and more technically complex, and the timetable is tight. Yesterday, I came upon Blake Brooker and assistant director Ken Cameron huddled intently in the Traverse's café/bar, trying to simplify* Thunderstruck*'s lighting cues. Tonight's opening went off without a hitch, but everybody is second-guessing the audience again.*

*"We got lots of laughs at last night's preview, they were really with us," said Clarke at the reception. "This audience was completely different." I reminded the company that tonight's show was full of overworked critics, who were probably too busy taking copious notes to respond freely. (Pity the frazzled lot. The chap beside me kept nodding off between his scribblings.)*

*So far this Fringe, the Traverse's big hit has been the premiere of* Further Than the Furthest Thing, *a new play by up-and-comer Zinnie Harris being co-produced by the Tron and Britain's Royal National Theatre. A drama about the simple inhabitants of a remote island, whose lives are irrevocably changed when civilization comes to call, its story is well told but its style is conventional. Nonetheless, critics are likely to warm to it more easily than to the unorthodox* Thunderstruck. *Even after seven visits to Edinburgh, OYR's splicing of physical theatre with poetic language remains an anomaly.*

*Back in Glasgow, Neil Murray said as much to me. "In Britain, if you're a physical company you don't use words, they're superfluous. And the other extreme is* [Further Than the Furthest Thing], *where you have a very dense text. In some ways it's very old-fashioned, I suppose, and those plays are still being written in Britain. Nobody's really combining both of those things the way the Rabbits do."*

John Murrell's *Death in New Orleans* is the closest the company has come to bringing a conventional play to Edinburgh and, not surprisingly, it proved to be one of its biggest critical successes.

Despite the fact that Murrell is a Calgarian, it took a long time for One Yellow Rabbit to enter his orbit. While the troupe was taking its first baby steps at the Off Centre Centre, the playwright was already moving in the major leagues. He'd made his name nationally with *Waiting for the Parade*, then gone on to savour international success with *Memoir*, his play about Sarah Bernhardt. The latter had been produced in Dublin and London with Irish leading lady Siobhan McKenna and ran for three years in Paris in a French translation, quaintly retitled *Sarah et le cri de la langouste* and featuring film star Delphine Seyrig. (Its popularity endures. It was revived in Paris in 2002 with another French celebrity, Fanny Ardant.)

"I was certainly aware of them," says Murrell of the Rabbits, but then admits to a rather hazy memory of a show done in a garage (no doubt the ION Centre).

But if Murrell was only dimly conscious of them, they knew Murrell quite well. His work was one of the rare sources of excitement in a dreary provincial theatre scene. Brooker and Clarke both remember going to see his tragedy *Farther West*, a play about the downfall of a frontier prostitute, which opened to great fanfare at Theatre Calgary in 1982, in a production directed by Robin Phillips and starring Martha Henry.

By the time One Yellow Rabbit was beginning to emerge as an important company, Murrell was undergoing a personal and artistic crisis. After the failure of *October,* a *Memoir*-ish drama about Eleonora Duse, and the death of his close friend and protege Doug Arnold, Murrell put aside playwriting for a time and took an appointment in Ottawa as head of the Canada Council's theatre section. When he returned to writing, and to Calgary, *Ilsa* had made OYR — to use a Blake Brooker word — "undeniable," and Murrell began to watch the troupe with growing appreciation. "I had made up my mind that I was going to do something with the Rabbits," he recalls, "if they were interested."

On the surface, it seemed an odd fit. Murrell wrote text-heavy — indeed, at times prolix — plays that read beautifully but challenged the finest directors to animate them on stage. (Even Chris Newton, an expert at staging that windbag Bernard Shaw, was defeated by Murrell's word-drunk *Democracy.*) Besides, the middle-aged playwright appeared to have very different tastes. He listened to Italian opera, he translated Chekhov. While the Rabbits championed the Beats, he admired Proust. Underneath, however, there was a bond. Murrell in his own way — and a decade earlier — had been attempting the same thing as Brooker. Both were literary men who wanted to turn poetry into theatre. Having tasted both success and failure in the big theatres, Murrell was ready to consider One Yellow Rabbit's alternative approach. After seeing the successful 1996 revival of *Mata Hari*, Murrell says he went backstage and told the Rabbits, "Have I got a show for you!"

The show was *Death in New Orleans*. Putting aside his predilection for famous people and historical periods, Murrell had begun writing a contemporary tragicomedy set in the crime-ridden Deep South and dealing with issues of racial, sexual, and cultural identity. It was about a University of Calgary anthropologist named Brenda who makes a trip down to New Orleans to claim a house inherited from a dead lover and to resume his archaeological dig in search of a lost pre-Colombian tribe. Joining her are a couple of callow pals: Lyle, who wants to cruise the gay bars and learn about voodoo, and Koontz, an amateur musician who hopes to find his artistic voice in the birthplace of jazz. Their encounters with the locals — including a surly white hustler, an angry black shop owner, and a gentle gospel singer — lead to a painful loss of innocence.

While Murrell was working on the play, he also got involved with OYR's first Summer Lab Intensive, a course designed to teach the troupe's creative techniques, and helped local audiences get their first taste of Murrell *à la* Rabbit when he suggested Denise Clarke be cast as Sarah Bernhardt in a Theatre Calgary revival of *Memoir*. To many older theatre patrons, Murrell's involvement with OYR was a seal of approval: The Rabbits were respectable.

Once *Death in New Orleans* entered rehearsals in the summer of 1998, Murrell quickly discovered what other Rabbit collaborators had learned — that the company's methods of preparation were a complete reversal of those used in traditional theatres. "The usual mainstream experience is that you start with the outside of the play — the lines, the stage directions, the set, and costume designs," he says. "You put together the exoskeleton and then you try to discover the heart of the play. The Rabbits work the other way round. They go right for the vital organs of the piece and only once they've found them does the production begin to take shape. I had worked with people in theatre who *claimed* to take that approach," he adds, "but when it got down to rehearsals, they didn't really do it. The Rabbits actually did. It was really utterly different working with them than anywhere else I'd ever worked."

The size and racial requirements of the show meant that OYR had to pull in three guest actors. Rodeo fave Doug Curtis played Alex the hustler and Barbara Barnes-Hopkins was Yvonne the gospel singer. Andrew Moodie, a Toronto-based actor/playwright, took the part of Rice, a bitter African American smouldering with resentment that his own father named him Edgar Rice Burroughs after the creator of that white colonial hero, Tarzan. Denise Clarke, Andy Curtis, and Michael Green were cast as Brenda, Lyle, and Koontz respectively, while Elizabeth Stepkowski was given a rather vague role as a Mahalia Jackson–style singer hovering on the fringes of the action and adding to the atmosphere.

It was a complex play, dark and splenetic but with lyrical passages and a leavening of humour. Blake Brooker played editor, carving Murrell's wordy script down to a workable length. The play benefited from the Rabbits' minimalist approach, in which Richard McDowell's aural sketches took the place of decor, evoking a crowded French Quarter bar or a sultry Mississippi riverbank purely with sound. And the Rabbits benefited from Murrell's challenging material, which forced them to stretch as actors. Green, as the foolish, frustrated Koontz, and Curtis, as the endearingly pathetic Lyle, were in top form.

The production received one preview in Calgary, on 20 August, then headed straight for Edinburgh. The frantic activity of moving the show into the Traverse's studio theatre, where it opened 26 August, left Murrell in a bit of a daze. He sat in the house that opening night — something he seldom does — and got no sense of whether the play was going over well or not.

Early the next morning, in the house where Murrell had been billeted with two or three of the actors, the phone rang. The playwright, still in his dressing robe, picked it up. "I just assumed it wasn't for me," he says, "but I answered it because no one else was up. They said 'We're calling from the Traverse and *Death in New Orleans* has won a Fringe First Award. Could some of you come down to receive it in an hour?'"

Murrell was flabbergasted. "It almost seemed like somebody's idea of a bizarre joke. The putting together of it had been such an adventure that it no longer seemed relevant whether anyone liked it or not."

*18 August 2000 — Back in Glasgow, and away from the crowds — if you don't count those 1,500 pop music fans queuing outside the Virgin megastore, waiting for autographs from Posh Spice, a.k.a. Victoria Beckham, who has recently extended her short stay in the spotlight by marrying football hero David Beckham. As I prepare to head back to Calgary, I grab Friday editions of the* Scotsman *and the* Herald, *the papers with the most extensive festival coverage. No review in the* Scotsman *yet, but the* Herald *has published its critique, by one Elizabeth Clark: "Like a bolt of lightning, Canada's One Yellow Rabbit has once again brought a piece of electrifying theatre to the Fringe with* Thunderstruck. … *Go steal a little of their thunder." An unqualified rave. There are going to be some happy Rabbits in Edinburgh today.*

# 8. On Tour II - Ecstasy in Mexico

**O**ne Yellow Rabbit's most memorable tour began in hell and ended in heaven.

The tour was a 1996 visit to the southwest US and Mexico with *Permission* and a work called *Hunger's Brides*. The latter was a dramatized reading of portions of a novel-in-progress by Paul Anderson. Once again, the Rabbits were hitching themselves to a personal obsession, only this time it was the *idée fixe* of a friend. Over the years, Anderson had become entranced with Mexico, the Spanish language, and, most particularly, a certain lady named Sor Juana Inés de la Cruz. The first great Mexican poet and one of the world's great feminist forerunners, Sor Juana, as her name implies, was a nun who lived in seventeenth-century Mexico and whose brilliant accomplishments brought her fame far beyond the walls of her cloister. In addition to poems, she wrote plays, essays, and learned treatises and turned her convent locutory into a salon, where she dazzled the aristocracy with her erudition and wit. However, she eventually ran afoul of her superiors when she dared to criticize a sermon by a respected Jesuit priest. After penning a powerful defence of women's right to education (the *Response to Sor Filotea de la Cruz*), she renounced her literary career and died a few years later while nursing her sister nuns during an epidemic. Her work went through a long period of neglect before being rediscovered in the twentieth century.

Among those who led the rediscovery was a fellow poet, Octavio Paz, whose monumental Sor Juana biography is, in the words of Anderson, "the Himalayas of Sor Juana scholarship." After reading Paz's *Sor Juana or, The Traps of Faith* (first published in English in 1988), Anderson was inspired to write a novel that would re-examine the life of Sor Juana within the context of modern Mexico and Canada. He started it in 1991, working on it intermittently until he received a grant in 1995 to make a six-month research trip to Mexico. While there, the Canadian Embassy invited him to give a reading from his manuscript at the 10th Guadalajara International Book Fair. The fair, one of the major literary festivals in the Spanish-speaking world, had chosen Canada as its guest nation for 1996 and was seeking Canadian participants. One day, while visiting the embassy in Mexico City, Anderson also happened to overhear a request from a cultural group that was looking for information about a Brad Fraser play. He volunteered his help and learned that the group consisted of several well-heeled offspring of the Mexican ruling class, including Pablo Raphael de la Madrid, the nephew of former Mexican president Miguel de la Madrid Hurtado. Pablo Raphael and his compadres had big plans to launch a restaurant-cum-arts centre in Mexico City called El Octavo Día (the Eighth Day). Among its features would be a new theatre and, while it was still under construction, they were already thinking about programming. Anderson got them interested in One Yellow Rabbit.

Back in Canada, Anderson approached the Rabbits with an idea. Instead of just doing the standard author's reading, what if he brought the whole troupe to Guadalajara to give the book a dramatic presentation as part of the fair's accompanying cultural festival? They liked the proposal. Anderson also shared his plan with Alberto Ruy-Sánchez, the distinguished Mexican novelist and publisher, who was associated with The Banff Centre. Using his contacts, Ruy-Sánchez helped get some money for the project from FONCA, the Fondo Nacional para la Cultura y las Artes — Mexico's arts funding agency. Soon a tour began to take shape. OYR would not only play the book fair, but also help christen the new Octavo Día and then pay a special visit to the shrine of Sor

Juana scholarship, the Universidad del Claustro de Sor Juana, a small liberal-arts university located within the walls of the poet's former convent in Mexico City.

In the spring of 1996, Anderson returned to Mexico with long-time pal Blake Brooker to finalize the arrangements. During their stay, they attended a sumptuous dinner party with the Octavo Día partners, where one of the guests happened to be a Mexican celebrity. Zaide Silvia Gutiérrez was famous for her starring role in *El Norte*, Gregory Nava's acclaimed 1983 film about two young Guatemalan refugees trying to rebuild their lives in the promised land of America. Gutiérrez had given a heartbreaking performance as Rosa, the baby-faced peasant girl who braved sewer rats and border patrols only to end up working in a sweatshop on the fringes of LA. But in the years since its release, she had become equally well-known to Mexican audiences as a theatre and TV actor who also worked as a director, teacher, and playwright.

Gutiérrez immediately took a shine to Anderson and Brooker. "She's a great deal of fun," says Anderson, "and Blake's a great deal of wicked fun and we just sort of clicked." When she learned about the *Hunger's Brides* production, she offered to be part of it. Anderson remembers being blown away. "It was kind of like going to a party in London and having Emma Thompson say she'd be interested in committing to your project." She also suggested the format for the show. In Mexico, it turned out, readers' theatre was a popular form, known as *teatro en atril* (literally, "theatre on music stands"). Gutiérrez had even performed on a TV show with that name, where actors gave dramatic readings of international literature.

The tour was set for the fall of 1996. The Rabbits would do a first read-through of the show while performing *Alien Bait* at Vancouver's Arts Club Theatre in October, then rehearse and premiere it the following month at Arizona State University in Phoenix, where Denise Clarke had been invited by a friend and faculty member, Marc Berezowski, to teach a series of master classes. Zaide Silvia Gutiérrez would join the tour in Phoenix. In addition to the *Hunger's Brides* reading, the troupe also planned to revive the hyperphysical *Permission* and give their American and Mexican audiences a double dose of Rabbit artistry.

Things did not begin promisingly. It must have seemed portentous for the Rabbits to start a tour in Vancouver on the tenth anniversary of their Expo '86 debacle, when *The Batman on a Dime* was shut down. Sure enough, this visit wasn't much better. *Alien Bait* stayed open, but played to pitifully small houses in the Arts Club's Granville Island theatre. For most of the run, Vancouver was drenched in dispiriting rain. Then Paul Anderson turned up with a final draft of the bilingual *Hunger's Brides* script, which was not just a selection of excerpts but almost a full-blown play.

The drama focused on a pair of contemporary academics, one Mexican, one Canadian, who are quarrelling over the unorthodox thesis written by a troubled young Sor Juana scholar. As they argue, parts of the thesis itself are played out in episodes that show Sor Juana's struggle for intellectual independence against the colonial arm of the Spanish Inquisition. Andy Curtis and Zaide Silvia Gutiérrez would play the professors and Elizabeth Stepkowski the scholar, while Michael Green had been aptly cast as the inquisitor. Clarke had the role of Sor Juana. Anderson remembers her reaction at the first read-through. "I could just see Denise's face sort of sinking. There was this dawning of the realization that it wasn't going to be that simple." Not only would the tall, blond actress have to convince audiences she was a Mexican nun, Anderson had given her some difficult soliloquies to deliver. She would have to learn them while also staging the movement for the show, and on top of that she had to re-choreograph and rehearse *Permission* in Phoenix as well as teach her university classes.

It got worse when they arrived in the States. Clarke discovered that she'd been scheduled to do more teaching than she'd anticipated and the classes were split between two of ASU's four campuses. The Rabbits were booked into a motel many kilometres from the university, which required a long daily commute by freeway. A bright spot was the arrival of Zaide Silvia Gutiérrez; although, when Paul Anderson and Grant Burns went to pick her up at the airport, Anderson brought along a photo. Months after their first and only meeting, he wasn't sure if he'd recognize her.

Gutiérrez herself wasn't too sure about what she was getting into. Would she be able to integrate herself into this close-knit foreign theatre troupe? As it turned out, she and the Rabbits were a perfect fit. She shared their no-nonsense professionalism and immediately warmed to their welcoming style. "I felt like an honoured guest," remembers Gutiérrez. "It was like being invited to be part of a family, which was a beautiful experience." Within a day, the Mexican actor was working so confidently with her English-speaking hosts that Anderson found his services as interpreter weren't required.

As part of their ASU residency, the other Rabbits were also invited to lead some classes — or, in one case, not invited. One skeptical professor refused to let Michael Green address his creative writing class. In a drama class with a more amenable prof, Green managed to get into trouble with a heat-packing campus security guard. Having begun to teach some basic trust-building exercises, Green took the class outdoors in search of a more dramatic height from which students could fall into the waiting arms of their classmates. They found a concrete-and-plastic sign about two and a half metres high and, in Green's words, "were going about our happy business" when the security guard came squealing up in his vehicle. "He jumped out of the car and told us to step away from the structure," recalls Green. "Unfortunately, a young woman was perched up there. It was easier to get up onto than to climb down from, so I instructed her to fall into our arms, and then we would be finished with our exercises. But when she did so, the guard pulled his gun and freaked out!" He was convinced to holster his firearm, but ended up taking down everyone's name, while the professor in turn took down his badge number and reported his behaviour. "In the end," says Green, "I agreed not to instruct students to hurl themselves from tall objects, and the offending officer had to take anger management and conflict-resolution training."

There was more trouble back at the motel, when Gutiérrez and her roommate, Elizabeth Stepkowski, returned one evening to find their room had been broken into. Among the items stolen were Gutiérrez's passport, visa, and airline ticket. Their mutual distress only brought Gutiérrez and the Rabbits closer together. "I think that night something happened between the Rabbits and me," she says. "If there was any ice left to be broken between us, it was melted. Everyone was very kind to me. I never felt like I was a foreigner."

Denise Clarke, meanwhile, was going through a different kind of crisis. For one of the rare times in her career, her remarkable self-confidence had been shaken. "It started to dawn on me as we got down to Arizona that I was going to play a Mexican icon," she says, "and I started panicking." The heavy teaching load meant she had to miss some rehearsals and, when she was able to attend, she was unable to make any progress with the role of Sor Juana. "Paul was listening as I'd read away, working at it, trying to see if I could get in my brain what to do with it, what it meant. And finally he would ask Blake [she speaks *sotto voce*]: 'Is she ever going to, like, do it *well?*' Finally, I saw him one day looking at me in distress and I said 'Paul, I might be really shitty for a long time.' And I felt so bad, I didn't know what to do, I couldn't find her character." Clarke's anxiety finally reached a peak one day in rehearsal, as she listened to Stepkowski and Curtis performing a dialogue between the student and professor. "Lizzybeth and Andy were just doing this scene like gangbusters, they were just sensational. I'd been off teaching a whole raft of classes and trying to build *Permission* on the side and I was exhausted, and I'm listening to these two sing like birds and I just decided I couldn't do it. I knew my scene was next and I thought: I'm going to have to quit theatre, because I know for sure I can't do this. It was a terrible moment in my life. I was sitting there, getting ready to say 'Okay, guys, I've got some terrible news for you, I've decided to quit.' And instead, when I opened my mouth, I just spoke my scene. Like that. And of course it was one of those special moments that's so invested with emotion. I was sure I had nothing left to lose 'cause I was so convinced I definitely cannot do this."

Despite that sudden respite, Clarke was still gnawed with anxiety right up until the show's public read-through at the university. "Denise will never give you less than she can," says Anderson. "It's a sacred thing with her. Blake told me 'She's the slowest pupil. She'll be fighting with it, struggling with it right up until the last minute. But you'll see in performance that she often goes the farthest. You'll be amazed.' And it was exactly that way. That day, she came back from this master class and asked me to run lines with her and talk her through some of the longer speeches. We did that for about a hour and a half. And one of the first great moments of the tour was when she walked out on stage that evening and absolutely nailed those long, difficult soliloquies. I was dumbstruck. I was so moved, so grateful."

Clarke had made the breakthrough. After that, the show began to gel. But this was shaping up to be a tour plagued with problems and there were more to come. After finishing up in Phoenix, the Rabbits hopped a plane to Mexico and the Guadalajara book fair. As they passed through Mexican customs at Guadalajara's Miguel Hidalgo y Costilla airport, Richard McDowell's flight cases packed with sound equipment were seized. "They asked for my paperwork," recalls McDowell, "but we hadn't been given the right papers, so they just said 'You can't have these boxes.'" Despite entreaties from Paul Anderson and a lawyer with the book festival, the customs men refused to release the equipment. It took more than a day of battling red tape to pry McDowell's synthesizers from their grasp, to the point where it looked like there wouldn't be enough time to set up for the show. "It came right down to the wire," says Anderson, who spent a tense twenty-four hours shuttling between the airport and the Canadian consulate. "We eventually got the stuff through just in time." The nail-biting was worth it. The Mexican media was fascinated by the idea of a Canadian play about Sor Juana, in part thanks to Zaide Silvia Gutiérrez's involvement, and descended on the Rabbits as soon as they arrived. The company performed *Hunger's Brides* and *Permission* — or *Las novias del hambre* and *Permiso* — in the 300-seat Teatro Experimental at the University of Guadalajara and was mobbed backstage by Sorjuanistas — devotees of the poet — and curious audience members. "They wanted to know all about us," says Anderson. "They couldn't believe that this six-foot, blond, spiky-haired Canadian woman was playing their Sor Juana."

Buoyed by the reception at the book fair and with their customs hassles behind them, the Rabbits headed east to Mexico City to open a brand-new theatre.

Only, as they soon discovered, there was no theatre.

The boys of El Octavo Día had promised more than they delivered. Their elegant restaurant, library, and cybercafé, occupying a mansion in the city's trendy Condesa district, showed no signs of also being a performance venue. Asking to see where they were supposed to play, the Rabbits were led to a two-storey cinderblock bunker in the back, without electricity, lights, or — crucial for *Permission* — a dance floor. Ralph Christoffersen, who had been dutifully faxing his technical requirements to the restaurant for months, couldn't believe it. Nor could Grant Burns. It was the Finborough Arms all over again — only worse. "We looked it over," says Christoffersen, "and wondered if we should even bother trying to perform there. Then we said 'Hell, let's do it.'" The guys who'd built the SkyRoom and the Secret and refurbished the Finborough snapped into action. They demanded that the owners provide some lights, which they helped to install. They scavenged a used lighting board. "It was from an old disco," says Christoffersen, "and it had had thousands of cocktails spilled on it." They hauled in some risers for seating. They built a makeshift dance floor. "We ended up having some scraps of kitchen linoleum from a discount store brought in, and carpet underlay," says Richard McDowell. "The floor had a sort of bizarre pattern on it where the seams had to be taped together."

Within three days, El Octavo Día had a functioning theatre. They had to siphon electricity off outdoor utility poles to run the lights (a not-uncommon practice in Mexico City) and plug McDowell's mighty sound system into a kitchen outlet normally reserved for the freezer. Apparently, nobody told the cooks. On the opening night of *Permission*, one of them wandered by, noticed that his freezer had been unplugged, and yanked out McDowell's extension cord. "Just as Michael started his opening monologue," says McDowell, "all my machines went dead. I looked over at Ralph. Ralph jumped up from his lighting board, ran out, and followed the cable into the kitchen." The Mexican staff was startled when a huge white-haired Norseman came storming in, making a beeline for their freezer like some ravenous beast. "He pulled the freezer plug out, plugged my equipment back in, and everything booted up five seconds before my first sound cue."

The actors had their share of problems, too. *Permission* was perhaps their most physically demanding show and they were trying to perform it in the midst of the dangerously polluted Mexico City at the time of year when the smog is at its thickest and oxygen is more than usually scant. To make it worse, the concrete bunker was filled with dust, and the floor, despite the padding, was hard. "It was like everything was conspiring against us," says Andy Curtis, who also remembers that their dressing room was tucked away in another part of the house and far from private. "We'd be standing there naked, getting changed, and five guys would troop through, stop, and look at us. I guess they'd never seen a dressing room. It was a different way of working, that's for sure."

There were some perks to make up for the pains, including delicious free meals in the restaurant. However, it quickly became clear that, while the Octavo Día partners may have been rich kids, they didn't have a lot of money themselves. Despite drawing good houses, the Rabbits left Mexico without being paid for their gig. A year later, Burns would still be trying to squeeze some pesos out of Pablo Raphael, but at length El Octavo Día folded and the house was put up for sale.

Now it was time to move on to the final stop of their ill-starred tour, which promised to be mercifully short. The company would give a couple of performances of *Hunger's Brides* at the Claustro de Sor Juana, 10 and 11 December, then fly back home to Canada in time for Christmas.

Wedged between rough streets in Mexico City's Centro Historico, the Claustro hardly seemed like a place of quiet contemplation, religious or secular. Its entrance was opposite a busy Metro station. Its historic chapel faced a shabby little square where kids regularly played soccer. But inside the walls were lovely patios, leafy courtyards, and the university itself, set amid the ruins of the Convento de San Jerónimo, where Sor Juana had spent much of her short life and where she was buried after her death in 1695.

The Rabbits would be performing in the chapel, now desanctified and used as a theatre. Its high windows were broken and its two massive wooden doors, which opened into the square, were riven with cracks. The noises of the world's largest city seeped into the dark interior where, four centuries before, Sor Juana would have knelt and prayed. On the first evening, as Paul Anderson took his seat next to director Blake Brooker in what was once the chancel and was now a technicians booth, he feared the outside racket would distract the actors and disrupt the performance. But as the stage lights went up and *Hunger's Brides* began, he realized something strange was happening.

As they watched, he and Brooker exchanged glances of silent recognition. "The actors were excited," says Anderson, "they were electrified." Behind the cracked doors came the scuffles and cries of young soccer players, backed by a chorus of dogs going through their nightly ritual of howling as the sun went down. From the windows could be heard the thrashings of passing helicopters and the flapping of pigeons and doves as they congregated on the bell tower. Inside the crammed chapel, the audience of academics was silent and rapt as four Canadians and a Mexican recounted the seventeenth-century life of Sor Juana to the accompanying soundscape of modern-day Mexico City at night. It was magical. "The work was partly about this interpenetration of two times and places," says Anderson, "and here we were, actually experiencing that."

By the time it was over, the actors felt almost delirious. As they left the chapel, Gabriella, a young Sorjuanista who had met the troupe in Guadalajara, ran up to Denise Clarke, bursting with excitement. "Oh, Denise, come next door! There's a huge fete for Octavio Paz. He's next door — come next door!"

As chance would have it, Octavio Paz, Nobel Prize–winning poet and leading authority on Sor Juana Inés de la Cruz, was attending the Christmas party of *Vuelta,* the literary magazine he'd founded in 1976. The party, on the Claustro's big patio, was a posh affair — waiters in livery serving canapés on silver trays, a chamber orchestra playing taste-fully in the background. Led by Gabriella, the Rabbits slipped in to mingle with the many guests. Among them was Alberto Ruy-Sánchez, who had just been to the play. He offered to introduce Paul Anderson to the man whose biography had inspired *Hunger's Brides.* By then, the formidable literary lion was eighty-two and in frail health, his body crippled by the long illness that would eventually kill him less than two years later. "You could see he wasn't well," says Anderson. "In his photo-graphs he has these beautiful, jade-clear eyes, and in them an unspar-ing, almost piercing clarity. These were not those eyes, and the man himself was very small and stooped." A retinue hovered round him and a steady stream of admirers approached to wish him well and ask for autographs. Anderson couldn't help but notice that virtually all of them were young women. No one in the troupe had a book for Paz to sign, so Gabriella ran off to fetch one.

Ruy-Sánchez presented Anderson and Brooker to Paz and told the poet about *Hunger's Brides.* When he mentioned that Paz himself figured in the play, the old man brightened and gave a half-smile. Anderson groped for words. He found himself stifling a lunatic urge to laugh at the sheer inadequacy of speech when confronting one of the great poets of the century and the man whose biography of Sor Juana has had such a profound influence on him. Zaide Silvia Gutiérrez wasn't quite so awestruck. As a Mexican, she had a more difficult rela-tionship with this living legend. She had seen Paz the arrogant genius, bawling out a disruptive audience member at a poetry reading, and she questioned some of his public stances on Mexican cultural issues. "At the time, I don't think I had settled my own feelings about Octavio Paz," she says. "For all my admiration for his works, I couldn't always follow his politics." Meanwhile, Gabriella came back with a volume of poems, which Andy Curtis got Paz to autograph. (Anderson claims it was actu-ally a collection by Paz's Chilean contemporary, Pablo Neruda. "God, was it?" says Curtis. "I don't remember that.") Then Curtis snapped a photo of Blake Brooker posing with the poet. Finally, Paz rose to leave, leaning on the arm of his wife, Marie Jose. He shuffled across the patio, seemingly staring at the ground, then suddenly stopped and redirected his steps to a table eight metres away.

Denise Clarke was hanging back from the crowd, sipping wine with a visiting Canadian journalist who was sharing the thrill of the evening and wishing she could meet the poet, too. "Well," said Clarke grandly, "you know, sometimes you just have to sit back and let things come to you in this world." As she spoke, she caught sight of Anderson and McDowell gazing over her shoulder in amazement. She turned to see a weathered hand come into view. "*Buenos noches,*" said the old man. "My name is Octavio Paz." "Ah! Señor Paz," Clarke exclaimed, and without missing a beat she proceeded to introduce her table companions. Paz briefly acknowledged them, then leaned over and kissed Clarke's hand. "It's lovely to meet you," he said. "No," she sweetly contradicted him, "it's lovely to meet *you.*" "Good night, my dear." "Good night, Senōr Paz." At that, the poet turned back to his wife and made his exit. "The whole party was hushed," recalls Clarke. "Paul was practically weeping. It was so moving. The next day, it was in the papers." Nobody knew if Paz had approached the actor because he knew she was playing his beloved Sor Juana, or if he was merely paying his attentions to an attractive woman. In any case, it was rare for the aging Nobel laureate to introduce himself to anyone. "Denise was radiant," remembers Anderson. "It was a lovely grace note to the evening."

After the following night's performance, the Claustro's faculty invited the Rabbits to a Christmas dinner hosted by the president and the rector of the university. The troupe was presented with gifts and showered with praise for its sensitive treatment of Sor Juana's story. Denise Clarke was over the moon. "Those last two nights at the Claustro turned into an over-the-top raison d'être for the entire tour," she says. "It was the absolute highlight of my career up until then. Struggling as hard as I did to play Sor Juana, feeling so shy about being this big Canadian prairie girl trying to play a Mexican icon, it was deeply fulfilling to have them embrace me so completely. They acted as though it was the most normal thing in the world that I would play her."

Andy Curtis, who'd never been to Mexico, spent his time off playing the wide-eyed tourist, bedazzled at the Basilica of the Virgin of Guadalupe, in awe of the ancient pyramids at Teotihuacán. Even an unfortunate incident, when he and his wife, Bo, were mugged on the Metro on their last day, couldn't dampen his spirits. "It was such an enriching time," he remembers.

One Yellow Rabbit left Mexico on a high. But no one was higher than Richard McDowell. He was in love.

While everyone else was enthralled by Octavio Paz and grooving to the spirit of Sor Juana, the Rabbit's soundman had been falling deeply, helplessly, for the delightful Zaide Silvia Gutiérrez.

There was one last, long night of partying and saying farewell before Gutiérrez returned to her home and the Rabbits got on a plane to Calgary. "As we were flying out of Mexico City," says McDowell, "I had this terrible feeling. I didn't want to go." As soon as he got back, he composed a love letter, opening his heart to the Mexican beauty, and sent it by express. She was stunned. "She called me and said 'Wow. Your letter — I had no idea.'" They were reunited less than a month later when Gutiérrez came to Calgary to perform *Hunger's Brides* at the High Performance Rodeo. When McDowell learned that his love was requited, he didn't waste time. "I packed up everything, sold most of my stuff, and took what I had left, boxed it up, and moved to Mexico in the spring of '97."

As of 2002, McDowell spends half his year in Calgary working with One Yellow Rabbit, and the rest in Mexico City, collaborating on theatre projects with Gutiérrez. Their work together, including a Spanish adaptation of Denise Clarke's *So Low,* has garnered a slew of awards.

For Paul Anderson, the Rabbits' Mexican tour administered a fresh shot of inspiration. "It gave me a sense of how the second half of the book should go. In fact, I have a chapter in the novel in which a Canadian theatre company comes to the Claustro to do what is essentially *Hunger's Brides.*" It also left him with renewed admiration for his theatre pals and their incredible stamina. "I had no idea how gruelling a tour was," he says. "And all I was doing was a little bit of translating, a little bit of media. They were working these full, long days and then partying till late into the night. I was in bed by ten or eleven. Denise would sort of shake me awake again. We'd be drinking in the hotel in somebody's room and she'd shake me and say 'You're bringing the party down. Go to your room.' I'd wake up and go back to my room and those guys would just continue partying."

This seems like the most felicitous spot at which to leave the One Yellow Rabbit tours. In its time on the road, the company has played to larger houses, in better-known theatrical venues (and certainly ones with better soundproofing), but the gig at the Claustro de Sor Juana stands out as one of those rare, serendipitous occasions when shortcomings became assets and all the hassles and craziness of touring were paid off a hundredfold in an intimate and magical communion between artists and audience. Perhaps it isn't entirely a surprise. For the Rabbits, the term "secret theatre" refers not only to an actual place but also to an ideal one — its performance nirvana. The first meaning of "claustro" in Spanish is "cloister" and the verb "to cloister" means to seclude or hide away. In Sor Juana's aged convent, for a few ecstatic hours, One Yellow Rabbit had found its Mexican secret theatre.

# 9. Get to Know Your Rabbits

**H**aving gotten this far, it's high time we zoomed in on the principal members of One Yellow Rabbit and examined them in more detail. Since 1989, the creative core has consisted of Michael Green and Blake Brooker, the co-founders and co-artistic directors; Denise Clarke, associate artist, and Andy Curtis, comic actor extraordinaire, who has appeared in virtually every OYR production since his debut as (the fictional) Jim Keegstra in 1987. However, the designation of "the fifth Rabbit" has shifted with time. For a season or two, it was actor Lindsay Burns. Then Elizabeth Stepkowski stepped in to replace her and fit so well with the ensemble that she stayed five years. As of 2002, the company had yet to settle on another actor to fill her shoes. One could consider songwriter/musician David Rhymer to be Bunny No. 5, but he remains after many years a valued guest artist who pursues his own projects when not collaborating with OYR. In fact, these days the label best suits composer Richard McDowell, who could also be called "the invisible Rabbit" (*pace* Mary Chase), and whose sound designs have enhanced the company's shows immeasurably as far back as *Changing Bodies* in 1986.

Now, without further ado, here's a close-up look at the madman, poet, diva, knob-twiddler, and clown who call themselves the One Yellow Rabbit Ensemble.

## Michael

When a man cites Frank Zappa and Spike Milligan as his major influences, is willing to strut buck naked in front of strangers on the least theatrical pretext, and changes his appearance as frequently as others change their shirts, you could say that man is not exactly normal. Then add that he's also an amateur UFOlogist who writes plays about drunken Quakers and singing severed heads and you may be ready to dismiss him as a borderline nutcase. But there's another side to Michael Green: the ringleader, the organizer, the master schmoozer, the guy with all the connections. "I've never seen Michael's address book," says Daniel MacIvor, "but I'm sure it's enormous and it spans the globe. He knows everyone, and people really respond to him." There's also a third Michael: the family man with a wife and a house and 1.0 kids, a doting dad who's worried that little daughter, Maya, is a bit too introverted.

She sure doesn't get that from the old man.

One July day in 2001, Michael Green decided to treat the students of One Yellow Rabbit's Summer Lab Intensive to one of his favourite party pieces. It began with him striding on stage, nude except for a pair of huge black rubber gloves, and thrusting his head into a metal bucket of water. As he swung his hair into the air in a great dripping arc, he surveyed the audience with maniacal eyes and bellowed forth: "I AM *THE WHALER!*" Ahab himself would've been freaked.

Michael's public exhibitionism has a long history, going back at least as far as that memorable Halloween night in the condemned house when, greased up and naked, he ripped his way out of a hanging sac with a hunting knife like some demonic thing that couldn't wait to be born. You could say the opening of *Meatsong* symbolized his birth as a theatrical avant-gardist, but Michael has wanted to entertain almost from the day he slithered out of the real womb.

"My parents say that when I was six, I was already telling people I was going to be a comedian," he reveals. Although his mom and dad weren't performers themselves, there was showbiz in the blood. "My father comes from a fairground family, carny folk. His cousins were all related to circus people." Back in England, grandmother Green drove the lorry that hauled the Ferris wheel from town to town. "She and her husband got out of the business after the Second World War," he says. "But my great-grandmother Little, who I actually met on more than one occasion, worked the fairground till the day she died." His mother's people, the Waddicars, were just as colourful. "Her side of the family, from what I can tell, is made up of mad, opera-singing Italian Irish. Quite an eccentric bunch."

His parents, Thomas Albert and Margaret Mary Green, were married in Bolton, near Manchester, and emigrated to Canada shortly afterwards. Michael Thomas was born a year later in Scarborough, Ontario, on 21 January 1957 — which, by remarkable coincidence, is two years to the day after Blake Brooker and less than a day before Denise Clarke. "I think I'm just a few hours older than her," he says. A younger brother, Eamonn, and sister, Deborah, would follow. The Greens quickly adapted to the Canadian mosaic — that is, they remained thoroughly British. Margaret ran out faithfully to buy the latest Beatles single as soon as it hit the stores. Thomas spent his leisure hours listening to his prized recordings of the BBC's classic *Goon Show.* Now, the *Goon Show,* while legendary in the UK, is not as well known in North America. A radio program of sublime silliness and pure Marxist anarchy (Groucho, not Karl), it aired from 1951 to 1959, in the midst of the drab post-war period, and anticipated the great wave of irreverent British comedy that would follow in the next two decades. Its most famous performer was Peter Sellers, who honed his gift for characterization while playing a bevy of bizarre characters, from the dyspeptic coward Major Bloodnok to that doughty Boy Scout, Bluebottle. The arch-Goon, however, was Spike Milligan, who wrote the show's hilariously chaotic scripts and served as a foil to Sellers — most notably in the role of the blissful idiot Eccles. Michael listened along, captivated by the craziness, and it was Milligan that he grew to admire — an unhinged comic genius with a taste for the surreal who would do anything for a laugh. "There could have been no *Monty Python* without Spike Milligan," he asserts. Or, one ventures to add, no *Dreams of a Drunken Quaker.* (It's revealing that

Michael identified not with Sellers, the consummate chameleon actor who immersed himself in roles beyond all recognition, but with Milligan, a much broader and zanier performer. It helps explain his own bold-stroke approach to acting.)

The Greens also made trips back to England and it was on one early visit that little Michael saw his first play and simultaneously made his stage debut. "I must've been three or four," he reckons. It was the traditional Christmas pantomime *Aladdin*, featuring those immortal panto characters the Widow Twankey and Wishy-Washy. "What I remember is Wishy hiding from his mom in the washing machine and coming through the wringer flat as a board. I remember thinking that was amazing. What I don't remember is that I was one of the lucky kids to be invited up on the stage and march around the piano with a balloon."

But at home, which had become Montreal, Michael grew up without seeing any theatre, apart from the odd school talent show, and didn't tread the boards again until the sixth grade, when he played Dick Deadeye in a production of *HMS Pinafore*. "I don't think I ever heard him say he wanted to be an actor," recalls his childhood friend, John Dunn. "I think he wanted to be a performer of some kind, though. He studied piano for a while, was in a Beatles cover band. He always had a creative bug." In Michael's early teens, his father, who'd already turned him on to one future influence with Spike Milligan, inadvertently introduced him to another. "My dad gave me my first Frank Zappa album," he says. "I guess I was about fourteen. He'd bought the album *Hot Rats* in the bargain bin 'cause he'd heard there was some good jazz on there, but he didn't like it at all. So he gave it to me — and I loved it." Zappa embodied everything that Michael enjoyed. Not only was the man a brilliant guitarist and ambitious composer, he was a leading (if not always appreciated) exponent of the musical avant-garde, plus a withering satirist and an early performance artist. He also had a uniquely weird sense of humour matched only by his friend and some-time associate, Captain Beefheart (another Green deity). Dunn was over at Michael's house when he first slapped that copy of *Hot Rats* on the turntable. He remembers his pal's delight. "That was the first real manifestation of Michael's taste for the unusual, for the artistically outrageous."

Michael and Johnny had met at the age of five, when their families both lived in Longueuil, on the south shore of Montreal. "I owned a pretty spiffy red tractor," says Dunn. "I pedalled it to the corner one day and this boy across the street went 'Wow! I really like your red tractor. Do you think I might come over and see it?' I said 'Yeah, that'd be great, but I'm not allowed to cross the street.' He said 'I'm not allowed to cross the street either. But I'm going to run home and ask my mom, so please wait there.' He ran home, got permission, and joined me. It turned out we were both starting grade one at the same time and we were going to the same school." Their friendship continued through school and even after Michael and his family left Montreal when he was fifteen.

Thomas, a mechanical engineer, had decided to move the clan to Calgary in the wake of the October Crisis of 1970, when Quebec labour minister Pierre Laporte was murdered and British trade commissioner James Cross kidnapped by French Canadian separatist terrorists. The Greens, steadfast Anglos who didn't speak French, began to feel threatened. Coming West did wonders for Michael. "I basically turned into another person," he says. "All the hormones kicked in. I had felt very shy in Montreal. My parents really had no intention of learning French and I was somewhat impressionable that way, so I could never be part of anything, could never really express myself. I felt almost like an outsider. But when I moved to Calgary it didn't take me long to realize this is a whole city full of people from other places, and Calgarians themselves were incredibly friendly and open."

If Milligan and Zappa were, in his words, "mentoring spirits," Michael found a more immediate mentor in high school teacher Gary Stromsmoe.

Raised in an Alberta farming community, Stromsmoe had had a theatre-free upbringing. In fact, he says his closest brush with anything artistic at all was designing a model pig farm out of matchsticks in a high school agriculture class. It wasn't until he came to the University of Calgary to take a degree in English that he became interested in drama

— inspired less by the plays he saw than by the theories he read. After graduation, he landed a teaching position in the English department at Western Canada High School. Three years in, he was asked to take over the vacant position of drama teacher. Having taught Peter Weiss's *Marat/Sade* in English 30, he decided the students should stage it as well. "It was a pretty chancey thing to do," he says now. "We weren't really aware of the enormity of it, or its controversial nature." Michael Green played a major role in the show and he, Stromsmoe, and several other students got so drunk on the experience that they decided to keep the party going. They formed Ikarus a year later, taking their name from the original teen rebel of Greek mythology. "We were going to fly as high as we could until the feathers burned off," says Stromsmoe. For their debut, they mounted a production of absurdist playwright Fernando Arrabal's *Automobile Graveyard* at the city's planetarium. Stromsmoe cheerfully recalls an irate couple getting up and making a noisy exit mid-show — a harbinger of the kind of response the company would get for much of its six-year existence. The young teacher, who'd been reading his Peter Brook, was trying to practise the sort of total theatre espoused by that seminal director. "It seemed to fit the interests of the kids," he recalls. "Their notion of theatre before that had been stuffy and traditional, so this was all brand new to them and very exciting." Michael was the most excited of them all. Theatre, he says, "didn't make any impression on me, until I met Stromsmoe."

He didn't quite leap in with both feet, however. Following graduation there was some typical post-high school floundering. Michael enrolled at the University of Calgary, where he smoked a lot of hash and barely cracked a book, then dropped out and moved to Toronto for a year. "I was really searching for myself," he says, "and at that point had no notion that I could make a living at theatre." As Dunn recollects, he ended up working at a SAAN store. After a year on his own, Michael returned to Calgary to find Ikarus had gone on hiatus. He quickly set the wings flapping again. "Within months we'd got our second production up — Jean Genet's *Deathwatch*. And that was it. I just committed my entire life, at that point, to theatre."

After taking a string of jobs — carpenter, taxi driver — to survive, Michael returned to the U of C and embarked on a drama degree. He found another guide there in professor Gerry Thurston, who cast him in a production of Arrabal's *Fando and Lis,* but he stuck it out only two years. The university's scholarly approach to theatre didn't suit him, and he devoted more and more time to Ikarus — apart from acting, he was now serving as a producer, director, and stage manager — until his studies suffered. Looking for an alternative, he auditioned for New York University's experimental theatre wing and was accepted, but couldn't afford to go. Instead, he took a job offer from Theatre Calgary's Stage Coach Players, where he met future wife Jan Stirling.

All this time, Michael was a whirlwind of theatrical activity, and John Dunn, who had just moved to Calgary, got swept up in it. "Michael was so driven," he remembers. One summer, Michael decided to mount his own touring play based on the Robin Hood legend and roped in Dunn and some other pals. "We built some backdrops, made some costumes, put everything in the back of Michael's yellow pickup truck, and we'd go to parks, set up, and perform it. We were theatre buskers, I guess. We didn't even pass the hat. We just did it for the fun of it." Along with Ikarus, Michael performed at Loose Moose and was involved in all the university's extracurricular theatre programs. "I can remember being more exhausted than I've ever been since," he says, "but it was invigorating, too."

Skinny, bespectacled, Michael was hardly the athletic type, but with Ikarus he began to throw himself bodily into his performances. "I always hated physical activity," he admits, "but when I got into theatre I realized the only theatre that I was interested in doing was physically very demanding. So I found myself doing things I never thought I was going to be doing in this lifetime. Gary Stromsmoe, although he would never call himself a physical theatre director, had a very strong vision of what a theatre performer should be able to do with his body. It was some kind of strange mix of Artaud and [the Russian director] Meyerhold, or something, but I really loved that vision and I wanted to be what he was imagining. My early expressions of physical theatre were hanging upside down in a closet, cutting myself out of plastic sacks, writhing in a flowerbed. I realized if I wanted to do it well, I had to get good at it." Ikarus gave him the opportunities, while later work with Richard Fowler and Edmonton's Small Change mime troupe provided the basic training. Then Denise Clarke came along and helped mould his movement skills into a definite style.

With Ikarus Michael also began taking his clothes off. Although nudity has become a Michael Green/One Yellow Rabbit trademark, he insists it was never intentional. Nor has he kept count of the times he's appeared on stage without a stitch. "It never seemed like a big issue to me," he says, adding that he doesn't know why he does it. "Maybe it's a kind of '60s thing." Certainly, mentor Frank Zappa had no problem being photographed naked sitting on a toilet (q.v. the classic "Phi Zappa Krappa" poster). As we discuss this, Michael is fully, not to say stylishly, clothed in black, and grabbing a quick bite in Drinkwater's restaurant before heading off to a meeting with the Alberta Foundation for the Arts. He gestures toward the lunchtime crowd. "I love clothing," he says, "but if we look around this room right now, everyone here is sitting on their genitals, and our skin pokes out the top of our clothes, pokes out the end of our sleeves. So, take the decoration away ..." When anyone asks him about the nudity, Michael likes to quote Denise Clarke: "It's a costume choice." Or, as he may have learned from Penny Arcade: "If you really want someone to pay attention to you, talk to them naked."

Nudity does, indeed, seem to be a costume with Michael Green. He, more than any of the other Rabbits, loves transforming his appearance for different roles. He'll get lightning bolts shaved into his temples, or cut off all his hair. One day he'll be shaggy, with his favoured Zappa/Zapata moustache and a goatee, the next he's clean-shaven with a short-back-and-sides. His eyewear always seems a step ahead of the latest trend. Look through the Rabbit photo archives and he's always the guy with the hunchback, the fright wig, the lobster suit. In Denise Clarke's *Featherland,* he played an eccentric ornithologist kitted out in cowboy chaps, a fencing mask, and a fedora.

Whatever his getup, Michael is a stage magnet. Former *Calgary Herald* critic Kate Zimmerman says he was the most riveting figure in the original Rabbit lineup. "I remember describing Green's delivery as 'orotund' in one review, and in those early days it was — he would intone things in a rather dramatic way onstage that, in combination with all the other unorthodox things going on, sometimes felt pretentious. On the other hand, he was always gripping, whether he was playing serial killer Charles Sobhraj or a clownish figure in a potato face [with Edmonton's Small Change troupe]." Audiences tend to remember his flamboyant comic characterizations, from the sentimental Nazi colonel of *Ilsa* to lewd, lecherous Baron von Tantamount, the obese restaurateur-cum-tinpot tyrant in the klezmer-rock opera *In Klezskavania*. There is, however, a fine, sensitive actor under the lurching and cackling and wildly rolling eyes. It's been evident in his low-key performances as the pathetic, white wannabe jazzman of *Death in New Orleans,* or the agonized trauma victim of *Alien Bait.* That's when another, hidden side of Michael Green comes out — maybe a throwback to that shy, funny-looking kid from Montreal. "Michael likes to call himself the nerd of the company," reveals OYR's former assistant director, Ken Cameron. "He probably feels that way next to Andy, who was clearly a handsome, dashing fellow in high school."

It was Michael's gung-ho performances with Ikarus that first attracted Denise Clarke. "I loved his physicality and his precision," she says. "I thought he was just a joy to watch." They first met socially and Clarke didn't know quite what to make of this freaky guy. "Then, when I saw him on the stage I was most impressed." She says her first experience of Ikarus was the outrageous *Meatsong,* "but the show that really blew my mind was *Robin Come Back.* I couldn't believe how intelligent and beautiful and odd and entertaining it was. And I was especially knocked out with Mikey. Up until then I'd always thought he was just an oddball. We became fans of each other around that time."

*Robin Come Back* was a drama of images inspired by a personal note Stromsmoe had found posted on a light pole in San Francisco. Like *Meatsong,* it was presented in the McPhail Secret Theatre, the original found space that preceded the Rabbits' secret theatres, big and small. That concept of theatre as a clandestine, possibly illegal and very likely subversive act is one of Green's main contributions to the OYR aesthetic, along with his taste for heightened performance. The old McPhail house, near the planetarium, was owned by the city and due to be demolished. The top floor had been occupied by an actor friend of Michael's who was moving out, and the city wasn't going to rent his suite when he left. At the same time, the place couldn't be torn down until the ground-floor occupant was gone — and he had a one-year lease. Unbeknownst to the city, but with the blessing of the remaining tenant, the Ikarus gang moved in and began a reno job on the vacant rooms. Green, Stromsmoe, Dunn, and another Ikarus colleague, Simon Dekker, knocked out walls, painted the interior white, and turned it into a tiny theatre with seating for about twenty. "We were squatting, basically," says Dunn. The ads for shows went out minus an address. "You had to phone in your reservation. We'd screen the calls and return those we thought were safe."

Michael Green's gutsiness goes beyond the stage. If he wasn't in theatre, he'd make one hell of a salesman, a foot in every door. Over the years, he's sold One Yellow Rabbit with remarkable effectiveness. Michael Dobbin, former boss of Alberta Theatre Projects, recalls when Green popped up at the conference of the Professional Association of Canadian Theatres for the first time, after OYR gained its professional status in 1985. "I remember he kept standing up in the meetings and saying 'I'm Michael Green from One Yellow Rabbit,' and of course no one had ever heard of this little theatre company with such a weird name. Nor had they ever heard a newcomer with such a determined point of view about issues. He was quite strident about certain things. Suddenly, the national theatre community was aware of One Yellow Rabbit." Once the Canadian arts scene knew OYR, Green went forth on a mission to sell the company abroad. Grant Burns remembers that he and Blake Brooker were skeptical. "He took off for six weeks and Blake and I sort of raised our eyebrows: 'Oh yeah, Michael is going to Ireland and the UK for six weeks. He's going to do a lot of work there, as in, a lot of work on his Guinness drinking. But in fact he made a lot of contacts." Out of that trip grew the Rabbits' first international tour. Dobbin, no mean hand at schmoozing himself, thinks Green's personal quirkiness works as an asset. "Part of it with Michael is that he's so peculiar, people are fascinated by him. He's an unusual-looking man, he seems fearless, and he's straight-down-the-line. When he engages in conversation, there's no small talk, and that's so disarming."

Perhaps the only time the famous Green gall failed him was when he met Lou Reed. It was at New York's Knitting Factory, where Laurie Anderson was launching a new CD-ROM, and Michael had managed to worm his way backstage in the hopes of meeting Anderson and trying to lure her to the High Performance Rodeo. Instead, he found himself in a nearly empty green room, standing next to the legendary Lou. "I was gobsmacked," he says. "I wanted to tell him 'I think you're great. I've got all your albums.' And I couldn't. Lou Reed was mad, he was banging the fridge door 'cause it was empty and there was no beer in there. I thought of saying 'I'll get you one, Lou!' Instead, I took out a pen and wrote a note on a piece of paper to Laurie Anderson and said 'Mr. Reed, could you give this to your girlfriend, please?' Even today my face goes all red thinking about it."

The Michael Green who can still feel like a tongue-tied kid in front of a favourite rock star is the one who has never lost touch with his youthful self. That's probably why he bends over backwards to encourage young people starting out in the theatre. When young actors send their resumés to the Rabbits, he's the one who writes them back. And the fresh and adventurous always attract him more than the polished and traditional. The man who can go to David Hare's acclaimed adaptation of Chekhov's *Platonov* at the Almeida in London and leave unimpressed will show up to a Rabbit rehearsal waxing enthusiastic about some little group of drama students he saw doing a play of their own in a converted warehouse.

Sometimes, however, his enthusiasm can be too much for his colleagues. Grant Burns, who spent his final year with the Rabbits (1999) solely producing the Rodeo, ended up locking horns with Michael over the latter's room-for-one-more approach to the festival. "He would hate to hear this," says Burns, "but the guy has to be reined in. He's like a child with way too much energy. He'd meet someone and they'd have an idea [for a show] and he'd say 'Great!' The Rodeo's already full but he'd throw them in there. So we'd end up booking them and, what with the tech and the box office, suddenly nobody gets a day off. I know he's the curator, but that's where I would go head-to-head with him and say 'No. I don't want it in there. It's one more thing to sell.'"

Burns thinks Michael is ideally twinned with Blake Brooker as his co-artistic director. Personality-wise, the two are a classic study in opposites. "Michael is always really busy, spending money, wants to fly somewhere to see something, superexcited, like a kid in a candy store," says Burns. "Blake's more like 'Okay, we've got to think about this. We've got to make a plan. Why are we doing this?' It's a good dynamic. Blake will question Michael's process, why he'll choose something [for the Rodeo], and he'll do it openly, and they'll have a wild confrontation over it. In turn, Michael will question Blake's process, how he directs and casts a piece."

In the theatre, the contrast between the two is made manifest. Playwright Brooker brews the elixir of words and actor Green serves it with panache. The erudite John Murrell sees the pair as Molière split in two. "If you took Molière apart and put the writer part on one side and the great clown he must have been on the other, you'd have Blake and Michael. Michael is well-read, well-versed, but for him his art resides in the moment of performance, when you electrify the audience, not the slow buildup to it or the aftermath when you analyze it to death."

Michael says the disparate personalities of all five Rabbits contribute to a certain degree of tension. "I think there's always a kind of low-level frustration that's present, partly because we're such different people and we're bound together by some kind of cosmic thread. I think it's natural." Outsiders marvel at how quickly and efficiently the ensemble can build a show, thanks to years of working together, but Michael says it comes with a down side. "Sometimes we frustrate ourselves because the shorthand means that we don't have to go through much of the creative process, which in fact is so important. Other times, we're frustrated if the shorthand isn't working. Frustration is not a theme, but it'd be ridiculous to deny it: It's there. It's the same way you're frustrated with your own family: Why does he always have to carve the turkey like that? But much more than frustration is the sense of, Well, we know what we're trying to do, so let's just get to work and do it." God knows, the troupe has weathered a lot of personal turmoil, including four breakups. "Mine was the first," says Michael. "Unfortunately for me, I was the pioneer. I went through it ten years before everybody else, so by the time everyone else was going through it, they'd conveniently forgot that I understood what was going on."

His marriage to Jan crumbled in 1987, after she had split with the Rabbits and left for Toronto. They were officially divorced five years later. By then, Michael had a new love in his life. She was Kim Arrell, an interior designer and a big One Yellow Rabbit fan who'd had her eye on the wild man for some time. She finally approached him one night at a club when he was pissed. "I was drinking tequila out of a wineskin," he recalls. "She came up and said 'Aren't you Michael Green?' Later, when I got sober, I looked her up in the phone book and called her." A black-haired, pale-skinned young woman who came across like a Goth girl with a sense of humour, she seemed the perfect match for Michael. "She's a creative person," he says, "but she doesn't consider herself an artist. She doesn't have an artistic temperament." The couple married in 1994 and their daughter, Maya Rose Green, was born three years later. Actor friend Christopher Hunt, who has two children of his own, says Michael loves to swap stories about the kids. "He's like a proper English family man, in some ways, the kind who wears slippers and reads the paper at home, but most people would never imagine that because he has this dynamic public persona."

It's a Sunday afternoon in autumn, when the average middle-aged Calgary male is either watching football on TV or cleaning the leaves out of the eavestroughs and *wishing* he was watching football on TV. Only today, a bunch of them are packed into the Auburn Saloon, the favoured watering hole of the city's arts types. This isn't the bar's usual clientele. Oh, here and there you spot a familiar face: Andy Curtis, or Judd Palmer, the philosophy student-turned-puppeteer of the Old Trout Puppet Workshop. But mostly these look like the guys who used to hang out and smoke pot in the high school parking lot, only twenty years older now. Many of them have long hair, most of them wear T-shirts and jeans, and all of them recognize the squawks and squiggles issuing from the Auburn's sound system — *Burnt Weeny Sandwich,* Frank Zappa and the Mothers of Invention, 1970. We are at the first meeting of Whip It Out: The REAL Frank Zappa Appreciation Society. Michael Green the instigator is at it again.

Michael is grinning through his goatee as he moves about the bar, dressed in tight white trousers, black leather jacket, and a T-shirt with a silkscreened photo of his musical hero. If he was planning a Zappa lookalike contest, he's already won it hands down. But he's smiling because the turnout is bigger than he'd expected. What he sees around him aren't just fellow Frank aficionados, they're also the potential audience for his next show. For years, Michael has nursed the idea of a play celebrating his favourite composer. That dream got a push forward when he hooked up with the Land's End Chamber Ensemble, a clutch of classical musicians willing and able to play Zappa's orchestral work. Now Michael needs to attract musicians from the other side of the Zappa equation — those with the chops to do his no-less-demanding rock-jazz-R & B riffs. To find them and, at the same time, gauge the interest in such a project, he decided to start a fan club.

As his friends note with a sigh, Michael Green has energy to burn. Not content to be a co-artistic director, festival curator, and lead actor with his own company, he has to find other things to do.

In recent years, his musical tastes have informed his various side projects. Michael inherited his father's fondness for jazz, but typically he prefers its most experimental mutations — faves include Peter Applebaum, Jon Hassell, and John Zorn. In 1996, he convinced the city's jazz festival to let him add a theatrical component to its programming with a staging of Michael McClure's *Minnie Mouse and the Tap-Dancing Buddha* — a riff on the sex lives of Walt Disney's cartoon characters — featuring a ten-piece jazz orchestra. He produced the show under the name of the Shiny Beast Collective — a nod to jazz-rock maverick Captain Beefheart and his 1978 album *Shiny Beast (Bat Chain Puller)*. He followed it up the next year with a more audacious Shiny Beast production: his gruesome Grand Guignol parody *Zertrummerung*, refashioned as a creepy musical with an industrial-jazz score played by Richard McDowell, saxman Dan Meichel, and drummer Peter Moller. Michael, at his most Mephistophelian, gnawed the scenery as sicko surgeon Dr. Panic, but Elizabeth Stepkowski stole the show as his decapitated wife, her head still alive and singing on a silver salver. Michael had written the play on commission for Calgary's Lunchbox Theatre, which was loath to serve up such ghoulishness to its lunch-hour patrons. Michael had hoped to turn it into an OYR production, but his colleagues balked. "I was so disappointed, just sick, when my fellow Rabbits refused to do it," he says. "So I assembled a company of crack actors and did it myself."

Michael was proud of *Zertrummerung*, which marked his move away from the cut-and-paste crutch he'd relied on in the past. Over the years, though, the company has come to discourage his writing attempts. While nobody can deny that his plays have provided some of the Rabbits' wildest work — *Dreams of a Drunken Quaker*, or that he-man hybrid of hunting and homoeroticism, *Naked West* — it's not the texts that people remember. Still, he has his fans. Among them is Sheri-D Wilson, who thinks Michael is closer in spirit to the Beat poets than Blake. "Blake doesn't have a lot of jazz going on in his writing, but Michael understands a huge amount about jazz. His writing is very musical." Nonetheless, these days he seems resigned to once more being the provocateur, as he was with *Alien Bait* and *Doing Leonard Cohen*. Watching the Zappa fans milling about the Auburn, Michael figures he might commission the script for this project from the Rabbits. They may turn up their noses, but then again, they weren't too crazy about alien abduction theories either. [1]

Don't underestimate his powers of persuasion or the fact that, while he sometimes puzzles his colleagues, they continue to find him endlessly fascinating. "I totally dig Michael Green," says Andy Curtis. "I don't necessarily understand his aesthetic, what the hell he's doing naked in a room with a bunch of feathers and bike tires, but he sure does some of the most interesting things I've ever seen." Michael, incidentally, does have an explanation for his twisted tastes. "All that weird stuff I like, that people talk about, just comes out of my sense of humour," he says simply. "I think that stuff is funny."

## Blake

It's a warm September night and Blake Brooker is sitting at the kitchen table of his new house in the old Calgary neighbourhood of Ramsay, sipping vodka and cranberry juice on the rocks and providing a play-by-play analysis of his work for One Yellow Rabbit. He's wearing shorts, and his boulder-solid body is draped in a mauve-grey, long-sleeved shirt, untucked and with the sleeves rolled up, exposing thick, hairy forearms. It's worth pausing over his appearance because Blake is not your run-of-the-café artistic type. He's short and sturdy, built like a fireplug, with a square head and a broad face, into which are set tiny, twinkling blue eyes and a nose so small and delicate that it barely breaks the surface in profile. The effect is a bit like one of those unfinished statues by Michelangelo, a rugged mass of marble into which fine, almost feminine features have been assiduously — and beautifully — chiselled. The contradictions between Blake's husky physique and the stereotypical image of a poet-playwright-director can be amusing. When he has adopted an arty look, wearing a long scarf and the latest in chic little wire rims, what would seem effeminate on a slender or softer man only appears incongruous — to twist one of his own similes, "like a pickle tied to a cowboy hat."

Yet, belying Blake's cinder-block build, there is something of the imp or sprite inside him. It gleams in his eye and dances on his thin, half-smiling lips. He can be coy. Actors talk about him teasing a performance out of them. He can be secretive. When he directs, he'll often take an individual actor aside and make suggestions in low, conspiratorial tones. And he can be mischievous. When he sits down for an interview, he'll slyly turn the tables and begin questioning the interviewer.

Tonight, however, he is firmly focused on his own writing. It may be because he has a new project on the go. At his elbow is a stack of books, most of them novels by William S. Burroughs: *Nova Express, Port of Saints, The Wild Boys,* and his personal favourite, *Cities of the Red Night* — tales filled with creepy drugs, cool weapons, grotesque sci-fi fantasies, and the homoerotic adventures of gangs of priapic youth. Tom Swift meets *Satyricon.* Blake is rereading Burroughs as he prepares his next play, a musical about the novelist and his partner in cut up Brion Gysin called *Dream Machine.* When you're writing something new, it's helpful to look back on your past efforts, identify the common themes, retrace the steps that led you here. Blake's memory may be fuzzy on the sources of inspiration and details of composition, but in each of his plays he can chart his growth as a writer. Upon arriving at *Alien Bait,* he also offers a peek at his working method.

"I can demonstrate it for you," he says, jumping up from his chair and disappearing downstairs. He comes back up a minute later, brandishing a used, two-hole spiral notebook. In 1994, after the Scottish tour of *Ilsa,* he and Denise took a two-week break and headed for Greece. "At the airport I bought this pad." He opens it at the first page, revealing his longhand — easy, flowing cursive, in pencil and quite legible. It fills one page after another. There are no cross-outs, no inserts, no palimpsest writing over eraser smudges. Kicking back on the island of Sifnos in the middle of the Aegean Sea, Blake wrote the bulk of *Alien Bait* in one first and final draft. "This is almost word for word what's in the play, each one of these scenes just coming right out of my pencil." Along with the characters' monologues, notes begin to appear suggesting props and costumes, and scenic diagrams crop up as the poetic playwright sporadically shifts into his director's mode, plotting the production even as he writes the play. It doesn't always happen this way, he says. But in the spirit of Kerouac, bashing out *On the Road* on a mile-long paper scroll, or Cohen, blazing through *Beautiful Losers* in a white heat on his own Greek island, Hydra, Blake's muse thrives on spontaneity.

"He has a tremendous amount of confidence," says Ken Cameron who, as an assistant director for One Yellow Rabbit, was Blake's right-hand man on many shows. "He has this ability to write on demand with a second's notice. I was often frustrated by him because it was my job to plan and I'm meticulous about organizing things. I remember when we were doing *Somalia Yellow* [for the 1998 High Performance Rodeo], I was panicking, saying, 'We should be doing the script. When are we going to write it?' Finally he said 'Sit down and type what I tell you.' I sat down at the computer and he literally wrote the entire script, dictated every single word to me. The man can write perfect, beautiful, poetic sentences just like that; they just come out of him."

Stephen Schroeder, who replaced Grant Burns in 1998 to become OYR's managing producer, understands Cameron's frustration. Blake would seem to extend the "secret theatre" concept to the very content of his plays. "I'm the producer and sometimes even I don't have a very good idea of what a show is going to be about," Schroeder says. "I'll sit down with Blake two months before a show is going to premiere and say 'Tell me what's in your head.' Blake knows what he's doing, but he's also a wily guy," he adds. "We joke about him being the International Man of Mystery. He leaves all his options open till the last possible minute."

Blake's preferred method of composition is a piecemeal approach, often with much of the script taking shape in rehearsal. "Blake is a non-linear thinker," says Cameron. "He's able to see the whole picture at once but he's only able to focus sporadically on pieces of it at a time. When one piece comes into clear focus, then so does something else, but it all comes together in a spotty way." Like American avant-garde director Robert Wilson, Blake sticks pages of script to the wall of the theatre rather than handing out a completed draft to the cast and crew. "He'll have ten pieces of paper posted on a wall," says Grant Burns. "They'll be lists of scenes. And then he'll start to put it together. He'll have bits of writing and then he'll make it into a whole. That was how *Alien Bait* was made. Michael had all this research, made the actors do this research for their characters, and then he culled it all. And then Blake put a story over the research, a narrative about a guy who goes to a [UFO] conference and meets these other people — a vehicle for Michael's research on all these paranormal events that he wanted to discuss."

As he flips through the *Alien Bait* notebook, Blake pauses to read portions here and there. His light, gentle voice is quiet and intense. It is a young poet's voice. Despite the advancing army of white bristles invading his brown-black hair, Blake still carries the aura of youth. It's in his tone and his attitude, the way he still discusses art and politics with the unquenchable enthusiasm of a student, as well as in his face. By the time some men hit their mid-forties, it has become impossible to see through the accretions of age to catch a glimpse of the boy beneath. With Blake, the boy is right there, still on the surface. You can easily see him setting fires in the junkyard with his brother, or poring over his stash of DC comics, or lipping off the old man.

Blake was born on 21 January 1955 in Vancouver, where his parents had moved during a brief, ill-fated business venture. Blake's dad, Howard Brooker, and his mother, Marguerite, née Black, came from families that had been in Calgary or the southern Alberta region since the 1890s. However, sometime in the 1950s, Blake's paternal grandfather, Sidney Brooker, decided to pull up stakes and resettle on the West Coast. A former head of operations at the Burns meat processing plant in Calgary, he now planned to run his own delicatessen. Howard came out to join his father in the enterprise but, despite Sidney's expertise, the shop failed. Blake puts it down to the family's English roots. "A deli has to be German, or European, to have credibility. Customers were coming in, speaking German, and nobody understood them." Rather than change their name to Buddenbrooks, Howard and Marguerite packed up and, with their oldest child, Cheryl, and baby Blake in tow, moved back to Calgary. Howard took a job as a process technician at the Imperial Oil refinery in the industrial yards of Ogden, and the family settled not far away, in the new southeast suburb of Forest Lawn.

"We lived on the edge of the city," remembers Kevin Brooker, who was born there in 1957. "Our house was uniquely situated in that it faced toward the south to infinity; there was nothing out there but countryside. For the ten years that we lived there, we roamed absolutely freely into the country, past the train tracks, past this incredible junkyard where we did endless amounts of fire-lighting, fort-building, glass-breaking, mouse-slaughtering, gopher extermination. Some of those grisly moments were among the first things that Blake wrote about as a poet — those teenage cruelties to animals. But we never did anything really bad."

At about the time Blake was reaching his early teens, Howard had his mid-life crisis. In 1968, at the age of thirty-eight, he quit his refinery job, enrolled at the university, and began building the family a new house with his own hands. It was an adventure that left a deep impression on his kids. He sold their house in Forest Lawn, recalls Kevin, "and we started renting another home while he was building a house from scratch on the north hill. And when I say from scratch, we dug the basement by hand — me, my father, and my brother. We had a pick, a wheelbarrow, and, I believe, three shovels. My father was superhandy and learned how to do it all. Designed it even. It still stands." The house is in the northwest district of Capitol Hill, on the edge of Confederation Park — the same neighbourhood where Howard and Marguerite grew up. A devotee of visionary architect R. Buckminster Fuller, who was then at the height of his popularity, Howard built the roof to geodesic specifications. (Fuller's environmentally responsible, "doing more with less" philosophy would later inform Blake's attitudes toward theatre-making.) The roof "took us months, as a family," says Kevin. "We all built it together, my mother and sister working the saw, handing up the boards, while the guys were placing them, gluing and nailing them. It took us three months." They moved in before it was finished, in 1969. "We lived in one room all summer, the five of us. It was pretty Spartan."

Blake remembers his father fondly (Howard died on 31 January 2001 at the age of seventy). "He was a creative guy," he says, "a guy who felt he could do things on his own, a guy who always used to bring ideas into the house. He was sort of like a working man's George Bernard Shaw. When I was six or seven years old, my parents took a trip to Europe and very soon after he came back he was inculcated with all these ideas about art and philosophy. He had this sense of European culture. He got into a phase where he used to buy art prints by avant-garde European painters and have them up around the house." At university, Howard majored in education and minored in art history. Although he had been a high school dropout, he excelled at the U of C, but in the end he never did anything with his teaching degree. He went back into business and ended up in industrial shelving, running a Canadian franchise of Lundia, the Swedish storage-systems giant.

Blake eulogizes his dad now, but Kevin says Howard was a strict disciplinarian and often punished his rebellious older son, who had already begun to automatically question authority. "Blake was recalcitrant — he couldn't just shut up and take the bullshit that comes down from above. As a result, he perceives his upbringing to be more harsh than I do. But he was mouthing off the old man and I was like, 'Dude, don't be a fucking idiot, man, you can't win.'"

"There was clearly friction between them," remembers Blake's friend Don Gillmor. In their twenties, the unemployed Brooker boys were often hired by their dad to help out on shelving installation jobs and they, in turn, recruited their pals. Gillmor was among them and witnessed the tension. But he also saw where Blake inherited his passion for perfection. "We'd be installing these big movable shelves in oil companies, $90,000 systems, and you'd lay down these tracks and one of them would be, like, 1/64 of an inch out, and Howie would say 'Tear the whole thing up. They're paying for quality, we're going to give 'em quality.' He was so meticulous, way more than his clients gave a shit about. He'd run around these office buildings with no shirt on. You'd be in some legal firm, and there's bare-chested Howie with his 1950s swimmer's build, this muscular old guy, running around like crazy. We called him 'Taz' as in the Tasmanian Devil. He was driven. You can see that quality in Blake now."

Apart from the art prints and a mother who played the piano, the Brooker household was not an artistic one. The boys were into athletics, doing gymnastics with the Calgary Gym Club, playing badminton and basketball. To this day, Blake is still a big hockey fan and faithfully follows the rocky fortunes of the Calgary Flames. He was also a typical Canadian boy in many other ways. He joined Cub Scouts. He read fantasy literature (Robert E. Howard's macho *Conan the Barbarian* tales were favourites). He was an avid comic-book buyer with a preference for the venerable DC brand over the younger, hipper Marvel. "I liked Batman, Superman, Aquaman. And Sgt. Rock." At Crescent Heights High School, he hung out with a bunch of fellow jocks. "They weren't offensively bastard, car-club dudes," says Kevin, "they were pretty good guys." And he let Kevin tag along. "We were always buddies. He was always good about incorporating me into his friends. He never shunned me."

After university, they ended up living together at the notorious 1313, then later Blake and Kevin moved to Vancouver, where they had a loft on Water Street in Gastown. They also travelled together in those reckless backpacking days that would inspire *Serpent Kills*. It was 1978 and Kevin was living in the popular French ski resort of Val d'Isère. "My brother, Gregg Casselman, and Warren Fick came over," he says, "and I had bought a van in Amsterdam and fixed it up. They met me in Val d'Isère, we hooked up and drove 25,000 kilometres through North Africa, up through Tunisia, to Sicily, Italy, Rome. We went through Switzerland, France, Spain, England, Wales, Scotland — we did this Grand Tour of Europe, which took about three or four months. Spent five weeks in Morocco, smoked a lot of hash. That was a fun trip. I had bought that van for five hundred bucks Canadian, sold it for a thousand in London, after 25,000 kilometres. That was sweet." By then, Kevin remembers, Blake had become an obsessive reader and his authors of preference were the Beats. It was a taste he shared with his brother and pals. Although they had been teens at the tail end of the '60s, and were therefore presumed citizens of Abbie Hoffman's Woodstock Nation, it was those post-war voices from the '50s that spoke most strongly to them. "We were never hippies," says Kevin. "We went straight from jock to Beatnik. You'll find not a trace of New Age in Blake."

While attending the U of C, Blake wrote poetry and short stories but even then he was performance-oriented. Writer Paul Anderson, who met him at university in 1975, says Blake loved to have his eloquence put to the test. "Although he was a good writer even then, he lived for the oral final. It didn't matter what class he was in, if he could arrange it so that the final could count for 100 per cent of his mark and it could be oral, that's what he wanted. It wasn't necessarily that he expected it to be a great advantage, it was more a sense of the adventure, of everything riding on that moment." Anderson read his friend's youthful work, but was more impressed with his spontaneous creativity. "A lot of his best compositions were the riffs I heard standing around at kitchen parties with him, Michael, and Kevin. Those three really knew how to improvise and keep a party cooking."

Another writer who got friendly with Blake in those salad days was Don Gillmor, who would go on to become an award-winning journalist and co-author the best-selling *Canada: A People's History.* A U of C grad, Gillmor had met Kevin when they were both ski bums in Val d'Isère and decided to look him up back in Calgary. When he knocked on the door of the Brookers' Capitol Hill home, Blake answered the door. "He was in his bathrobe," recalls Gillmor, "watching the afternoon matinee, drinking Kool-Aid, and looking at the want ads half-heartedly." It turned out they were both authors in search of a purpose. "We shared that sense that we wanted to pursue something, write something, but we didn't know exactly what that was."

That summer, when the boys moved out, Gillmor joined the non-stop party at 1313, which he remembers as being a hive of ceaseless creativity. "There were always bands being started, projects under way. Kevin was writing stuff for the *National Lampoon.* Everyone was trying everything. I even bought a guitar and hammered away at it for a while. I thought: Why not?" Kevin did learn some rudimentary bass licks and formed a punk band with Casselman and Richard McDowell called Rhythm and Bruise. Poet Murdoch Burnett was also part of the scene and was instrumental in importing Beat icons Burroughs and Ginsberg to do local readings. Blake began reading his own poetry and developed quite a theatrical delivery, Gillmor recalls. Still, he was surprised when Blake made his stage debut as the crippled Sam in *Creeps.* "I went with

Denise to see the show and I was bowled over by the fact that he'd just jumped into some other discipline completely."

It was another pal, Grant Burns, who commissioned Blake's first play, asking him to write a radio drama for CJSW, the U of C's campus radio station, back when Burns was station manager. He remains a huge fan of Blake's writing and regrets not being able to order more. "I love it," he says. "My favourite plays the company has done are his. I wish he would spend more time doing his own writing and less time fixing other people's. When I was with OYR, I wanted to act more as a producer, be able to say 'Here's $5,000, I'm commissioning you to write a play.' We used to pay him $2,500 to write a play. I think he got paid $1,500 to write *Ilsa*. I would have upped the ante and said 'Stop directing. Get the hell out of here, go to Greece, spend the next three months writing a play. Don't fix *Alien Bait*, or Denise's latest creation. You're more than a dramaturge, you're a great playwright.'"

Conversely, while Green and Clarke have no qualms about writing, Blake almost never acts. Few realize that he ever did. When, in 1999, it was announced that he would write and perform a solo show at the Rodeo, the news came as a surprise. Could Blake do it? Sure, he could direct a bunch of actors, but would he be able to hold an audience's attention with his own quiet, unassuming demeanour? *Blake with an Exclamation Mark* turned out to be a witty, low-key performance, with the barefoot, bed-headed Brooker perched protectively behind a music stand, playing up his lack of stage presence. Once he got going, however, he proved to have crisp comic timing as he delivered a classic Brooker-style meditation — this time on his own identity, compared and contrasted with those of three of his namesakes: the great poet-artist William Blake, the legendary hockey coach "Toe" Blake, and Blake Carrington, the jet-setting billionaire of TV's *Dynasty*.

What those with short memories had forgotten was that, quite apart from romping in a Paddington Bear costume, Blake had spent his early days at One Yellow Rabbit as an actor. He was Lasca, the capitalist charnel-house keeper, in the company's original Edmonton Fringe production of *Leonardo's Last Supper* (and got a good notice in the *Edmonton Journal*). He was also part of *Winterplay's* storytelling troupe. Laura Parken remembers seeing him make an impressive entrance during a performance at the Off Centre Centre. "As you walked into the gallery, in one corner there was this huge pile of dead leaves," she says. "There was this wonderful ambience, this cozy feeling, the smell of leaves in the fall. So we settled in, heard the first folk tale, and then, suddenly, out of these leaves bursts Blake Brooker, red-faced, sweaty, panting. He's telling this story of this young boy who has been in hiding, and I just was utterly captivated by that moment, that surprise, and by Blake's dishevelled appearance. I discovered later that he's got lots of allergies and he was lying under there, barely able to breathe."

Even when he finally wrote his first Rabbit play and found his forte, Blake wasn't above stepping in for one of its actors on late notice. "When we were doing *The Batman on a Dime* for *Café Theatre*," recalls George McFaul, "it was really on the wing a lot of times. The program changed every week. One week Denise couldn't be there. Marianne was already gone, so Blake played Catwoman. It still makes me laugh uproariously whenever I think about it." Parken, who participated in *Café Theatre* not long after, remembers Blake's cavalier attitude to acting. "There was this piece in the show that I believe George did, where he'd crack open a bottle of Bushmills on stage and have a swig. Then he'd bring it back into the dressing room and, since the seal was broken and the show was almost over, we'd all pass it around. I recall Blake once, picking up the bottle and saying 'Well, you people may come from the Richard *Fowler* school of acting, but I come from the Richard *Burton* school!' And then he chugalugged it." From then on, they referred to the Irish whisky as "Burton."

Blake's brief periods in the spotlight may have made him a more sympathetic director. Mark Bellamy has a telling anecdote from the time he performed in Michael Green's kinky hunting play, *Naked West*, which Blake directed. "We all started the show naked," remembers Bellamy. An actor and dancer whose experience up until then had been mostly in musicals, Bellamy had never done a nude scene. "The day we finally had to do the opening in rehearsal, Michael of course had no problem. [Fellow actor] Chris Hunt and I were like, 'O–kay …' Then I remember looking up and seeing that Blake was sitting in the audience and he was naked, too. And so was Richard McDowell. Blake said 'I'm not going to ask you to do something that I'm not willing to do myself.' I thought that was great. After that, it was fine."

When it comes to casting, Blake's choices can be unpredictable and inspired. He chose Hunt to play the most cold-blooded of the hunters in *Naked West* and, later, cast him as Forest, the disfigured, sado-masochistic villain of Brad Fraser's *The Ugly Man*. For the balding, bland-faced actor, more accustomed to playing Oscar Wilde dandies and providing comic relief, it was against the grain to say the least. "Blake is maybe the only person who sees me in those kind of sick, twisted roles," he says with a grin. "Nobody else throws them my way." Yet few could forget the savage Hunt imitating the scream of a dying stallion in *Naked West* — a chilling moment evoking a line from that other Blake, poet William, about the misused horse that "calls to Heaven for human blood."

Both Elizabeth Stepkowski and Andy Curtis say Blake is a hands-off director who lets actors develop their characters and steps aside after the play opens — even though, unlike the hired directors in the regional theatre system, he has the luxury of sticking around and tinkering with the production. "Blake always says 'This is your show,' and then he'll fuck off," says Curtis. He contrasts Brooker with ex-Rabbit Gyllian Raby. "She'd be there for the entire run of the show and she'd be backstage after every performance, hammering you with notes. She'd get some brilliant idea of how something should be changed, which I think wasn't always that well-considered."

At a surface glance, Blake's work in the rehearsal hall can look as subdued as his stage presence. One Yellow Rabbit productions are often credited as "directed by Blake Brooker, staged by Denise Clarke" — meaning Clarke devises and directs the performers' movements, which in a Rabbit show are to the blocking of most plays what a Bach fugue is to three-chord rock. Since Clarke is often performing as well as staging, she's always up on her feet, striding about the stage, explaining as much with her body as her words. Blake sits behind his favoured music stand, part overseer, part big-picture guy, a conductor rather than a choreographer. His Socratic love of questioning informs his direction. Working on a scene, he won't tell an actor what to do, instead he'll ask "What are you looking at right now?" or "What would you be thinking when he told you that?" His shrewd eye for detail, a trademark of his writing, is also an asset when he's directing. Both because OYR creates collectively, and because Blake as a director doesn't attempt to apply a heavy imprint of personal style, his handiwork is often subtle, anonymous, transparent. He's a writer's director as well as an actor's — he never lets his direction upstage the play.

"Blake has an ego," says Ken Cameron, his erstwhile assistant, "but what he's taught me is that directing is not about the director — you are not the centre of attention. It's all about the performers. If a director can't step back and disappear while in the process of rehearsal, then he's not a good director." In the rehearsal hall, the performers jokingly refer to him as "Uncle Blake." On the one hand, he's the protective member of their theatrical family, dealing with a show's technical concerns, communicating with the office, so that his colleagues are free to concentrate on their performances. In return, and out of respect for his spectator's viewpoint, he always has the final say. "There will be a bit of choreography that's totally precious to Denise," says Cameron, "but Blake will be forced to say 'It has to go.' And I'm sure it crushes her, but she accepts his judgment because she's inside the play and he's outside it."

Friends outside the company often wonder how Blake and Denise manage to still work together after their painful breakup. They've obviously handled it well, but the other members of the troupe remember some tense times, when the wounds were still fresh — a period when Denise wouldn't allow Blake in the same room with her. Ironically, while Denise had shuttled between Blake and Richard MacDowell in the early days of their relationship, and later had a brief affair with another man, it was finally Blake who broke up the marriage. When they separated, in the autumn of 1997, Denise kept their funky little house on the Elbow River (successor to the one on the Bow). Four years after the split, Blake told me: "I think I'm over it now. Finally. It took a while." In retrospect, it almost looked like part of a chain reaction. Richard McDowell left his partner of nine years, dancer/choreographer Hannah Stilwell, for Zaide Silvia Gutiérrez in December 1996. Then Grant Burns and Shawna Helland, who had been married with Blake and Denise in a double ceremony, called it quits in February of the following year. "Everybody I know, of my age, has been divorced," said Blake. "And virtually everyone has had two or three significant relationships. I think that's how it goes now — but I'm not sure, because I'm not hooked into the deep suburbs at all." It has probably helped that both Blake and Denise went on to new relationships — Denise with Calgary artist Chris Cran, Blake with Toronto actor/director Karen Hines. Still, MacDowell thinks the separation has affected Blake's creativity. "Life has been fairly traumatic for Blake since he and Denise split up. Some people might be fuelled by that, but I don't think he's done his best work when he's in emotional distress."

But now *Dream Machine* has got his juices flowing. Reteamed with his old musical partner, David Rhymer, Blake is on a songwriting jag. The two men have been taking long walks on these warm autumn days, discussing the ideas and themes in the work of Burroughs and singing and humming bits of lyric and melody into a tape recorder. When they are finally showcased in a cabaret presentation at the High Performance Rodeo, they'll prove to be some of the most diverse and sophisticated songs the pair has yet produced.

Blake considers Burroughs the foremost — and furthest-out — spokesman of the Beat philosophy, with its rebellion against the military-industrial complex and the consumer-driven society. It's a philosophy that has informed Blake's and One Yellow Rabbit's work for twenty years. It inspired their youthful urge to rebel and create, but also to find an alternative way of creating. "We had an evolving aesthetic that was personal," he says, "and didn't necessarily have to do with performance. We wanted to be people who made things, not people who took things apart, not people who just shuffled things that had already been made, not people who destroyed things. We wanted to add value to the society we lived in by making things. And, in doing so, make them in a way that wasn't physically toxic — there was a real naive environmental sensibility involved!" In fact, he sees OYR partly as a theatrical expression of the theories of British economist/ecologist E. F. Schumacher, author of *Small Is Beautiful.* "We always wanted to be small and beautiful, local and authentic. Schumacher was referring to sustainable developments. We were into sustainable development in theatre as well — making things that are small, minimal, repeatable, so that once you developed something you could redevelop it and do it again and again. It would have a kind of life that didn't depend on other people picking it up.

"Part of our development is a philosophical and economic argument," he continues. "Certainly it's been a successful economic argument, to have started something like One Yellow Rabbit in a putatively or, possibly, culture-hating town and a largely art-ignoring culture. It was remarkable that we could hatch ourselves and fledge and now still be flying around bringing worms back to the nest."

When Blake puts his work in the broader context of economic and social theories, you're reminded of the essential difference between him and the other two artistic helmsmen of One Yellow Rabbit. You can't imagine Denise Clarke or Michael Green having a career outside the world of entertainment. They were born to bask in the spotlight. If Green wasn't an actor and impresario, he'd be the ringmaster of a circus or, at the very least, truck that Ferris wheel from fair to fair. Even if Clarke retreated to a pillar in the desert, there'd be a flock of disciples surrounding her and she'd devise some fancy footwork on her perch. Blake, however, is a writer and thinker who just happened to choose theatre as an outlet for his talents. And after all these years, he remains somewhat aloof toward the industry he works in. Blake and Green "are polar opposites in that respect," says Grant Burns. "Michael's been to every show in Calgary, I'll bet. He doesn't miss anything. Blake goes to very few. I'm not sure why. Maybe he doesn't want to be corrupted by other people's theatres and their ideas. Maybe he just doesn't like theatre." "If you asked me if I'm a theatre person," says Blake, "I would say, definitely not. I'm not a theatre guy, I'm an art guy. I'll go to something if someone says 'You've gotta go see this.'"

During the High Performance Rodeo, or on tour, Michael Green is glad-handing, networking, slapping fellow artists on the back and buying them a drink. If he loves a play, he'll lead the audience in laughter and applause. Blake is more stinting in his praise and has no qualms about openly criticizing shows even when they're playing in his own theatre. At the same time, his enthusiasm for a performance can be deliciously genuine. In 1993, while he and Clarke were creating *Dance Freak*, OYR's comic homage to classical ballet, she described to me his "unique" love of the art form: "Sitting with Blake at the ballet, with all the people who think they know exactly what they should be doing there — which is wearing their best scratchy clothes and way too much perfume — and watching them react to Blake reacting to the ballet, is really quite an experience," she said. "He'll watch the character dancers on stage, fulfilling their highly ritualistic roles, and he'll laugh loud and lasciviously and appreciatively at the smallest detail" (*Calgary Herald*, 25 February 1993).

He may appear thoughtful and intense, but Blake leads his fellow Rabbits in their rich, ribald sense of humour. In fact, Ken Cameron disputes Michael Green's image as the troupe's wild man: "Give Blake a chance and a) he'll be weirder and b) he'll drink Michael under the table." Sheri-D Wilson still laughs at the memory of a raucous night partying with Blake at their mutual friend Martin Guderna's Vancouver studio. The poet found herself the lone female at an all-male gathering and decided to do a little research. "I asked them 'How many times a day do you masturbate?'" Not shy about taking matters into his own hands, Blake boasted that he sometimes did it twenty times a day. "He turned it into this real competition," says Wilson. "Then Martin said that he masturbated in front of all his paintings, one at a time. It was so funny. And everybody was so open and frank about how they did it. I didn't know that men masturbated all over the house. Blake told me sometimes he'd just throw himself down at the bottom of the stairs and jerk off." She went away that night and wrote the hilarious masturbation riff for her erotic play/poem *Hung, Drawn and Quartered*. Of course, when it was staged, it was Michael who delivered the monologue, wanking on a fearsome rubber dildo, naked but for a gold earring.

Blake's own writing also tests the boundaries of taste, often in more daring ways (such as *Ilsa* with its sexy Nazis). The one line the Rabbits have seldom crossed since the days of *Krebbs* is grossing out the audience. They don't seem to have the temperament — or inner torment — to create deliberately vile plays such as Sarah Kane's *Blasted* or Mark Ravenhill's *Shopping and Fucking*. Even the violence of Danis's *Thunderstruck* and Murrell's *Death in New Orleans* is given an abstract or understated rendering. "Theatre is watched, so it has to be watchable," says Blake. "It has to be entertaining, diverting, attractive to one degree or another. It's fun to read about repulsive theatre and it would probably be fun to do it, but you really can't do it and survive. It has to be attractive on some level. We always do the kind of stuff that we'd like to see ourselves."

For a Beat disciple, he's keenly aware of consumer tastes. Grant Burns says Blake involves himself more than the other Rabbits in the marketing and publicity for shows. When Burns was GM, the two would spend days just debating the marketability of a play's title. "Our acid test was: Is it sexy? Is it funny?" says Burns. "I mean, even if the play wasn't, we knew if it sounded sexy and funny it would sell." The classic example being *Ilsa*. "Sure, it's a play about Jim Keegstra, but look at our poster image, look at our title: It looks like a comedy that's sexy. These were the kinds of things that Blake and I would fight over. In the office, after work when we went for drinks, then he'd phone me at ten o'clock at night: 'I still want to call it *Blah blah blah.*' And I'd say 'Fuck off. Why? Because that's what you put on the grant form? The title sucks.' And we'd be on the phone for half an hour, till our wives told us to get off. Then we'd be back at it again at work the next day. But we'd work it out."

The shock tactics of Kane, Ravenhill, and the other young playwrights who emerged in the late '90s have been labelled "in-yer-face theatre." Their methods may reflect a desire for attention, to make a big noise. Blake shares that motivation, but again he's taken the broader view and coined his own term: "undeniable theatre." It refers to something more enduring than the one play that causes a scandal or sensation. "As a director, I always wanted to have a *performance group* that was undeniable," he says. "In other words, it cannot be dismissed. I suppose that comes from a defensive position, because it's so easy to be dismissed as an artist. Whether people like it or not, whenever they come to One Yellow Rabbit they're going to see something that can't be denied."

In that same feisty spirit, he refuses to call his company an alternative theatre. "It's a ghetto-izing term," he says. "Alternative to what? Something that's better, or worse? We're citizens, we're human beings, our expression is as appropriate and valid as anybody else's."

It would be glib and inaccurate to call Blake Brooker the brains of the operation, given that the others in the company are also thoughtful, astute, and well-read. Instead, just call him the brainy one. Daniel MacIvor says he knows he can always count on Blake if he wants to get into a deep conversation about, say, the significance of theatre — a question he doubts that Green, and certainly Clarke, would ever ask. Trying to describe the personalities of the three Rabbit leaders, he comes up with a great street-level analogy. "Michael is a bit of a grifter," he says. "Somewhere in his past, in some other life, you can see him doing the old shell game in Times Square. But there's none of that in Denise. There's a pea under every shell in Denise's game. Everybody's a winner. And then there's Blake, just standing back from the crowd, trying to figure out how to win."

### Denise

Like Michael Green, Denise Clarke has no qualms about disrobing on stage.

15 November 2001. The opening night of *Sign Language: A Physical Conversation Performed by Denise Clarke.* The show is an experiment in presentation — part dance solo and part "salon" — its implicit

intent being to help demystify the oft-hermetic world of interpretive dance. Its first half consists of a seventy-minute abstract piece created and danced by Denise, inspired by Radiohead's "Fitter, Happier" litany on the *OK Computer* album and touching on everything from the events of the day — the war in Afghanistan in the wake of the terrorist attacks in the US — to Denise's own personal concerns, including her disputatious relationship with God. Early on, she slithers out of her tight black mini-dress and for a good portion of the work she dances nude. At forty-four, she is still in splendid shape but, like Mark Morris, she is one of those defiant dancers who is not afraid of aging and imperfect flesh. At one point, she sticks out her glorious buttocks like a horse's croup and then, discovering that they jiggle, she turns it into a joke, playfully hopping and jiggling across the stage.

After the interval comes the salon portion of the show, in which Denise, clothed, re-appears to discuss the making of the dance piece and answer questions from the audience. On this night there are many friends and fans in the Big Secret Theatre, and as the house lights go up, Denise spots her greying, well-dressed parents sitting amid the black-clad arts crowd, looking like an elderly couple that came to see a Broadway musical at Theatre Calgary and ended up in the wrong place. Denise introduces them to the audience and suddenly the diva becomes a daughter. "Sorry I showed my boobs, Dad," she mock-apologizes. "Sorry I shook my bum." Then she explains to the rest of us that whenever she does a nude performance, her father just raises his eyes to the lighting grid. "Yes," quips John Clarke, "and I've nearly gone blind staring at those darn lights!"

This leads Denise to muse over what she calls the "taking-off-my-clothes thing." She thinks it goes back to her childhood. "It's related to being three years old and getting out of the bath and just running around," she says. "I find I cannot lie when I'm naked."

Denise Elizabeth Clarke was born on 22 January 1957 at Calgary's Grace Hospital. The fourth and youngest child of salesman John and his wife, Betty, a homemaker, Denise grew up in Acadia at what was then the southern edge of the city. A lower-middle-class neighbourhood made up mostly of tiny bungalows, Acadia "was a horrible suburb at the time," says Denise. "I hated it." However, like the Brooker boys, she has fond memories of living on the verge of the countryside. "It was kinda cool for the first three years; my brother Peter and I could play out there." The two of them took long bicycle trips to the town of Midnapore — now a part of Calgary — and Fish Creek. But before long, the prairie scrub was gobbled up by new and bigger suburbs. "Willow Park went up, then [Lake] Bonavista — it continued on from there."

Denise speaks warmly of her parents. She calls John a "very gregarious, very funny man. He's a serious hero of mine, my dad. He had a violent temper as a young guy. He was one of those kind of guys who's so much fun, so handsome and delightful, and then [also has] a wild, raging temper. Then he had his first heart attack when he was in his early fifties and the guy just completely changed. I saw my father turn into a real sweetheart, very thoughtful, very kind, sort of a Zen guy." Her mother Betty is "a really elegant, beautiful woman" whose interest in ballet sparked her daughter's career.

Little Denise looked up with awe at her big sister, Susan, who is eight years older and, as a teen, twirled a mean baton. "She was a rockin' baton twirler, was in the [Stampede] parade with Bing Crosby, wore this purple satin baton outfit. To this day I'm really impressed by baton twirling. It kills me. I always used to bruise my elbows when I tried it." But as a kid she was closest with her second brother, Peter, who is only eighteen months older. "I always fantasized that we were twins."

When Denise was three, Betty took her to see a film of the Bolshoi Ballet's *Swan Lake,* starring the celebrated Maya Plisetskaya as Odette, and the little girl was hooked. "That was it," says Denise. "I just drove her insane until she got me into a class." She took her first ballet lessons with Rosalee Carter, then later was taught by Lynette Fry, who had been a soloist with the Royal Winnipeg Ballet and who ran, with husband Jock Abra, the Calgary Dance Theatre. She glissaded blithely through her preteen years at the barre, a happy child with natural talent. "I remember I was always very surprised as a little kid if anything good happened to me. I was always surprised to find out that I was pretty talented. I loved dancing so much that I just thought I was so lucky to get to do it. So I always had a really nice relationship to a very fucked-up scene — until I was about fourteen."

It was then that she received the Royal Academy's Solo Seal, which precipitated a falling-out with her ballet teacher at the time. "It was very rare for someone my age to pass that exam," Denise says. "My teacher was very cross with me and told me not to get a big head. I didn't get to have one second of glory or pleasure. And I just started thinking: Oh, fuck you. I felt rebellious and I thought: I'm not dancing with you again. That's why I went to Edmonton. I tearfully told my mom one night, 'I have to dance and I can't do it here. I have to go to Edmonton and dance with the Alberta Ballet.' I thought it was going to be several months of family discussion, but my mom came downstairs an hour later and said 'Okay.' And a week later I was living in Edmonton, alone."

Denise also convinced her parents to let her drop out of Lord Beaverbrook High School although she'd just started grade twelve — the final grade in Alberta's secondary school system. Once a model pupil, she had lost interest in formal education. "I was an extraordinarily attentive student as a kid," she says, "almost an obsessive-compulsive child — really, really organized mentally. Then, when I hit high school, I started smoking pot."

She joined Alberta Ballet at fifteen and two years later moved east to continue her training at the more prestigious Royal Winnipeg Ballet. It was there that she had her first career crisis. "I'd really injured my foot," she recalls, "and the world of ballet is so crazy that nobody had said 'You have to heal your foot,' so I had seven compound injuries, to the point where it became really dangerous. And besides, I was just so thin. Near the end, I was doing diet pills and sleeping pills to sleep 'cause I'd hurt my foot." After taking time off to nurse her injuries, she returned to the company a physical wreck. "I was super-skinny, big black circles under my eyes, and I walked into class thinking: Oh, they're going to know I've been doing drugs, they're going to tell my mom. And I walked in and everybody said 'Oh, you look fantastic!' Finally, the alarms went off. I just realized: this is crazy, this is sick."

She bid adieu to the RWB and, in the fall of 1975, moved to Quebec to begin an apprenticeship with Les Ballets Jazz de Montréal. She also found freelance work at Radio-Canada, the French-language arm of the Canadian Broadcasting Corporation, as one of the dancers on a cheesy variety show called *Monsieur B.* "We were like Solid Gold Dancers," she says with a laugh. "The highlight of that experience was dancing in complete gold body paint while Shirley Bassey sang 'Gold-finger.'" At Les Ballets Jazz, Clarke's defiant nature surfaced again and led to a clash with co-founder/artistic director Eva von Gencsy. At first, she and the charismatic von Gencsy got along well. "I really liked her," says Denise, "and she befriended me and took me on as her star new-comer." But their relationship soon turned sour. "It got to the point where a choreographer from New York had come and he said he wanted to work with me, and Eva said 'No, you can't work with her.' I was in the room and overheard this and I said 'Why not?' And then she got all angry and made me dance in a different studio by myself. I thought: This is really weird. I don't want to do this. These people are crazy. So then I thought I'd be a poet."

Denise had been writing poetry for her own amusement since the age of fourteen. Like Brooker and Green, she has a literary side and has always been a voracious reader. As a kid she devoured everything from the pulpy Nancy Drew/Hardy Boys series to children's classics. "*Treasure Island* was, for me, just a magical book. And a book that never left my consciousness was *The Water Babies.* I would read it over and over to myself as a poetry book and an imagination book; I would dance that book and think about that book." Later, she raided her parents' library for the best-sellers of the day — such as *On the Beach* by Nevil Shute and *The Naked and the Dead* by Norman Mailer. "My parents never censored anything. If the book was in the house, you could read it." The first poet to catch her fancy was Emily Dickinson. "She didn't make sense to me particularly as a kid, but I just really liked her." Then, in her early teens, a friend turned Denise on to the mystical writings of Herman Hesse, which led her to discover Allen Ginsberg and the other Beats. Now, at eighteen, let loose in Canada's sexiest city, she embraced the Beatnik lifestyle with enthusiasm, living on the knife-edge of poverty, kicking at the doors of perception.

"I did a lot of drugs in Montreal when I became a poet," she says. "I ran into a bit of trouble with that. I did a lot of mescaline, for a long period of time, and got a little bit disassociative. I'm really lucky, 'cause in the nick of time I suddenly woke up and thought: Hey, maybe I shouldn't do all these drugs constantly. But you know the extreme lifestyle of checking out the street. It was pretty radical for a sweet little bunhead. My poor parents — had they known, they would've died. My mother still just freaks whenever I talk about it. But it was very important to my development. And I felt invincible. I was basically homeless for several months and never worried about it. The thing I remember the most about it was that I was never afraid. I was sad, sometimes, but never afraid."

She ended up sharing an apartment with two young men. "Their names were both Brian, but one guy said to call him 'Byron.' He was a Dylan freak. And when I moved in, they showed me a bag of mescaline and they put it in a drawer — it was brown-powder, old-fashioned, old brown mescaline — and there was a bag of capsules beside it. And they said 'Just scoop out a cap and help yourself.' And so, it was like, Oh, gee, I think maybe I'll have some mescaline. It was stupid naïveté. I actually thought I was living a mature lifestyle. I really was living a bohemian existence. There was no money. We ate carrot sandwiches and stuff. I hung out in a pretty wild scene. In those years, in '75, '76, it was really hard to know who was a criminal, who was a drug dealer, who was a law student, who was a real writer, who was a hack. Everyone looked the same. Bikers looked the same as law students. The element that I mixed in and ran around with was so diverse. But it was powerfully, intellectually stimulating."

Denise also learned that there was another dance world outside classical ballet, jazz, and modern, and other reasons for dancing besides artistic self-expression. "I had one boyfriend who was insistent on my education in strip bars. He took me to these really raunchy strip clubs. He was actually a hipster, he knew what he was doing; he knew I was a dancer and he was like, 'You know, there's other kinds of dancers and they make a thousand dollars a week.' And I was like, 'Oh? Doing what?' And he said 'C'mon, I'm going to show you.' So I had this incredibly wild education in stripping. Then he'd show me a low-end stripper and say 'Now check out this girl, now this is a junkie. Look at this bar, look at the difference. She makes three hundred bucks a week.' It was a world I sure had no idea about. Absolutely none."

Ever since leaving Edmonton, Denise had stayed in touch with Richard McDowell, whom she'd first met in high school. "He was what really saved me," she says. "We were in constant contact with letters. We were writing fifteen pages a day — this was pre-Internet, and we had no money for the long-distance phone. We essentially received a letter a day from one another. He burned all mine and I kept all his," she adds, laughing. "I could just kill him for that." It was McDowell whom she finally returned to when being down and out in Montreal lost its charm. They were reunited in Edmonton, then moved south to Calgary to be close to Denise's family when her oldest brother, John, had a kidney transplant. Back in Calgary, Denise got her act together. Ending her hiatus from dancing, she returned to the studio and rediscovered her first love. "It suddenly occurred to me that what had bugged me was not doing what I wanted to do," she says, "and what might appeal to me would be to make my own dances." She got a job teaching dance classes — ballet to children, jazz to adults — with Dance Incorporated, a school run by Teri Willoughby, one of her childhood dance pals. "She was this remarkable creature," says Denise. "The worst businesswoman in the world at that time, but with an unbelievably generous spirit, just a great dame. She essentially became my patron." Willoughby had a studio above a natural bread store in the funky Hillhurst-Sunnyside district and she gave Denise the run of the place, rent free. "At the age of twenty-one, I had a studio, sound system, access to dancers — just a dream come true. And I practically lived in that studio; I worked like a maniac."

If Willoughby gave Denise a place to create, another young woman introduced her to the techniques that would come to inform her style.

Anne Flynn was a New York dancer who had studied at SUNY Brockport and at the Eric Hawkins and Merce Cunningham studios. Arriving in Calgary in the late 1970s to take a teaching post at the U of C, she was frustrated to find there were virtually no other modern dancers in the city. That changed when Denise Clarke appeared on the scene. Flynn remembers being thrilled by Denise's performance of a piece by local choreographer Vicki Adams Willis called *The Peacock and the Crane*. Not long afterward, Denise was hired by the university to fill in for a dance teacher on maternity leave. "At the time she was working on a solo concert," recalls Flynn, "and I had done a solo concert — mostly because I didn't have anybody to dance with here. I approached her and said 'Do you want to put our solo concerts together on the same program?'" In May 1981 they gave their first joint concert, which included some duets and marked the beginning of a six-year partnership. They would go on to create four more full-length concerts together, play the Canada Dance Festivals, and perform countless other gigs. They also became fast friends. "It was a real meeting of kindred spirits," says Flynn. "When we danced together for the first time, we knew there was something special between us." Their teamwork led to an exchange of methods and styles. While Denise had taken the classical route, Flynn's New York education had centred on postmodern and improvisational dance. "Denise and I had hugely contrasting backgrounds, we really had nothing in common in terms of our training, and it's something we played around with choreographically. It was an unusual combination to have this postmodern improviser and this very traditionally trained ballet and jazz dancer." Denise says Flynn "was a huge influence" who introduced her to the theories and methods of Irene Dowd, Bonnie Bainbridge Cohen, and Moshe Feldenkrais. "They're all about efficiency of movement and their work was so profoundly beautiful. For the first time in my life, suddenly my technique was serving me, instead of me serving the technique." When, in September 1981, choreographer Twyla Tharp premiered *The Catherine Wheel*, a major work danced to a richly textured score by Talking Heads' David Byrne, Flynn insisted that Denise go to New York and see it. Denise says she was turned on by Tharp's barrier-busting. "In the snobby days of new modern and classical modern dance, she was doing this break-through work where she would involve every aspect of her background. She had been one of those small-town kids who did tap and gymnastics and baton and ballet — you name it, she did it — and it was all there in her work."

Tharp soon entered Denise's pantheon of dance heroes — along with superstar Mikhail Baryshnikov, the great Broadway choreographer Bob Fosse and … Prince. The flamboyant, multi-talented rock musi-cian had come strutting onto the scene at the end of the '70s and, while a lot of people thought he was a joke, Denise became infatuated with him. "I was mad for Prince," she says. "I knew he was a little greaseball, but I just could not get over him. He was such a renaissance cat. Here's this guy my age, I'm listening to his music and he's playing all the instruments, he's just dressed in the most godawful getup, but you lis-ten to him and he can sing deep down in this huge bass voice, he can twitter up high almost comically. He was super-theatrical to me and, most importantly, his freedom and audacity just rocked my world. He was kind of unfashionable at the time amongst a lot of my friends, but I didn't care. He also made me laugh; I got such a sense of humour from him. And when I watched him dance I'd think: That's what people want to look at. That's so much fun, this outrageous, sexy dancing. And he could do it — it wasn't embarrassing. I could always dance like that and I used to try not to. And then I thought: Well, I'm not going to har-ness that anymore, I'm just going to let it play where it wants to."

It wasn't Anne Flynn, but Blake Brooker who had turned Denise on to Prince. Shortly after coming back to Calgary, she and Richard McDowell had met Blake, Kevin, and the rest of the 1313 posse. Denise was immediately taken with Blake. "I just loved him. He was so funny and unbelievably lively." At about the same time, she became pregnant by McDowell and was determined to have the baby despite the misgiv-ings of her friends and family. When she lost the child, a boy, five-and-a-half months into her pregnancy, everyone was relieved except Denise. "I was horrified and so sad," she says. "I guess my first really serious, deep depression settled in. Everybody said 'Well, it's for the best.' But it shattered me, it broke my heart. And Blake was around then and he cheered me up. He and I and Shawna Helland — who was my best friend — we formed a very intense friendship and really rock-and-rolled around intellectually and laughed our heads off together." Brooker read Denise's poetry and encouraged her writing, exchanging poems with her. Still, it would be a long time before she was able to resolve her conflicted feelings for McDowell and Brooker. "We had a strange triangular love life for five years in our twenties, which was very difficult," she says. "It was awful and sad and tricky. And, at the risk of sounding a bit melodramatic, it was probably pretty much the reason we are all the kind of artists we are. Because it was really hard, and it was judged harshly by our peers. They were really dismayed. It was like, Smarten up! And when you're living in a radical arts scene, it seems surprising when people are mad at you for doing something like that."

Despite the emotional turmoil, for most of her twenties Denise enjoyed a pretty sweet life. Along with Anne Flynn and Vicki Adams Willis, who would co-found the successful Decidedly Jazz Danceworks, she was one of the brightest lights in the city's small dance community. The high school dropout was suddenly earning $5,000 a month teaching full-time at the university, in both its fine arts and physical education faculties, as well as giving concerts and choreographing like crazy. "I made something like sixty dances at the university," she says. "Solos and group dances for fifteen and twenty — which I still cannot believe, when I know now how hard it is to make a dance. And I was getting paid handsomely to do what I considered to be research — how to get people to move well and interestingly." She taught everybody, from dancers to athletes, kids to grandparents, and her classes were enormously popular. "There'd be fifty, sixty people packed into her jazz classes," recalls Flynn. "It was unbelievable." Denise's secret was that she taught everyone the same thing. "I kept realizing fundamentals are fundamentals," she says, "and what you do within that is simply shape-changing stuff. It allowed me to devise this way of introducing physical notions to people that they could do and own and interpret, so that they didn't have to look awkward or goofy. They never had to deal with that problem on the stage of thinking: Oh, I feel dumb doing this. They could just do it. That was probably my biggest breakthrough as a choreographer up to then."

It was in 1986, in her thirtieth year, that Denise experienced her second career crisis. It was brought on by a bout with Graves' Disease, a hyperthyroid condition, which first began to manifest itself during her unhappy stint with One Yellow Rabbit in *The Pageant of the Comet* at Expo '86. At the time she didn't realize she was sick. Victims of Graves' can be nervous and high-strung, symptoms that Denise mistook as signs of a psychological problem. "You don't sleep, you're kind of crazy, you're really emotional, difficult, irrational. I thought: Oh my God, I'm crazy. I'm one of those crazy choreographer/actor types." Finally, Betty Clarke realized her daughter was ill. "I was still doing a lot of dance work with Flynn and my mother came to see a show of ours called *Red Dress Journey,* and she said to me 'Something's wrong with you.' She insisted that I get looked at and I had this disease. It put me on my back, stopped the presses, for a good four months.

"I just reassessed my life during that time," Denise recalls, "and I realized if I didn't quit the university, I would never quit, I would stay as a teacher. And I loved to teach. It was a great passion of mine. But I thought: No, I'm going to devote myself to performing. And that very quickly translated into devoting myself to the Rabbits. The dance world didn't appeal to me, the level of intellectual companionship I had in the dance world didn't satisfy me, and so I let that go and concentrated on theatre. I almost immediately realized what I really wanted to do was concentrate on acting, and just develop myself as an actor."

Denise had already taken an acting workshop at the U of C and now she set about learning how to use her voice as capably as her body. "I embarked on my own training program of reading out loud a couple of hours a day — classics, poetry, Shakespeare, whatever touched my fancy," she recalls. "And I really started to sing a lot. I was way too nervous, every time I tried to take a singing or a voice lesson; I was completely confused and my voice would disappear. So I had to do it myself."

The first evidence that Denise Clarke could really act came with *Serpent Kills,* when she turned in a sharp performance as Sobhraj gang member Barbara, a tough Australian chick who shaved her legs with a straight razor and who was as streetwise and pragmatic as the heroine, Marie-Andrée, was gullible and romantic. But Barbara, like Ilsa, Mata, and Martha in *Permission,* was a character that fit her own independent, defiant nature. As with any actor, Denise delights in the roles that go against type — her nerdy scientist in *The Land, The Animals* or her teenage boy in *Thunderstruck.* Yet her most daring performance, in some ways, has been her Sarah Bernhardt in John Murrell's *Memoir* at Theatre Calgary.

Denise has worked countless times at TC and other big regional theatres as a choreographer, but no one had had the wherewithal to invite her on stage. That changed in 1998, when young director Nikki Lundmark bypassed an impressive list of Canadian grandes dames suggested by the theatre's administration and picked her to play the septuagenarian French actress. The choice came with the blessing — indeed, encouragement — of Murrell. "I knew it would make it an adventure, as opposed to just putting together a sellable commodity," he says. "Besides, if we have a true diva [in Calgary] who would understand the kind of demon that drove an artist such as Bernhardt, someone with that same kind of supra-normal juice as a performer, it would be Denise."

Sure enough, displaying a minimum of old-age makeup and a maximum of theatrical flair, the forty-one-year-old Clarke pulled it off. It was, as Murrell anticipated, not a feat of sedulous impersonation but a radiant embodiment of Bernhardt's spirit. She knew Sarah in her bones. (At the end of one performance, when Denise stepped into the wings, overcome with emotion, she leaned on her co-star, Christopher Hunt, who portrayed her faithful servant Pitou, and shed a few tears. Then she departed to her dressing room. The theatre's new general manager, a former banker, was watching. "So what's her problem?" he asked Hunt brusquely. "She's playing the great Sarah Bernhardt," Hunt patiently explained to him, "and Sarah Bernhardt is dying.") Later that same season, Denise invaded Theatre Calgary again, bringing with her Elizabeth Stepkowski, David Rhymer, and other partners in crime, and gave its conservative patrons an unexpected blast of sexy OYR energy as they made a heroic effort to dirty up Andrew Lloyd Webber's pallid concert musical, *Song and Dance*.

It was a pointless task. But, like Denise's other sallies into middle-of-the-road theatre, a profitable one. For a stretch of time in the 1990s, she spent two or three months a year choreographing musicals for major regional companies such as Toronto's Canadian Stage Company, Calgary's Alberta Theatre Projects, and Edmonton's Citadel Theatre. "They were big contracts, upwards of $20,000," recalls Grant Burns. "It was as much as she was making with the Rabbits all year. It used to be a little frustrating, but we decided that we were going to work around her schedule. Then we had a summit meeting one year where Denise said 'I'll give up all that shit if we're going to build a really hot show.' That's what she chose to do. She pulled herself back out of those high-earning gigs on a decision by all of us that we were going to make better shows and tour them."

It wasn't all shit, mind you. Denise has had a particularly fruitful association with Bob Baker in his time as artistic director of Canadian Stage and, later, the Citadel. A glimpse at her work with him reveals how her choreographic method is suited even to conventional theatre and traditionally trained actors.

Baker first hired her in 1992, on the recommendation of director Peter Hinton, who had staged the original *Serpent Kills*. Her introductory assignment was a sizeable one: choreograph the movement for Canadian Stage's ambitious mounting of Shakespeare's Wars of the Roses cycle. Clarke did the stylized fight choreography for the three *Henry VI* plays, presented al fresco in the theatre's Dream in High Park summer season, as well as *Richard III*, which opened its main-stage season at the St. Lawrence Centre. On top of that, she also acted in *The Queens*, Normand Chaurette's play about the women in the histories, which launched the second-stage season at the Berkeley Street Theatre.

"I have a background as a choreographer and dancer," says Baker, "so I really notice things that other choreographers do. In her morning warm-ups for the actors, Denise would also be developing a physical vocabulary for the show that she would use later on. Those warm-ups were just fabulous. It was the highlight of my day to be part of that. She focused everybody, had a strong discipline and yet a sense of fun and creativity. I could see a variety of actors of different skills and experience levels responding as an ensemble. No one stood out because they could jump higher or pick up the movement quicker. I'd never seen that before." She also tamed some male egos in the process. "There were some jock-mentality, alpha-dog-type guys who wanted more traditional sword fighting," says Baker, "but it was evident that if they opened up and allowed a more movement-based fight, it was better for all, and they went along with it." As a treat one day, Denise asked permission to perform excerpts from her latest solo work for the company on its lunch break. "She knocked everybody out with this powerful piece of acting and dance," recalls Baker. "From that point on, I realized this person was extraordinarily talented."

Baker subsequently worked with her on a superb 1996 production of Stephen Sondheim's *Into the Woods,* co-produced with Theatre Calgary. When Baker returned to his hometown of Edmonton in 1998 to take the wheel of the Citadel, he re-teamed with Clarke for a revival of the Sondheim, followed by a production of her favourite musical, *Cabaret.* "I didn't want to shy away from any of the sexuality of that show, or the dangerous side of its world," says Baker, "and I knew she wouldn't have any qualms about taking such risks."

Baker says Denise is "more organic than most choreographers. It is never just about movement or dance, it's always integrated into thinking and feeling. That is, if the mind understands what's going on, the body will move in the right way, as opposed to 'Now your left foot goes here and your right there.' She doesn't choreograph to the numbers so much as to the idea." She also does most of her creating in the rehearsal hall, shaping movement to the physical type and ability of the individual actors, as opposed to making them fit a preconceived choreographic plot. "It always feels to me like she's making it up on the spot, following her instincts, which I'm so impressed by."

At about the same time as she started to ease herself into acting, Denise also dipped her toe in the playwriting pool. Like Michael Green, she began by screwing around with an existing text, the vintage radio melodrama that formed the basis of *The Erotic Irony of Old Glory*. She went further with her next dance drama, a piece again created with her *Erotic* co-star, Mark Christmann. A serious chronicle of a cooling marriage, climaxing in an explosive confrontation between husband and wife (he's gay and cheating on her with a man), it required more than borrowed words. "In *Touch* there was out-and-out, huge monologue writing and big scene work," she says. During that project, her shyness about dramaturgy melted away. "I felt really like I was ready to just go ahead and write the thing. Just because I really liked the idea and wanted to get the work done."

Finally, in 1993, she set out to write a full-blown play. *Breeder*, conceived and started in Singapore, was a science-fiction satire set in a ravaged future world where most of the population is sterile and the few fertile females are an elite corps who sell their services like high-priced whores. The concept owed a debt to Margaret Atwood's *The Handmaid's Tale* and Aldous Huxley's *Brave New World*, but also to Denise's impressions of Singapore as a wealthy society that used affluence as an opiate to stifle dissent. In the course of the play, Tim (Clarke), one of the breeders, begins to question her luxurious life as a "fetal factory" as evidence surfaces of a eugenics plot by the suavely totalitarian government. When it premiered in the winter of 1994 at the Uptown Stage, *Breeder* was a smash hit. Blake Brooker directed and Richard McDowell did the score, while Lindsay Burns and Tanja Jacobs co-starred as Tim's fellow procreators and Mark Bellamy camped it up as their gay overseer and resident stud. (It was Michael Green and Andy Curtis's turn that year to play Theatre Calgary. They were off being Rosencrantz and Guildenstern and enlivening an otherwise dreadful production of *Hamlet*.)

Before that summit meeting described by Grant Burns, Denise still considered herself to be loosely affiliated with One Yellow Rabbit.

Even her own theatre projects weren't Rabbit ones, per se. "Those were things that I was going to do, regardless," she says, "and One Yellow Rabbit was welcome to produce them, or not. And they always wanted to." It wasn't until after OYR produced *Breeder* that she began to re-think things. "I felt afterwards that it wasn't very fair because [the show] didn't involve the ensemble [Green and Curtis]. That's when we all realized we should do work with the ensemble and that way we could tour it and it would have a future."

*Breeder* confirmed Denise's box-office clout with the company. Apart from Brooker's *Ilsa,* her shows were consistently its top draws. "Every show she's ever done has been commercially successful," claims Burns. "There's something about Denise. She's not as poetic as Blake, and Michael likes to shock for the sake of shocking, but Denise is into telling stories. Also, Denise was a star as a dancer, became the star of *Ilsa,* and, thanks to us always putting her face on posters, she's become a Calgary star. She's an icon in a sense and she has a lot of fans. So whenever Denise had an idea I was always in favour of putting it in the season."

Her next idea was to graft the dance solo to the monologue form. In *So Low,* she wrote and starred as a self-absorbed radio personality named Louise Metcalfe, who gets the kiss-off from her boyfriend on what was supposed to be the evening of their engagement, causing her to re-evaluate her solipsistic ways. In part a comic look at the life of a single, thirtysomething career woman (imagine Bridget Jones with an ego), it was also a sincere reflection on the "victim" culture of the '90s, as Louise cast the blame for all her problems on others to the point of hilarious and pitiful absurdity. The writing was sharp and amusing, but what separated *So Low* from the myriad of monologues besieging theatres then and now was Denise's use of dance as an alternative form of expression when words wouldn't do. The show opened with a crazy, slapstick ballet, Louise precariously clutching an armful of groceries, and climaxed with her slowly, literally spiralling into an abyss of despair.

*So Low* bracketed Denise's own heartbreak. Between its premiere in 1996 and its remount in 1997, Brooker decided to leave her. (Ironically, it was Brooker's friend Bruce McCulloch who had provided the voice of Louise's jilting boyfriend, delivering the *coup de grâce* on her answering machine.) According to Denise, the breakup was triggered by her infatuation with another man four years before: "that foolish, immature, and cruel attempt [to walk out on the marriage and the company] wound up being the reason Blake left me." Artist Chris Cran, invited back to redesign *Permission* for its revival in the Big Secret Theatre, caught her performance in *So Low* in the fall of '97 and saw her afterwards. "She was in a pretty rough way emotionally," he says, but already she and Brooker were facing the work-versus-relationship dilemma. "Right after that, *Permission* was up next, so they had no time not to work together, they had too much on their plate."

In the new year, the Rabbits toured *Doing Leonard Cohen* to Toronto's Factory Theatre. It ought to have been — and in commercial and artistic terms, it was — a highlight of the company's sixteen-year existence. The reviews were terrific. The houses were packed. Canadian celebs flocked to the Factory and congratulated the cast afterwards. Yet Andy Curtis remembers climbing into a taxi every night after the show with a weeping, devastated Denise. Even four years later, while rehearsing the Cohen play for an engagement at the Citadel, the memory still stung. She was hard put to get through her tender recital of "Suzanne" at the end of Act 1 without breaking into tears.

For a tense time, fans and friends of the Rabbits waited anxiously to see what would happen. Would one of them leave? Would the troupe split up, too? Stephen Schroeder, who had joined OYR as Grant Burns's assistant in 1995, watched the fallout from the inside. "It was made extraordinarily clear at the time that nobody wanted anybody to leave," he says. "They realized they had a great thing going. I think Blake and Denise always liked each other underneath, they've always been of major importance to each other's lives, and a divorce wasn't enough to make that go away." As well, he adds: "It almost seemed to me that neither one wanted to be seen to have quit for that reason. As Denise has put it herself many times, what we've embarked on is a grand experiment, and I think that's what helps keep the group together. We had a lot of late-night, beer- and wine-fuelled conversations when she was going through her breakup with Blake and she often said to me that, for all this heartache and turmoil, the experiment is just too interesting to stop."

Step into Chris Cran's cluttered studio, formerly the garage of a converted fire station, and your eye is sure to hit on something amusing. This time it's a big, bright, cartoon painting leaning up against a chair: Archie Andrews, the comic-book teen, naked with long orange hair, crouching in the pose of Goya's horrific Saturn and clutching a beheaded and dismembered body, a wide grin on his freckled face. The title: *Archie Devouring Reggie*. Cran, needless to say, has a twisted sense of humour to rival the Rabbits'. Among his finest and funniest works: the mock advertisement *My Face in Your Home;* a picture of Cran and a curiously hatted stranger taking in an exhibit of Warhol silkscreens, entitled *Self-Portrait Just Two Maos Down from Some Guy with a Goddamned Tea Cozy on His Head;* and, of course, the sublime *Self-Portrait with the Combat Nymphos of Saigon.*

Cran began his full-time career as a painter just a year after OYR formed, but he didn't move in the Ten Foot Henry's circle or go to the theatre much. "I was married with six kids," he explains. However, he did eventually meet Denise Clarke at a party and, after that, made a point of checking out the Rabbits' work. Denise, in turn, became a fan of his paintings and asked him to do the set for *Breeder.* It was his first attempt at scenic design and he was all at sea. "I didn't know what to do, so I just made a painting for it. Denise restructured the play around it." The painting, which dominated the breeders' boudoir, was an idyllic landscape copied from the seventeenth-century French painter Claude Lorrain. However, it concealed an optical trick. On its surface Cran added a second, pop image with invisible fluorescent paint that could only be seen under black light. The second image — a ventriloquist's dummy glaring down at the breeders like Big Brother — was revealed with a surprise lighting shift near the end of the play.

The next time the Rabbits requested a set, Cran got more ambitious, creating the '60s-kitsch decor for *Permission,* plus another painting. Along the way, he became a Rabbit junkie. "I think I've seen *Permission* almost thirty times," he says.

Denise was amazed at his capacity for observing new things with every viewing. "After a performance I'd say to him 'You're back! So what did you see in it this time?' He'd say 'Oh, subtle things. The way the light played, the changes in your eyes.' I'd say 'You can see that?!'" Cran doesn't think his repeated viewings are so odd. "It's like playing an album over and over again. Parts that I'm moved by, I'm not moved any less by for having seeing them a number of times. The hook is always there." However, among visual artists he admits he's atypical. "In the art world, there's been a real aversion to theatre," he says, "like the difference between Catholics and Jehovah's Witnesses or something. I have a lot of friends who just think theatre does not work as an art form."

In the months following Denise and Brooker's separation, Cran — divorced since 1982 — started hanging with her, and soon after they became lovers. So you could say Denise is a touch prejudiced when she makes the case for theatres using visual artists instead of scenic designers. "It worked for Diaghilev," she asserts, referring to the great impresario's hiring of Picasso to design sets for the Ballets Russes. "These are people whose lives are devoted to visual aesthetics. Give them a theatre to work with — they're brilliant. No offence to the designers out there in the universe, but good painters are, hands down, way cooler."

Like Brooker, Denise defies the classic pain-equals-good art equation. She seems to do her best work when she's happy. Since hooking up with Cran, she's written another full-scale play. *Featherland*, which premiered in the winter of 2001, tells the tale of Canadian husband-and-wife ornithologists Adele and Cecil Hyndman, eccentrics whose passion for their birds verged on bestiality. Based on a sympathetic biography by British Columbia journalist Bill Burns, the play treats Adele and Cecil with both humour and affection, capturing some of the absurdities of their avian obsession yet never mocking their ardour. It is a play about love, written with love, and in her dramatization of the Hyndmans' story, one detects Denise's identification with these "brave oddballs" who embarked on their own grand experiment in defiance of convention. At *Featherland*'s moving close, Cecil (Michael Green) triumphantly declares: "I would never trade my life. … I lived exactly as I chose! What caused me pain also afforded me the chance to know I was alive and balanced a kind of ecstatic existence that was my own design."

That might be Denise speaking for herself and the other Rabbits. Only, the Hyndmans, who ran a quaint bird sanctuary-cum-tourist attraction on Vancouver Island, had a hard time getting serious attention or respect for their work when they were alive. Denise is so admired that one could write a chapter consisting of nothing but testimonials from her fans and peers. Here's Michele Moss, artistic director of Dancers' Studio West in Calgary: "I always find her compelling. She's expressive, she's passionate. Her performances are big and boldly outlined, they aren't finely etched in pen-and-ink, but they're great to watch and they run the gamut of emotions." Anne Flynn: "She's a magnificent dancer. Forget the acting, forget the singing, Denise could have had a complete career just as a dancer. In dancerly terms, she's a uniquely talented person." Don Gillmor: "She's always had tremendous confidence. Even if she didn't have extraordinary depth as a performer, I think she'd still make it just through sheer force of will." Michael Dobbin: "I could watch Denise Clarke read the phone book."

But wait — is this a dissenting opinion we hear? "Denise is a diva," declares old Rabbit Kirk Miles. "Always will be. When we went to Vancouver [for Expo '86], she was a diva. She's always had an incredibly big ego. And for good reason — she's amazing."

One doesn't have to be a member of the Denise Clarke fan club, however, to acknowledge her crucial role in making One Yellow Rabbit a theatre to be reckoned with. If Blake Brooker wanted an undeniable company, she's made it so. Her distinctively choreographed movement, supple or hard-edged, vibrantly aggressive or small and gentle, is the Rabbits' indelible signature. It's why they stand out everywhere they go. Even the weariest critics at the late-night opening of *Thunderstruck* in Edinburgh were startled awake by the scene in which Denise toys with the show's precise choreography by having her, Green, and Curtis suddenly repeat an entire routine in reverse. In Europe, "physical theatre" often means the familiar acrobatic mime taught by Jacques Lecoq and practised by such celebrated disciples as Théâtre de Complicité and Steven Berkoff. It doesn't mean the kind of quirky, sexy, one-of-a-kind theatre ballets created by Denise Clarke.

"She's the connecting tissue of the Rabbits," says Dobbin. "There've been lots of influences from the other members, but hers is the one continuous thread that runs through all the work. It's that movement. It gives them more than a style, it gives them a presence and character and personality that's theirs alone. Compare Michael Green's physical capacities now, as a middle-aged man, with the limited ones he had when he was a young, lithe fellow at university. Michael can do anything now, thanks to Denise's physical vocabulary."

To help build those capacities and keep the ensemble in shape, Denise introduced yoga to the Rabbit regimen in the early 1990s. "I was worried about Andy's knees — he had bad knees when he was young — and Michael's very tight upper body," she says. "I knew that was going to be problematic in the future." She began by teaching them a basic yoga exercise, the *surya namaskarah* or "sun salutation." Today, every Rabbit rehearsal begins with an hour-long yoga warm-up, which in addition to tuning the performers' "instruments," is also, says Denise, a means of recognizing and purging any negative moods before getting down to work. Denise discovered yoga herself at the end of the 1980s, after years of trying to design some kind of compact dancer's warm-up that could be done anywhere. "I'd been trying to invent a practice to do in a little area, when I suddenly went 'Oh, look at yoga! It's exactly what I want.' That's all I was looking for. Something practical you could do on a mat." She also swiftly realized that the ancient Indian system was the perfect complement to her dance training, its poses with their emphasis on inner balance being the opposite of the outwardly rotating movements used in dance. Yoga is "all about aligning the body on the truest axis and the most efficient alignment principles," she says. "Once you have a lot of dance technique, it's the most efficient way to use your body to stay in shape. The more you outward rotate in dance, the more you weaken your body, because it's so hard on the human body to always be rotated in those dance positions."

Although a dedicated yoga practitioner, Denise is not so strict as to follow only one method or school of teaching. She learned the popular Iyengar method of hatha yoga from Shirley Johanssen, who was taught in turn by European yoga theorist Dona Holleman, a protege of B. K. S. Iyengar himself. However, she also draws on the ashtanga or "power" yoga of another Indian master, Pattabhi Jois, and has even studied the trademarked method of Bikram Choudhury, Beverly Hills–based "guru to the stars" who, like one of his stellar clients, Madonna, prefers to be known simply as Bikram. "I thought he was a joke," says Denise, "until I went and learned his practice at one of his studios in Vancouver. He developed it for [basketball star] Kareem Abdul-Jabbar, whom I admire very much." Bikram's method concentrates on balancing, which Denise credits with helping her cope after the breakup with Blake. "I found, especially after my divorce, that balances were unbelievable psychological developers," she says. "Standing on one foot became really important to me and, the better I got at that and doing other really hard things, the better I felt. I don't believe our society and culture, or our schooling, provide any kind of rigorous process to combat sorrow and anxiety. The yoga practice is completely designed, from ancient sources, to do just that."

Like Bikram, Denise could trademark her choreographic and physical theatre techniques. As it is, in recent years she's begun passing them on, yoga style, to disciples at OYR's annual Summer Lab Intensive. She prides herself on being able to turn anyone into a dancer, or at least make them move well and feel comfortable about it. She's the opposite of the snob artist, believing the professionals could learn from the amateurs. "I think for Denise, having an ordinary person on stage is more interesting than having an actor on stage," says Daniel MacIvor. "It's as if she's convincing actors to be more like people and less like actors." She also defies the us-and-them mystique of the theatre by always holding open-door rehearsals. When One Yellow Rabbit is at work, everyone is invited to come in and watch. And if what they see looks dumb or lousy, hey, it's just part of the creative process — trial and error. "I have no shame about that," she says. "We're allowed to be really hacky."

All this sharing has its pros and cons, says Grant Burns. The positive thing about the creation of the Summer Lab is that it's helping others to better understand One Yellow Rabbit's style of theatre. The down side? "They're giving away some of their language [methods]. There's going to be a lot more work that looks like Denise Clarke's on stages in Alberta and all across Canada in the next few years. It's going to make what the company does seem less unique.

"Although," Burns concedes, stating what has become patently obvious, "no one can do Denise like Denise does Denise."

### Andy

There's a telling line early in *Alien Bait,* when Andy Curtis, as the 7-Eleven night manager and alien abductee Frank, asks us not to be deceived by his "freckled ordinariness." Curtis could be speaking for himself. Appearance-wise, the other Rabbits are a striking bunch — Clarke the big, sleepy-eyed lioness, Green the sinister-beaked freak — but Andy's downright average. Try as he might — funky glasses, beard, tonsure — he can't help looking like the guy next door. You can see him cheerfully mowing the lawn, maybe stopping to tell the kids to be careful climbing that apple tree. Or taking the family on an outing to the local mall. Not long ago, One Yellow Rabbit fans were startled to see Andy, perched on a carousel horse and smiling sheepishly — just a big kid at heart — in large bus-board ads promoting a suburban shopping centre.

"I think I'm fairly able to communicate that banality, that regular-guy-ness, to make somebody empathetic," Andy says modestly. Ever since his brilliant turn as Jim Keegstra in *Ilsa, Queen of the Nazi Love Camp,* OYR has been taking advantage of that inherent likeability. Sometimes Andy gets typecast — as Albee's amiable Nick in *Permission,* or nature-loving author Bill Burns in *Featherland* — but his juiciest roles are the ones that play on the irony of his appeal, such as Keegstra or F., the outrageous guru-satyr of Leonard Cohen's *Beautiful Losers* who, in the words of the novel, "died in a padded cell, his brain rotted from too much dirty sex." If Curtis made the Eckville crackpot seem sympathetic, his kinky F. was positively charming.

The truth is that Andy Curtis really is likeable. But, as Frank in *Alien Bait* says, there's more to him than meets the eye. Behind that wholesome Jimmy Olsen appearance lurks a surrealist comedian, an art-loving hipster, and the Rabbits' own Elastic Lad.

Like Brooker and Clarke, Andy is a child of the Calgary suburbs who grew up — take a guess — on the edge of the city. Only, being several years younger than them, the edge was a few suburbs farther out. The Curtis family moved to the northwest district of Dalhousie in the early 1970s, when it was still in development. If Clarke and Brooker had the prairie as their backyard, Andy was in the foothills that led to the Rockies. His memories read like Brooker's monologues for *The Land, The Animals*: "We had deer come through the neighbour-hood," he says, "and one year they shot a little bear cub that had gone quite far into the suburb and climbed up a tree. I was a paper boy in grade six or seven, and one day as I was walking down the sidewalk by the school fields, which sloped down to a chain-link fence, pulling my little red newspaper wagon, I saw this elk with huge antlers running back and forth on the field. He came running down the hill, put his head down and smashed into the chain-link fence, so hard that he bent it and the antlers snapped off and blood just splattered all over."

His other recollections of Dalhousie betray a streak of youthful mischief. "Once in a while," he says, "for pure nostalgia, I'll drive up to that neighbourhood because I have so many memories there: 'Oh, yeah, we broke a window in that house one midnight, and trashed those kids' snow fort because they egged our house. That's the place where I first smoked a cigarette, and that's the place where I first smoked a joint.' I can relive my delinquent past."

The peregrine Curtises had come to Calgary from Yellowknife in the Northwest Territories. Prior to that, they had lived in Vancouver, Fernie, and Trail, British Columbia — in the last of which Andrew David Curtis was born on 1 March 1963. Dad Douglas Curtis worked largely in the mining industry, like his father before him. "His father had been gassed in World War I and worked for Cominco [the major lead-zinc smelter] in Trail," says Andy. "When my dad was born, my grandfather was terrified that the smelter pollution would ruin my father's lungs, like the gas had ruined his lungs, so he shipped my dad north to live in a little village — which is now underwater. It was flooded when they built a dam on the Arrow Lakes. I always loved that image of history and memory buried under the water. Every time I take the little ferry from Nakusp to Fauquier across the Arrow Lakes, I think that somewhere under there is the farmhouse that my dad grew up in." But for all that, Doug ended up following his father's footsteps, also serving in Europe during the Second World War, then coming back to Trail, where he got a job at Cominco and married Andy's mother, Joan.

The Curtises weren't arts people. "I had an uncle who glued little eyes onto seashells and put them on driftwood," says Andy. "That was about the extent of the artistic endeavours in my family." However, he and his little sister, Michelle, did a lot of playacting as kids. "My sister was always pissed off because I always got to be Gandalf in *Lord of the Rings* and she had to be a dwarf or some little thing. I liked to boss my sister around and direct her, and the kids in the neighbourhood." The first production he remembers was a little puppet show. "It was in the basement, in a closet, which sort of served as our stage. My sister and I built a big cardboard set and cardboard puppets on sticks." When Andy got his first cassette tape recorder, they began taping their own plays and sound effects, or they'd do a little jamming in the kitchen. "We'd get out all my mom's pots and pans — she was off at work, so we could make a hell of a mess and clean it up before she got home — and we'd be banging on them, sort of Peter Moller style, only without his skill or talent. Just loads of passion. I loved doing that."

Andy also loved cartooning, imitating the grotesque style of *Mad* magazine's Basil Wolverton and the prurient underground comix of Robert Crumb, which appealed to his adolescent sense of humour. One day in math class, he was caught passing one of his dirty cartoons to a buddy and hauled down to the vice-principal's office. As he recalls, his masterpiece depicted the math teacher on his knees, begging to suck the vice-principal's gigantic cock. Parents were called and Andy was livid with shame. "I just felt filthy, like I was the dirtiest little son-of-a-bitch bastard," he recalls. He couldn't get over the feeling he was some kind of pervert. Then, years later, while touring schools doing children's theatre, Andy ran into his old vice-principal, who recognized him. "He said to me 'Andy Curtis, how ya doin'? I always knew you'd turn out okay.' With those words, the curse of the previous ten years was broken. 'Mr. Rosewarn said I was okay. I'm not a sicko. Yay!' At least," he adds under his breath, "they don't *think* I'm a sicko ..."

Andy's interest in art was serious, however, and he enrolled at the U of C to study it. The experience was discouraging — he remembers one drawing professor grabbing a sketch he was doing in class and tearing it in half — and boring. "Some of the profs were just so bloody dry," he says. The lone exception was David Bershad, who taught art history. "He'd finish up a lecture with 'Come back next Wednesday — sex and death in the sixteenth century with Caravaggio! Don't miss it!' His class was constantly packed. There was something about his passion that seemed more instructive to me than memorizing dates and styles and movements in art." In his second year, he picked up some drama courses and fell under the spell of an even more influential teacher.

"Keith Johnstone's class was in improvisation, which I just took to immediately," Andy says. "There was something absolutely fascinating to me about it — just the joy, to just jump up and do it and not worry about failing; that, in fact, failure is a good thing. Having failed a number of classes, that was a notion that appealed to me: Failure is a good thing? Hey, I like this!" What he learned in that class has stayed with him to this day. "One of Keith Johnstone's great lessons for me was that the stage is a safe place," he says, "and you can do absolutely anything on stage. And the audience wants you to. They want to see you go places that they will never go. It's that sacred open space and anything goes."

By then Andy had already begun hanging at Loose Moose and taking Theatresports classes with the likes of Bruce McCulloch and

Mark McKinney. "Boy, it sounds so cliché, but I guess I walked in and went 'Wow, this is magic, man! This is fuckin' cool!'" In addition to Theatresports, the company was going full-throttle at the time, staging new plays, kids' plays, famous plays *(The Caretaker, Arsenic and Old Lace)* and its own loose-and-lively adaptations of classics such as *Ben-Hur.* McCulloch, McKinney, Gary Campbell, Norm Hiscock, and Frank Van Keekan were also doing *Late Nite Comedy,* a weekend series of skits and routines in the *Saturday Night Live*/Second City mould. They let the new kid join them and contribute. "We had regular Wednesday night writers meetings, when we'd write the show," says Andy. "At that point I was purely a novice. I would drag in my one or two ideas every week, and once in a while one of them would get in. You had to sell your ideas, which was another skill I didn't possess at that time — the pitch. Whoever was the appointed secretary would write them all down. We'd have a list of titles. Then we'd go around and do a little vote. It was done democratically. The funniest ideas generally made it in; it seemed like a pretty fair system. Money had no bearing on it, it wasn't about making a living, it was purely about coming up with great ideas and whipping a show together. And I loved the flurry heading into Saturday night, collecting all your shitty cardboard props, going to the Salvation Army and buying a flea-bitten toilet-seat cover because it was a prop you required. That was my first real taste of show-biz." It was also his introduction to the mysteries of group dynamics: "who wanted to stick around and stick it out and who didn't, and seeing how different styles meshed. There were definite partnerships that came and went. It showed me that people with different ideas can co-exist in one space."

When McCulloch and McKinney headed for Toronto, Curtis went on to help pilot a spinoff, *That Comedy Thing,* which evolved into a comedy troupe of the same name that played gigs at what he describes as "cool restaurants and dingy little bars." He dropped out of the U of C without finishing his third year and decided to make comedy a career. His parents voiced no objection. "They certainly would have preferred something more regular, something with more of a financial future," he says, "but they've always been incredibly supportive of whatever the hell it is I wanted to do. Except acid. They didn't like that very much." However, Andy hadn't lost his love of art. Laura Parken was part of the troupe and recalls that he used to apply his cartooning skills to the program. "He'd write and draw the whole thing himself. They were just a scream — these hilarious, off-the-top-of-his head ramblings." Like many a company-band-marriage, That Comedy Thing struggled along bravely, only to break up when it finally became successful. While playing full houses at Edmonton's Princess Theatre during the Edmonton Fringe, the group's leaders, Andy and Reid Sinclair, clashed over their differing ambitions — Reid wanted to emulate mainstream stand-up, Andy wanted to go for the wacky and surreal. "I never liked his song-and-dance, chipper-Wayne-and-Shuster material," says Andy, still curling his lip at the memory. He, in contrast, was doing skits about necrophilia and M. C. Escher. "We had a big meeting on the Fringe site and the group just — pow! — split in two. I think that was the first personal blow in showbiz that I'd ever had." Besides, he adds, while he and his art-school buddies were listening to the Clash and the Jam, Reid was into Duran Duran. "The whole thing just *had* to fall apart."

By then, Andy already had an eye on another bunch of entertainers who seemed closer to his offbeat tastes. One Yellow Rabbit could be surreal and literate and funny, all at once. In addition, while That Comedy Thing was shamefacedly slapdash — "I think on a few occasions we gave people back their money and said 'Sorry!'" — OYR was slick. "I remember watching *Café Theatre* [at Beggar's Banquet] and one of the first things I thought was: These guys are tight. Being a stranger to the concept of rehearsal at that time, I was quite impressed with what a little practising could do."

When Andy finally gained entrance to the troupe in 1987 with the role of Keegstra, he arrived at the right time. The collective had come apart and OYR was in a state of flux. Andy started popping up in just about every Rabbit project, from *Mata Hari* to the notorious *Krebbs*. In 1990, when he co-starred with Clarke and Green in the first *Ilsa* revival, OYR's new ensemble was unofficially born.

The Rabbits helped Andy discover and exploit comic gifts he didn't realize he had. Clarke, in particular, showed him how to use his reedy frame to full effect, beginning perhaps with *Dreams of a Drunken Quaker.* "I remember being called a physical comedian," he says, "and I'd never really thought of myself as one — you know, the rubber face, the elastic boy. Suddenly, to meet up with Denise was to encounter a wealth of technical knowledge I could really use." As an actor, says Andy, he's still a cartoonist at heart — "but I don't need a pen and paper anymore. I'm a human cartoon."

As he was joining the Rabbits, Andy Curtis also met his future wife. Bo Morrisette was an actor from Montreal who'd met the company, sans Andy, at The Banff Centre during the making of *Tears of a Dinosaur.* Later, she and her identical twin sister, Willa, would participate in some of the early High Performance Rodeos. In 1988 Bo had just moved to Calgary and was waitressing at an eatery called Sparky's Diner. Andy had a crush on her and used to hang out there in hopes of getting her attention. He finally did, but he had to shave part of his head to do it. During his run in OYR's *Lives of the Saints,* where he sported a monk's tonsure for the role of St. Francis, Andy attended a post-show party, hiding his semi-nude scalp under a cap. Bo was there and had obviously seen the play. "She came up to me, whipped off my cap, and rubbed my bald spot," he says. "Bo doesn't usually drink a lot, but that night she had this bottle of brandy. We ended up sitting on the steps before the front door, drinking this mickey, and smooching like crazy. Everybody told us later 'Yeah, we had to step over you. You two were lip-locked.' It's lucky she married me and bore my child, or that might be an embarrassing story today."

Morrisette went on to become a drama teacher in the Catholic school system. Their daughter, Arielle, was born in 1998 — one month premature and so small that she recalled one of Ariel's songs from *The Tempest:* "In a cowslip's bell I lie ... On the bat's back I do fly." Hence her pretty name. "She was so little and sprightly, like one of those nymphs or dryads or whatever they're called," says Andy lovingly. "Normally I hate cute, precious theatrical names for kids. I never would've imagined I'd end up naming my daughter after a character in a Shakespeare play that I've never even read all the way through."

Andy was involved in writing *Lives of the Saints,* but since then his role with One Yellow Rabbit has been almost exclusively that of an actor. It appears to be his own choice. "If Andy ever wanted to present [a project] to us," says Denise Clarke, "we'd be most interested in looking at it and producing it." Curtis happily defers to his colleagues. "Michael, Denise, and Blake are the prime movers and shakers," he says. "When it comes to plans for the company, I can trust those guys to come up with something that I'll be into." He shares most of their obsessions anyway. As a teenager, he read *Beautiful Losers* and was blown away. He thought he was the only guy who took Frank Zappa seriously — until he met Michael Green. As an art student, he was drawn to the Dadaists and Surrealists and the crossover literary experiments of Burroughs. "There was something about that spirit that wowed me and I knew for sure I wanted to explore those ideas," he says. "Sketch comedy didn't really allow for any real exploration of that, but working with these guys has brought me back to things that, in my younger days, had really intrigued me." In One Yellow Rabbit's work he says he finds the same incongruous magic summed up in that favourite Surrealist statement from the Comte de Lautréamont's *Les Chants de Maldoror:* "Beautiful as the chance encounter, on a dissecting table, of a sewing machine and an umbrella."

Andy does take the occasional vacation from the ensemble. Over time, he has quietly built up a list of directing credits, staging shows for Doug Curtis's Ghost River Theatre and Ground Zero Theatre in Calgary, and Edmonton's Generic Theatre and Three Dead Trolls in a Baggie. Christopher Hunt, who co-starred in Doug Curtis's *Mesa,* says Andy brings what he's learned with the Rabbits to his direction. "He loves Doug's storytelling but he's always aware of the theatricality, the physicality. He'll say 'Okay, Doug, we've heard you talk enough, let's do something funny.' He likes to shake things up." Even in the director's chair, Andy won't stash the comedian side of his personality. "He's wildly funny," says Hunt. "I'm astounded at the way he can sustain a comic riff. In rehearsal it just goes on and on and gets hysterically funny. My gut gets sore just thinking about it." For years, Andy got his fix of "cheapo comedy shtick" by doing one-off shows at the High Performance Rodeo, often with ex-Troll Neil Grahn. More recently, he likes to slip into his sleazy alter ego, the oleaginous emcee Anthony Curtola, for OYR cabarets and the theatre's major fundraiser, the Big Rock Eddies beer-commercial competition.

Then there's Andrew D. Curtis, thespian, who has been known to play the occasional classic role at more traditional theatres — including Bluntschli in Shaw's *Arms and the Man* at Theatre Junction and Guildenstern (or was it Rosencrantz?) in *Hamlet* at Theatre Calgary.

The latter experience, in which he and Michael Green turned in witty cameos as the hapless courtiers of Shakespeare's tragedy, is a prime example of why he seldom seeks work in conventional theatre. "I loved doing the play, but the [rehearsal] process just *sucked*. Seeing the lack of respect for the people backstage drove me fuckin' crazy. Some of the lead actors were unbelievably demanding divas. We make it an unspoken policy [at One Yellow Rabbit] to go out of our way to be friendly and respectful to everyone who's working for us. It pays off in spades."

Besides his distaste for that neurotic, "temperamental artiste" behaviour, which Denise Clarke also rails against, Andy doesn't find much to challenge him in ordinary theatre. Give him the rigours of a Rabbit show, with its complex choreography and shifting realities. "It makes roles in other companies seem like such a breeze," he says. "A conventional play is just a snap; I only have to worry about playing the through-line. I don't have to worry about four through-lines that only connect through context." With the Rabbits, a role may require him to act naturalistically at one point, then suddenly switch into an abstract dance or directly address the audience. The word used constantly in a Rabbit rehearsal is "transition" — so much, in fact, that Clarke has abbreviated it to "transish." "You can't play a continuous psychological through-line," says Andy, "therefore certain Method acting notions must be dispensed with. So Denise and I have coined this term: Method externalism. Sometimes you're in a scene, acting intensely, and you just have to drop that and go someplace else."

Perhaps the chemistry — or, in their critics' eyes, the inconsistency — of the OYR ensemble exists in their varied backgrounds and different approaches to acting. Andy sees himself as a character comedian, akin to Sid Caesar or Peter Sellers. He has to make sense of a role, even in a play as nonsensical as *Dreams of a Drunken Quaker*. "I can't help but try to fill it from the inside. It's just the way I work," he says. "Then there's Michael, with his plastiques and his externalisms and his iconic style of acting. He doesn't tend to work in the same fashion at all. And Denise is, of course, a mix: grand expertise on the outside but dark, hidden depths of empathy for people."

Despite their differences, the three mesh beautifully in performance. They seem to be hyperattuned to one another. John Murrell compares them to a seasoned string quartet. Andy, however, says acting with OYR is more like playing jazz. "You're doing your own thing, but you also have to pay attention to what the bass player is doing, and the drums." It harkens back to his early days doing improv, when he learned from Keith Johnstone that the essence of good acting is interaction and listening to one another. "If I come in a little early one night, Denise is on it. If Michael's timing is slightly off, I'll be there to respond. We're so inside the play, and so inside each other. Man, it's such a great feeling."

Yet, after all these years, Andy Curtis still feels he has to measure up. "My desire to be good for my colleagues is paramount, because *they're* so good," he says. "It's taken me awhile to get a sense of belonging, to feel as though I've carved out a niche for myself that's on an equal footing with them. They snapped me up when I was pretty young and didn't really know a lot. Now, I don't know what I'd do without them."

## Richard

Sound designers seldom bask in the spotlight at the best of times, but Richard McDowell seems to actively seek the shadows. When he appears on stage, he's usually tucked in a dark corner, hidden behind a bank of keyboards and computers. During rehearsals, he squirrels himself away in an adjacent room. Pay no attention to the man behind the curtain. He's busy sampling and splicing — maybe re-editing the chorus of Dylan's "Rainy Day Women #12 & 35" into a groggy mantra or turning a drum into an eagle's scream.

He must communicate with the other Rabbits by telepathy. When he emerges, he always has the sounds they need.

"I usually have a general sense of what the play's about, having read the script," he explains, "but I don't go through the long process that they do in the beginning of poring over and analyzing it. I need the time to just go and play with sounds and ideas. I go away to my room and I come out as soon as I have samples to play them. They never sit down with a checklist to say 'We like this, we don't like that.' Denise will always be listening for something that she can use. Blake will sometimes go through a script, if there's a complete one, and say 'Here's where I think we're going to need music.' But he'll never say what kind of music it should be. I hunt for things that please me and start stitching them together in little or large chunks. Then I play them back and I'll stretch them or shrink them or discard them," depending on what the show requires.

About the same time One Yellow Rabbit was shedding its original collective, Richard McDowell the club owner/rock musician was remaking himself as a sound wizard. It would prove to be the most lasting and satisfying incarnation for a man who spent more than a little time finding his forte.

Richard was born 3 September 1954 in Stettler, Alberta, a true child of the oil patch. His father was a professional drilling engineer and Richard and his parents lived in a trailer by the edge of a drilling rig for the first few months of his life. The family spent three years in Indonesia when he was a toddler, then returned to Canada, and Richard grew up in Edmonton. A teen athlete turned dropout, at seventeen he quit high school and came to Calgary. "One the first people I met was Denise," he says. "It was through high school buddies. A friend of mine had moved down and she was one of the girls that ran around in his little high school posse." Clarke, fourteen at the time, was knocked out by Richard's sense of style. "When I met Richard he wore K2 sunglasses — red, white, and blue — K2 ski pants, K2 gloves — and I'd never seen K2 before him," she laughs. "He was sooo cool. A powerfully individualistic kid. Nobody I knew was like that — they did not possess that kind of extraordinary sense of self that he had."

For all his outward assurance, Richard had no clue what he wanted to do. He calls his period between sixteen and twenty-six his "ten lost years" of drifting. It was his reunion with Clarke in Edmonton, after she'd quit Les Ballets Jazz, and their subsequent return to Calgary that began to put him on the right track. He found himself hanging with musicians, poets, artists — all of them energized by the punk/new wave movement. Richard decided to learn to play the guitar — something he hadn't considered before. "I had never been steered toward music when I was younger. My father was naturally musical, but he was never trained. He learned how to play harmonica, loved to sing along with his favourite pop records of the '40s. My mom had no training either. They loved music — jazz. I listened to a lot of that when I was a kid." He formed a band called the Satellites, a politically conscious punk outfit on the model of the Clash, whose members included poet Murdoch Burnett (drums) and artist Gregg Casselman (bass). Later, he moved over to the Rip Chords, where he switched from lead guitar to bass.

Writer Don Gillmor, who worked with Richard doing landscaping jobs during the day and partied with him after hours, recalls that his twin enthusiasms at the time were music and the occult. While the other nascent Rabbits were hooked on the Beats, "Richard had a much more mystical bent. He was always reading things like the diaries of Aleister Crowley. And at the same time he always had these weird bootleg tapes of people you'd never heard of, or rare outtakes of Jimi Hendrix, stuff you couldn't find anywhere."

It was during a trip to northern Europe with the Chords' drummer, Peter Moller, that Richard got the inspiration for Ten Foot Henry's. Its prototypes were the Studenterhuset in Copenhagen and Melkweg in Amsterdam. "They were these multi-level clubs that had alternative music and alternative film and video, and poetry readings, as well as bars and restaurants. It was just a fabulous place to hang out. In Copenhagen, we spent three or four nights at [Studenterhuset] and I thought: Wow, this is great." This was what Cowtown needed. "The oil economy had crashed by that time, so Calgary was relatively dead and there were a few vacant buildings around. When I got back, I was full of enthusiasm, went and found one, and it just snowballed from there."

Henry's opened in the summer of 1982, on the site of a former disco at the northwest edge of downtown. It was a tiny, out-of-the-way club that held two hundred at most, yet there was nothing else like it in the city. It was as if Zurich's legendary Cabaret Voltaire had been relocated at New York's CBGB. "There were a lot of the hipsters, a little older than I was, who got involved in the early days," says Richard, "and they provided it with a real unique flavour. People like Brad Struble [later the visual designer for *Alien Bait*]. He used to go and rent NFB films and project them onto screens we had built, then bounce slides on top of those. Then there'd be live bands playing and Brad had a small assortment of theatrical lighting which he'd lend to us, bring it down, and set up great visual displays."

At the time, it was a strange, arty anomaly. Calgary was still a pretty raw and unsophisticated town, where most of the bars catering to young people were big, 500-seat rooms attached to hotels that, as Don Gillmor recalls, could be as rowdy as Wild West saloons — "There were always, like, thirty-two fights in the parking lot at the end of every night." Sheri-D Wilson remembers how cool and welcoming Henry's appeared to a baby poet and aspiring bohemian. "The first time I walked in there, the Rip Chords were playing, Murdoch [Burnett] was sitting in a chair reading his poetry, and Denise and Anne Flynn were dancing on the dance floor. It was a real playground. It was a little hub of experimentation and improvisation. For young artists, there are very few places you can go to improvise, to just try stuff, and that's what Ten Foot Henry's was." Richard ran it on a shoestring. "We never did have a [liquor] licence, so it was always a bit of a struggle," he says. "The only thing we could make money on was admission at the door." And the deposit on the empty bottles and cans of booze that people were allowed to sneak in. "The police were pretty cool at that time. They said as long as we're not selling booze and don't have people coming outside, making noise on the street, they were not obligated to bust us. I think we were shut down maybe three times in those three years."

Henry's closed for good late in 1985 (the building itself was later torn down), and Richard would eventually pass on its ten-foot cartoon icon to the Night Gallery, another little club with the same grungy artistic spirit. About the same time that he was getting out of the nightclub business, he was approached by Michael Green to create a score for *Changing Bodies,* which would mark his OYR debut. He laid down tracks using fellow Chords Moller, keyboardist Kevin Labchuk, and vocalist Adele Leger, working under the tongue-in-cheek name Infra-dig. When the Rip Chords disbanded in the fall of '86, Richard decided to go it alone. He went up to The Banff Centre the following autumn and spent three months learning about electronic music. "That was my introduction to early electronic and computer-controlled synthesizers, being able to build sequences. I thought: Wow, this is great. I can be everything — drummer, keyboard player, everybody." While in Banff, he scored the Rabbits' *Tears of a Dinosaur* and played a minor role in its original production. At the same time, he also created the music for *The Blind Struggle,* Denise Clarke's Olympic dance commission.

"It was an extreme amount of pressure," he recalls. "I was working twelve, fourteen hours a day and another full five or six days past the time everyone went back home from Banff for Christmas. All the staff was gone, there were no services left. I had a key and I would just go and let myself into this room and churn away. I arrived back in town a couple of days before Christmas, got off the bus from Banff, and walked through the falling snow with no money in my pocket, but this big fat reel-to-reel in my backpack of Denise's Olympic score. I was destitute but real happy. It turned out to be a good thing. Denise kicked ass at the Olympic festival."

After that, Richard put down his bass guitar and put on his wizard's hat. "I have a good musical ear which allows me to do what I can do, but I'm not a trained musician," he says. "Therefore, when I make music I have to work real hard. The giver of my freedom has been electronic instruments and software — essentially my private band. I can introduce their parts to them slowly and they'll play them back over and over while I hunt for the melody or things that please my ear. You can't do that with a real band — make them play the same groove for half an hour while you look for the right line."

As a neophyte composer, Richard McDowell wore his musical influences on his sleeve. His score for OYR's *Lives of the Saints* used backwards tapes in the time-honoured tradition of the late-period Beatles. His *Passing the Bally Hoo!,* a musical satire he helped create for the 1988 High Performance Rodeo, and, later, the sound design for Michael Green's *Naked West,* looped and manipulated televangelists' sermons and the soundtracks from hunting videos in a style that mimicked David Byrne and Brian Eno's *My Life in the Bush of Ghosts.* Since then, however, his scores have tended to be more atmospheric, closer perhaps to Eno's ambient creations, and at times subtle to the point of subliminal. "I like to float around behind things," he says. "I like to fade some things out real slowly, so that you almost don't know that they're going away till they're gone. And I like to work at low ranges. I like to step out of the middle range, where the voice is, and go low. Low stuff is great for being present and still allowing the actors' voices to be heard." His designs reflect his own changing tastes, which have evolved over the years from a teenage love of British and Southern-boogie rock to a current passion for world music. "When I first came out of playing in bands, I was interested in creating, in an electronic way, the kind of music I had been playing, beat-driven rock-pop. But I'm not so concerned about that anymore. I like textures more than a pop sensibility now."

If his music is subtle, Richard's methods of creating it are often playful. For the *Permission* score he improvised sections live during every performance using the old Mattel PowerGlove — a video-game toy from the mid-'80s that allowed gamers to control the action by wearing a piece of handgear that emitted ultrasonic pulses. "A bunch of freaks in France and the United States realized this thing was just spitting out a string of numbers to the controller on the television," he says. "So if you put those through a little box [an interface] they could be routed into a computer instead." At various times in the show, Richard would track the actors' movements with the glove, sending signals to his computer that allowed him to paint simultaneous soundscapes. "I'd do my little hand dance with them, and by flexing, opening, or bending certain fingers, I could inject streams of sound and change effects on my machines."

It seems a shame that so much of this sonic magic goes unseen, or that audiences don't always know what kind of electronic alchemy has produced a memorable score. The creation of the sound effects or Denise Clarke's avian fantasy *Featherland* is a case in point. Since its real-life hero, ornithologist Cecil Hyndman, had taped hours of bird vocals, Richard hoped to employ the authentic material in his score. He was disappointed to find that most of Hyndman's old recordings had so much surrounding noise they were all but unusable. He was able to salvage, by chopping up and filtering them, only a few small segments — none of them containing the cries of Susan the golden eagle, the play's principal bird character. He searched in vain for a recording of an eagle screeching to accompany a crucial scene. The final solution came partly by accident. One day, while working on the score, he took a drumbeat from one of Michael Green's esoteric CDs and fed it into a software module as an experiment. The module, he explains, "basically chews apart digital samples and stitches them back together, and you have very little control over what it's going to sound like. I dropped the drumbeats onto this module, went away for lunch, came back to give it a listen and, good God!, there were these horrible screaming sounds." When heard during the performance, at the height of Susan's rage, Richard's ersatz eagle scream proved weird and chilling.

Unlike Clarke and Curtis, Richard has rarely worked in the mainstream theatre. In the mid-'90s he was hired by one big company to score a couple of plays, a gig he calls "the most unrewarding of any of my theatrical experiences. I didn't fit in there. It was not conducive to good creative stuff. Nobody knew what they wanted, nobody could make a decision. They were driven by stage managers and paperwork." After Richard spent countless hours building one sound design, the show's director decided he didn't want an original score and opted for a compilation of pop oldies — an all-too-frequent cop-out in contemporary theatre, borrowed shamelessly from the no-more-original movies. Aside from the work of a few fellow sound sorcerers, such as Richard Feren of Toronto's da da kamera, McDowell doesn't care for the music he usually hears in the theatre. "So much of it is boring or it's so traditional-sounding. It doesn't do anything for me at all." When he creates a score, his bywords (lifted from an early review of his work) are "eerie and haunting." "That's been my handle since 1989," he says. "If it's eerie, that means that it's not normal. And if it's haunting, that means it might stick with you a little bit longer than normal."

Of course, Richard McDowell isn't like the sound designer in a conventional theatre. First of all, the dance-based work of the Rabbits makes the musical component more important than in the average play. His stuff isn't just mood-setting filler for scene changes. Second, he may be concealed in a tech booth, but he's still one of the performers. Where other touring companies would hand a pre-recorded tape and a list of cues to a local technician, Richard travels with the troupe, operating sound and mixing his score live at every performance. He talks about his job like he's the bass player for King Crimson or the drummer for the Stones. "It's great to be a Rabbit, it's like being part of an older rock band in many respects," he says. "When I travel with the company, I don't really care how we do critically, it's just fun to know that you're part of a long tradition and to be proud of the work and the group."

When Richard does fly solo from the Rabbits, it's with his new creative partner in his new home. In 1999, Denise Clarke's *So Low* had its Spanish-language premiere in Mexico City in a production directed by Richard and starring Zaide Silvia Gutiérrez. Richard and Gutiérrez had adapted Clarke's one-woman dance comedy into what he calls "physical storytelling" as a vehicle for the Mexican actor. "Richard had this beautiful idea," says Gutiérrez, "so we asked Denise's permission and then I translated it and Richard and I produced and directed it." *Sola!* was a big success, running weekly for close to a year at the Teatro Helénico, with Gutiérrez sweeping the three major Mexican critics' awards for best monologue performance. "In a city of twenty million," says her admiring boyfriend, "that's pretty good."

As we speak, Richard is midway through the Calgary half of one of his typical Calgary/Mexico years. It's mid-afternoon and he's hanging in the vacant Big Secret Theatre. "Even when I'm not working on projects, I'll often come down here," he says. "One of the things that stuck out in my mind so strongly when I came back from Mexico after first working there, and got to sit in this theatre again, is that what we have built here is so spectacular and desirable and special. To know that you had a hand in it and know that, while it ain't perfect, it's still a pretty great place to do your work, gives me a great deal of pride. I got all teary-eyed on a couple of occasions, simply because there are theatre practitioners in that huge Mexico City who would just die to be able to call this kind of place home." He gets up from a table, goes round to the back of the theatre's bar, and pours himself a fresh coffee. It strikes you that, in some ways, the Big Secret is as much a successor to Ten Foot Henry's as it is to all those little self-made theatres the Rabbits grew up in. It's not only where they work, it's where they play. "Everyone involved with the Rabbits feels like this is their place," Richard says, "and they can invite people in: 'Welcome to my home. Come on in. Enjoy yourself.'"

1    In September 2002, the seeds of Green's Zappa scheme began to bear fruit. He assembled a band of fourteen musicians, singers, and actors, and orchestrated an impressive live interpretation of Zappa and the Mothers of Invention's 1968 anti-flower power album, *We're Only in It for the Money*, for three workshop performances. Fellow Rabbit and Zappa freak Andy Curtis was one of the vocalists.

# 10. Here Come the Wild Boys

*"Sticking it half an inch into your eye."*
— *"WE ARE THE BEATS" (THE DREAM MACHINE CABARET)*

**W**hat is it about the Rabbits that they attract the bad boys, the troublemakers, the scapegraces, the *enfants terribles?* It could be because One Yellow Rabbit is a great place to break the rules and remake them after your own fashion.

It was to the Rabbits that a precocious string-puller named Ronnie Burkett turned when he wanted to create his first dirty, adult puppet show — a jab in the eye at cute Muppets and time-honoured traditions. And it was to the Rabbits that he returned a decade later, having established himself as Canada's master of marionette mischief, to cultivate his darker, serious side — re-emerging triumphantly as a brilliant puppeteer/playwright of international renown.

Maybe it's because One Yellow Rabbit is a great place to let out the beast within, or just let your hair down.

It was to the Rabbits that mild-mannered Daniel MacIvor came to unbottle his Mr. Hyde — that angry, neurotic motormouth Victor — and make his breakthrough as a solo performer. To the Rabbits that Bruce McCulloch comes when he wants to escape the creative headaches of Hollywood and indulge in his loopy comedy-rock jams.

Or perhaps it's because the Rabbits are feisty champions of their fellow rebels.

When Brad Fraser was feeling the heat over a play that everyone else was ready to write off as a disaster before it had even opened — a play that would make his name and go on to worldwide success — it was OYR that encouraged him with word and example.

Over the years, One Yellow Rabbit has associated in one way or another with most of Canada's theatrical avant-garde. It may be pure coincidence that its closest links have been with young men who have "bad boy" images and reputations — a rap that, as Orson Welles and Lord Byron could attest, is just about impossible to beat. These "boys" are all older and, perhaps, mellower now, but the films, the fame, the greying hair have failed to make them safe and boring. Burkett is still trampling down the fences of his once-innocuous art form. MacIvor digs ever deeper into his psyche to thrill and move us. Fraser still flips the bird to the middle-class theatre audience with plays that provoke. Bruce McCulloch and his comrade-in-laughs, Mark McKinney, are still, at heart, "kids" in the hall — comedy punks with a college-campus cult following.

Now, is it also a coincidence that the first three of these wild boys are gay and the other two like to wear dresses?

## Ronnie Burkett

Medicine Hat is a small city in southeastern Alberta, one of whose few claims to fame is that it caught the fancy of poet Stephen Vincent Benet, who mentioned it in his popular poem "American Names" (the one that ends with the line "Bury my heart at Wounded Knee"). The name may intrigue poets and children, but many Albertans, for whom the image of the "plumed war-bonnet" either holds no charm or has become commonplace, simply refer to it as "the Hat." Then there's the local chamber of commerce, which apparently has no sense of double entendre. Because Medicine Hat is built upon vast natural gas reserves, it likes to have the place known as "the Gas City" — at least to judge from the highway signs proudly greeting visitors. Little kids must love that.

Certainly, it's the kind of thing that would make Ronnie Burkett giggle. Inside this worldly, sophisticated theatre artist, there's a naughty little boy who never has any trouble getting out.

But when Burkett really was a boy, it was the Gas City he wanted to escape. "I had a sense that Medicine Hat was a place to get out of," he says. "I remember thinking, I'd better just grow up and get out of here so I can go be a puppeteer."

You see, at the age of seven he had an epiphany over a volume of the *World Book Encyclopedia* that would shape the rest of his life.

Like many dutiful parents in the 1960s, Ray and Eileen Burkett had bought the twenty-volume encyclopedia on the instalment plan to enrich their child's education. One day, seven-year-old Ronnie was annoying his mother as she made his lunch, and Eileen, realizing they had a rather expensive diversion sitting on their bookshelves, told her son to go look at the encyclopedia. "I grabbed a volume at random," recalls Burkett, and it fell open at the entry "Puppet." There, in a black-and-white photo reprinted from *Life* magazine, were husband-and-wife puppeteers Bil and Cora Baird, grinning happily as they posed with their motley family of marionettes and hand puppets. "I remember distinctly thinking: Oh, that's what I'll do! Something just clicked. I said to myself, That's the life for me. My mother called me for lunch, I closed the book and announced that I was going to be a puppeteer." While other kids might start with the sock or paper-bag versions, Burkett was immediately drawn to the most complex species of puppet. "There were instructions in the *World Book* on how to make a marionette out of dowls, so I cut up a broom in the basement and tried to make it into one." He also hit the library and began to read every book he could find on the subject. As he pored over the pictures, he realized that a seven-year-old hadn't the skill, the know-how — or the allowance — to build the puppets he saw there. He resolved to one day acquire the knowledge.

In the meantime, Burkett became a puppet fan. In 1965, *The Sound of Music* skipped its way onto cinema screens and Burkett joined the many repeat viewers, but in his case simply so he could see the Bairds' marionettes perform "The Lonely Goatherd" over and over again. When he read in a children's magazine that Baird operated his own puppet theatre and workshop at 59 Barrow Street in Greenwich Village, he fired off a letter. It was the first of many. "I wrote him repeatedly over the years, telling him that he should hire me and I would leave my family and come live in New York." Years later, when he finally did get a job with Baird, Burkett discovered that his mentor had saved all those boyhood entreaties. Another American puppet master, Martin Stevens, was also a big influence and Burkett subscribed to his correspondence course.

Dead certain of his destiny, young Ronnie went about the business of growing up so he could get out of town. His parents were, in his words, "not at all" artistic, but Ray, a probation officer, and Eileen, a homemaker, didn't discourage their son's dream — even if they weren't too sure what it meant. "In Medicine Hat, no one really knew what a puppeteer was," says Burkett. "You had to explain it. Once Jim Henson started getting really popular in the mid-'70s and started doing American Express ads and stuff, it became a recognizable career to the general public. But before his big success, it was still kind of mysterious — you didn't know of many people who did it." Burkett's self-portrait of his teen years is that of the classic nerd who knew what he wanted to do long before any of his peers and probably missed out on a few good parties thanks to his obsession. "I hear some of the Rabbits' stories now and I go 'Man, you had good teenage years! All these wild, drunken, drug-filled sex stories. I was always in the basement building puppets.'"

Both his best friend and his high school drama teacher were Mormons, which led Burkett, with the impulsiveness of adolescence, to embrace the religion, too. After graduation, he headed south to Utah and Brigham Young University, a squeaky-clean Mormon kid on a puppetry scholarship. One shudders to think that bad boy Burkett might have ended up doing pious kiddy puppet shows on the order of *Davey and Goliath* — but thankfully it was not to be. "I went there thinking I'd be able to do all this wild, experimental puppet work in the theatre program. As it turned out, puppetry was relegated — as it is pretty much everywhere — to theatre for young audiences and developmental drama. I realized I would probably be nothing more than a teaching assistant making paper-bag puppets." Within a week, he'd switched his major to musical theatre. Within a semester, he had quit. "I remember one night writing Bil Baird this desperate plea for help, saying 'You have to hire me. You have to get me out of here.'" Baird didn't reply, so Burkett went home to Medicine Hat, got a job, saved his money, and, in the spring of 1976, flew to the then-Soviet Union to attend an international puppet congress in Moscow. There, he ran into Baird, who finally invited him to stop by 59 Barrow Street on his way back to Canada. Burkett dutifully showed up at the theatre on 10 June, his nineteenth birthday, did an audition, and was hired. That fall, he moved to New York and embarked on his professional puppetry career, working on the show *Davy Jones' Locker* from the Baird repertoire.

Burkett was finally living his boyhood dream — but the bubble soon burst. Baird's Greenwich Village operation, which had opened in 1966, was on its last legs. "I actually went there thinking: Yay, I'll work here for the rest of my life! But halfway through the season the theatre closed." However, in New York he had finally found a community of puppet artists and craftspeople who were a lot more fun than the Mormons. "I learned to drink and smoke from puppeteers," he says. He also got his first taste of success, when a friend from Brigham Young received a grant to produce a children's show for the Public Broadcasting System and asked Burkett to help him. "I came back to Canada for the summer, built all these TV puppets, and then went to Provo, Utah, and did this thing called *Cinderabbit*. I got an Emmy for it and then went back to New York."

It was a great time for the puppet industry. Henson and Frank Oz had parlayed their success with *Sesame Street* into a spinoff Muppet TV series and a hit Hollywood movie with all-star cameos. In the entertainment industry, however, a little innovation leads to a lot of imitation, and Muppetry was where it was at. "Even though a lot of puppet kids, as we are known, grew up dreaming of marionette shows, when the Muppet boom happened, a lot of us said 'Ah, this is the future. We're going to stick our hands in foam-rubber things and stand in front of TV cameras.' I kind of went along with that wave." Again, we may have lost another Canadian talent in the gaping maw of American showbiz, if Burkett hadn't gotten a piece of sage advice from an elderly colleague.

"When I was in New York, there was a guy who had been head designer for the Muppets who had died quite unexpectedly. I didn't know the guy, but the week he died I was on the street and I ran into an old puppeteer. He asked me what I was doing and I told him what I really wanted to do was marionettes. And he said that's what this guy at Muppets wanted to do his whole life and he never did. Then the old puppeteer looked at me and said 'Get out of this city. Go home. Go back to Canada and do it. 'Cause if you stay here, you'll never do it.' A month later I was back in Canada."

So the young Emmy Award–winning TV puppeteer began re-inventing himself as a one-man marionette theatre. He settled in Calgary, a three-hour drive from his hometown, and built a little show — *The Plight of Polly Pureheart* — which he could literally carry on his back. "I wore a backpack stage, the puppets hung around my waist and there was a kazoo around my neck. I think I did twelve hundred performances of that, from schools to adult conventions and Armed Forces tours. It was this dream, take-anywhere kind of show." Sure enough, as One Yellow Rabbit was also discovering, raw Alberta was a wide-open field for the arts. "When I told people I did marionette shows," Burkett recalls, "they would just look at me blankly and say 'Cool!' There was no community of puppeteers going, 'Oh, no one does *that* anymore.'" However, there *was* a theatre community, ready to embrace him. "Back then I didn't know anybody. I was doing this little show, driving around the province and staying in any cheap motel I could find. It was the theatre people who sought me out, dragged me out for drinks." When he took *Polly Pureheart* to the inaugural Edmonton Fringe, he realized he wasn't the only guy doing offbeat stuff. "That was when I felt there was a theatre scene that I belonged to. Suddenly, I didn't feel so much like an outsider." However, it wasn't until his first visit to Ten Foot Henry's that Burkett met the Rabbits.

Keith Marion and Damon Johnston, friends of the OYR gang, were starting up a management company and trying to woo Burkett as a client. They suggested he do *Polly Pureheart* at the new club, which Burkett hadn't heard of. He remembers walking into Henry's and

WILD THEATRE

seeing Peter Moller of the Rip Chords on stage, thrashing away with his
drumsticks on a giant Coca-Cola sign. "I saw that and thought: Oh,
man, what a bunch of freaks. I also thought: Oh, they're going to hate
my stupid little puppet show! But I got up and did it anyway and it was
one of those brilliant little experiences. The room totally got it. And
immediately after the show, I met Denise Clarke. She just came up to
me and said 'We should work together.'" Clarke was serious. Soon, she
and Burkett were teaming up to do a show called *Together Again for the
First Time,* a lumpy blend of dance and puppetry that had a three-night
run in the University of Calgary's Reeve Theatre. Neither participant
was too thrilled with the outcome. "I remember that night in the dressing room before we did the first performance, Denise and I just freaked.
We looked at each other and said 'I really love *you,* but I hate this
show!'" He had also met Blake Brooker and, not long after, the two
embarked on a more successful collaboration — *Fool's Edge,* which
marked Burkett's move out of his one-show-fits-all *Polly Pureheart*
phase and into ribald, adults-only comedy.

In between, Burkett shacked up with Brooker and Clarke. For a
year, the three shared a house owned by Clarke's aunt in the southwest
neighbourhood of Killarney. Burkett had a studio in the basement and
he remembers, "We were all horribly poor. We called it the Kraft Dinner
house, because we would keep trying to think of things to add to Kraft
Dinner." Not that they didn't have fun. When they went out to bars,
Burkett and Clarke, both tall, striking blonds, liked to pose as brother
and sister. At home, Burkett invented an alter ego, a campy showbiz
character named Go-Go LaFontaine, which became their private joke.
In fact, Burkett probably gets the credit for introducing Brooker to
camp. During the making of *Fool's Edge,* which was composed by
Edward Connell and directed by Allen MacInnis, Brooker was the only
straight guy on the creative team. Not long afterwards, Burkett recalled
to me that Brooker was often confused by all their gay innuendoes and
references. What was this obsession with Judy Garland and Tallulah
Bankhead? Today, that's no longer the case. "He has definitely caught
up," says Burkett, laughing. "Now he phones me and leaves the lewdest

messages. I actually feel like the straight one around Blake." Brooker, in turn, had encouraged Burkett to let out his own crude sense of humour — part scatological little boy, part tart-tongued queen bitch. Not to mention that inordinate fondness for puns and double entendres. Burkett would go on to dub his production company Rink-A-Dink Inc. and create characters with names like Beatrix Poppers (a lesbian novelist), Melba Dangereuse (a black chanteuse who's "the toast of Paris"), and the Rev. Onan Ramsbottom (a pedophiliac priest). It made you wonder sometimes if it was really just a coincidence that Burkett's own name looked like an amalgamation of those pun-struck British comics Ronnie Barker and Ronnie Corbett.

After Brooker wrote the script for *Fool's Edge,* Burkett returned the favour, first by originating the title role in Brooker's *Ilsa, Queen of the Nazi Love Camp,* and then by co-designing his *Tears of a Dinosaur.* He was also tabbed to play his pet character, Go-Go LaFontaine, in the latter show's first, Banff Centre incarnation, which premiered in the fall of 1987. On the *Tears* project, Burkett had a hard time dealing with Brooker's write-as-you-rehearse style of creation. "The hook to get everybody [to Banff] was that we were going to be in the mountains and relax and create this piece of work," he recalls. "There'd be no pressure like there is at home. I found it really stressful, actually, because I was down in the cabaret space with a makeshift puppet studio set up, trying to build puppets and not knowing what the heck we were doing. Then, to my horror, I found out I had to wear this loincloth with everyone else and work this giant dinosaur marionette." Go-Go and his loincloth were subsequently cut when Brooker reworked the play, although Burkett's puppets remained.

By that point, the careers of One Yellow Rabbit and the Ronnie Burkett Theatre of Marionettes had become closely entwined. In the winter of 1988, *Fool's Edge* played the Rabbits' Secret Theatre during the Olympics and in the spring it toured to Toronto's World Stage festival, playing alongside the reworked *Tears of a Dinosaur.* The Toronto critics noted the overlapping talent in both shows and began to sense that something exciting was happening way out west in Stampede City.

Christopher Newton, with his nose for new talent, was already one step ahead of them. The artistic director of the Shaw Festival had happened to catch *Fool's Edge* while in Calgary for the Olympic Arts Festival and extended an invitation. The following summer, Burkett would be at the Shaw in Niagara-on-the-Lake, making a brave effort to breathe life into Shaw's lone, late puppet play, *Shakes Versus Shav,* a silly bit of ego-stroking from the great man's dotage. (Shaw, it should be noted, appreciated the art of puppetry and was not being facetious when he said actors could learn from watching marionettes.)

With the success of *Fool's Edge,* Burkett felt he'd found his niche as a puppeteer — risqué musical parodies of theatrical genres. After skewering *commedia dell'arte,* he slashed Victorian operetta *(Virtue Falls),* sliced up Punch and Judy *(The Punch Club)* and made mincemeat of the Gothic murder mystery *(Awful Manors).* He also found his way into mainstream theatre. None of those productions were seen at One Yellow Rabbit. The first two were one-acts presented at Calgary's Lunchbox Theatre, a company catering to downtown workers during the lunch hour. The last and most lavish, the full-length *Awful Manors* with its cast of forty-six — count 'em, forty-six — puppets, had its premiere at the Canadian Stage Company, Toronto's major public theatre, to sold-out houses in the fall of 1991. By then, Burkett had arrived. His work was becoming known nationally, and Adrienne Clarkson was soon touting him on her CBC-TV series with a profile shot in Calgary and Medicine Hat while *Awful Manors* ran at Alberta Theatre Projects in June 1992.

Once again, Burkett thought he had realized his dream. At the age of thirty-four, he had his own company, was doing the marionette theatre he wanted to do, and theatres across Canada were clamouring for it. Yet something was missing. Being the bad boy of puppetry, titillating regional theatre audiences with playful smut and camp while simultaneously dazzling them with his skill, was admittedly a great gimmick. But all boys have to grow up. Even the ever-youthful Ronnie, whose shock of yellow hair and impish smile gave him the appearance of a dirty-minded Peter Pan as he dangled his little wooden dolls in full view of the audience. Burkett had already successfully battled the North American attitude that puppetry was just children's entertainment; now he was out to show that it was also a noble art form. He'd been reading about the gutsy political puppeteers in occupied Czechoslovakia, who had subverted the Nazis by putting on secret puppet plays mocking the Third Reich. Their underground shows were called "daisy plays," apparently because daisies are able to grow in the dark. Burkett, living in a province with a bluntly conservative, subtly homophobic regime, thought Alberta could use its own subversive satire. It was then that he turned back to his pals at One Yellow Rabbit.

He had a new kind of play in mind, one that would incorporate topical humour and commentary, much of it ad libbed every night. It required some preliminary experiments and the Rabbits had the right lab in which to perform them. *The Daisy Theatre* kicked off OYR's 1993–94 season, in the tiny Secret Theatre, and it was a revelation. Gone were the scripts, the elaborate decor, the carefully plotted staging. With nothing but a miniature proscenium stage and a stable of marionettes at his disposal, Burkett proceeded to wing his way wickedly and hilariously through the day's headlines, the latest local and national controversies, with plenty of bitchy asides about the city's arts scene. He came prepared with a cast of new puppets, including some *Spitting Image*–style grotesques of Alberta Premier Ralph Klein — depicted as a florid-faced drunk — and Kim Campbell in her short-lived role as Canadian prime minister. Then there was the power-mad Canada Council officer named Phyllis Stein, an oh-so-serious German performance artist called Helmut Head, and, most remarkably, a sweet, dumpy, mildly befuddled lady from small-town Alberta named Edna Rural, in whom Burkett had succinctly embodied all the contradictions of the provincial character. Edna volunteered for Calgary's AIDS agency and planned to vote for the morally conservative Reform Party.

Burkett's "Daisies," so popular they returned later in the season for an encore, were the basis for his next big project, the first play in what would become an amazing trilogy of adult puppet dramas unlike anything anybody had seen. *Tinka's New Dress* was a fable inspired by the Czech puppet resistance, set in a fictional totalitarian state ruled by an oppressive regime called the Common Good. While young puppeteer Carl and his sister, Tinka, decide to vent their outrage at the government by secretly staging satirical shows in a ghetto cabaret, Carl's rival, Fipsy, sells out to the state and prospers as a puppet propagandist. By play's end, the decent and defiant outcasts are being rounded up and sent off to the death camps. Within this framework story, partly built with borrowed bits from Orwell, *Cabaret,* and Martin Sherman's *Bent,* Burkett set his *Daisy Theatre*–type improvs. When Carl's puppets, Franz and Schnitzel, take the stage, they engage in sidesplitting comic riffs on our own current events. Depending on the time and place, the duo might make a mockery of Quebec's separatist referendum (Toronto, 1995), ridicule British Prime Minister Tony Blair (London, 1999), or do a scathing parody of Theatre Calgary's financial crisis (Calgary, 1996). Apart from marrying the past and the present, the concept also allowed Burkett to neatly divide his serious, slightly sentimental side and his old campy persona, with its fiendish delight in bad puns and bitchy put-downs. The production saw a return to a large puppet cast and elaborate decor *à la Awful Manors* — Martin Herbert's revolve set took the form of a gorgeous old-time merry-go-round — while retaining the cheeky spontaneity of the Daisies. What was new was Burkett's bid to move audiences to tears as well as laughter and make a dramatic statement.

"*Tinka* was probably the biggest risk I ever took," says Burkett. "It broke the mould of what I had been doing. In fact, a lot of people said to me 'Oh, you've changed your style.' And I remember saying 'No, I think I've found my style.' I wanted to do something that was important to me and I wanted an audience that would come along on that ride." They did. *Tinka* was a ripping success. Apart from being a box-office blockbuster for the Rabbits and an award-winning hit at other Canadian theatres, it blew 'em away at New York's Public Theater and the Dublin International Theatre Festival. In New York, *Tinka* won an off-Broadway OBIE Award and in Dublin it grabbed the *Evening Herald* Samuel Beckett Award for best international production. Burkett had dived into the world theatre market with a big splash. And while his fable may have seemed a touch quaint to some critics, audiences at a festival in Germany responded to it as though it had rubbed a raw wound. "Even though I never say 'Holocaust' in the play, I had people after the performance say to me 'What do we have to do as a German people to let this be forgotten?'" Burkett told me during a *Calgary Herald* interview (15 November 1998). "My only response is that it shouldn't be forgotten."

Burkett's own struggle at that time wasn't between subversion or submission, but between producing real, provocative art or lucrative pablum. For a long time, he took pride in the fact that he didn't apply for arts grants, but paid his own way via well-paying TV work. The creation of *Tinka* was financed by television — specifically, by kiddie shows produced in Montreal, where Burkett spent almost half the year. He worked on two series started by Desclez Productions, *Chicken Minute* and *Little Star,* doing, by his count, 156 episodes of the latter. Even after *Tinka* took off as an international touring show, Burkett stuck with the TV gigs so he could buy a bigger studio to accommodate what was becoming a small puppet-making factory. He now had a handful of employees building, in his adjectives, "derivative, Muppet-type" knockoffs for commercial clients. The pace was brutal. "There was a period there when I was touring *Tinka* and *Old Friends* [a children's play] and doing TV work in Montreal for four or five months at a time. I'd get a week or two off, fly somewhere and do *Tinka,* then fly back and continue with the TV. It was exhausting — not the schedule, but going from doing my work in the theatre before a live audience to being back in a studio at eight in the morning doing this stupid filler material." Finally, he says, "it just came down to the feeling that, no matter what the money from TV was, it wasn't worth being away from home and my studio to do work that I didn't really get much from. I felt kind of empty and rootless." By then, he had his own Bil Baird–style headquarters, *sans* theatre — a 4,358–square foot, two-storey home/office/workshop tucked away among the old houses in Calgary's Ramsay neighbourhood. It had formerly been a Buddhist monastery.

On Halloween night in 1997, the studio became a target for vandals, who soaped homophobic hatred on the windows and left Burkett seething with anger — an anger he would channel into his next play, a scorching satire called *Street of Blood*. If *Tinka's New Dress* came wrapped in the mists of the past, with its suggestions of Europe during the Holocaust and its Old World characters and carousel, *Street of Blood* was undeniably here and now. Its subjects included terrorism, AIDS and the tainted blood scandal (then plaguing the Canadian Red Cross), gay bashing, the loss of religious faith, and the '90s vampire vogue. It was also Burkett's most personal play, set in small-town Alberta and featuring the *Daisy Theatre*'s lovable Edna Rural — a character modelled partly on Ronnie's own mother — and Edna's angry gay urbanite son. Burkett described it as "a big, sprawling, Gothic prairie epic." If it had any kind of equivalent, it could only be Tony Kushner's *Angels in America*. Perhaps it didn't have Kushner's intellectual underpinnings, but it did have his scope, wit, and passion — as well as scenes of almost heartbreaking tenderness. Audiences wept for gentle Edna and her stoic husband, Stanley, as if they weren't constructions of wood and cloth and wire but flesh-and-blood human beings. Already, critic Michael Feingold in the *Village Voice* had written of *Tinka's New Dress:* "I deny the existence of a puppeteer: this is a great ensemble of actors." With *Street of Blood* there was no longer any question that Burkett had made a rare transition. He wasn't a puppeteer anymore. He was a remarkable playwright and actor who just happened to use puppets. The work won Burkett Toronto's Floyd S. Chalmers Canadian Play Award in 2000.

(A side note: Burkett, unlike Edna's son, Eden, has remained close to his parents. Not only do they attend all his shows, they've also been known to furnish the occasional bit of set dressing. When Burkett couldn't find any gold brocade fabric to make Franz and Schnitzel's backcloth for *Tinka,* he rang them up in Medicine Hat. "I said 'You need to bring me your bedroom drapes!' So they drove up with them, cut them up, and [Eileen] sewed them into a little backdrop. They've always been really good sports." The published script of *Street of Blood* is dedicated to them.)

Both *Tinka's New Dress* and *Street of Blood* were huge successes for One Yellow Rabbit. *Happy,* the third play in what had become the *Memory Dress Trilogy,* was co-presented by OYR and Alberta Theatre Projects, in the latter's 400-seat Martha Cohen Theatre — because, Burkett maintains, the set was simply too large for the Big Secret Theatre, although clearly he could pack ATP's space as easily as OYR's. He still considers One Yellow Rabbit his home theatre, a tribute to the company's sizable influence on Theatre of Marionettes. At the start, he says, "I used the Rabbits as a kind of model. I was going after their audience. They had already started creating an audience in Calgary. Without their work, I don't know if *Fool's Edge* would even have had an audience in the beginning." Blake Brooker's script for that show also determined that Burkett's style of puppet play would be text-based — a fact that has proved a delightful novelty with international audiences accustomed to seeing puppetry as primarily a visual entertainment.

Later on, Denise Clarke would get Burkett to rethink his staging and adopt a more comfortable physical presence. Already Burkett had broken one of the unspoken taboos of puppetry, by appearing in full view of the audience. Other puppeteers sometimes remained in plain sight, but never drew attention to themselves. In situations where Bil Baird couldn't conceal himself, he saw to it that a spotlight kept the spectators focused on his marionettes and left him cloaked in shadows. Burkett, in contrast, became part of the show. Beginning with *Fool's Edge,* when he appeared clad as a seventeenth-century cavalier, he would wear costumes, play ironic minor roles (such as the butler in his whodunit, *Awful Manors*), and occasionally "talk back" to his puppets. Still, he continued to adhere to some ingrained rules about his art that no one had questioned. Until Clarke came along.

"At my request, she sat in for a week in the middle of rehearsals for *Tinka,*" he says, "where I had multiple characters on stage and I was just walking back and forth, back and forth on the set to go get them or hang them up again during all these scenes. At one point, Denise jumped up and said 'You've got to stop doing that. Can you hang lines above the stage and just hang the puppets up, just let them stand there?'

I remember my complete horror, saying 'No, you have to keep them moving all the time! You *never* hang a puppet up on stage.' In *Awful Manors,* I was like a streaking projectile 'cause nobody got hung up. It was entrance-exit-entrance; I was running like crazy. I was doing the same sort of thing in *Tinka* and she said 'No, you've got to hang them up; it's getting really monotonous. Humour me.' So she had the stage manager rig some fishline above the set and she said 'Just try it.' And that's where a whole new exploration of vocabulary started, because of Denise's insistence. I began doing that in *Tinka* and it continued on in *Street of Blood.* And in *Happy,* I have the character of Carla just sitting there still, in repose, for most of the time, and I talk for or about her from the other side of the stage. That's a direct result of that one little seed that Denise planted in my head." She also suggested that, instead of moving back and forth between two marionettes while they're talking, the puppeteer should simply crouch down between them and shift the focus with his voice. "Denise's influence in terms of movement freed me to think more about the actual acting of the characters," he says. "It freed me from just jiggling puppets all the time."

Burkett laughs that Clarke is still giving him notes. In *Street of Blood,* he took his visible presence a step further, playing on the whole God-as-puppet-master image by appearing to his characters as Jesus Christ Himself. (Eden complains that Christ now looks like "an aging club boy.") In one scene, Ronnie/Jesus gives a great, sweeping gesture with his arm, which in the early performances was somewhat tentative. "Denise came to the opening night of *Street of Blood* at OYR," he recalls, "and she came backstage and it was a typical Ronnie-and-Denise moment — Denise was sobbing her fool head off, she was really moved and charged. She was crying and hugging me and in the middle of it she dried her eyes and said 'Okay, Go-Go, just one tiny note: When Jesus appears, do this.'" And she made a grand, slow sweep with her arm. "'Take a breath,' she told me, '*own* it.'" In other words, if you're going to be God, then really *be* God. "From that moment on, I've not been ashamed to do that move," says Burkett. "That's my association with Denise; she's always able to give me one little hint to improve things."

Burkett remains close to Clarke and Brooker. "I really feel like I grew up with those kids in a way — though we weren't even kids when we met. It's funny that we're all middle-aged now and Blake and Denise and I all had our mid-life crises happen not too far from each other." Burkett's occurred at the end of the '90s, when he and his longtime lover and creative partner, Larry Smith, split up. Burkett shut down his Calgary studio and moved to Toronto to be with his new flame, musician John Alcorn. In his wake, however, he has left a taste for experimental puppet theatre among both Calgary artists and audiences. Of late, the Rabbits have been fostering the funky Old Trout Puppet Workshop, a multi-talented collective of young artists and craftspeople who, in true neo-hippie, retro-'70s style, created their first show while living communally on a southern Alberta ranch and gave their premiere performance to an audience of neighbouring Hutterites.

"Who would have thought Calgary would have all this puppet activity?" muses Burkett, who modestly denies any direct influence. "I can only think it's the same reason I did my work here. You just can. You can actually afford a studio here, which for puppeteers is a big deal, but also there are things like the High Performance Rodeo to showcase it." Looking at the novel work of Old Trout, he's forced to admit that he and the Rabbits are, perhaps, becoming *passé*. "We're not the cool, hip avant-garde now," Burkett sighs. "We're just a bunch of middle-aged freaks."

## Daniel MacIvor

When Daniel MacIvor made his first Calgary appearances, nobody took much notice. As far as anyone knew, he was just another young unknown actor from Toronto hired to fill a role on the Theatre Calgary stage. In the spring of 1988, he played a minor part in TC's Johnny-come-lately staging of Tom Stoppard's early '80s London/New York hit, *The Real Thing*. The following season, he was back in a leading role, that of Tom the frustrated young writer in Tennessee Williams's *The Glass Menagerie*. Still, nobody came to TC to see *him*. The drawing cards were

Dawn Greenhalgh and Samantha Follows, mother and sister, respectively, of Megan Follows, then at the height of her popularity as TV's Anne of Green Gables. During both shows, MacIvor got a distinct feeling this wasn't where it was at.

"I remember hearing about the Rabbits," he says, "and feeling I was working in the wrong theatre."

There was something happening in that little black box on the +15 that sounded a lot more fun than trudging through stolid versions of an oh-so-English comedy and a forty-four-year-old American play. "Without even knowing what their work was, I just thought it must be the coolest, hippest thing ever in terms of what I'd seen going on in theatre in this country."

As it happened, MacIvor wasn't just another young unknown Toronto actor — he was also a young unknown Toronto playwright. Born the youngest of five children in a working-class family in Sydney, Nova Scotia, in 1962, MacIvor had studied theatre at Halifax's Dalhousie University and Toronto's George Brown College, settling in the latter city. Although he got his start doing fringe-y work for Buddies in Bad Times, Canada's foremost queer playhouse, by the end of the 1980s he had been taken under the wing of Urjo Kareda's Tarragon Theatre. One of Toronto's primary sources of new Canadian playwriting, the Tarragon boasted an impressive roster of big names — Michel Tremblay, David French, Judith Thompson — and development programs for new writers. It was also a resolutely literary theatre, with no time for collective and multidisciplinary work. At the Tarragon, MacIvor had met John Murrell, who made mention of a bunch of young rabble-rousers back in Calgary called One Yellow Rabbit. MacIvor was intrigued, but at the same time he was locked into the Tarragon mindset of the well-made Canadian play. The Rabbits and a guy named Daniel Brooks would change all that.

In 1990, MacIvor made his Tarragon debut with *Somewhere I Have Never Travelled*. The title was borrowed from E. E. Cummings, the style from the Tarragon's stockroom. The play was not a success and, to add insult to injury, MacIvor's own contemporaries appeared to be making fun of it. Daniel Brooks, a sharp, witty young playwright/director who loved baiting the Toronto theatre elite, just happened to be staging a parody of the Tarragon fare with his group, the Augusta Company. It consisted of a mock Tarragon play called *Sometime Come Often*. The similarity with MacIvor's title was a coincidence, says Brooks, but sure enough, MacIvor took it personally. He went to see the show and, when he got over his mortification, fell in love with its brashness. He joined the cast for drinks afterwards and, before long, he was asking Brooks to help him create something new with a distinctly non-Tarragon flavour.

By now, MacIvor had seen his first OYR play, *Tears of a Dinosaur*, and gotten a sense of how they collaborated. "I could see that they were using their own relationships in the work they were doing. There was this investment of their own lives in the work." He wanted to aim for that same kind of intimacy and he found it with Brooks, who egged him on, urging him to explore all the aspects of his personality in his writing. Out of that grew *House*, in which MacIvor unbolted the doors of his imagination and let all the wild, dark, crazy things run loose.

Following a pilot run at the Factory Theatre Studio Café in May 1991, the show visited the Rodeo late the same year. If Brooks had spurred MacIvor to greater heights, OYR and its audience made both men realize they were on to something good. "The Rabbits gave us permission to do what we were doing," says MacIvor. "The reaction to the work in Calgary was proof that people did want to see this and it was important and, just because we liked it didn't mean it wasn't any good — which is *so* Canadian." Soon after, Toronto also gave its stamp of approval with the 1992 Chalmers playwriting award. With that, MacIvor slipped from under the shadow of the Tarragon and began to build his own little company, da da kamera, with Brooks and producer Sherrie Johnson, taking part of his inspiration from his new pals in Calgary.

"One of the things I stole from the Rabbits was the human element of the work," he says, "which sometimes means failure or imperfection. That's part of their process. With the Tarragon you're going for a kind of airtight, hermetically sealed, perfect play. And you're not going to get that. I found that incredibly frustrating and demoralizing. It almost made me question whether I wanted to work in this field. The Rabbits offered another view of the process." MacIvor also lifted the Rabbit habit of touring. *House* went on the road in 1992, playing dates in Israel and England (Manchester and Brighton) before winding up back in Calgary for a second OYR-sponsored run at the Garry Theatre. "It was the strangest tour — it didn't make any sense," he says, "but it was the beginning of something."

MacIvor was starting to get cozy with the Rabbits, and his November gig at the Garry Theatre would lead to a close friendship with Blake Brooker. The Garry was a former movie house that had ended its reel life as a porn cinema before playwright Sharon Pollock and her son, K. C. Campbell, remade it into a scrappy little live theatre. It was in Inglewood, an inner-city neighbourhood with some rough and seedy patches, and unsavoury types were known to wander into the place from time to time. "For the opening of *House* at the Garry, there were two people in the audience who, I found out later, were high on solvents," says MacIvor. "They found the show very funny. But they found it *too* funny. They wouldn't stop laughing. It got to the point where the audience was turning round and looking at these people. I had to sort of stop the show a little and say 'Look, it's not that funny.' Then, it was even more funny to them, that I was speaking directly to them. Finally, I had to say 'Someone please get these people out of here!' I had to say it two or three times and the only person in the audience who knew I meant it was Blake. He got up from his seat, went and escorted them out of the theatre. Apparently they threatened to come back and get me the next night. That was certainly a bonding moment for Blake and I, when he played bouncer for me."

MacIvor stayed with Brooker during the run and the two bonded for other reasons as well. Both were going through the relationship blues. "We were both incredibly miserable," says MacIvor. "We drank a lot of vodka and listened to a lot of Indigo Girls. We talked a lot about what is theatre, what is writing, and why bother. And in the face of all this misery in our lives, we kind of realized this is what we had to do.

In the end it was a very positive, affirming thing about where we were at in our work. I remember it was [Blake and Denise's] house by the river and the house was really cold. I have a lot of photographs from the time of Blake wearing a scarf, sitting at the dining room table with a glass of vodka."

During those early visits to Calgary, MacIvor noted how cleverly One Yellow Rabbit sold its product using intriguing photo images and graphics. "I was struck by the Rabbits' incredible sense of how to present themselves to the mainstream, to the world at large, as a company," he recalls. "In some situations and cities, you'd find [other avant-garde theatre] people embracing the dirty obscurity of their work, essentially saying 'We don't even want you to come.' That was not part of the Rabbits' appeal. There was no 'us and them' about the Rabbits and the audience. It was open to anyone, and anyone could potentially have a good time." He remembers watching the company members at one of their Dust It Off fundraising parties, seeing them mingle with the suit-and-tie crowd as easily as with fellow artists. "Blake and Michael were introducing me to people and, being the cynical, crusty bastard that I am, I was seeing a lot of people that I probably would have disdain for, for various reasons. But Blake and Michael were as inclusive and generous with them as they might have been with, say, Karen Finley or Penny Arcade. It really showed me something about respect for the audience — that the potential for these people's lives to be transformed by the theatre was just as great, if not greater, than people who maybe had a bit more knowledge of what was going on. I've always been humbled by the Rabbits' respect for the people they perform for."

There was a four-year gap between MacIvor's second *House* call and his third visit to OYR, in 1996 with *Here Lies Henry*. He arrived to celebrate the first Rodeo in the Big Secret Theatre, thrilled that Michael Green had booked him to play back-to-back with Penny Arcade. "Michael and I share this New York fetish, which I had had from the time I was in high school. I was fascinated by Warhol and that whole Factory scene, and I knew about Penny Arcade, so the idea of actually being on a bill with her made me weirdly starstruck." He also saw that with the Big Secret, the Rabbits had attained their ideal theatre where they could party as well as work and let the audience hang with them after the play. And as far as he could tell, success hadn't spoiled them. "I've often been around companies where, when they're hungrier, they're better," he says. "You have that fear all the time that when people get the thing they want or the space they need, that they'll become complacent. But it never happened, in my view, with the Rabbits. And I think it's because they're so involved with one another's lives and there's so much struggle in keeping that together. The work continued to be vital and interesting and edgy, despite the fact that they had slightly cushier surroundings."

MacIvor himself had enjoyed no little measure of success since *House*. Between touring his international one-man shows, he veered off into movies and TV, scripting an award-winning short film, *The Fairy Who Didn't Want to be a Fairy Anymore*, co-starring in Don McKellar's quirky *Twitch City* series on CBC-TV, and picking up a Genie Award nomination for best actor for his performance as Robert, the scent-obsessed house cleaner, in Jeremy Podeswa's film *The Five Senses*. Despite his higher profile in recent years, One Yellow Rabbit remains a favourite test house for his new work, often one of the first stops on his tours. He finds the Calgary audience friendly and open — but it can also be demanding. He has a reputation to live up to.

MacIvor remembers the first night he performed his funny-scary solo piece *Monster* at the 1998 Rodeo. "It was terrifying," he says — and he's not referring to the play itself. "It was really early in the process — I think it was our second time doing it [after the premiere in Nova Scotia]. We had our dressing room in the basement and we had to come up the elevator and I remember thinking all the way up: Oh, you know, I don't think I can do this. My, uh, leg hurts. I don't think I can stand … I was just desperate not have to go out on stage." The theatre was dark and deadly quiet when he walked out to centre stage and began to set the play's eerie mood. "I did this thing I do at the beginning, where I go 'Ssshhh, ssshhh.' And somebody kicked over a beer bottle — as would only happen in the Big Secret Theatre! — and I spontaneously went

'Shut up, asshole!' Then all of a sudden, the show took a step up to a whole new level. As soon as I felt the freedom to say that to the audience, we were somewhere else. And the audience loved that I was calling one of them an asshole." It became a scripted part of the show.

MacIvor appreciates the irony that One Yellow Rabbit and the Rodeo flourish in what is traditionally considered to be Canada's most conservative — or, to put it less politely, redneck — province. "When people talk of Alberta to me in terms of national politics, the image they present to me is nothing like the Alberta I know," he says. "I enter Alberta through the Big Secret Theatre, so I have an entirely different perspective on what the place is. But then, whenever you've got some very right-leaning force you're going to have the opposite happen. Isn't that physics or something?"

In the summer of 2000, MacIvor and the Rabbits did the ships-in-the-night thing at Edinburgh's Traverse Theatre. MacIvor was finishing up a Fringe run with his poignant two-hander about love and loss, *In On It,* while OYR was on its way in with its production of *Thunderstruck.* MacIvor, who hadn't seen the play, sat in on a dress rehearsal all by himself. That powerful show, not easy to assimilate on a first viewing, seemed to encapsulate the thrill he gets from the company's work.

"At the end," he says, "because I was alone, I didn't have to just applaud, so I yelled out 'I don't know what the hell that was, but I loved it!' Which to me is what the Rabbits allow an audience member to feel. At a certain point, you feel their craft and their vision and you give over to them and let go trying to understand it. They allow you to not have to understand it. They allow you to just love it, to be alive in it."

## Brad Fraser

The first two months of 1989 were, in retrospect, a watershed for Calgary and Canadian theatre. True, Daniel MacIvor was still stuck in the regional-theatre rut, doing his best southern accent for Theatre Calgary's *Glass Menagerie,* but next door Denise Clarke was busily creating One Yellow Rabbit's prototype dance drama, *The Erotic Irony of Old Glory,* and in another corner of the city's arts centre something just as significant was about to explode.

Alberta Theatre Projects was preparing to unveil its third play-Rites festival, which was not, in itself, cause for any great excitement. The national event, while big on production values and festive hoopla, had yet to premiere anything of substance, and 1989's lineup didn't look all that promising, either. A yuppie comedy set around a Jacuzzi, a play about a modern religious miracle, a jokey adaptation of a lesser Jules Verne novel. The only item that sounded half interesting was a script by a young Edmonton playwright, and that mainly because of its strange long-winded title: *Unidentified Human Remains and the True Nature of Love.* How is any theatre going to fit that on a marquee? Don't these greenhorn playwrights have any marketing smarts?

Then the rumours began to trickle out from the maze that is ATP's backstage. Susan Ferley, the director of *Unidentified Human Remains,* had quit in the final week of rehearsals. The playwright himself had intervened and was trying to direct his own show. One of the designers had pulled his name from the credits. Soon, warning signs were being posted in the ATP lobby. Brace yourself for "crude language, violence and nudity." ATP had earlier shown reservations about staging the play and, of the four shows, it had been the only one that couldn't entice a corporate sponsor. Was the theatre about to spawn a disaster?

The opening night audience filed into Brad Fraser's play not knowing what to expect. It emerged at the interval, breathless, agitated, eager to go straight back in. Fraser did indeed have marketing smarts but, better, he was a funny, daring, and inspired writer with a keen sense of the theatrical. The compound title said it all. This was a play about sad young people wandering a soulless urban landscape, seeking love but often settling for sex and friendship instead. It was also a gripping thriller about an unknown sociopath on a killing spree. It was by turns creepy and moving and, quite often, hilarious. By the end of the night, it began to dawn on some of us that Fraser had done the unexpected:

beneath the nudity, the gore, the spook-house lighting and sound effects, he had written his generation's *Look Back in Anger*.

By the end of the run, Fraser, a self-assured twenty-nine-year-old with wavy black hair and a Clark Gable moustache, had his own play-Rites fan club. Thus *Human Remains* began its journey to national and then international success: a sold-out Toronto production by Crow's Theatre starring Brent Carver; an off-Broadway run with a rave from *Time* (and a snooty dismissal from the *New York Times*); a UK premiere at the Traverse that transferred to London, wowed the critics, and won Fraser the *Evening Standard* and *Time Out* Awards. Along the way, it also became a disappointing Denys Arcand film under the truncated title *Love and Human Remains*.

Fraser, meanwhile, shaved his head, donned skirts, and quickly surpassed Sky Gilbert of Buddies in Bad Times as Canada's most famous bald, gay, won't-go-away playwright.

When he came back to playRites in 1992, he'd moved from being the dark horse to the sure bet. And, once again, he blew away the competition with a sexy, bloody, darkly funny bagatelle called *The Ugly Man*. A homage-cum-spoof of Middleton and Rowley's old Jacobean shocker, *The Changeling*, set on a western ranch, it was a slighter effort than *Human Remains* but hugely entertaining. Some in the ATP audience found it grisly and gratuitous. Blake Brooker couldn't stop laughing.

Fraser and the Rabbits were friendly, going back to the golden days of the Edmonton Fringe. At the 1985 festival, Fraser was doing a nasty little thing called *Chainsaw Love* when he heard about a show from Calgary that had to be right up his alley. It had all his favourite ingredients: sex, camp, comic books. "Paul Thompson and Gerry Potter, all the artistic directors who were at the Fringe that year, all said 'You've got to go see Blake's work, you'll really enjoy it,'" Fraser recalls. He braved the queues to check out *The Batman on a Dime* and "absolutely loved it."

Later, when Fraser moved to Calgary and landed a position as ATP's playwright in residence, he hung with the Rabbits and shared in their restless, rebellious nature. "I felt that kinship with Blake," he says.

"We used to get together and have drinks and bitch about the existing artistic directors and theatres." It only remained for the playwright and the company to team up. That opportunity arose in 1993. Given that the Traverse loved Fraser and OYR, it was a natural that OYR should bring Scotland the latest Fraser play.

"I've always thought that the Rabbits are probably the most innovative and creative theatre company in Canada," says Fraser. "I've seen everything of theirs that I can and I've never, with one exception, been less than absolutely enchanted or blown away by what they do." That one exception? "I hated their production of *The Ugly Man*."

Fraser's play, about the heartless daughter of a wealthy lady rancher, who enters into a compact with her mother's brutal, disfigured chauffeur to kill her unwanted fiancé, was pure comic-book horror, but it did have a sombre, chilling side to it that Bob White's ATP production had captured and the Rabbits chose to ignore. "I know Blake felt it was my funniest play," says Fraser, "but it's also very black, and I felt as if they were playing it as a kind of a lark." OYR's humorous, stylized staging emphasized the play's western comedy at the expense of its Gothic side. Fraser thinks it was simply a case of two opposing aesthetics bumping up against each other. "I am so text-based and genre-oriented — most of my plays come out of a pop culture style I want to explore — and I just felt that what they did, and what I do, while it was an interesting experiment, didn't really mesh very well. I felt like the script got short shrift in their process and became a venue for the performers to do the things they wanted to do. Which is not a bad thing, but what it does with that kind of a piece is make something which is already fairly thin, even thinner."

He's philosophical about it now, but at the time Fraser was furious. He hadn't been involved in the production or seen its handful of Calgary previews prior to its Traverse debut. "I'm such a huge fan of their work it never even dawned on me that I maybe wouldn't like what they had done with the show. I was just so thrilled that they were doing it." He made the trip to Edinburgh at the company's invitation, where he saw it for the first time on opening night. Actor Christopher Hunt, who portrayed the monster of the title, remembers seeing Fraser in the bar post-show and asking him ingenuously if he liked it. An upset Fraser's terse reply: "I'll be speaking to the director." To make matters even more awkward, the playwright was sharing digs with Brooker and Clarke. "Of course, I'm staying in a fucking house with them for the next seven days," he says with a laugh, "which did make things pretty tense. Although we did ultimately talk about it. It was a very difficult thing, though, because Blake was a bit defensive anyway because it wasn't getting the kind of reaction that he had hoped it would."

Well, maybe. Ian Brown, the Traverse's artistic director at the time, recalls things a bit differently. "I seem to remember it did quite well," he says. Certainly, critic Colin Donald in the influential *Scotsman* hailed it as "another dizzy display of virtuoso physical acting and quick-thinking literate theatre," and Neil Murray of Glasgow's Tron Theatre credits it as the show that turned him on to One Yellow Rabbit. (Personally, I agree with Fraser's assessment of the OYR treatment.)

It's all water under the bridge now and, anyway, while in Scotland, Brooker made it clear that he respected his colleague's work. At one point, Fraser participated in a panel discussion on international playwriting at which Maurice Podbrey, the grizzled artistic director of Montreal's English-language Centaur Theatre, was also present. "The panel was talking about my work specifically," says Fraser, "because it had only been done in the small houses in Canada, and at that time the Traverse and various larger houses in Britain were doing it. And Blake just lit into Maurice for not ever having produced one of my plays! He pointed out that everyone was talking about how progressive Canada was and yet their best-known playwright in Britain had never been produced in an 'A' house in Canada. I've always appreciated the fact that Blake has never been shy or scared of expressing those kinds of opinions or standing up for the people he believes in."

Fraser had, of course, been produced in one Canadian 'A' house (the highest category of professional theatre, based on box-office gross), but his relationship with Alberta Theatre Projects deteriorated in the '90s. His last work there, as of 2002, was an elaborate 1993 workshop production of *Outrageous!,* his musical version of the 1970s Canadian cult film that made a star of female impersonator Craig Russell. After a long gestation that included a change of composers, it would finally premiere in 2000 at Toronto's Canadian Stage. Despite critical success and controversy in Britain and the US, Fraser's next play, *Poor Super Man* — a comedy/drama in which the death of an AIDS-infected transsexual parallels that of the Man of Steel — has yet to be produced in Calgary, the place in which it is set. (For the film version, *Leaving Metropolis,* Fraser relocated the story to Winnipeg.) Nor, apart from the second-stage of Canadian Stage, has he seen his work presented by other major Canadian regional theatres. His stubborn insistence on making libidinous gay men his main characters and his fondness for dragging sex acts out of the bedroom and onto the stage are enough to scare away any artistic director fearful of offending middlebrow audiences and corporate sponsors. In recent years, Fraser has premiered his plays at Manchester's Royal Exchange, a 750-seat theatre the size of most Canadian 'A' houses. "They said they'd produce anything I wanted to do — they wanted to be the people who did the first productions of my work," says Fraser. "Nobody in Canada was making me that offer. The kind of relationship I once had in Calgary, I now have in Manchester."

At forty-two, Fraser looks back, not in anger, but with fondness at his time as an *enfant terrible,* raising shit at ATP and getting support and inspiration from the Rabbits in his battle against deadly theatre. "Had the Rabbits not been right next door, I might not have struggled as much as I did to make sure that *Human Remains* opened as the play I wanted it to be," he says. "If you don't have someone whose work you admire, who you aspire to and want to compete with in a constructive way, it's easy to just sit back and let things happen. Having the Rabbits in that space, especially in the late '80s, kicked other people up a notch in terms of being innovative and rebellious and interesting, too. That certainly happened for me. When the director wasn't doing the work that I thought she should be doing, and I didn't feel I was getting the support from the theatre that I needed, Blake was very much there as someone to encourage me to fight for what I wanted."

and financially — fun, challenging, and satisfying. In this last rehearsal process for *Somalia Yellow* we've been able to explore these questions and we're still in the process of figuring it out.

GREEN: In our situation, we need to keep our environment a lively and nurturing one, in which we feel safe growing up next to each other and being ourselves for the rest of our lives.

BROOKER: Or as long as this [company] lasts. Whichever comes first!

*At any point, have you discussed the possibility of a finality to One Yellow Rabbit?*

BROOKER: We're just trying to keep ourselves interested and challenged. In most traditional workplaces, and certainly in theatre, your work companions change project by project, so this question doesn't come up. But it does come up with us and we do have to talk about it. We've been talking about all kinds of options and possibilities in order to take into consideration the growth of our aspirations.

*Last winter, some of you went on a retreat to discuss the company's future. What came out of that?*

GREEN: There were some very practical things. For instance, what are we going to do with our beautiful theatre? It would be nice to find ourselves in a situation where we don't have to rent it out to anybody who can afford it, but instead be in a position where we're able to present our favourite artists from around the world, or even just down the block. It would allow us to participate to a greater extent in our community.

CLARKE: We came up with this concept of the theatre as a creation house, where we slowly begin to implement several arms or branches of activity, such as salons. We wanted to do more small shows, like *Somalia Yellow* and *Sign Language* this year, where we wouldn't be as freaked about the box office, where the emphasis is more on outreach, on really talking to your audience, going back to building a dialogue. And [we committed to] working with the youth — finding them, engaging them, training them.

BROOKER: Also to participating more as a company in the Rodeo. We want it to be more strongly identified as our enterprise. We want to perform in it as a company, but also participate in the work of the other groups, whether directing them or performing with them. The other thing that came out of that retreat was a decision to explore other media, particularly video. We'd just done that movie *[Beautiful Jew]* and we hope to do more. We also want to find ways in which our live performance can interact with that.

GREEN: It was very much a "taking stock" of where we're at — what we have done and what we do. We've got so much going on here — the school, the festival, the international touring — but we needed to step back and take stock of all that, of where our power is, where our reserves are. Rather than just blindly swinging from one tree to the next, we had to sit back and try and imagine the future and plot some strategy. I'm reminded that, when we first started in 1982, we had a seven-year plan — to make our livings doing this — and we achieved it in five years. We've never sat down since and figured out what our next five- or seven-year plan is.

*How do you see the ensemble evolving?*

BROOKER: First of all, my idea of the ensemble is to try to create a circumstance of emotional and psychological stability for the participants, which doesn't exist in the jobbing artist's solo career. It's something that's virtually unknown in our business, outside of the great unionized ensembles of Europe. The evolving idea is how to keep it going so that it can also accommodate its members if they want or need to go away and do something else, and still know that they can come back.

CLARKE: I suspect that's why Elizabeth [Stepkowski] retired from us — that she didn't really feel that was an option. For her, other [offers] were leaping out to her, and she needed to be able to come to us and say she wanted to take a year off and do some other kinds of theatre. She didn't even attempt that. When she left she told me "I feel like I'm breaking up with you!" It was very emotional, as though she didn't know what to do. So she left, in her own words, abruptly and kind of inappropriately. She honestly didn't see another way to do it. She didn't feel at the time that we would be going "Hey, take a year off if you need it."

GREEN: We have actually been talking about the fact that each one of us individually has earned a sabbatical by now, and we should be able to figure out how to do that.

CLARKE: The problem with taking a sabbatical one at a time is, who goes first? And what great thing gets happening with the company that that person isn't involved in? That's always a risk.

MCDOWELL: The other side of course, is that you'd go away and have a great sabbatical and look back and the company would be suffering and you'd say "Ah, they can't function when I'm gone!"

*You've been pretty much building your own model of creation theatre, but do you ever look at some of the other creation companies, say Carbone 14 in Quebec, and see how they are doing things?*

BROOKER: At one time we went and looked at Carbone 14 and other companies in Quebec, but their theatre-making culture is so vastly different. They have unpaid rehearsals for God knows how long —

GREEN: Endless tours —

BROOKER: Only one production a year. We're a strange creature in comparison.

GREEN: I feel as though we've outlived every model I ever looked at. So I don't know. Now maybe we have to look at a different *planet*. *[Laughs]*

BROOKER: Norman Armour of Theatre Rumble [that is, Rumble Productions in Vancouver], who goes around and sees a lot of theatre, has said to me "You guys do four major things where most companies your size dedicate themselves to just one or two of them." We tour, we present a season, we mount a festival, and we run a school. We're always spreading ourselves out. Now, whether we're spreading ourselves thin …

GREEN: But we've always done it. Always.

CLARKE: I suspect it's our greatest strength and our greatest flaw. We just don't do one spectacular thing and explode. But I no sooner have that thought then I think: That's why the work remains authentic and true to us. We never hit so big that we lose each member to Hollywood or somebody gets lured away and the company gets fractured. Chris Cran always repeats this quote about how the best things are things just before they hit. That's when the work is best.

GREEN: And we're doomed to stay at that point!

CLARKE: Sometimes I wonder. Or, are we late bloomers? Are we tremendously fortunate and is the roll of the dice such that the great fortuitous event will occur when we're slightly older, so that we don't have to suffer the horrors of being youthful stars?

CURTIS: You'll become famous when a young Gwyneth Paltrow plays you in the biopic.

CLARKE: Nah, she's getting too old. *[Laughs]* But if you look at us as middle-aged now, then supposedly we have another half-life to go.

*Looking at that half-life and considering that you do physical theatre, how is that going to change as you get older?*

CLARKE: The yoga practice will never end. It shouldn't. That being the case, you may not be able to leap into the air, Andy might not be able to jump on my back anymore. But if distilled movement is our great passion, which I think it is, and "economy, precision, and relaxation" are our credo, which I think they are, then we should be able to continue expressing ourselves as a physical theatre company, perhaps with even greater effect. I don't personally have any of those fears that dancers or hockey players have. I don't share that at all. I know that all three of us are moving better now than we did ten years ago.

GREEN: I think my stilt-walking career is behind me, quite frankly.

CLARKE: Yeah, that's really sad.

CURTIS: I don't know how many more years of leaping around, doing *Permission*-style shows, I have in my body.

*That brings up the question of your repertoire. Would you ever consider staging* Permission *again with a cast of younger actors?*
BROOKER: That might be an interesting experiment.
GREEN: Actually, my forty-five-year-old body is stronger and more flexible than it's ever been. It just doesn't like the punishing bruising quite as much as it used to.
CLARKE: Not to harp on about yoga, but there are certain things we can learn from it. It's a tool for longevity for sure. One thing you learn as you get deeper into the practice is that the rejuvenative work is way important. That just does not occur to you when you're younger and trying to do your headstand and handstand and the rest of it. Andy and Michael are interesting for me to observe from the way they approach their yoga practices, which is possibly a bit lazy but also intuitively correct. They may do ten minutes [of exercises] instead of forty-five, but they answer their own body needs. They don't have a yoga dancer's fit about having to do their hour a day. They relax and do rejuvenative stuff, simple twists, which may be smarter than knocking yourself out.
BROOKER: Of course, you're a yoga mistress and you attack it hard. These guys may be lazy as yoga practitioners, but they aren't lazy actors.
CLARKE: No, I'm using "lazy" as a positive term. I'm saying I think it's probably smart.

*Let's talk about some of your current theatrical formats, both the cabaret — which you've been doing in one form or another since* Café Theatre *— and this new one, the salon.*
CLARKE: For myself, the salon was something that has fascinated me ever since [doing] *Mata Hari*. She did the bulk of her body of work — which was pretty slim, to say the least — in salons. It occurred to me that it was a really healthy way to stay in touch

with your audience, to be able to talk to them. Johnny Dunn did a bunch of research on it for me and got this thing off the Net about changing the world through the salon, one conversation at a time. That really appealed to me as a way to re-introduce conversation. Obviously, we're a fairly literate theatre and we challenge the audience each time with something new and provocative. There's always "for" and "against" at our theatre, a show is rarely a nice cozy, comfy, happy hit. There's always plenty to discuss.

GREEN: And as for cabaret, we've just always done that.

BROOKER: We've just decided to amp it up.

GREEN: And there are different ways of doing it. Sometimes it's all written by Blake. Sometimes, it's a mixture of things. Sometimes, like in the old days, we go away and all come back with fifteen minutes worth of stuff and jam it together.

BROOKER: We decided at the retreat that we were going to explore it.

GREEN: And we certainly have.

BROOKER: A couple of the things we like about it are the interaction — like Denise says with the salon — and we like having guest acts we can hang out with. And sometimes there's a feeling from audiences that a formal play isn't as fun or as interesting. There are different ways of getting information out on stage than telling a story.

CLARKE: Then there's the community effect, too. We've always had this Rolling Thunder Revue[2] going — it's a really tiny revue *[Laughs]* — but we've certainly always carried the party with us. It influences us to this day. We like to provide a good time; we like people to enjoy themselves around us, whether or not the work is fun and funny. We like people to feel there's an intellectual life to pursue, that you can go somewhere and be with people who are lots of fun and will drink with you and don't have too many rules. For me, the Summer Lab only really kicks into gear when I can get these guys [the other Rabbits] to commit to being around for the whole time. It's super-effective when all the Lab participants get to meet everybody and hang out and the faculty are listening to one another talk and sharing ideas. We were able to bring a similar feeling to the Rodeo this year, because we were down here three nights a week doing the show [the *Dream Machine Cabaret*]. It was a party, but it was also a genuine cultural exchange.

BROOKER: This place was like a cross between a theatre and a nightclub in a way. We've always liked to think that we're doing something that we wish we could find. We wish there was something like this in our city, so, okay, we're going to do it. Am I right?

MCDOWELL: From a distance, looking back — 'cause I leave for long chunks of time to be in Mexico — there's no place like this. Michael's seen more theatre and been to more places — probably Blake, too — but I think they'd agree. I can't count the number of theatres we've been to where, when the show is over, you're hustled out of there, and maybe there's a bar nearby, but the theatre itself dies. A perfect recent example is the Citadel in Edmonton [where they'd just performed *Doing Leonard Cohen*]. The Rice Stage is a lovely space but the moment that the audience leaves there's an IATSE [union] technician waiting to climb the ladder, to kick the breakers off, and shut the sound system down. Everyone is gone within fifteen minutes. This space is always alive, any time of day, in one way or another.

CLARKE: The crowds for *Somalia Yellow* have not been huge, it's been quite intimate, and it's surprising how many people stick around to talk to us.

MCDOWELL: Every show is different, but you always end up with some people hanging out at the bar afterwards.

CURTIS: I'm always amazed on those occasions when someone will tell you "I can't believe I'm standing here, talking to you!" In places like Theatre Calgary it's difficult even to get backstage to see the actors.

MCDOWELL: For most people, it's sacred ground. You're not supposed to go there.

CURTIS: Then there's us with our little clubhouse. C'mon in and play with us.

MCDOWELL: We're trying to do that even more. This year with the

Rodeo, everyone [in the company] was here most of the time and that is the way it should be.

CLARKE: And it really allowed us to see everybody else's work for a change. In the past, who knows why, you'd find yourself two weeks into the Rodeo and, God, you'd only seen one show! This year I saw almost everything. As Michael puts it, we've had a meaningful cultural exchange as a result and it was a gas. Lots of marijuana was involved, too, let's face it.

The conversation turns to exchanges with the audience. Denise tells of a recent encounter with a longtime Rabbit watcher who was incensed by *Somalia Yellow* — "She was incredibly mad at us. Furious! She said 'You people shouldn't have made this show! It doesn't gel. Nothing happens in it. It's pathetic!'" Then Michael mentions an e-mail he'd just received from the public relations officer at the US consulate, complimenting OYR for doing shows that "have engaged me and made me think."

*People do go to your shows presumably expecting experimental theatre, and* Somalia Yellow *is an experiment.*

GREEN: I have a kind of affectionate bitterness for our audience. I know they love nothing more than to toast themselves at their cocktail parties that they support way-out theatre by coming to One Yellow Rabbit. But as soon as we give them something that really fits that description, well, they just don't come. It's always been like that. It will never change.

CLARKE: I'm not so sure. One thing about the salons is that I've met so many people this season who are here for the first time, or maybe saw one thing ten years ago. Some of them are just getting the hang of it, saying "Oh, wow! This is great! How long has it been here?" And I have to say "Like, twenty years." *[Laughs]*

*How does it feel to have lasted that long as a company?*

CLARKE: Something that's really caught my mind these days is this sensation that we're at a halfway point. And that, in the future, there will be dissolution and we'll just fall apart and become drunks. *[Laughs]* But seriously. There are so many young theatre students interested in us these days; there are constant requests for interviews and discussions. They want to know how we do this. And we don't know what to say. Michael and I have described it as being idiot savant–like. There was no design, we didn't sit down and say "Well, we thought we'd do seven different things at a time, all the time, juggling them brilliantly and precariously in the air." But coming back to this feeling that we're at a halfway point, I'm equating it with my personal feelings as a middle-aged person. I'm sure this hits everybody when they're forty-five. There's some sense — and believe me, it's as exciting as it is nerve-racking — of "Now what? Is the second half of the adventure beginning?" It's a different feeling and I really like it — this idea that you are genuinely, truly grown up and that possibly these are the power years, the years where you're effective and you'll be taken seriously if you want to be. I wonder how it's going to affect us? For instance, these guys [Andy and Michael], being dads, are much more concerned now about organizing their time better.

GREEN: I'm sure Andy feels the same way I do, but I've got another whole dynamic reality by which to measure the passage of time, and that's my five-year-old. I've got a whole other world, a parallel universe, with all these responsibilities. My life feels very different now than it did for the first fifteen or so years of One Yellow Rabbit.

*How is that new reality going to change the operations of the company? Will there be a point where you say you won't tour as much or produce as much, or you'll bring in younger people to, say, tour one of the shows while you stay here and organize the Rodeo?*

GREEN: One thing's for sure, we're certainly not as interested in long tours as maybe we were once upon a time. We've been talking about possibly going on an extended tour to New York, which makes me feel like I'm in some kind of version of the military. If we get called up, we can't not go. You can't spend your whole life trying to get a gig in New York and finally get one and say "Sorry, we can't do it."

BROOKER: Although we haven't spent our whole lives trying to get a gig in New York.

GREEN: Many people in our business do.

BROOKER: Yes, and we'd be willing to do one, but that's not the point with us, that's not what we're aimed at. We're aimed at creating undeniable performance theatre in our own community and maybe taking it elsewhere when it warrants it.

CURTIS *[pointing at the Big Secret stage]*: This is my Broadway.

BROOKER: Yeah, it's my Broadway, too. We've got a great audience in Calgary, we really, truly do — a group of intelligent, sensitive, adventurous individuals that we've never underestimated and we've always respected. I don't necessarily want to go be at the mercy of people who get offended if you swear, or get angry if you do something they didn't like. We want people to come on the adventure with us; we need talented audience members to collaborate with us. That's what we require. We're not *Phantom of the Opera*, we're not going to tell you how to feel. You have to navigate it yourself, you have to bring your own imagination.

CLARKE: Yes, but that being said, sometimes, as we well know, if you can establish a reputation outside of your own burg, you make your audience super proud of you and it affords you a few opportunities. I think the dilemma for us is: How can we capitalize on all this, on our beautiful audience and our beautiful body of work that we've invested so much in, so that we can *make more money?* So that we can afford to keep doing this? For me, that's the hardcore reality we're all facing now. Our income is making it increasingly difficult to, you know, make that mortgage payment, without having to take on a lot of other things that cut into your time with the company.

BROOKER: You know what we should do? A contemporary family drama full of dirty realism. Like a Raymond Carver story come alive, only taking place in Calgary. I'd love to go see that. Wouldn't you love to go see a skilful, incredible family drama?

CLARKE: Yes, but what we need is something that we can commodify — and not hand over to Hollywood, or even the Canadian film companies, where they always want to get another writer to re-write your screenplay.

*You discussed the film option on your retreat. What's come out of that?*

GREEN: We have three cameras.

CLARKE: And I have two deals in development. I am absolutely determined that that's going to be a way to commodify this company. We have to get our work out beyond here, to the level of [John] Malkovich and [Gary] Sinise and [John] Cusack. Those actors are guys I truly admire, who haven't sacrificed their integrity to make films and still play in the theatre. We are really capable of doing that.

CURTIS: We could set our theatre up as a TV studio.

GREEN: Or a soundstage. For a project or two.

CLARKE: But the very real question of commodification for a group of true freaks like us is not one we should be afraid of.

CURTIS *[to Green]*: Maybe we could get the TV rights to all the things you bring in [for the Rodeo] and start creating a series we could sell.

GREEN: That's an idea.

CLARKE: One of our ideas was to televise the cabarets and build these fabulous variety shows.

GREEN: It just seemed like too much at the time. We were so busy making the cabaret, we didn't have time to also film it.

BROOKER: It's hard enough to run a theatre company, let alone a theatre company *and* a TV company.

CLARKE: Yeah, but *I* don't run this company. That's the difference. I'm realizing a way to stay with the company would be to do something outside of it and that makes use of its resources. I don't want to make films with other actors, I want to use you guys.

GREEN: I guess this is probably one of the reasons why we remain the way we are and work the way we do. We have these different passions. I get all excited when I hear Denise talk about her film passion and if she can show me how to be a part of it, I'll do it. Meanwhile, I've got this passion with the Rodeo and everybody's getting involved in it now. And Blake's got this idea for a new play he clearly needs us to do.

CLARKE: I'm just saying, we should take our strongest work and commit it to film projects. It's not like we're doing a whole new thing. And say we had a couple of young actors in one of those shows and they turn into stars and that reflects back on our company, like with Steppenwolf [the Chicago theatre company], and allows us to flourish. I think that's not at all impossible to do.

GREEN *[to Clarke]*: One of the things I love about what we do, notwithstanding all these projects and visions, is that when the three of us, you, me, and Andy, are on stage in this theatre, doing what we do, it's incredible. We are, in those moments, arguably among the best examples of contemporary performance anywhere. Now, how do you make that transfer to another medium?

CLARKE: Well, I'd love to try.

GREEN *[to me]*: The passion that I feel for being on stage with these two, in this environment that we've all created, is greater than the passion I feel for almost anything else.

CLARKE: Well, that's it. And if we want to do it for another twenty years, I'd suggest we have to make more money so we can afford to do it. I've just accepted that. It's not a negative thing at all. *[To Brooker]* I know the concern about "branding" our work doesn't bother me as much as it does you. But I don't know if we haven't already branded ourselves, so why not profit a little more from it?

CURTIS: Yeah. Put that little yellow rabbit everywhere.

So there you have it. A band of auteurs, all with separate enthusiasms, trying to stay on the same page — or get the others to turn to their page. It's how One Yellow Rabbit has created for two decades. "This is probably why we're not way bigger stars," says Clarke. "Unlike a Lepage or an Édouard Lock [leader of La La La Human Steps], who says 'This is what I want. We're focusing on this exclusively,' we have to focus on what three or four people want to do."

It can be frustrating, it can be messy, things can slide in all directions. When their passions converge, however, it can be as thrilling as it is indefinable. "This is a kind of theatre that I've never seen or known," says Brooker. "It's a kind of theatre that we're in the process of imagining."

Flashback to 1985, and once again young Michael Green is being interviewed by critic Louise Bresky, who asks the inevitable question: Why is your funny little group called "One Yellow Rabbit"? Ah, it's very significant, says Green, bluffing beautifully. (You can imagine him cocking a coal-black eyebrow.) "One" stands for unity among the collective. "Yellow" is the colour symbolizing intelligence. And as for "Rabbit," well, um, er …

It's okay, Michael, we know the answer now. A rabbit is an animal that's just about impossible to pin down.

1    The *Somalia Yellow* tour eventually played Prague's Ponec Theatre in the Czech Republic (18 October 2002) and Glasgow's Tron Theatre in Scotland (30 October to 2 November 2002).

2    A reference to Bob Dylan's legendary tour with old friends in the mid-1970s.

# Epilogue – Where Are They Now?

The other original Rabbits, that is.

Jan Stirling lives in England and teaches drama therapy in St. Albans, north of London.

Marianne Moroney lives in Toronto, where she has done film, TV, and commercial work and runs two street businesses — a jewellery kiosk and a hot-dog cart.

Kirk Miles still lives in Calgary and is still a One Yellow Rabbit board member, still a poet, and still a clown. A book of his poetry, *The Last Six Minutes of Elvis,* was published in 2002.

George McFaul also remains in Calgary and, like Denise Clarke, has become a serious yoga practitioner. He instructs it full-time when he isn't occupied raising his three daughters. He also continues to do clown performances at big events, including Calgary's children's and folk-music festivals.

Gyllian Raby turned to an academic career after leaving Northern Light Theatre. Nigel Scott went back to school and studied architecture. The two are still, in Raby's phrase, "a love unit," although work opportunities have meant their family has had to live apart from time to time. Scott's career has taken him to the United States, as a designer of theme parks and state-of-the-art rides. In 2001, Raby accepted a post at Brock University in St. Catharines, Ontario, as an assistant professor, teaching drama in its School of Fine and Performing Arts. She still pines for One Yellow Rabbit.

"To me, in some ways, it's like a paradise lost," she says. "I'm still looking for an ensemble of people like that. Everywhere I go, I find small pockets of people that I develop a vocabulary and a rapport with, but I haven't stuck in one place for long enough to develop what the Rabbits have developed. As a result, my expectations of them are so high, I don't think they could ever reach them. I'm fiercely proud of them and the work that they do."

# List of Productions

**Calgary Seasons**

All shows listed from the 1995–96 season onward were presented in the Big Secret Theatre, unless otherwise indicated. From 1987 until the 1995–96 season, all shows were presented in the Secret Theatre, unless otherwise indicated. The various venues for shows prior to 1987 are included in the listings. In the case of guest productions, the production company or artist is also listed.

2001–2002 — Ronnie Burkett Theatre of Marionettes: *Happy* (co-presented with Alberta Theatre Projects; Martha Cohen Theatre), 18 September to 7 October 2001; *All Fours* (co-presented with Dancers' Studio West), 24–27 October 2001; *Sign Language*, 13–24 November 2001; High Performance Rodeo (Big Secret Theatre, Engineered Air Theatre, Jack Singer Concert Hall, Art Gallery of Calgary, and other venues), 3–27 January 2002; *Dream Machine Cabaret* (presented at the Rodeo), 4–19 January 2002; Old Trout Puppet Workshop: *Beowulf*, 26 February to 16 March 2002; *Somalia Yellow* (remount), 9–27 April 2002.

2000–2001 — *Fall Cabaret*, 12–28 October 2000; Old Trout Puppet Workshop: *The Unlikely Birth Of Istvan*, 7–25 November 2000; High Performance Rodeo (Big Secret Theatre, Engineered Air Theatre, Max Bell Theatre, and the "engine room" of the Arts Centre), 4–28 January 2001; *Featherland*, 13–31 March 2001.

1999–2000 — da da kamera: *Monster*, 30 September to 10 October 1999; *These Girls*, 23 November to 11 December 1999; High Performance Rodeo (Big Secret Theatre, Engineered Air Theatre, Jubilee Auditorium, The Banff Centre), 6–30 January 2000; *Radioheaded* (presented at the Rodeo), 21–24 January 2000; *The History of Wild Theatre*, 28 March to 15 April 2000.

1998–1999 — *Death in New Orleans*, 6–24 October 1998; Ronnie Burkett Theatre of Marionettes: *Street of Blood*, 17 November to 19 December 1998; High Performance Rodeo (Big Secret Theatre, Max Bell Theatre), 4–24 January 1999; *Blake with an Exclamation Mark* (presented at the Rodeo), 11–13 January 1999; *Thunderstruck*, 23 February to 13 March 1999; *Doing Leonard Cohen* (remount), 13–24 April 1999.

1997–1998 — Northwood Productions: *Frida K.*, 30 September to 18 October 1997; *So Low* (remount), 4–15 November 1997; *Permission* (remount), 25 November to 6 December 1997; High Performance Rodeo (Big Secret Theatre, Max Bell Theatre), 5–25 January 1998; *Somalia Yellow* (presented at the Rodeo), 7–10 January 1998; *In Klezskavania*, 24 February to 14 March 1998.

1996–1997 — Ronnie Burkett Theatre of Marionettes: *Tinka's New Dress*, 10 September to 19 October 1996; High Performance Rodeo, 6–26 January 1997; *Hunger's Brides* (presented at the Rodeo), 8–11 January 1997; *Doing Leonard Cohen*, 20 February to 8 March 1997; *Mata Hari: Tigress at the City Gates* (remount), 1–13 April 1997; Bruce McCulloch: *Slightly Bigger Cities* (University Theatre, University of Calgary), 16–17 May 1997.

1995–1996 — *Conniption Cabaret* (Big Secret Theatre debut), 21 November to 9 December 1995; High Performance Rodeo (Big Secret Theatre, Jack Singer Concert Hall), 8–21 January 1996; *Mata Hari: Tigress at the City Gates*, 15 February 15 to 3 March 1996; *So Low*, 9–27 April 1996.

1994–1995 — *Alien Bait*, 10 November to 4 December 1994; High Performance Rodeo (Secret Theatre, Jack Singer Concert Hall), 10–22 January 1995; *Permission*, 11 May to 4 June 1995.

1993–1994 — Meta-Physical Theatre: *Emotional Baggage/Earthlings*, 23–25 September 1993; Ronnie Burkett Theatre of Marionettes: *The Daisy Theatre*, 28 September to 24 October 1993; High Performance Rodeo (Secret Theatre,

Uptown Stage, the New Gallery), 8–21 November 1993; *Breeder* (Uptown Stage), 24 February to 13 March 1994; Ronnie Burkett Theatre of Marionettes: *The Daisy Theatre* (encore), 15 March to 3 April 1994; *Ilsa, Queen of the Nazi Love Camp* (Uptown Stage), 5–10 April 1994; *The Ugly Man* (Uptown Stage), 14–31 July 1994.

1992–1993 — English Suitcase Theatre: *Decadence/Autogeddon*, 26–30 August 1992; Egg Theatre: *See Bob Run*, 29 September to 4 October 1992; Andrew Akman/Diane Flacks: *Wild Abandon/Myth Me*, 7–10 October 1992; da da kamera: *House* (Garry Theatre), 17–22 November 1992; *Naked West*, 5–22 November 1992; High Performance Rodeo (Secret Theatre, Theatre Calgary rehearsal hall), 4–17 January 1993; *Dance Freak*, 23 February to 21 March 1993; Clare Coulter: *The Fever*, 6–11 April 1993; Ghost River Theatre: *The Cruise*, 13–18 April 1993; Egg Theatre: *To Hear with Eyes*, 20–25 April 1993; *Ilsa, Queen of the Nazi Love Camp* (Uptown Stage), 3–8 May 1993; *The Ugly Man*, 13–15 August 1993.

1991–1992 — Screwtape Theatre: *The Last Temptation of Christopher Robin*, 7–11 August 1991; Hamlet Enterprises: *Moon Robe*, 10–15 September 1991; *The Two-Headed Roommate*, 17 October to 2 November 1991; High Performance Rodeo, 2–15 December 1991; *Rabbit Dance*, 17–22 December 1991; *Serpent Kills*, 28 January to 16 February 1992; *Banned in Alberta Benefit Cabaret* (Pumphouse Theatres), 3 April 1992; *Hung, Drawn and Quartered*, 17–28 June 1992.

1990–1991 — English Suitcase Theatre: *Billy Budd/Macbeth*, 29 August to 1 September 1990; Hamlet Enterprises: *The Dime Store Dreams of Mr. Boat*, 4–8 September 1990; *Touch*, 27 September to 20 October 1990; *Exit the King*, 29 November to 15 December 1990; *The Land, The Animals*, 31 January to 23 February 1991; High Performance Rodeo, 29 March to 13 April 1991.

1989–1990 — *Mata Hari*, 27 September to 21 October 1989; *Barbarians*, 23 November to 9 December 1989; High Performance Rodeo, 1–13 January 1990; Rodeo Darlings (hold-overs from the Rodeo), 18–20 January 1990; *Dreams of a Drunken Quaker*, 6–24 March 1990; *Ilsa, Queen of the Nazi Love Camp*, 26 July to 18 August 1990.

1988–1989 — Alan Williams: *King of America Trilogy*, 20 September to 1 October 1988; *Lives of the Saints* (co-produced with Live Arts Theatre Alberta), 16 November to 3 December 1988; *The Erotic Irony of Old Glory*, 18 January to 4

February 1989; High Performance Rodeo, 6–19 March 1989; *Horse Killer,* 4–13 May 1989; Hamlet Enterprises: *Desperately Seeking Stooge,* 4–8 July 1989; *Serpent Kills* (co-produced with Crow's Theatre), 12–29 July 1989; Primus Theatre: *Dog Day,* 1–6 August 1989; Calgary Fringe Preview, 10–12 August 1989; Mump and Smoot: *Something,* 16–18 August 1989; *The Erotic Irony of Old Glory* (encore), 30 August to 2 September 1989.

1987–1988 — *Fall of the House of Krebbs,* 30 September to 17 October 1987; *Changing Bodies* (remount), 21–24 October 1987; Ronnie Burkett Theatre of Marionettes: *Fool's Edge,* 14–30 January 1988; High Performance Rodeo, 14–27 March 1988; *Tears of a Dinosaur,* 5–21 May 1988; Crow's Theatre: *Quartet,* 8–18 June 1988; Rough Theatre: *Born in the R.S.A.,* 22–25 June 1988; Calgary Fringe Preview, 3–7 August 1988.

1986–1987 — *Changing Bodies* (Pumphouse Theatres), 15 October to 1 November 1986; Secret Elevator Experimental Performance Festival (SOMA Building), 31 January to 8 February 1987; *Disrobing the Bride* (Secret Theatre debut), 6–21 March 1987; *The Field* (school tour), 1 March to 10 April 1987; *Rembrandt Brown,* 23 April to 10 May 1987; *Ilsa, Queen of the Nazi Love Camp,* 28 May to 20 June 1987.

1985–1986 — *Josephine: The Mouse Singer* (SkyRoom Theatre), 31 October to 16 November 1985; *Buy In/Sell Out* (school tour), winter 1986; *Changing Bodies* (SkyRoom Theatre), 22–24 January 1986; *The Pageant of the Comet* (various locales), 18–27 June 1986.

1984–1985 — *Juggler on a Drum* (ION Centre), 30 August to 3 September 1984; *Winterplay II* (various locales), winter 1984–85; *Leonardo's Last Supper* (SkyRoom Theatre debut) 15 March to 13 April 1985; Denise Clarke and Anne Flynn (SkyRoom Theatre), 4–13 April 1985; *Ides* (SkyRoom Theatre), 21 June to 11 August 1985; *Café Theatre* and *The Batman on a Dime* (Marty's Café), summer 1985.

1983–1984 — *Winterplay* (Off Centre Centre), 16–20 November 1983 (plus school tour); *Mr. Green Goes to Bottle Street* (Off Centre Centre), winter 1984; *Café Theatre* (Beggar's Banquet Bistro), winter-spring 1984; Richard Fowler: *Wait for the Dawn* (ION Centre), 20–23 June 1984; *Festival Performance* (various locales), June 1984; *The Batman on a Dime* (Beggar's Banquet Bistro), 13 July to 5 August 1984.

1982–1983 — *Leonardo's Last Supper* (Off Centre Centre), 13 August 1982; *The Crusader* (Off Centre Centre), 9–13 November 1982; *The Only Jealousy of Emer* (Off Centre Centre), 18–22 January 1983; *Juggler on a Drum* (Loose Moose Simplex), 20–24 July 1983.

## Touring Shows

### Alien Bait
Tron Theatre, Glasgow, Scotland, 1995
Traverse Theatre, Edinburgh, Scotland, 1995
Factory Theatre, Toronto, Canada, 1996
Arts Club Theatre, Vancouver, Canada, 1996

### The Batman on a Dime
Edmonton Fringe, Edmonton, Canada, 1985
Expo '86, Vancouver, Canada, 1986

### CD Dance
Edmonton Fringe, Edmonton, Canada, 1991

### Changing Bodies
Edmonton Fringe, Edmonton, Canada, 1986
Vancouver Fringe Festival, Vancouver, Canada, 1986
Project Artaud, San Francisco, USA, 1986
The Banff Centre, Banff, Canada, 1987
Factory Theatre, Toronto, Canada, 1988
Old Court House, Red Deer, Canada, 1988

### The Crusader/The Only Jealousy of Emer
The Banff Centre, Banff, Canada, 1983
Canmore Scout Hall, Canmore, Canada, 1983
Edmonton Fringe, Edmonton, Canada, 1983

### Death in New Orleans
Edinburgh Festival Fringe, Traverse Theatre, Edinburgh, Scotland, 1998

### Doing Leonard Cohen
Philadelphia Fringe Festival, Philadelphia, USA, 1999

Vancouver East Cultural Centre, Vancouver, Canada, 1999
Tron Theatre, Glasgow, Scotland, 2000
Citadel Theatre, Edmonton, Canada, 2002
Eastern Front Theatre, Halifax, Canada, 2002
Théâtre la Chapelle, Montreal, Canada, 2002

## Doing Leonard Cohen/Permission

Factory Theatre, Toronto, Canada, 1998

## Dreams of a Drunken Quaker

Edmonton Fringe, Edmonton, Canada, 1990
Vancouver East Cultural Centre, Vancouver, Canada, 1990

## The Erotic Irony of Old Glory

Edmonton Fringe, Edmonton, Canada, 1989
Canada Dance Festival, Ottawa, Canada, 1990
Tarragon Theatre, Toronto, Canada, 1990
Firehall Arts Centre, Vancouver, Canada, 1991
Zap Club, Brighton, England, 1991
Finborough Theatre, London, England, 1991
Belltable Arts Centre, Limerick, Ireland, 1991
St. John's Arts Centre, Listowel, Ireland, 1991
Triskel Arts Centre, Cork, Ireland, 1991
The Green Room, Manchester, England, 1991
Vooruit Centrum, Gent, Belgium, 1991
Traverse Theatre, Edinburgh, Scotland, 1991

## Hunger's Brides

Universidad del Claustro de Sor Juana, Mexico City, Mexico, 1996

## Hunger's Brides/Permission

Arizona State University, Phoenix, USA, 1996
Feria Internacional del Libro, Guadalajara, Mexico, 1996
El Octavo Día, Mexico City, Mexico, 1996

## Ilsa, Queen of the Nazi Love Camp

Edmonton Fringe, Edmonton, Canada, 1987
Northern Light Theatre, Edmonton, Canada, 1992

Firehall Arts Centre, Vancouver, Canada, 1993
Belfry Theatre, Victoria, Canada, 1993
The Banff Centre, Banff, Canada, 1993
du Maurier World Stage, Toronto, Canada, 1994
Edinburgh Festival Fringe, Traverse Theatre, Edinburgh, Scotland, 1994
Tron Theatre, Glasgow, Scotland, 1994
Festival of Perth, Perth, Australia, 1995

*Juggler on a Drum*

Edmonton Fringe, Edmonton, Canada, 1984

*Leonardo's Last Supper*

Edmonton Fringe, Edmonton, Canada, 1982

*Mata Hari: Tigress at the City Gates*

Citadel Theatre, Edmonton, Canada, 1997

*Mr. Green Goes to Bottle Street*

Chinook Theatre, Edmonton, Canada, 1985

*The Pageant of the Comet*

Expo '86, Vancouver, Canada, 1986

*Serpent Kills*

Tarragon Theatre, Toronto, Canada, 1989 (co-produced with Crow's Theatre)
Edinburgh Festival Fringe, Traverse Theatre, Edinburgh, Scotland, 1992
Les 20 jours de théâtre à risque, Quebec City, Canada, 1992

*Slightly Bigger Cities* (Bruce McCulloch)

University of Alberta, Edmonton, Canada, 1997
McPherson Playhouse, Victoria, Canada, 1997
Vancouver East Cultural Centre, Vancouver, Canada, 1997

*So Low*

Edmonton Fringe, Edmonton, Canada, 1996
25th Street Theatre, Saskatoon, Canada, 1997

*Somalia Yellow*

Ponec Theatre, Prague, Czech Republic, 2002

Tron Theatre, Glasgow, Scotland, 2002

*Tears of a Dinosaur*

The Banff Centre, Banff, Canada, 1987

Quinzane Festival, Quebec City, Canada, 1988

du Maurier World Stage, Toronto, Canada, 1988

Centaur Theatre, Montreal, Canada, 1988

Edmonton Fringe, Edmonton, Canada, 1988

Vancouver Fringe Festival, Vancouver, Canada, 1988

*Thunderstruck*

Edinburgh Festival Fringe, Traverse Theatre, Edinburgh, Scotland, 2000

Factory Theatre, Toronto, Canada, 2000

*The Ugly Man*

Edinburgh Festival Fringe, Traverse Theatre, Edinburgh, Scotland, 1993

Tron Theatre, Glasgow, Scotland, 1993

*Under the Bed* (co-produced with TheatreWorks)

Drama Centre, Singapore, 1993

# Selected Bibliography

Given the heavy literary influences on One Yellow Rabbit, a full bibliography for this book would contain at least as many works of fiction and poetry as those of non-fiction and reference. For the sake of simplicity, I have omitted the former, as well as any dramatic literature apart from published works written by the members of One Yellow Rabbit themselves.

Bercuson, David, and Douglas Wertheimer. *A Trust Betrayed: The Keegstra Affair*. Toronto: Doubleday Canada, 1985.

Brooker, Blake. *Ilsa, Queen of the Nazi Love Camp and Other Plays*. Red Deer, AB: Red Deer College Press, 1993.

*Canada on Stage: 1982–1986* and *Canada on Stage: 1986–1988*. Toronto: PACT Communications Centre, Professional Association of Canadian Theatres, 1989 and 1991.

Foreman, Kathleen, and Clem Martini. *Something Like a Drug: An Unauthorized Oral History of Theatresports*. Red Deer, AB: Red Deer College Press, 1995.

Goldberg, RoseLee. *Performance Art: From Futurism to the Present*. London and New York: Thames & Hudson, 2001.

Green, Michael. *Dreams of a Drunken Quaker, Naked West & Yowl — Two Plays & a Rant*. Halifax: AB Collector Publishing, 1992.

Johnston, Denis W. *Up the Mainstream: The Rise of Toronto's Alternative Theatres 1968–1975*. Toronto: University of Toronto Press, 1991.

Johnstone, Keith. *Impro: Improvisation and the Theatre.* London: Methuen, 1981.

Macpherson, Susan, ed. *Encyclopedia of Theatre Dance in Canada.* Toronto: Arts Inter-Media Canada/Dance Collection Danse, 2000.

Mertl, Steve, and John Ward. *Keegstra: The Issues, The Trial, The Consequences.* Saskatoon: Western Producer Prairie Books, 1985.

Miles, Barry. *William Burroughs: El Hombre Invisible.* London: Virgin Books, 1992.

Millan, Jim, and Blake Brooker. *Serpent Kills.* Toronto: Playwrights Canada Press, 1994.

Nadel, Ira B. *Various Positions: A Life of Leonard Cohen.* Toronto and New York: Random House, 1996.

Nikiforuk, Andrew, and others. *Running on Empty: Alberta After the Boom.* Edmonton: NeWest Press, 1987.

Roose-Evans, James. *Experimental Theatre: From Stanislavsky to Peter Brook.* London: Routledge, 1989.

Stenson, Fred. *The Story of Calgary.* Saskatoon: Fifth House Publishers, 1994.

Usmiani, Renate. *Second Stage: The Alternative Theatre Movement in Canada.* Vancouver: University of British Columbia Press, 1983.

Wallace, Robert. *Producing Marginality: Theatre and Criticism in Canada.* Saskatoon: Fifth House Publishers, 1990.

# Index